P9-ART-793

Social Work
in Rural
Communities

Social Work in Rural Communities

Fifth Edition

EDITED BY

Leon Ginsberg

COUNCIL ON SOCIAL WORK EDUCATION

Alexandria, Virginia

Copyright © 2011 Council on Social Work Education, Inc.

Published in the United States by the Council on Social Work Education, Inc. All rights reserved. No part of this book may be reproduced or transmitted in any manner whatsoever without the prior written permission of the publisher.

Library of Congress Cataloging-in-Publication Data

Social work in rural communities / edited by Leon H. Ginsberg. — 5th ed.
    p. cm.
    Includes bibliographical references and index.
    ISBN 978-0-87293-146-6 (alk. paper)
    1. Social service, Rural—United States. I. Ginsberg, Leon H.
    HV91.S625 2011
    361.97309173'4--dc23
                                2011039165

Printed in the United States of America on acid-free paper that meets the American National Standards Institute Z39-48 standard.

Council on Social Work Education, Inc.
1701 Duke Street, Suite 200
Alexandria, VA 22314-3457
www.cswe.org

Fifth Edition

Contents

Preface to the Fifth Edition

This fifth edition of *Social Work in Rural Communities* represents the latest book in some 40 years of attention that the Council on Social Work Education (CSWE) provides to the education of social workers in smaller communities and rural areas. As is mentioned in the Introduction, the effort was initiated in 1969 at the Annual Program Meeting, which was held in Cleveland, OH. Dr. Richard Lodge, then dean of the Virginia Commonwealth University School of Social Work, had been involved earlier in the reaffirmation of accreditation of the West Virginia University Division of Social Work. When he was asked for recommendations for a new director, my name was one he proposed. I was invited to fill the position after 5 years as a faculty member at the University of Oklahoma social work school. Dick Lodge was also chair of the program committee for the Cleveland Annual Program Meeting. He and the committee asked me to organize a workshop for the meeting, and that began the extensive efforts that CSWE and, later, the National Association of Social Workers, began in understanding and providing assistance to social work in rural communities. Dick became executive director of CSWE and later a professor at Adelphi.

There had been earlier efforts and some literature about social work in rural communities, but most of it had become inactive by the 1960s, with that decade's emphasis on urban issues, metropolitan social problems, and social work practice in the cities.

Many comparable efforts also contributed to the profession's rural emphasis. The annual institutes on social work in rural areas began in 1977 in Knoxville under the auspices of the University of Tennessee and have continued each year. The most recent was in the summer of 2011 at Northwest State University of Louisiana in Natchitoches.

Personally, although I was raised in San Antonio, TX, my orientation was to the small communities of East Central Texas—places such as Columbus, Gonzales, Schulenburg, and Weimar, where I have family members. I spent my social work education and practice career (as West Virginia commissioner of human services and chancellor of higher education) in smaller communities: West Virginia, which is by some measures the most rural state in the United States; South Carolina, which is nearly one-half nonmetropolitan; and, most recently, on the faculty of Appalachian State University, whose enrollment is larger than the population of the town in which it is located (Boone, NC). When I served as Jewish community activities director in Tulsa, a moderately large city, I published my first article— about the special nature of organizing a program in a small Jewish community. I've long been attracted to small town environments, which also is true of the contributors to this volume.

One of the principal uses of this book has been as a text for social work education courses on rural practice, policy, and behavior. That is not surprising, because so many American colleges and universities are located in small towns. In many cases, the college or university is the main industry in these small communities. That means that course and field instruction is likely to take place in small towns and nonmetropolitan agencies. We hope that students and practitioners who read the book find it interesting and useful in advancing their professional social work careers.

Each edition of this book has been substantially different from its predecessor. Each edition has contained specialized content, and some educators and practitioners continue to use earlier editions.

For this edition the editor and CSWE conducted a membership-wide call for chapter submissions. The result was that many seasoned rural social work scholars and practitioners, as well as relative newcomers to the field, contributed to the volume. Many of the authors had held an interest in the scholarship and practice of rural social work for many years but had not written about those interests until now, whereas others have had a long history in writing about rural issues in the profession. Each author is identified in the part introductions and in the list of contributors at the end of the book.

The overall proposal for the book was reviewed and accepted by the CSWE Council on Publications. The editor and the authors are grateful to the Council members for their thoughtful help. The book is better because of their insights.

We are all also grateful to Elizabeth Simon, the CSWE manager of publications, who suggested this fifth edition and shepherded it from its beginnings. Our accrediting body was fortunate to have found and employed her. Thanks also go to CSWE's executive director, Julia Watkins, who is leaving that post too soon. CSWE has flourished under her leadership, and we are pleased to have been a part of her administration.

It has been our pleasure to develop and prepare this edition, and we hope our readers enjoy reading and using this edition as much as we did writing it.

Leon Ginsberg
Boone, North Carolina
July 2011

PART I

Basics of Social Work in Rural Communities

When the first edition of this book was published in the 1970s, it looked more like a pamphlet than a textbook, compared to the substantial volume that is this fifth edition. Although social work in rural communities was a continuing, albeit small, emphasis in the social work literature, there had been no major works published for several decades. With help from a foundation supported by funds from the United Parcel Service (which has also funded the Annie E. Casey Foundation, an important social welfare institution), the Council on Social Work Education embarked on its rural project. Many of those who helped define the field and develop its modern theoretical foundations have moved on to other emphases or retired, but many others have taken their places and become significant contributors to the literature. This edition's contributors include scholars and practitioners from many locations, and the content these contributors provide is diverse—some of it on subjects that were not conceptualized in the 1970s. Many are from smaller social work education programs in nonmetropolitan areas. Some chapters are written by social workers in larger communities who have developed or retained their interests in rural issues.

Part I of the text is designed to lay the foundation for what follows. Understanding precisely what is meant by social work in rural communities—or even what is meant by *rural*—is a longstanding issue in the literature. There are many different ways of defining rural life, each of which serves purposes for the agencies and institutions that use them. It is a characteristic of much of the rural social work literature, at least since the 1960s, that authors use to define their understanding of the term. Throughout the text there are repetitions of rural definitions from a variety of sources. These are useful for expanding reader understanding of the diversity of the field. In some cases, information such as definitions is cross-referenced to earlier chapters, especially those in this first part of the book. In other cases the authors begin with their conceptions of the subject matter.

This introduction explains the practice of multiple definitions of rural social work, because each of the chapters confronts rural social work in a different way and deals with different dimensions of the subject. Taken as a whole, the chapters in Part I lay the groundwork for the rest of the book.

Chapter 1 is the editor's new introduction to some of the basic concepts of rural social work, as well as some examples. Of course, the field has changed, and that is made clear in Chapter 1. Other authors have also contributed extensively to the basic social work in rural communities literature—especially O. William Farley and his colleagues at the University of Utah; Emilia Martinez-Brawley of Arizona State University, the author of several books tracing the historical antecedents of rural social work; T. Laine Scales of Baylor University; Calvin Streeter of the University of Texas; and Nancy and Roger Lohmann of West Virginia University are among some of the more prominent and recent rural social work authors. Several authors in the United Kingdom, Australia, and various other parts of the world also write about social work in rural areas. So what had been a minor area of concern in social work education has become a significant part of the scholarship and literature of social work.

Chapter 2 highlights festivals, buildings, traditions, and other artifacts that can be called rural treasures. The authors, Iris Carlton-LaNey and N. Yolanda Burwell, discuss their concept of rural treasures, which is original and makes a new and valuable contribution to the rural social work literature.

Interest in rural social work extends worldwide. Internet searches will identify books, articles, and specialized journals dealing with the subject in Europe, Oceania, and the nations of Asia. The one non-U.S. contribution in this edition is Rambaree Komalsingh's Chapter 3, describing an effort to empower the people of Mauritius and eradicate the absolute poverty faced by many of its inhabitants. Of course, the approaches used and the solutions proposed in the United Nations project have applications in other parts of the world and in the United States, where similar problems exist.

Chapters 4 and 5, by Karen Harper-Dorton and Glenn Stone, respectively, discuss the significance of technology in social work from two different perspectives. In recent years, as is discussed in Chapter 1 and elsewhere, technological innovations by organizations such as the National Association of Social Workers (NASW) and the Council on Social Work Education (CSWE), began making a difference in social work practice and education. NASW's online educational activities make licensing requirements more accessible for rural participants, and online approaches to social work education simplify and make major changes in the educational quality control processes.

Lois Bosch and Laura Boisen are the authors of Chapter 6, which discusses and analyzes the issue of dual relationships in rural areas. Of course, since the early days of the literature of social work in rural communities, social workers have emphasized the pervasive, and at times uncomfortable, phenomenon of running into one's clients in the grocery store or finding that clients or their family members are also affiliated with local government and businesses. The NASW Code of Ethics deals with dual relationships and discourages—perhaps even prohibits—them. Social workers in rural communities, however, recognize that some are unavoidable.

Educating social workers for service in rural areas is the subject of Chapter 7, contributed by Michael R. Daley and Barbara Pierce. Given the critical shortages of professional social workers in rural areas, social work education has a responsibility to address the preparation of social workers for rural practice both in terms of increased numbers of programs offering rural content and also the addition of enhanced rural content in curricula. Chapter 7 identifies key conceptual and content issues that can be used to support the development of the idea of rurality in the education of social workers.

Paul Force-Emery Mackie reflects on the rural social work labor force in Chapter 8, a persistent problem in social work in rural communities. His research and scholarship is largely about filling the needs for social workers in nonmetropolitan areas.

In Chapter 9 Vanda Galen and Dexter Alexander provide some insights into the rural settlement movement that should lead to revisions of all the textbooks (including this editor's) that trace that movement to urban centers such as Hull House in Chicago and Toynbee Hall in England. In fact, Galen and Alexander point out that there were rural settlements, principally in the Kentucky mountains, that adapted the kinds of programs found at Hull House to rural areas. The principal examples were the Hindman Settlement School in Hindman, KY, and Pine Mountain

Settlement School in Harlan County, KY. The authors also note the work of the Council of the Southern Mountains, which dealt with rural education and development in Southern Appalachia, which was in operation from 1925 through 1989.

With these chapters, Part I deals with many of the longstanding, as well as current, issues defining social work in rural communities.

1   Introduction to Basic Concepts of Rural Social Work

Leon Ginsberg

In many ways, social work's roots are tied closely to urban life in England, as well as to metropolitan America and its cities. Organized efforts such as the Charity Organization Societies and the settlement movement, which began in Buffalo, NY; Chicago, IL; London, UK; and New York, NY, were all urban and metropolitan. Only passing attention was given in social work's earlier days to rural or nonmetropolitan areas. In fact, little special attention was given to American rural life in general, because most of the population was rural, and rural life was not the source of social and economic problems that affected the cities. The concerns facing large cities and metropolitan areas were great, and, therefore, less attention was given to rural America.

Beginning with the 20th century, however, America's elected officials and policy makers began to take note of issues facing rural people, some of which resulted from the migration of large numbers to the cities from smaller towns and abroad. The extensive population of cities by immigrants from other nations was another public concern and a source of some conflict. Irish, Italian, and Russian immigrants (many of whom were Jewish and from parts of the Russian sphere of influence that are now independent nations) changed the cities and required integration into a nation that was previously populated primarily by people from England and Germany.

In 1909 Theodore Roosevelt, one of the nation's most innovative presidents, dealt with the rural American population. He reported to Congress on his appointed Country Life Commission. He said,

I warn my countrymen that the great recent progress made in city life is not a full measure of our civilization; for our civilization rests at bottom on the wholesomeness, the attractiveness, and the completeness, as well as prosperity of life in the country. (Roosevelt, 1909)

The Commission recommendations enacted into law by Congress, along with the Department of Agriculture, began the implementation of a variety of rural services, such as Agricultural Extension and Land Grant colleges, designed to improve agriculture and rural home life at a time when developments in cities were a national preoccupation.

Roosevelt began the White House Conferences on Children at about the same time—conferences that led to the creation of child protective services, especially in rural areas, and, eventually, Social Security. He also helped to establish the Children's Bureau, which became a reality in 1912. In some ways Theodore Roosevelt was the founder of much of early social work and, in particular, national concern about life in rural areas.

The metropolitanization of the world, which is as true for the United States as it is for other nations, results in part when people find that they cannot survive economically in rural areas. One author (Beattie, 2009) notes that, beginning in 2007 or 2008, a majority of the world's population became urbanized. Beattie (2009) says that 180,000 people moved from the rural areas to cities. The transition was not steady, and the growth has been recent. Many cities, Beattie (2009) reports, took centuries to grow from relatively small towns to enormous metropolises, and most of the growth was in the 20th century.

Farming, the most common rural occupation, no longer provides adequate earnings for many rural people, who find they can earn more in cities. Industrial accidents in agriculture cause more serious injuries and fatalities than in more urban occupations. According to a survey conducted by Purdue University (Stewart, 2010), farm personnel have a fatality rate of 31.6 deaths per 100,000 workers, whereas the death rate in all nonfarm industries is 3.5 per 100,000 workers. Mining, another common rural occupation, uses fewer people and more machines. The work is also considered hazardous, but mining fatalities are less than 1 per 200,000 hours worked (U.S. Department of Labor, 2010). Media coverage of mining fatalities is much more dramatic than coverage of farm accidents that commonly claim only one or two people.

Of course, as students of rural life have long noted, these phenomena change. In the summer of 2011 *Time* reported that farmers were prospering because of increases in food prices and the growing use of biofuels (Gandel, 2011). Gandel's article reported that farm income was up by 27%, whereas the total U.S. economy was growing at a rate of only 1.9%. And although urban real estate prices are depressed, farm land doubled in value during the first decade of the 21st century.

Another historical era in the United States was the specific, internal "Great Migration" in which millions of rural, Southern African Americans, who faced discrimination at minimum and lynching for many, relocated to the urban North. According to Jill Lepore (2010), 6 million African Americans left the South for the North during the 20th century. Clearly, the changing demographics of rural America are important to understanding and practicing social work in nonmetropolitan America.

This book is the fifth in a series of compendia on modern approaches to social work in rural communities. The series began with the first edition in 1974, which was supported by a grant from a foundation financed by the United Parcel Service to the Council on Social Work Education (CSWE). The grant provided funds for two seminars on social work in rural areas in addition to the financing of the first book. Subsequent editions were supported by sales of the book to social workers, libraries, and social work students by CSWE.

The idea that social work needed an emphasis on rural problems and practice was reiterated in 1968 at the Annual Program Meeting of CSWE, when a workshop on the topic was presented. It attracted dozens of educators from all over the United States. Some of those participants, augmented by others with rural interests, founded rural caucuses for CSWE and also within the National Association of Social Workers (NASW). In 1977 rural social work advocates organized the first National Institute on Social Work in Rural Areas (also known as the National Rural Social Work Caucus), first at the University of Tennessee in Knoxville and subsequently every year since then at sites throughout the United States. For a time social work educators at various universities founded and published a journal, *Social Work in Rural Areas*, which eventually ceased publication. The Caucus also has a new electronic journal, *Contemporary Rural Social Work*, which is published by the University of South Alabama (www.ruralsocialwork.org). Beginning in the 1970s NASW's *Encyclopedia of Social Work* included articles on social work in rural areas.

Emilia Martinez-Brawley of Arizona State University published a book in 1981 on the larger history of social work in rural areas called *Seven Decades of Rural Social Work: From Country Life Commission to Rural Caucus*, which highlights the lengthy efforts by many social workers to add a rural emphasis to the profession

(Martinez-Brawley, 1981). Scales and Streeter (2003) and Lohmann and Lohmann (2008) wrote recent texts on rural social work practice. Farley and Griffiths (1982), with a foreword by Francis J. Turner, also wrote on rural social work.

What is Rural?

In spite of all the discussions and scholarship on the issues of social work in rural areas, it is now clear that there is no universally accepted definition of what *rural* means. Two researchers at the Economic Research Service of the U.S. Department of Agriculture, which is a major force in developing data on rural issues, attempted to catalogue the various ways in which *rural* is defined. John Cromartie and Shawn Bucholtz (2008) discuss nine different ways in which *rural* is defined by U.S. government agencies.

Depending on what definition is used, the rural population of the United States may be as small as 16% (according to an Associated Press story released on July 28, 2011) or as large as 63%. Different definitions, Cromartie and Bucholtz (2008) suggest, are chosen for the purpose of the research or the program being used. Some definitions define the rural population as those living in areas with 2,500 people or fewer, which is the classic definition. Others use a metropolitan and nonmetropolitan distinction, viewing the rural population as those who live outside metropolitan areas. Others focus on the commuting time and distance from various locations.

For social work researchers and students, it is probably sufficient to suggest that the U.S. rural or nonmetropolitan (a term that is perhaps more recognized by rural demographers and researchers) population is between one-fifth and one-fourth of the total U.S. population. And that, in a population that exceeds 300 million, is a lot of people—60–75 million.

Several of the other chapters in this text deal with definitions of rural areas and rural social work. As Cromartie and Bucholtz (2008) suggest, differing definitions are part of the process of understanding rural life for differing purposes.

Obtaining Supervision and Overcoming Isolation

One of the primary issues that make social work in rural communities a matter of special interest for the profession is that workers tend to be employed alone or in very small groups. The resulting lack of supervision and the professional isolation are sources of concern for social work practitioners in nonmetropolitan areas.

Of course, the professional and personal isolation that has long been a concern of people in smaller communities is mitigated by modern communication. The Internet, perhaps more than any other resource, has reduced isolation through the electronic interconnectedness of all people. A rural dweller has as much access to the news and media as do the residents of the largest American cities. Two chapters in this book discuss the impact of electronic communication and the Internet on rural practice.

Entertainment was once severely limited for rural people. However, cable and satellite television, with their hundreds of channels, and services such as Netflix, which make any movie available in a person's mailbox within 1 or 2 days, have revolutionized small town entertainment. Live, professional theatre is still largely limited to the major cities, but rural people have long entertained themselves and their fellow residents with community theatre, school plays, and talent shows. Of course, live sports entertainment, especially high school sports, is a key feature of small town life, perhaps more than for citizens of cities. There may be no professional teams, which are found in a few cities, but access to NBA and NFL games is available through television and the Internet.

Supervision remains a problem for many rural social workers. However, the Internet also provides opportunities for electronic supervision—sharing case materials and receiving responses by e-mail. Video cameras for computers are also convenient and inexpensive. Long distance telephone calls, which were once expensive, are now much less so or are included without additional cost in telephone service. So, electronic supervision and consultation are now possible and more or less efficient. However, positive interactions between social workers and those from whom they receive consultation and supervision require some face-to-face interaction, which can be accomplished through periodic personal visits by either the supervisor or consultant or by those with whom they provide supervision and consultation.

Social Problems in Rural Areas

Rural area residents face most of the same social problems as their urban and metropolitan counterparts. Access to health care, which may be addressed for many by the Patient Protection and Affordable Care Act of 2010, is a problem for large numbers of low-income, uninsured Americans in all parts of the nation. Rural communities may have hospitals, but they are usually primary care facilities that treat fractures, infections, and give immediate attention needed for heart attacks, strokes, and cancer. However, the more complicated treatments, such as heart bypasses and transplants, must often be performed in tertiary care, large city facilities. Medical evacuation by helicopters is often available in such cases. Internet streaming is an important part of technology in rural areas. Telemedicine, often provided by such streaming, is also used in many rural communities. Physicians, sometimes with the patients present, consult with distant specialists, who guide primary care physicians in treating rural residents. The Medical College of Georgia, which serves large numbers of rural communities, is a pioneer in providing sophisticated health consultation through computers and closed circuit television. Chapters on oncology care and other specific health issues are discussed in later chapters, as are rural mental health services, domestic violence services, and the reentry to the community issues faced by those who leave penal institutions.

Housing is also a problem for the rural and metropolitan low-income population. However, as the *People Left Behind* report showed, inadequate housing is more problematic in rural areas (President's National Advisory Commission on Rural Poverty, 1967). The stock of available housing is greater in urban and metropolitan areas, although it may also be substandard.

Domestic violence, including child abuse, may be as severe in rural areas as in the cities. It may also be more hidden because of the widespread patterns of housing and the smaller population cohorts.

The one problem that stands out as more difficult for rural people than their urban counterparts is transportation. Many rural communities have little or no public transportation. Therefore, rural residents need to rely on private automobiles, which are costly; taxis; and rides with friends or neighbors, which are not consistently available. Therefore, even when services are available, rural residents may have difficulty accessing them. The scale of life and small populations often make it difficult for rural residents to obtain necessary transportation. Of course, there are exceptions. The Boone, NC, area has a highly reliable and free bus system that reaches people in all parts of the area, all day, every day. Policy makers find it less expensive than constructing parking lots for the thousands of Appalachian State University students, who park in a few central lots and use the bus system to reach their classes. Nonstudents are equally free to use the buses for shopping, health care, and whatever else they may need.

Rural employment also lacks the diversity of jobs found in metropolitan areas, and the wages are typically not as high as in cities. That may be a particular problem for rural youth. A chapter on some of the characteristics and problems of rural youth is included later in this volume. Much of traditional rural work, such as mining and farming, is also more dangerous than in more urban industries, as mentioned previously in this chapter. However, farm employment, also mentioned previously in this chapter, has increased, as has farm income and economic development in rural areas.

Need for Rural Attention

Clearly, many social workers need special knowledge and skills for working in rural communities. Many social work jobs are in smaller communities outside the metropolitan areas. Fields of service such as public human services, mental health, developmental disabilities, and substance abuse are all represented in rural areas. Some social problems, such as the production and use of methamphetamines, are more pronounced in some nonmetropolitan areas than in cities.

It is also clear that rural populations often face more extensive and more severe social problems than do their metropolitan counterparts. One exception may be mental illness. *Time* ("Big City, Big Risks," 2010), citing the *Archives of General Psychiatry*, reports that severe mental illnesses, such as psychoses, are less prevalent in rural than in metropolitan areas. The magazine adds,

> while genetics and personal circumstances are primarily responsible for the development of psychoses, the social fragmentation and disconnected nature of city life help explain why the rates of these disorders are higher in urbanites. Strengthening community ties, they [a team of mental health researchers] say, may help lower the risk of mental illness among city dwellers. (p. 20)

Rural transportation, health care, employment, and equal rights enforcement are also less than adequate, as discussed in this introduction, and continuing to be special problems for rural people.

Meeting the social work needs of the rural population and helping rural people overcome the problems they face are skills that many social workers need now and will continue to need in the future. It is also clear that many social work education programs, both graduate and undergraduate, are located in communities that meet at least one and often several definitions of *rural*. That means that many practicum or field instruction placements are in rural areas, which suggests that students, as well as their field liaison faculty, need understanding of rural community life if the practicum experience is to be optimal.

Several of the chapters in this book deal with education for social workers about rural issues. Michael R. Daley of the University of South Alabama and Barbara Pierce of Northwestern State University of Louisiana provide in Chapter 7 insight on educating for rural social work.

The Scale of Rural Life

Our social science colleagues help explain rural life with the distinctions between *gemeinschaft* and *gesselschaft* populations (Tönnies, 2001.) The *gemeinschaft* orientation is to a larger, impersonal, community system. Activities are instrumental, and involvement is on a business-like basis, focused on achieving the task at hand. Interactions in an urban motor vehicles office is perhaps a good example. Achieving the auto registration task by mail or online is perhaps an even better example. But rural areas are more likely to be oriented to the *gesselschaft* orientation in which face-to-face, rather personal, interactions prevail. Renewing a driver's license in a rural area might entail discussions with the issuing clerk about family matters on both sides, because both parties know members of each other's families, went to high school together, are members of the same church, or have children who study and play together. In many rural communities there are no impersonal interactions.

The classic metropolitan institution is likely to be governmental—with interchangeable personnel and impersonal transactions. Those same institutions in small towns—a rural post office, for example—involve some personal discussions and interactions between the postage purchaser and the clerk. It is likely that the clerk is also a member of the customer's Sunday school class or that both are active in the same Parent–Teacher Association.

In other words, much of life in metropolitan areas is *gemeinschaft*, whereas life in rural areas is more likely *gesselschaft*. The typical metropolitan institution is likely impersonal and instrumental. The typical rural institution—school, café, church, even political organization—is likely highly personal. Rural community institutions are more like families than are their metropolitan counterparts.

Implications for Practice

Successful social workers in rural communities soon learn that they must involve themselves with the people of the community, the leaders, the grass roots community members, local clergy, and local elected officials, in the process of working for community change or even in initiating direct services to clients. Outsiders are not always welcomed enthusiastically, no matter what their credentials, if they seem aloof or otherwise distant from the community's members. Of course, good social work practice takes such concerns into consideration. Many kinds of organizations that employ social workers operate as if they are small communities. New faculty in social work education programs often explain that their full involvement requires weeks of getting to know colleagues before they can fully participate in educational activities. New staff of community mental health and other agencies often report similar experiences. Therefore, many students of effective social work in rural communities think such work is comparable to effective social work anywhere. However, the results of failing to build relationships with colleagues and the community are often more dramatic in rural communities than in other social work settings.

Program Development

Social workers in rural communities often find that one of their major tasks is in the development of programs—either building new and improved functions onto existing programs or working to start new programs. A clear characteristic of social workers in rural areas, as Vanda Galen and Dexter Alexander suggest in Chapter 9, is the need to play many roles. Sometimes the direct practice worker finds it necessary to be a program developer, if a gap in service is the necessary solution to the problems faced by many clients. Although many direct services workers have minimal exposure to program development during their educations, that kind of macrowork may be the most logical approach to meeting their clients' needs. Some consultation with program development experts and developing program development skills through reading and other research may need to become part of the practice skill that social workers in rural areas develop.

Of course, when taking steps to develop programs, workers need to be attentive to some of the methods of community work suggested in the preceding section. They should also understand that many rural institutions are exceptionally powerful because of the involvement and support of large numbers of community residents. Churches tend to play a larger role in rural communities than they might in metropolitan areas. They are often primary, *gesselschaft* organizations, rather than secondary, less personal institutions, as they might be in large cities. Other important institutions include local government, schools, and financial corporations, such as banks. Many banks in rural areas have meeting rooms that are used by community groups, even friendship groups. Innumerable other organizations, such as civic clubs and veterans' organizations, may play major roles in rural service development and in addressing social problems. For those reasons, social workers in rural communities, no matter what their specific roles, often find it worthwhile to visit and connect with rural institutions that may not be as important in metropolitan or urban areas.

Chapter 9, which also discusses the importance of multiple tasks for rural workers, discusses the ways in which rural communities adopt and use the settlement
house approach, even though settlements are usually found in urban rather than
rural areas. Chapter 9 points to the importance of community development work
in rural social work and to the multiplicity of roles that social workers must play
in smaller communities.

One lesson learned and communicated by social workers in rural communities is
that, although there may be no formal professional agencies or structures delivering
services, there are probably many services provided informally or by other designations. For example, the small community may appear to lack resources for serving
the homeless. Homeless people may appear in the community and require lodging
and food for a period of time—perhaps only a day or two or, in the case of persons
trying to reestablish themselves and become self-supporting, several weeks or
months. The community, in this case, may have no formal homeless shelter or meal
services. However, looking around the community and speaking with its leaders may
reveal that the local law enforcement officials provide housing to homeless people in
cells that are open and unused. Many rural counties have jail facilities that are often
vacant. Those facilities may be available for temporary shelter. Or local churches may
sponsor daily lunches for people who would otherwise have no way of feeding themselves, even though the lunches are not advertised. Local people simply "know" that
the Presbyterian or Roman Catholic Church provides lunches daily.

Many rural communities often offer job placement for unemployed people with
moving companies, landscaping services, or even public schools. The service may
not be registered with any local employment services office, if such an office exists,
but local people know about it. Of course, formal services such as job training,
emergency assistance, and food stamps may be available through local public
human service agency offices, but there may be a delay between needing the services and becoming eligible to receive them. Or the office may be some distance
from the community. Those who need the help may find it necessary to arrange
transportation to a county seat or wait for an out-stationed representative of the
agency to arrive in the community, which is often only once weekly or monthly. Or
a family that needs counseling may be involved with a local church's minister, who
may have some training in pastoral counseling. Displacing that existing service
with the efforts of a social worker may meet significant resistance from community
members. The lesson for rural social workers is to be cognizant of existing community services, which may not be formally designated as services.

An example is a social worker employed by a small Jewish community to organize recreational and social activities for young people and the aged Jewish population. The worker was assured that there were no existing services in the community, but on arriving in the city where the community was located, the worker discovered that the local synagogue already had an active recreation program for youth. The synagogue sponsored soccer and basketball teams that were part of the city's recreation program. Older adults had weekly luncheons at the synagogue, and it was also involved in the community's program of senior centers. Arts and crafts activities for young people and the elderly were sponsored by the city recreation center, and many in the Jewish community were participants. So the worker's task became connecting with the existing services and organizing new programs that were not already provided. Liaison with and coordination with the synagogue's services became priorities. Many years later the Jewish community built and financed a Jewish Community Center that, as was the pattern in the city, involved both Jewish and non-Jewish people of all ages in a variety of activities.

Rural Population and Leadership Groups

As suggested by the foregoing example, rural communities come in many configurations. A Jewish community (or more correctly, subcommunity) may exist within a larger city and may have rural characteristics. Other subcommunities, such as the Amish and American Indians, are described in other chapters, as well as in this introduction.

An effective social worker in a rural area must come to understand and relate to the broad range of communities that he or she encounters. Getting to know some members, especially those recognized as leaders, is an important part of working in rural areas. Some examples, by no means exhaustive, are described in following paragraphs.

Ethnic Groups

Ethnicity may be more pronounced in smaller communities and in the subcommunities of metropolitan or urban areas. Such groups may support primary values that are different from those found in mainstream America. Some of them may be about food, dress, and socialization. Groups such as Czechoslovakians, Croatians, Slovenians, and other Eastern European ethnic groups may maintain strong identities and carry out periodic social and cultural activities, such as festivals and meals on important ethnic holidays. Cities such as Pittsburgh, PA, maintain large numbers of diverse Eastern European ethnic groups, as well as others, which are recognized in such institutions as the University of Pittsburgh Hall of Nationalities. The Museum of Texas Cultures in San Antonio recognizes dozens of Texas ethnic groups, many of which are more strongly identified in the rural parts of the state than in its large cities.

Chinese, Greek, Japanese, and Korean communities are often significant and strong subcommunities in rural areas. Many sponsor their own schools and religious organizations, such as churches. Other groups, such as those of Cambodian, Laotian, and Vietnamese origins, are often significant groups in some rural areas. In some rural areas, ethnic groups dominate. Hasidic Jewish communities in parts of rural New York are an example. Some Massachusetts towns are largely populated by people who are of Portuguese ethnicity.

As previously discussed, 6 million African Americans left the South for the North in the 20th century (Lepore, 2010). Today, Lepore reports, there are more African Americans living in Chicago than in the entire state of Mississippi. However, there are still large numbers of low-income, disadvantaged, rural, Southern African Americans, although there are few African Americans in the rural North and West. It is also true, however, that in some rural areas African Americans are top leaders, such as town or county council members, mayors, state legislators, sheriffs, and police chiefs. Many rural areas have African American majority populations and, with the voting rights acts of the 1960s, many African Americans, who were once excluded from voting, now hold office.

Migrant laborers from both within and outside the United States are a significant population in rural areas. Often, they have needs that go beyond the ordinary for education, health care, and child and family services. A variety of organizations operate with migrant groups and many include social workers. Coming to know and working with those organizations are often important tasks for the rural social worker.

New immigrants are a source of social policy and social services concern in many parts of the Unites States. Recently, there were controversies over an Arizona law, replicated in other states, which allowed law enforcement officials to question the legality of anyone appearing to possibly be an illegal immigrant and to stop and question such individuals. That law, which was of special concern to human rights groups and immigrants, as well as to U.S. citizens of Latino origin, was challenged in the courts.

So a competent rural social worker knows the ethnicity of the community. In some ways that ethnicity will affect the ways in which social work is practiced and life in the community is lived. Food choices; religious celebrations; concepts of family life; parent–child relations; and appropriate, as well as inappropriate, recreational activities are often determined by the community's ethnic composition. A fundamentalist Christian community may oppose dancing. A Muslim community may object to serving pork, as well as non-Halal meats, and nonreligious activities on Fridays. A community that is largely affiliated with the Roman Catholic Church will have other norms and priorities.

Latinos, now the largest single ethnic minority in the United States, are often well-represented as a rural population group. At times family members may be bilingual, and the rural social worker who can communicate in Spanish is often especially valuable and effective with the Latino population.

Native Americans or American Indians (both terms are used in social science and other literature) are a largely rural group, especially for those who live on reservations. Although the urban American Indian population is large and growing, reservations are located in rural areas. So, reservation-dwelling Native Americans remain an important rural ethnic group. Dr. Patricia Conway contributes Chapter 13, dealing specifically with Native Americans.

Moving around the community, talking with the leaders of the various subcommunities, and becoming aware of what is and is not important are critical beginning activities for a newcomer to rural social work practice. Of course, the list of groups is not exhaustive. Communities differ, and the key factor is developing an understanding of the various groups that comprise them.

Dual Relationships

One difficult problem for rural social workers is that of the frowned-on existence of dual relationships. As previously alluded to in this chapter and mentioned in several subsequent chapters, social workers in rural areas often find dual relationships with clients unavoidable. A social worker's client may also be his or her children's teacher or the spouse of his or her health care providers. Ideally, social workers in rural areas, as anywhere else, work to avoid dual relationships that can cause conflicts of interest. Chapter 6 is devoted to this specific issue.

Professional Isolation

One of the problems often encountered by social workers in rural communities is isolation from other social workers, as previously suggested in this chapter. Because the rural worker may be the only social worker in the agency or even in the agency's locale, it becomes particularly important for social workers in small towns to participate actively in programs of NASW and other organizations that have social work membership. Attending monthly or quarterly meetings is important, even if they are held at some distance from the social worker's employment site. Many state chapters of NASW hold annual meetings in central locations, and attending those may have higher priority for rural social workers than for their urban and metropolitan colleagues. Such meetings also provide avenues for earning the continuing education credits required by most state social work licensing boards.

National meetings of organizations, such as the National Network for Social Work Managers and other specialized social work groups, are also valuable assets for the social worker who feels isolated in a smaller work environment. Joining and being active in such groups is sometimes more important for the rural worker than for others.

Keeping up with the professional literature through the numerous publications provided by social work organizations is another way to avoid isolation and remain current. Although there were once only a handful of social work journals, there are now dozens, at least one of which covers the specialized responsibilities of most social workers.

Again, the Internet provides special opportunities for staying abreast of trends in the profession. NASW sponsors periodic educational programs by Internet for which social workers may enroll and often earn continuing education credits. Therefore, isolation need not always be a special problem of social workers in rural communities.

Rural Social Work Research

Several of the chapters in this volume deal with research on social work practice in rural areas, social problems in rural areas, and social data on rural residents.

Most U.S. government agencies, such as the National Institutes of Health, the Children's Bureau, the U.S. Department of Labor, and the U.S. Department of Agriculture, provide for research applications that deal with rural issues and populations. These agencies also provide occasional research that they conduct themselves.

The Rural Assistance Center is a project of the U.S. Department of Health and Human Services, which began in 2002 as part of the department's rural initiative. It provides information and assistance on rural health and human services issues. Information on the Center is available at its website: www.raconline.org. It also has a toll free telephone number: 1-800-270-1898. Programs and data dealing with most of the programs of American health and human services, such as mental health, child protective services, financial assistance, and others, are available through the website.

Perhaps the most extensive research on rural communities is that conducted by the Economic Research Service (ERS) of the U.S. Department of Agriculture. Because agriculture is predominantly rural, the ERS conducts research, disseminates data, and responds to questions from rural practitioners and researchers. Its website is www.ers.usda.gov. Because the Department of Agriculture also includes the Food and Nutrition Service, which administers the food stamp and nutrition programs for schools and other institutions, it has more connections with social work, particularly rural social work, than its name implies.

Conclusion

It should be clear from the suggestions in this chapter that working in rural areas is different for social workers—different, perhaps, from what was taught in baccalaureate and graduate social work courses, as well as different from information read in text books.

The special skills and knowledge needed for social work in rural communities make a difference in practice effectiveness. The remaining chapters of this edition focus on some specifics of that work and the knowledge and skills appropriate to it.

References

Beattie, A. (2009). *False economy: A surprising economic history of the world.* New York, NY: Riverhead Books.

Big city, big risks. (2010, September 20). *Time Magazine.* Retrieved from http://www.time.com/time/magazine/article/0,9171,2017223,00.html

Cromartie, J., & Buckholz, S. (2008). *Defining the rural in rural America.* Retrieved from www.ers.usda.gov.AmberWaves

Farley, O.W., & Griffiths, K. L. (1982). *Rural social work practice.* New York, NY: Simon & Schuster.

Gandel, S. (July 11, 2011). Want to make more than a banker? Become a farmer! *Time,* 38–42.

Lepore, J. (September 6, 2010). The uprooted. *The New Yorker,* 76–83.

Lohmann, N., & Lohmann, R. A. (2008) *Rural social work practice.* New York, NY: Columbia University Press.

Martinez-Brawley, E. (1981). *Seven decades of rural social work: from Country Life Commission to rural caucus.* New York, NY: Praeger.

President's National Advisory Commission on Rural Poverty. (1967). *The people left behind.* Washington, DC: U.S. Government Printing Office.

Roosevelt, T. (1909). *Report of the Country Life Commission.* Washington, DC: U.S. Government Printing Office.

Scales, L., & Streeter, C. L. (2003). *Rural social work: Building and sustaining community assets.* Pacific Grove, CA: Brooks-Cole.

Stewart, J. (2010). *Farm Fatality Summary brings safety to the forefront.* Purdue University News Service. Retrieved from http://www.purdue.edu/newsroom/outreach/2010/100609DeboyFatalities.html

Tönnies, F. (2001). *Community and civil society.* Cambridge, UK: Cambridge University Press.

U.S. Department of Labor. (2010). Injury trends in mining. Retrieved from www.msha.gov/mshainfo/factsheets/mshafct2.htm

2 Historical Treasures of Rural Communities: *Special Characteristics of Rural Places*

IRIS CARLTON-LANEY AND N. YOLANDA BURWELL

Rural communities have a plethora of traditions that both strengthen and challenge their stability in the 21st century economy. Part of strength-based social work practice asks that social workers identify, use, build on, and reinforce people's strengths and abilities. Those strengths are embedded in the history of people, places, and events. Building on strengths demands knowledge, awareness, understanding, and appreciation of history and culture as it plays out in the everyday lives and interactions of people in rural communities.

This chapter discusses historical treasures in rural communities—treasures that are hidden in plain view. These treasures include a number of activities, organizations, entrepreneurial ventures, buildings, and traditional celebrations such as local harvest and heritage festivals. These historical treasures have supported local communities, given them a sense of pride, and provided venues for recreation, celebration, and economic development.

This chapter describes these treasures and identifies ways that social workers can learn from them and ways that the sense of community is enhanced by their existence. Understanding the sense of community will allow social workers to develop the critical consciousness needed to support social capital, community collaboration, and coalition building.

Many rural communities are struggling to stay viable as they deal with loss of traditional industries and populations, persistent poverty, and aging infrastructures.

Rural poverty is pervasive, and pockets of poverty in these areas have experienced persistent poverty. About 7 million people in the rural United States lived in poverty in 2003 (Weber, Duncan, Whitner, & Miller, 2003). Five hundred or more of the rural counties in the United States are persistently poor, which means they have had poverty rates of more than 20% since 1960 (Locke & Winship, 2005). Rural poverty is both people based and place based. People based poverty concerns personal initiative, poor money management, and decision-making as explanations for low education, poor job performance, and unplanned pregnancies. Place based poverty addresses the absence of viable employment, aging water and sewer systems, poor schools, inadequate housing, and a limited number of helping services to assist people in need.

Moreover, many rural communities are losing youth to out-migration, resulting in a shrinking population. These communities are increasingly populated by elders, which can often mean they also lose tremendous quantities of owned assets that are transferred to the next generation of family who do not live in the communities and have no plans to return (Carlton-LaNey, 2005).

Additionally, these communities are often class and race divided, with embedded norms and behaviors that reinforce such separation. These divisions tend to further deflate the sense of community, deny access to resources, promote out-migration, and discourage economic development as families of prominence fail to relinquish power and control. Trends that have perpetuated these practices of excluding and marginalizing large groups of people based or class and race are gradually changing (Ritzer, 2007). Increasingly, as these communities struggle against decades of decline, some are recognizing the need to seek outside support from universities, rural economic development groups, and private consultants. Members of these communities are learning that partnerships and coalitions are preferable to practices of exclusion, if they want to survive.

Many rural communities with strong histories of racism and prejudice are also learning that marginalized people are incredible resources with rich traditions of leadership and organization. These marginalized groups must be actively included and encouraged to claim the entire community as their own. Some rural communities recognize and rely on social capital—the glue that makes things happen in these communities. It reflects the connections among individuals, groups, and organizations (Lohmann, 2005) and helps expand the sense of community. When people are committed and willing to work hard for their communities, positive change and growth are more likely to result.

Traditional activities within these marginalized communities that were largely ignored by the dominant sector are now being claimed as sources of "pride" for the larger community. Within the past 25 years, the histories and traditions of African American and American Indian communities have attracted more widespread interest (Wellman, 2002).

This critical change in attitude and perception has contributed to tremendous investment in rural communities' cultural capital. Cultural capital can be a tangible or intangible asset that contributes to cultural value. Tangible cultural capital assets exist "in buildings, structures, sites and locations endowed with cultural significance...artworks and artifacts" and intangible cultural assets include "the set of ideas, practices, beliefs, traditions and values which serve to identify and bind together ...with the stock of artworks, existing in the public domain as public goods" (Throsby, 1999, p.7). Flora, Flora, Fey, and Emery's (2007) effort to describe how communities work describes a Community Capital Framework, which includes natural, human, social built, political, financial, and cultural capital. They say that cultural capital

includes the dynamics of who we know and feel comfortable with, what heritages are valued, collaboration across races, ethnicities, and generations, etc. Cultural capital influences what voices are heard and listened to, which voices have influence in what areas, and how creativity, innovation, and influence emerge and are nurtured. Cultural capital might include ethnic festivals, multilingual populations or a strong work ethic. (Iowa State University, 2011)

Essentially, Flora and his colleagues (2007) believe that cultural capital is also the way people act in and know their world.

The hidden treasures discussed in this chapter reflect valued heritages, long term and more recent, and illustrate rural communities' emerging innovative approaches to the preservation and marketing of history and historical practices and traditions. The hidden treasures that are subsequently presented include beach resorts and their historical legacies, Underground Railroad sites, powwows, festivals, and buildings, such as the Rosenwald Schools, all of which have left historical legacies.

Rosenwald Schools

Rosenwald Schools are an excellent example of early built material culture in rural areas. Between 1912 and 1932 Julius Rosenwald, president of Sears, Roebuck, and Co., and Booker T. Washington, head of the Tuskegee Institute, implemented a grant program to seed the building of schools for African American children during the Jim Crow era. By the end of the program this grant had helped finance 5,357 buildings, which included 4,977 schools, 217 teacherages or teacher homes, and 163 industrial shops in 15 Southern states, from Maryland to Texas (Fairclough, 2000). Many of these buildings were located in small towns in rural counties on land donated by African Americans as part of their contribution to the effort to educate their children. Although many have been destroyed, it is estimated that 10% to 20% of the school buildings have survived.

> The Rosenwald program typically covered less than a third of construction, but it launched African American communities into creative fund-raising efforts and encouraged the black community to work with local school systems. Penny drives, charitable giving and self-sacrifice provided the money to match the grants. Even with the added financial burden of community fund-raising by those who could least afford it, thousands of schools were built across the rural South. (Perry, 2009)

Today many of these same communities are renovating and adapting these buildings for various community uses such as senior citizen centers, community outreach centers, and museums or cultural heritage centers. In 2002 the National Trust for Historic Preservation identified Rosenwald Schools as some of America's most endangered historic places. Both the federal impetus and grant funding have contributed to the wave of Rosenwald school renovations taking place throughout the South. The federal initiative also indicates recognition that these iconic schools are a critical part of American history and that they recall a chapter in rural American life when marginalized people, specifically African Americans, were denied public education. The schools stood as testament to African Americans' active participation in establishing their own institutions (Fairclough, 2000). The Rosenwald funds helped change the attitudes of White Americans toward the education for African Americans and established a collaborative partnership that included African Americans, Whites, and the Rosenwald Fund.

Renovating and revitalizing these Rosenwald school buildings as valuable community gathering places has encouraged the entire community to take advantage of these tangible pieces of cultural capital. Community members bring to the restoration of these schools the same sense of pride and self-help, fund-raising, and community development skills that their earlier counterparts did. They are becoming community showplaces and providing sites of interest for tourists and community residents alike. Many communities highlight their Rosenwald school sites on their websites, providing travel directions and inviting visitors to stop in. The small, neglected, wooden structures are coming back to life and bringing rural low-wealth communities with them.

Onslow County, North Carolina— Bear Island Hammocks Beach State Park

The Barrier Islands' Hammocks Beach State Park is another type of cultural capital, hidden away in a fairly isolated coastal community in southeast North Carolina. Today more than 200,000 people visit Hammocks Beach State Park and enjoy its natural beauty and boating and fishing activities. Most people are unaware of its unique history. Dr. William Sharpe, a wealthy New York neurosurgeon, purchased The Hammocks as hunting, fishing, and farming retreat. The Hammocks included more than 4 miles of beachfront and woodlands and an abundance of fish and fowl. John and Gertrude Hurst were the African American caretakers of the 4,600 acres of land during Sharpe's absence. A local school teacher, Gertrude cooked for the Sharpes when they vacationed at the retreat. Sharpe (1952, p. 204) describes The Hammocks in his autobiography:

> The property was ideal for my purposes; at the same time it was excellent for rais-ing cattle and hogs and farming cotton, tobacco, peanuts, watermelon, and the usual garden crops. I confess that the farming was of little interest to me com-pared with the hunting of quail, turkeys, ducks, and geese, the fishing for chan-nel bass, bluefish, mackerel, spearing of flounders at night—and, perhaps above all, the eating of hard-shelled clams, oysters, crabs, and shrimp which abound everywhere. During the past thirty years (with all telephone lines purposely torn out and no electric service) The Hammocks has been a paradise for my family and professional colleagues, especially with John and Gertrude supervising.

William Sharpe had a unique relationship with John Hurst. He admired Hurst greatly for his knowledge of farming and fishing and for his personal character. He did not tolerate or acquiesce to the attitudes and behaviors of racial superior-ity that governed that time. Sharpe was challenged by local Whites about allow-ing John Hurst to manage his enormous property, but Sharpe did not give in to the threats he received. Instead, he offered $5,000 for information leading to the arrest and conviction of any person who damaged the personnel or property at The Hammocks. He had no further trouble from local residents.

Sharpe's original intent was to bequeath The Hammocks to the Hursts for their loyal service and love of the land. Instead, at Gertrude Hurst's urging, he deeded The Hammocks to the North Carolina Teachers Association in 1949. Gertrude Hurst reasoned that The Hammocks would provide "vacation and assembly facilities for the many classroom teachers in North Carolina whose limited income would not finance vacations at costly resorts" (Murray, 1984). Sharpe honored her request and wrote in 1949 that he had transferred the acreage that constituted The Hammocks to the 8,000

Negro schoolteachers of North Carolina under an arrangement whereby we may share it with them so long as we live, as may also John and Gertrude Hurst while they live, as we agreed to match every dollar they themselves raised for improving it. So vigorous and successful have they been in raising funds that it's going to cost us a tidy sum of money, but nothing that we have ever done in our lives has given us more happiness (Sharpe, 1952, p. 216).

At the time The Hammocks was worth more than one-half million dollars. Negotiations to acquire the land began in 1946. There were conditions attached to its transfer. The state had to agree to build a bridge over the water to provide better access to the land. Sharpe agreed to give the land and provide matching funds, if the North Carolina Teachers Association, the state professional organization for African American educators, would raise $100,000 for the development of the property.

Two years later, the Hammocks Beach Corporation was established

"to provide, maintain and administer the properties or interests therein which may be acquired by this corporation in the property known as the "Hammocks" in Onslow County, North Carolina, and its assembly, vacation, and recreation facilities primarily for the teachers in public and private elementary, secondary, and collegiate institutions for Negroes in North Carolina who may which to use the said facilities as individuals or groups subject to regulations set by the Board of Directors" (Murray, 1984, p. 76–77).

The North Carolina Teachers Association envisioned the Hammocks as a conference/retreat center for all the African American professional, civic, and church groups such as the New Farmers of America, State Congress of Negro Parents and Teachers, and the State Nurses' Association. It was not intended to be a playground for the general public (Murray, 1984).

The first campaign to raise the $100,000 began in 1950; each teacher was assessed $13.67. The initial campaign was successful.

Unfortunately, progress was stymied by several stumbling blocks. The state's promise to construct the bridge from the mainland to the beach park still had not been fulfilled by 1955. This was troubling to Sharpe, who was equally disturbed by the teacher association's plans to make The Hammocks a segregated facility. Sharpe was reluctant to proceed with transferring the land, if his requirements and stipulations were not met (Murray, 1984). Complicating matters further, no provision for the matching funds was stated in Dr. Sharpe's will when he died in 1960.

Plans and fundraising continued around the development of this land into the early 1950s. The grand opening of the Hammocks Beach project took place May 1952. Featured at the opening was a large assembly hall named in honor of Gertrude Hurst. A motel that could accommodate 24 people and a bath house were in operation. Various African American associations with special campsites erected buildings to accommodate their memberships (Murray, 1984).

In 1960, 750 acres of beach land was deeded to the North Carolina Park Commission to develop a state park. The state hard surfaced the roads, built picnic areas, added personnel quarters, and provided a ferry service. The beach officially opened to African Americans only in 1961, but with the passage of the Civil Rights Act of 1964, the park was made available to all, regardless of race.

Such struggles to establish and maintain facilities for the creation of wholesome and healthful gathering spaces for a marginalized group are a pervasive aspect of American history. Today Hammocks Beach is part of the Jacksonville-Onslow African American Heritage Trail. This trail represents the combined efforts of Onslow County's tourism industry, county museum, and minority business services division of the Chamber of Commerce. Information about the park and beach is advertised on the Onslow County Tourism Official website. North Carolina boasts that thousands of people visit Bear Island to enjoy the unspoiled barrier island and its lovely unspoiled beach front.

The Underground Railroad

Like other hidden treasures, the sites of the Underground Railroad have become important cultural capital. In 1996 the U.S. Department of the Interior released a

National Park Service Study that explored options for preserving and commemorating the historical Underground Railroad. This study focused on the "sites, routes and other resources that remain available for public education and appreciation" (PWTS MultiMedia, 2011). Although this treasured piece of cultural capital is not a specific place, it does represent a movement that pulled diverse people together for a common goal of freedom for enslaved Africans. It has come to represent one of the most powerful forces for freedom in recorded history (PWTS MultiMedia, 2011). In 1998 Senator Carol Moseley Braun (D, IL) introduced a bill to commemorate the sites on the Underground Railroad. Cosponsored by Congressmen Rob Portman (R, OH) and Louis Stokes (D, OH), the bill was signed into law in 1998 by President Bill Clinton. The law authorized the National Park Service to "link sites of the Underground Railroad, produce educational materials and commemorate the 19th century escape route" (Johnson, 1998). Many of these escape routes have been destroyed and, due to the clandestine nature of the Underground Railroad, it is challenging to produce historical documentation to prove that a specific site was actually part of the route. Like the federal government's role in uncovering and preserving Rosenwald Schools, interest in the sites along the routes of the Underground Railroad has been rekindled. Wellman describes this phenomenon as "scholars...running to catch up with this re-fueled freedom train" (2002, p. 211), which had been largely ignored by historians, historic preservationists, and archaeologists.

Scholars have undertaken the daunting task of identifying sites and providing that evidence to the National Register of Historic Places. For example, the work of a team of scholars, volunteers, and students in New York used a variety of sources to conduct their research. Among other things they used published articles in local history publications, minutes of antislavery meetings, personal letters, and diaries; family stories printed on obituaries; and "city directories, deeds, maps, assessment records, mortgages, wills, and physical evidence from the sites themselves" (Wellman, 2002, p. 14).

Archaeologists, like other scholars, are acknowledging their role in the negligence of African American history and its preservation. However, LaRoche (2005) laments the undervaluation of archaeological contributions to African American history and encourages the use of the powerful tool of archaeological inquiry to expand historical approaches. She notes that

Through a combination of archaeological, family, and historical records, archaeologists are realizing that free people of color involved with the Underground

Railroad adopted a radical stance in helping one another, often risking their own freedom to ensure the escape of family, friends, or loved ones, as well as strangers. One must literally create this history by first identifying and confirming sites and then looking at census data, deed books, slave schedules, and old maps in order to formulate historical perspectives and create a thematic presence. Heritage resources cannot be effectively established until after historical analyses have been completed. (LaRoche, 2005, p. 36)

As scholars are engaged in documenting the historic sites along the Underground Railroad routes, local municipalities are busy building these sites into their tourism programs. Of the 1,001 Vacation Ideas in Pennsylvania, the state tourism website boasts some 20 different sites that involved the famous Underground Railroad. Other communities provide tours of their Underground Railroad sites along with elaborate activities for children to demonstrate, with costumed guides, the life of farm families engaged as conductors along the route.

Festivals

Festivals provide an important form of cultural capital that enhances community identity and pride. One of the major reasons given for hosting festivals is to "generate profits for local business and to raise funds for civic and charitable purposes" (Janiskee, 1991, p. 32). Festivals in rural communities can also bring publicity for the area and its sponsoring organizations, "foster civic pride and community spirit, and can boost morale in a declining area" (Janiskee, 1991, p. 32). Furthermore, festivals give rural communities an opportunity to demonstrate their individual character and allow them to include and spotlight community ethnic groups' culturally distinctive contributions. Festival season usually takes place between April and October. Festivals are "formal periods or programs of pleasurable activities, entertainment or events having a festive character and publicly celebrating some concept, happening or fact," generally lasting 1–2 days (Janiskee, 1991, p. 34). Most rural festivals rely on volunteers and donations and are simple, inexpensive, family-oriented events. South Carolina claimed that its rich history and proliferation of festivals placed a festival event within an hour's drive for every state resident. The names and types of rural festivals include food, heritage, and harvest celebrations, such as the Watermelon Festival and Salley's Chitlin Strut.

Several states host azalea festivals, which celebrate spring along with beautiful gardens, history, culture, and charm. North Carolina' Azalea Festival is a 5-day

event with entertainment, street fairs, concerts, pageantry, and a parade. This festival, which has celebrated its 64th year, attracts more than 300,000 visitors to
Wilmington and is billed as "the best party in the South" (North Carolina Azalea
Festival, 2011). The large and impressive Azalea Festival is not in a rural community, but it spills over into the surrounding rural parts of the state, providing fun,
pageantry, opportunities for fellowship, and temporary employment.

Heritage festivals are also part of the culture capital of rural communities. North
Carolina hosts two Scottish Highland Games. The Grandfather Mountain Highland
Games is a 4-day festival in the mountains, and the other is a 1-day event held in
the southeastern part of the state in Robeson County, called the Flora Macdonald
Highland Games (Chhabra, Sills, & Cubbage, 2003). People attend heritage festivals to enjoy friends, family, and food along with the competitive games. Ten surrounding counties benefit from the economic profits of the games in the mountain
county, because there are not enough hotels and eateries to accommodate the needs
of the visitors in the host county alone. The overall economies in these communities benefit from these games and can bank on this infusion of money into their
economies, because the games are annual events with large numbers of repeat and
new visitors (Chhabra et al., 2003).

In the West and Midwest, festivals and tourism are likely oriented toward agri-
tourism and outdoor adventure with nature-based activities that are associated
with public lands and frontier assets (Wang & Piaster, 2008). Various other types
of festivals also exist throughout the country. A small rural community in western
Colorado hosts the Carbondale Mountain Fair, which is now enjoying its 40th anniversary. This festival brings high-quality and unique art and crafts to the valley
and more than 20,000 visitors. It boasts a family-friendly environment of music,
art, and entertainment (Long & Perdue, 1990).

Long and Perdue (1990) posited that it is often difficult to ascertain the profits
that rural festivals generate, because the rural communities lack opportunities for
people to spend money and each festival is unique in terms of composition of ex-
hibitors, attendees, and community character. Nonetheless, it is, beneficial for festivals to support local cultural groups, artists, musicians, food service entities, and
others in the promotion of the festivals and the rural communities overall.

The Chitlin Strut in Salley, SC, is a celebration of "chitlins" (chitterlings), which
are minced and fried pig intestines. At the first festival in 1966 more than 600
pounds of chitlins were served. Today thousands of pounds of chitlins are con-
sumed by the 25,000 people who attend this popular festival. The International

Chitlin Strut festival has generated substantial revenues that have been used to completely equip Salley's fire department and provide "free garbage collections, a police car, lighted tennis courts, a jail renovation, new town well and water lines, new sidewalks and a new town hall completed with a lighted fountain" (Janiskee, 1980, p. 102).

Rural festivals have become part of the formal economy of these communities and even receive public assistance seed money in anticipation of profits. However, it is prudent to remember that with the influx of large numbers of visitors to poor rural communities, opportunities for informal economies are also more readily available. An informal economy is any economic activity that is not reported and that operates without administrative monitoring and control (Ratner, 2000). Informal economies can be criminal, such as drug dealing and prostitution, along with other illegal economies such as that produced by people working at exhibit areas for vendors who do not record the work or the pay and other similar opportunistic activities. These informal economies are common among low-wage, marginalized workers and have become a widely accepted and eagerly anticipated part of their survival system. Many of these informal economies associated with festivals are clandestine and, as such, contribute to the difficulty of assessing the extent of the contribution of festivals to local economic growth. Yet these informal economies are also very valuable to the individuals who are involved and to the local community's economy. Individuals (and family groups, as well) use festivals as an opportunity to earn extra money, peddle their arts and crafts, develop marketable skills, and cultivate a market for their wares. Although this is difficult to measure as one looks at the overall economic value of festivals, these individuals benefit greatly, have more disposable income, and ultimately contribute more to the local economy.

Powwows

Powwows are celebrations of American Indian culture and spirituality. These celebrations feature American Indian drums and dance, along with crafts and foods offered by vendors. Cultural identity among American Indians has been fragile because of the decades of discrimination, prejudice, maltreatment, poverty, and community devastation resulting in out-migration to urban centers (Goertzen, 2001). For some tribes powwows were and continue to be a response to the assaults on these communities. By definition, powwows are not tribe specific, and they convey the role of "contemporary Indianness, and as such are a complex interplay of communication regarding tribal, intertribal and cross-cultural concerns" (Sanchez, 2001, p. 66–67).

Powwows are a form of cultural capital that American Indians make available to the larger rural community. But unlike many of the cultural capital rural community assets described, powwows are very controlled environments. They allow and encourage non-Indian participation, but on Indian terms. The emcee at the powwow continuously provides introductions, information, instructions, and directions, while reminding non-Indian visitors that this is Indian space and they are to respect the sacredness of the arena by entering only when an invitation is extended. Powwows often provide a brief list of "dos" and "don'ts" to non-Indian guests as well. As non-Indians attend powwows, seeking the American Indian experience or, ideally, to better understand and appreciate their marginalized neighbors, they are encouraged to "re-think the accustomed power differential (Sanchez, 2001, p. 63).

In North Carolina the powwow has become one of the primary tools for displaying and defining American Indians' collective identity to non-Indians. Powwows in this state, and others as well, have adopted some of the practices of plains American Indians. North Carolina American Indian powwows "slid smoothly into an existing ceremonial niche" (Goertzen, 2001, p. 61)—the Protestant revivals. This church-centered event has critical features of powwows, such as the sharing of food, assembling and celebrating, and interacting with old friends and making new ones.

Some mid-Atlantic American Indians' heritages have been downplayed and even denied by their local communities. As one Waccamaw-Siouan tribal leader stated, "We were afraid to even say we were Indian because we were laughed at. We don't care about being laughed at anymore." She further indicated that they were no longer "hiding in the swamps" but were using their powwows to educate people about their culture and heritage (Museum of the Native American Resource Center, 2005). This reluctance to self-identify has basis in the genocidal Trail of Tears, which forced five tribes in the Southeast, including North Carolina's Cherokee nation, to relocate to Oklahoma. For some of these tribes, their public emergence as Indians came with their first powwows (Goertzen, 2001).

Powwows contribute to the local economy in minimal ways and, unlike the hidden treasures previously discussed, have not become part of the community's local economy. Among some tribes, such as the Ojibwe-Anishinaabe of Minnesota and Wisconsin, both the traditional powwow and the contest powwow are held.

Much discussion of the merits of one over the other has taken place. Some of the disenchantment with contest powwows is that they have made the powwow a commercialized venture with fees for admission, dance politics, and judging favoritism and bias. DesJarlait (1997) believes that both have merit. He identifies the merits of both, indicating that the "Drum, which symbolizes peace and goodwill between communities" (DesJarlait, 1997, p. 126) ensures that the traditional powwow remains strong and that the traditional powwow helps to retain and express tribal-centricity. Conversely, the contest powwow helps individual dancers "build confidence, character, stamina, and balance," allows spectators see the best dancers in each category, and has created a renaissance in powwow music (DesJarlait, 1997, p. 126).

Powwows are a representation of American Indian values and help illustrate and reinforce the primacy of spiritual health and a sense of community wellbeing over material possessions. Powwows are intertribal in many regions, which facilitates the sharing of dancers and musicians, many of whom travel to numerous powwows throughout the season. In one sense, powwows represent a singular political voice of Indian unity and serve as an opportunity for American Indians to negotiate their relationship with non-American Indians (Goertzen, 2001; Sanchez, 2001).

Conclusion

These rich sources of cultural capital are evident throughout rural America but tend to be hidden in plain view. They represent valuable community resources, power sources, and, to varying degrees, needed economic and image boosters for poor rural communities. The individuals and organizations engaged with these hidden treasures also are critical community assets, and their value-added roles must be considered in any rural community practice.

Several practice themes have been identified among scholars as essential to rural social work. They include "the social worker as generalist, an emphasis on community development, the importance of external relations, the importance of cultural influences and desirable personal and professional traits" (Locke & Winship, 2005, p. 5). These themes support a community practice model approach in rural communities. Community practice recognizes the need to work with community leaders, elected officials, professionals, task groups, agricultural extension agents, and marginalized groups (Weil & Gamble, 1995). The coalition model of community practice is ideal when helping communities invest in themselves. Through coalitions separate groups can work together for collective social change. The work of coalitions includes organizing for such issues as affordable housing or against gang violence. Efforts to enact legislation, involve the National Park Service in initiatives to preserve historic sites along the Underground Railroad routes, and identify and preserve the iconic Rosenwald Schools involved coalition building and political action.

Similarly, the work of community festivals relies on the strength of coalitions. Festivals can have multiple effects on communities. They can "serve the needs of residents, can protect the natural environment through increased attention to it, increase social equity by providing residents with a participatory role and provide a vision for participation" (Derrett, 2003, p. 36). Because coalitions have a limited life span, their work of producing a community festival would end with the festival event. Through their multiorganizational power base, impressive enough to draw down funding to respond to their common interest, local rural festival coalitions can affect the life of their communities by enhancing the livability and well-being of its residents. Social workers engaged in community practice are invaluable as leaders and spokespersons able to communicate with the various factions and use mediation and negotiation skills to keep the coalition focused and balance tensions (Weil & Gamble, 1995).

Powwows, as critical cultural capital, illustrate the importance of identity, independence, interdependence, and sense of self. American Indians, as a marginalized group, might find that the community practice model of political and social action best serves their interest. Social workers in political and social action accept the roles of advocate, educator, and organizer. The role of social work is to assist group members in becoming their own advocates. Most of the work is to facilitate leadership and capacity building. Rural communities are not always receptive to outside intervention, even when invited. American Indian tribes are a unique rural community with strict rules for membership, which is tribal enrollment. A social worker who is enrolled in the tribe is best positioned to engage successfully in the political and social action community practice model. She or he is already an accepted member of the community with knowledge of the history, heritage, and tradition. These attributes facilitate her or his involvement and add credibility.

A community social worker's role in rural communities is critical to helping these communities thrive and grow. Their work involves multiple approaches and strategies and is valuable when working in collaboration with numerous stakeholders.

The use and promotion of cultural capital in community growth and development provides an ideal role for social workers to build on the strengths and existing resources within the community.

References

Carlton-LaNey, I. (2005). *African Americans aging in the rural south: Stories of faith, family and community*. Durham, NC: Sourwood Press.

Chhabra, D., Sills, E., & Cubbage, F. (2003). The significance of festivals to rural economies: Estimating the economic impacts of Scottish Highland Games in North Carolina. *Journal of Travel Research 41*, 421–427.

Derrett, R. (2003). Festivals & regional destinations: How festivals demonstrate a sense of community & place. *Rural Society, 13*(1), 35–53.

DesJarlait, R. (1997). The contest powwow versus the traditional powwow and the role of Native American community. *Wicazo Sa Review, 12*(1), 115–127.

Fairclough, A. (2000). "Being in the field of education and also being a Negro...seems...tragic:" Black teachers in the Jim Crow south. *Journal of American History, 87*(1), 65–91.

Flora, C., Flora, J., Fey, S., & Emery, M. (2007). *Community capitals framework brief*. Retrieved from http://education.byu.edu.libproxy.lib.unc.edu/ellsymposium /documents/community_capital.pdf

Goertzen, C. (2001). Powwows and identity on the Piedmont and Coastal Plains of North Carolina. *Ethnomusicology, 45*(1), 58–88.

Iowa State University, Department of Sociology. (2011). *Community capitals*. Retrieved from http://webcache.googleusercontent.com/search?q=cache:NpwIGm 7vxuIJ:www.soc.iastate.edu/staff/cflora/ncrcrd/capitals.html+flora+and +Flora,+community+cultural+capital+framework+2011&cd=7&hl=en&ct =clnk&gl=us&client=firefox-a

Janiskee, B. (1980). South Carolina's harvest festivals: Rural delights for day tripping urbanites. *Journal of Cultural Geography, 1*(1), 96–104.

Janiskee, R. (1991). Rural festivals in South Carolina. *Journal of Cultural Geography, 11*(2), 31–43.

Johnson, R. E. (ed). (1998). President Clinton signs Underground Railroad Act to preserve sites of historical slave escape routes. *Jet* 94(11): 24. Retrieved from http://books.google.com/books?id=Y8QDAAAAMBAJ&pg=PA24&lpg=PA24&dq=Car ol+Moseley+Braun+worked+on+the+underground+railroad+act&source=bl&ots=BbU GBX08Rc&sig=bxBC-ps0FWereZQ8n1gmruM-wS8&hl=en&ei=mfehTdTeAq HD0QGFmdWTBQ&sa=X&oi=book_result&ct=result&resnum=3&ved=0CCcQ6AE wAg#v=onepage&q&f=false.

LaRoche, C. (2005). Heritage, archaeology, and African American history. *Society for American Archaeology Archaeological Record, 5*(2), 34–37, 44.

Locke, B., & Winship, J. (2005). Social work in rural America. In N. Lohmann & R. Lohmann (Eds.), *Rural social work practice* (pp. 3–24). New York, NY: Columbia University Press.

Lohmann, R. (2005). The third sector in rural America. In N. Lohmann & R. Lohmann (Eds.), *Rural social work practice* (p. 86–102). New York, NY: Columbia University Press.

Long, P., & Perdue, R. (1990). The economic impact of rural festivals and special events: Assessing the spatial distribution of expenditures. *Journal of Travel Research, 28,* 10–14.

Murray, P. E. (1984). *History of the North Carolina Teachers Association.* Washington, DC: National Education Association.

Museum of the Native American Resource Center. (Producer). (2005). *In the heart of tradition: The eight state-recognized tribes of North Carolina and the NC Commission of Indian Affairs* [DVD].

North Carolina Azalea Festival. (2011). 2011 North Carolina Azalea Festival. Retrieved from http://www.ncazaleafestival.org/

North Carolina State Parks. (2011). Hammocks Beach State Park. Retrieved from http://149.168.1.195/~habe/history.htm

Perry, R. (2009, August). The story of the lost schoolhouses. *Southern Living.* Retrieved from http://trustworthyimage.com/gallery/clips/clips2.pdf

PWTS MultiMedia. (2011). *National Park Service.* Retrieved from http://www.harriettubman.com/nps.html

Ratner, S. (2000). *The informal economy in rural community economic development.* [TVA Rural Studies/Contract Papers 00-03]. Retrieved from http://www.rural.org/publications/reports.html

Ritzer, G. (2007). *The McDonaldization of society.* Los Angeles, CA: Pine Forge Press.

Sanchez, V. (2001). Intertribal dance and cross cultural communication: Traditional powwows in Ohio. *Communication Studies, 52*(1), 51–69.

Sharpe, W. (1952). *Brain surgeon: The autobiography of William Sharpe.* New York, NY: Viking Press.

Throsby, D. (1999). Cultural capital. *Journal of Cultural Economics, 23,* 3–11.

Wang, Y., & Pfister, R. (2008). Residents' attitudes toward tourism and perceived personal benefits in a rural community. *Journal of Travel Research, 47,* 84–95. doi: 10.1177/0047287507312402.

Weber, B., Duncan, G., Whitner, L., & Miller, K. (2003). Still left behind, but gaining ground: Rural poverty in America. *Perspectives on Poverty, Policy, & Place, 1*(4), 3–5.

Weil, M., & Gamble, D. N. (1995). Community practice models. In R. L. Edwards (Ed.), *Encyclopedia of social work*, 19th ed. (p. 577–594). Washington, DC: NASW Press.

Wellman, J. (2002). The Underground Railroad and the National Register of Historic Places: Historical importance vs. architectural integrity. *Public Historian*, 24(1), 11–29.

3   A Case Study of Empowerment Interventions for the Eradication of Absolute Poverty in Southeast Rural Coastal Villages of Mauritius

KOMALSINGH RAMBAREE

The Island of Mauritius is situated in the Indian Ocean. It has a land surface area of 1,865 square kilometers and is considered to be peaceful, politically stable, multiethnic and multicultural, and making steady socioeconomic progress. According to the 2000 census report (Central Statistics Office, 2000) Mauritius has a population of about 1.2 million with the following ethnic composition: 52% Hindus, 16% Muslims (both of Indian origin), 27% Creoles (Mauritians of African descent), 3% Chinese, and 2% European decedents (mostly of French origin).

From 1638 to 1968 Mauritius was successively a former colony of the Dutch, the French, and the British. Since gaining its independence from Britain in 1968, Mauritius has been making remarkable socioeconomic progress. For instance, since the early 1980s Mauritius has had an average annual economic growth of approximately 5%, and, simultaneously, continuous efforts have been maintained by successive governments to consolidate the welfare state. During the past few decades Mauritius has shifted from being a predominantly agriculture-based economy to an economy based on an additional four pillars: manufacturing, tourism, financial services, and information communication and technology. The Mauritian welfare state is consolidated through an extensive set of social policies and programs, including free education at all levels, free health care, a universal basic retirement pension, assistance to families with special needs, and social aid/cash transfers (Government of Mauritius, 2006). According to the International Fund for Agricultural Development

(IFAD, 2005), Mauritius stands out as a social, economic, and development success story within the African continent.

However, the eradication of poverty has been a major challenge for several years in Mauritius. In particular, the United Nations Development Programs (UNDP, 2008) reports that in Mauritius

> The proportion of poor households below the relative poverty line increased from 7.7% in 2001/02 to 8.0% in 2006/07... and the Gini coefficient increased from 0.371 in 2001/02 to 0.389 in 2006/07 indicating an increase in income inequality. (p. 1)

According to official figures there are 7,157 families living in extreme poverty in 229 deprived regions of Mauritius (Ministry of Finance & Economic Development, 2009). Some 12% of the Mauritian population is estimated to be poor, based on a poverty benchmark calculated at 50% of the median monthly household expenditure (Ministry of Environment & National Development Unit, 2010). The Central Statistic's "Household Budget Survey," based on data collected during 2001–2002 and 2006–2007, reports that poverty has worsened in Mauritius (Ministry of Finance & Economic Development, 2009). In a similar manner, the Poverty Observatory Bulletin (2009, p. 4) concludes that the "clear consensus evident from this study was that for the poor life is more difficult nowadays in comparison with 12 months ago."

The main reason for rapidly rising rates of poverty over the past few years in Mauritius is commonly explained by two major phenomena—postcolonialism and globalization. Since the colonial period a particular section of the population has been marginalized. For instance, after the abolition of slavery the descendants of slaves did not have the savings and means, as unpaid laborers, to buy parts of the land occupied by the French settlers in Mauritius, whereas the descendants of the Indian immigrants worked on job contract and managed to save money to buy land, which helped them to attain socioeconomic mobility. Therefore, the marginalized group has been sinking into poverty.

Additionally, there is the effect of the neoclassical/neoliberal wave on the Mauritian economy. For instance, the Mauritian sugar industry is affected by the review of the African Caribbean Pacific–European Union trade and World Trade Organization agreements, whereby preferential tariffs are being dismantled. The textile industry also no longer has the reserve quotas and duty-free access to some international markets that it had under the multifiber agreement (Rambaree, 2009). It is also commonly known that the neoclassical/neoliberal wave makes the poor poorer in difficult circumstances (Stiglitz, 2002). For instance, poor people are often informally employed in vulnerable positions and conditions. As a result of job loss, poor people sink into further poverty.

In Mauritius billions of rupees (RS) are spent on poverty alleviation programs, and a priority has been set for the Eradication of Absolute Poverty (EAP). In this context, the National Empowerment Foundation (NEF) was set up in 2006 with an initial lifespan of 5 years and a budget of about USD 170 million (RS 5 billion; 1 US dollar is equivalent to approximately 30 Mauritian rupees) to fund various empowerment programs such as adult literacy, employability, life skills training, learn to earn, and so on (NEF, 2009a). Moreover, the Trust Fund for the Integration of Vulnerable Groups, another body within the government sector, was established in 1999 with a total budget of USD 17.9 million (RS 500 million) and has been working with some 60,000 vulnerable men, women, and children in rural and urban areas of Mauritius (IFAD, 2005).

In addition, in Mauritius all profitable firms are required to spend 2% of their profits on corporate social responsibility (CSR) activities approved by the government or otherwise transfer funds for use in the fight against poverty (Government of Mauritius, 2010). In 2010 the CSR contribution from all profitable companies was estimated at approximately RS 1 billion per year. After the legislative election of 2010, the new government of Mauritius set up the new Ministry of Social Integration and Economic Empowerment (MSIEE) to focus and coordinate the fight against poverty. The MSIEE brought together parapublic agencies and corporate partners involved in empowerment. The NEF, in addition to fulfilling its mandate, provides an overall coordinating framework for the programs to fight poverty undertaken by the Trust Fund for the Integration of Vulnerable Groups, EAP, the Decentralised Cooperation Programme (initiated by the European Union), and the programs of corporate partners (African Development Bank, 2009).

Several nongovernmental organizations (NGOs) also are actively involved in empowering people and communities. Most NGOs in Mauritius are affiliated with an umbrella organization called Mauritius Council of Social Services (MACOSS). MACOSS is planning to set up a strong coordinating team with 30 NGOs engaged in poverty eradication in Mauritius (MACOSS, 2010). The Mauritian NGOs obtain grants and funds from a variety of sources, such as international donors/funders, local sources such as the NGO-Trust Fund (government subsidies to the NGOs), and corporate bodies (as part of their contributions through CSR). In addition, several corporate bodies—such as Rogers, Beachcomber Hotels, Medine Sugar Estates, and so on—have set up their own internal organizational structures to contribute toward empowerment and to fight poverty in Mauritius. Altogether, it is estimated that more than 200 field social workers (from NGOs, government, and the private sector) are engaged in empowerment initiatives and the fight against poverty in urban and rural parts of Mauritius. The majority of the field social workers have university degrees either in social work or social sciences, and they are regularly involved in ongoing training courses and seminars related to poverty alleviation. The University of Mauritius is the only local tertiary institution that provides bachelor's level social work education, with an annual output of about 20 graduates.

According to IFAD (2005), the distinction between rural and urban areas is not always clear-cut in Mauritius because of the small size of the island, fairly good roads, and a growing economy from the tourism industry, which is mainly based in the rural coastal areas. Public service and infrastructure in most of the rural areas are similar to those in most of the urban areas in Mauritius. Usually, rural areas are characterized by having different lifestyles, livelihood strategies, and cultural patterns (Perpar, 2007). However, in Mauritius several rural and urban areas have similar characteristics, although cultural practices and traditions and livelihoods based on fishing and agriculture are somewhat more predominant in the rural parts. In Mauritius, *rural area* is defined in accordance with the boundaries of four districts and 124 village council areas; *urban area* is defined by the boundaries of five municipal council areas (IFAD, 2005). In making the distinction between urban and rural areas in Mauritius, the Ministry of Finance and Economic Development (2006) states:

During the past two Household Budget Surveys, all the five Municipal Wards of Mauritius were categorized for statistical purposes as urban except for some regions found in remote urban areas which were considered as either semi-urban or rural. Some villages having infrastructural facilities such as hospitals, schools and shopping centers were classified as semi-urban whilst the other villages were classified as rural.

Given the small size of the island and the close boundaries between rural and urban areas, the majority of social workers in Mauritius have experience in working with both urban and rural communities. Generally, rural social work can be viewed from two different perspectives. The first perspective in rural social work is focused on the place/setting—rurality—and looks at social work issues within such a context. The second perspective is based on the practice of social work, taking into consideration the knowledge and skills required for social workers to operate within such a context (Ginsberg, 2005; Pugh & Cheers, 2010).

Within rural social work some researchers and academics have reported certain distinct characteristics in the practice, such as being a generalist in orientation, community development focused, and sensitive to the rural cultural traditions (Cheers & Pugh, 2010; Ginsberg, 2005; Locke & Winship, 2005). Saltman, Gumbert, Allen-Kelly, & Zubrzycki (2004) argue that studies specifically focusing on the identification of differences between rural and urban social work practices have found little variation. In this sense, it is recommended that the study of rural social work focus more on bringing in-depth knowledge about the practice of social work from different corners of the world to have a better and broader understanding of the practice of rural social work within different contexts of rurality (Locke & Winship, 2010; Saltman et al., 2004). In this connection, this chapter considers the case study of empowerment interventions undertaken by the social workers for the EAP in the Southeast Rural Coastal Villages (SRCVs) of Mauritius.

Methodology

This chapter is grounded on the findings gathered from three rural villages: Old Grand Port (also referred as Vieux Grand Port), Bois des Amourettes, and Grand Sable. The data were collected through 22 semistructured interviews, 12 with social workers and 10 with groups of beneficiaries (individuals receiving services) of empowerment interventions in the regions. The social workers were interviewed individually via telephone, whereas the individuals receiving the empowerment services where interviewed in groups of four to six persons. The interviewees were selected on a convenience basis, and, among the social workers, there were representatives from government, NGOs, and private organizations. The interviews were conducted in the Creole (local lingua-franca) and/or English languages. Some observations of the regions were also carried out, and photographic evidence was collected to enhance the data from the fieldwork.

The sample size (22 interviews) was theoretically determined by the process of data collection for generating theory. As a first round, data were collected from three social workers and one group of beneficiaries. As per the rule of grounded theory, the data collected from the first round were analyzed to give a sense of the emerging theory. Then, successive interviews were added to the already existing set of data and analyzed immediately after the collection through a constant comparison method. A central feature of grounded theory is its method of constant comparative analysis (Glaser & Strauss, 1967), in that data collection and analysis occur simultaneously, and each item of data is compared with every other item of data. In other words, successive layers of data were added to the existing data set until saturation (or theoretical fit) for the emerging theory was achieved.

All of the 22 semistructured interviews were recorded on a digital voice recorder. For data analysis, Atlas-ti 5.2 (a computer-aided qualitative data analysis software) was used. The analysis of the data began through the open coding process, whereby theoretical quotations were identified and codes were assigned. For instance, when a quotation such as "we got all the facilities available for them, sometimes we go to their place to make them understand that it is important to have a job, earn a living" was identified, codes such as "giving facilities," "going to their place," "making them understand," and "importance of having job," were assigned. These codes were then theoretically linked for building theoretical explanations. For instance, codes such as "giving facilities," "building houses," and "buying books for children" were theoretically linked to the concept called *enablement*, and then theoretical discussions were created based on interlinkages between such concepts.

Because a grounded theory approach was used, the data collection tools were continuously improved over successive data collections. To bring rigor to the research through enhancing the validity, some of the findings from the interviews of the social workers were brought to the beneficiaries and vice versa. Moreover, important aspects highlighted in one interview were checked again during following interviews. To further enhance the rigor in the research process, an intracoder reliability check was carried out. In other words, the researcher repeated the coding process of a sample of two data sets independently of each other to verify consistency within the coding process. Most of the codes used in this chapter were consistent. Furthermore, Family Manager under the Memo feature within Atlas-ti 5.2, which is useful for sorting, filtering, and managing the researcher's written reflections about the project, data, participants, and self, was used for the reflexivity analysis (Rambaree, 2007).

Using a grounded theory methodology, with a case study approach, this chapter seeks to (a) analyze the conceptualization of empowerment and (b) identify and discuss the challenges related to empowerment of rural communities in social

work. For the presentation of the analysis, a comparison between the central concepts emerging from the findings of the case study and some existing relevant theoretical and conceptual literature is carried out, using a constant comparison
method.

The Context of the Case Study: Rural Southeast Coastal Villages

The southeast costal region of the Island of Mauritius includes several rural villages located in the district of Grand Port (see Figure 1). The population of the
studied villages, estimated by the Central Statistics Office (2010), was as follows:
Old Grand Port approximately 3000; Bois des Amourettes approximately 2000,
and Grand Sable approximately 2000.
The working population in these SRCVs
consists of mostly "low-skilled" and
"manual workers," such as fishers, seasonal laborers, part-time construction
workers, and factory workers. The SRCVs
are considered the least "developed" small
villages of Mauritius and are regularly followed by several social workers working
for the empowerment of these rural communities to eradicate absolute poverty
from the region.

FIGURE 1: Map of Mauritius.

The SRCVs of Mauritius have fewer
hotels and public service facilities such as banks, pharmacies, or supermarkets
compared with the other rural parts of the island. Most of the SRCVs are located
at the foot of the slope of Grand Port Mountain Range (see Figure 2). During heavy
rainfall, several places (such as shown in Figure 2) are flooded, and soil, rocks,
and sewage are drained to the sea, passing through vulnerable houses. A study of
the region carried out by UNDP (2001) reports:

> Most houses are made up of corrugated iron sheets… inhabitants suffer tremen-
> dously during heavy rains… water coming from mountains over-floods their toi-
> lets and creates a highly unhygienic condition.

The Central Statistics Office (2002) carried out a ranking exercise (from 1 for
the highest to 145 for the lowest) based on the Composite Relative Development

FIGURE 2: The landscape in the southeast of Mauritius.

Index for small areas. In this particular exercise some coastal villages of the southeast part of Mauritius (out of 145) ranked as follows: Grand Sable, 136; Old Grand Port, 117; and Bois des Amourettes, 138. In particular, research commissioned by UNDP (2001) identified the southeast coastal regions of Mauritius among the most deprived and vulnerable in the country. The majority of the poor people from the southeast coast region of Mauritius tend to rely heavily on fishing and microscale farming for subsistence, and cash income from informal labor (IFAD, 2007). The Ministry of Environment and National Development Unit (2010) states, "As a result of overfishing, a general decline in fish catch has been observed in lagoon fishery which has resulted in some degree of poverty in coastal villages."

This means that a number of poor people from the southeast coastal villages of Mauritius who earn their livelihoods through small-scale fishing are experiencing socioeconomic hardship (Sobhee, Jankee, & Rambaree, 2007). The poor people in the southeast coastal villages also earn their livelihood from low paying jobs such as seasonal labor on the sugar cane plantations, part-time construction work, and factory-based manual work. In addition to being low-paid, such jobs are also unstable, unsafe, and insecure. Since February 2009 many people from the SRCVs have lost their jobs as a result of restructuring at Ferney Spinning Mills, the only major textile industry of the region (Chutto & Ragoo, 2010). The major concern within the restructuring process at Ferney Spinning Mills was job cuts. Within this context, IFAD (2007) also mentions:

> In the wake of the recent exposure to global competition, and the consequent decline in the production of sugar and textiles for export, rural poverty is on the rise across the country. Unemployment is increasing, and those who are already disadvantaged are sinking into deeper poverty.

Moreover, the relatively low level of education, together with unemployment and the absence of acquired skills, further inhibits the chances of people from these coastal areas getting out of the poverty trap. In a similar vein, Sobhee (2004) writes that, among students who left primary school (at approximately age 10) in the region of Grand Port, less than 50% enrolled in secondary school in 1998. For instance, in the region of Bois des Amourettes, UNDP (2001) reports that most of the males and females consulted had "dropped out of school prior to Standard VI (usually 10–11 years old), with only a small number having reached Form III at secondary level (usually below 16 years old)." Furthermore, a study carried out by Sobhee and colleagues (2007) found that the majority of uneducated fishers in the country were from the district of Grand Port.

Housing is another major problem of the region. Several inhabitants of the SRCVs have squatted on state-owned land to construct their shelters. Figure 3 shows an example of houses constructed in such areas. The houses are constructed without building permits and, therefore, are not officially registered in the housing register. Consequently, almost all such houses have no access to electricity, water, and sewage collection facilities (at least during the early periods, for about 2–3 years). In addition, most such illegal constructions do not follow the building regulations or sanitation norms. They are very vulnerable to cyclones and floods and pose several health and safety risks. Access to low-cost housing for the squatters is among the major government projects. The National Audit Office (2010) mentions that, from "December 1991 to September 2000, there were some 2,249 squatters spread over the country…5.2% of them in the region of Grand Port."

Within this context, several organizations are involved in empowering individuals, groups, and communities from the SRCVs of Mauritius to eradicate absolute poverty. Social workers from various organizations are engaged in programs such

FIGURE 3: House on squatted land.

as community work, support for access to housing, facilitation in agricultural development, and training for employment and livelihoods. Social workers identify
the poor people through the community welfare centers, citizen's advice bureau,
and village councils. Activities that are typical within the "empowerment programs"
include organization of life skills courses, training in entrepreneurship for women,
work placement for young people, support for the construction of houses, and
supply of school materials (books, uniform, meals, etc.) for children's education.
It can be said that, without any doubt, the activities undertaken by various organizations to fight poverty in the SRCVs are helping the targeted populations to some
extent. However, are the communities/beneficiaries empowered?

   According to Fook (2002), the idea of empowerment is attractive in social work,
because it is a relatively easy concept to understand and promises a ready framework for application in direct practice. Adams (2003) argues that empowerment
is fundamental to the central and energizing feature of social work practice.
However, Sheppard (2006) contends that empowerment provides a very poor basis
on which to found the aims, and even processes, of social work. In particular,
Sheppard (2006) argues that empowerment is not a coherent concept, and, therefore, it cannot lead to a coherent practice in social work. Using the case study of

SRCVs from Mauritius, therefore, this chapter analyzes the conceptualization of empowerment and the challenges related to empowerment of rural communities in social work.

Empowerment: The Conceptualization

One of the foci of this case study—based on social work in rural communities in Mauritius—is to analyze the conceptualization of empowerment. It is difficult to understand empowerment, unless it is defined within a context (Adams, 2008; Askheim, 2003; Chamberlin, 1997). In particular, empowerment often is conceptualized differently within different contexts, as well as differently linked to various other concepts, such as power, control, self-realization, and participation, in accordance to the context within which it is used (Jönsson, 2010). Roy (2010) states that empowerment is a potent theoretical concept that is discussed in multiple social sciences; however, the interdisciplinary nature of the concept makes a coherent definition of the term problematic. Thus, in studying the conceptualization of empowerment, it is important to keep a focus on the context.

Within the context of social work, empowerment is regarded as one of the central concepts and a core intervention strategy. In social work interventions empowerment is considered both a process and an outcome. IFSW (2004) defines social work as, "a profession that promotes the empowerment and liberation of people to enhance well-being." Dubois and Miley (2011) state that when people experience empowerment, they feel effective, conclude that they are competent, and perceive that they have power and control over the course of their lives. In particular, power and control are the central components within the conceptualization of empowerment. Adams (2008) defines empowerment in social work as

the capacity of individuals, groups and/or communities to take control of their circumstances, exercise power and achieve their own goals, and the process by which, individually and collectively they are able to help themselves and others to maximize the quality of their lives. (p. 17)

The conceptual construction of empowerment, therefore, is based mainly on the notion of dealing with the transmission of power (Askheim, 2003) to beneficiaries of programs and services to help them rise out of positions of helplessness and confusion, (re)claim control of their lives, and discover their own "inner strengths" (Tew, 2006, p. 34). Within social work practice, social workers are trained to make their clients autonomous by having control over life situations and circumstances, rather than to become dependent and passive users of services. Empowerment is regarded as a transformational activity, and social workers try to render their practice transformational (Adams, 2003).

Within the field of social work for poverty eradication and social exclusion, empowerment is linked to the central concept of accretion of power to exercise choice regarding how one should direct one's life to become socioeconomically autonomous and self-reliant and, thus, avoid dependence on social aids and welfare benefits. Given that poverty is associated with a lack of power and control, the idea of empowering poor communities seems to fit neatly within social work's core practice (Sheppard, 2006). In analyzing the conceptualization of empowerment within certain contexts, therefore, it is important to look at how power and control are seen, organized, and experienced.

However, one should bear in mind certain important aspects related to power. First, power can be relative and lies in a continuum (Anderson, 1996). For instance, a person is powerful in relation to another. Second, power has a structural dimension. For instance, political people within the government are considered powerful. Third, power is something people use and create, rather than simply possess (Fook, 2002). For example, powerful people create and exercise power to achieve certain objectives.

From the analysis of social work in SRCVs, two important aspects related to empowerment emerge, both of which are subsequently discussed.

Enablement

In this case study, concepts such as facilitation, support, and care are dominant within the social workers' interventions and discourses in rural areas. One can argue that what social workers are practicing in the regions is more enablement than empowerment. In particular, it seems that, within the conceptualization of empowerment, power/control is not centralized toward the poor people. Instead, people from rural areas are looked at as vulnerable and easily exploited by others who have more power. Therefore, the social workers of the regions feel that poor people from the SRCVs need to be protected and given care and support. For instance, in relation to rural communities, some of the interviewed social workers mention:

Social worker 08: *"dimounes dans la campagne zotte facilement laisse zotte embete"* ("people in the rural areas get easily influenced/cheated")

Social worker 012: "rural people are more traditional, and they have low level of education and skills...they are easily exploited by others, such as by their employers, politicians, etc."

Social worker 07: "People, in general, have a tendency not to care for them (poor people from the rural areas) but use them for their own advantages in life."

In the majority of the interviews social workers tend to define *empowerment* from an enablement perspective. Following are a couple of the quotations gathered from the interviews on how empowerment is accomplished by social workers:

Social worker 11: "We try to enable them in getting job, building their house, sending their children to school."

Social worker 04: "We give social housing to landless people. ...we provide training for people to get employment."

Through the adoption of an enabling perspective within the empowerment process, therefore, power is further centralized toward professionals and authorities, which also undermines the empowerment interventions (Pease, 2002; Simon, 1990). Payne (2005) argues that empowerment is not limited to allowing or assisting people to take actions but is aimed at relinquishing and transferring power for people to permanently take control over their own lives. By adopting an enablement approach within the empowerment strategies, social workers risk making poor communities simply recipients of benefits and services, rather than creating autonomous groups able to make active choices to have better control over life situations and circumstances (Payne, 2005). When social workers were probed about the outcome of empowerment interventions, some concerns related to dependency and passivity of the beneficiaries were, indeed, mentioned:

Social worker 06: "We got all the facilities available for them, sometimes we go to their place to make them understand that it is important to have a job, earn a living. We even look for jobs for them, but some are not even willing to go to attend interviews. They prefer getting their pension as a source of income, instead of trying to earn a living through a job."

Social Worker 04: "We have the training and placement unit, which works for unemployed persons—linking them to potential employers. People don't take up job opportunities provided to them. Reasons: hours of work, distance to travel, fear of no more being eligible to social aid benefits if they take up jobs."

There are some risks of misusing empowerment as an enablement concept in social work practice. As Adams (2003) cautions, there is a danger of attaching empowerment to social work activities in an inappropriate way, thereby reducing its scope and power to improve people's circumstances, leading to another form of an enabling act by professionals. Social workers, by the nature of their profession and their closeness to authorities (such as government), have already centralized power toward themselves. By approaching empowerment from an enabling perspective, social workers create an oppressive practice. Oppression is another aspect found to be central to the conceptualization and practice of social work in this particular case study.

Oppression

Oppression is understood as the power domination of subordinate groups in society by politically, professionally, economically, socially, and culturally powerful group(s) (Mullaly, 2010). The phenomenon occurs when power is centralized in an unjust and cruel manner. At the end of the 1970s the term *empowerment* was widely used to refer to power for women's movements, liberation movements in former colonies, different kinds of self-help organizations, social activism, social mobilizing, and protest movements (Jönsson, 2010). The theoretical conceptualization of empowerment that followed was influenced by the ideologies taken from the work of Paulo Freire (1993)—"Pedagogy of the oppressed"—where the focus was on the social mobilization for justice, rights, and freedom of the oppressed groups (Askheim, 2003, p. 231).

In trying to do good for the beneficiaries, social workers sometimes unintentionally and/or unwillingly engage in an oppressive relationship. For instance, when empowerment is dominant through enablement, social workers centralize more power toward themselves and force the beneficiaries to develop an inferior/dependent/powerless identity (Dominelli, 2002; Fook, 2002; Payne, 2005).

This power imbalance between social workers and beneficiaries becomes a prolific ground for the emergence of oppressive practices in social work (Dominelli, 2002; Strier & Binyamin, 2010). In empowering rural communities, social workers need to be cautious not to create oppressive relationships and structures that will make those temporarily in need become long-term service- or benefit-dependent. Thus, rural social work as a nonoppressive practice must focus on understanding the objectives of empowerment right. As Fook (2002, pp. 53–54) puts it, "when using the empowerment model, unless we ask the more important questions like 'empowerment for what?' and 'for whom?' we are left with the possibility of perpetuating oppressive structures for someone."

Payne (2005) argues that, within empowerment, social workers should avoid oppression by enhancing the people's autonomy. In rural social work, empowerment can be conceptualized as emancipation of individuals/groups/communities from oppression (Adams, 2008). Thus, it is important for social workers to identify the forms and sources of oppression and work toward opportunities for emancipation of their clients from oppressive conditions and circumstances (Danso, 2009; Tew, 2006). In emancipatory social work practice, empowerment is mainly related to active participation of the client's consciousness-raising, helping the client overcome barriers and oppressive forces, and giving clients access to personal or collective power to control life situations and circumstances (Payne, 2005).

In this particular case study, the social workers were unable to recognize their approach as being oppressive. They believed that the poor rural communities were oppressed in a number of other ways. According to the social workers, one of the frequently mentioned forms of oppression within their empowerment initiatives emanates from politicians. Social workers also report that a number of people have been promised land, housing, jobs, and benefits by politicians and their agents operating in the region. For the social workers of the regions, empowerment has a very strong political dimension in Mauritius. Social workers state that they are pressured by politicians, particularly those in power (government), to create a caring and supportive image of the government. Most of the activities related to poverty eradication in the region are done with the intention of helping the politicians maintain power in coming elections.

Moreover, the social workers also report that there is too much political interference regarding how to empower people. Local politicians and top officials, such as advisers to ministers and managers or directors of parapublic organizations—who are mostly politically nominated and often do not have the right qualifications and experience in the field—directly or indirectly influence social workers to consider the people from the community as voters or potential voters who have been supporting or can support the political parties. Such nonprofessionally led programs to eradicate absolute poverty through empowerment reflect the exploitative or oppressive power structures (Adams, 2003) that exist within Mauritian society. In the context of this case study, social workers report that they are compelled to make the communities feel that the government is responsible and caring. For instance, Social Worker 04 states: "a lot of resources are spent because [a member of the parliament] wants his/her people to believe in him/her so that they can vote for him/her."

From the gathered evidence, it also seems that authorities, and even the social workers, do not appreciate that people from the community stand up for their rights and speak their minds in public, especially on private radio stations. In Mauritius there is a perception among the majority that the state-owned radio channels are used for government propaganda. The introduction of private commercial radio broadcasters, beginning in 2000, has provided an outlet for the general public to express its views in a more democratic manner (International Institute for Democracy & Electoral Assistance, 2006). As one of the social workers reports:

> Social worker 07: "We have to cater for so many needs...we do not want people going on radio or complaining...actions are taken so that people can trust us...sometimes, we have to give them hope and pretend things will be done for avoiding attention of the media."

To promote empowerment in rural communities, social workers need to work toward the emancipation of the beneficiaries. In social work, emancipation means liberating a person from oppression (Adams, 2003). One of the ways for people to become emancipated is by making their voices heard. In particular, social work practice in rural communities should focus more on the importance of making space for difference and including voices and perspectives of people in the rural communities to help overcome the power that tries to keep the poor silent (Eyben, Kabeer, & Cornwall, 2008). As Lord and Hutchison (1993, p. 21) put it, "While power cannot be given to people by professionals, concerned professionals can work to eliminate the systematic barriers that have been created which oppress, control, and dis-empower vulnerable citizens."

Furthermore, interviews with beneficiaries of the empowerment interventions confirm that poor people from rural communities are victims of oppression from powerful corporate interests operating in the region, such as textile companies, sugar cane plantation owners, and wealthy business owners. Most poor people are employed in casual and seasonal jobs and have no coverage in terms of occupational social protection. Additionally, there are very few economic opportunities in the region, such as in hotels, restaurants, shopping centers, and so forth, and some of the business owners and investors take advantage of the rural poor communities as cheap and unregulated labor. Although social workers recognize this form of oppression, not much is reported or done in relation to occupational welfare. For instance, none of the social workers mention interventions for empowering people for *decent work*. Decent work is based on the principle of social justice (Rambaree, 2009). The International Labour Organisation (1999) states that "decent work means productive work in which rights are protected, which generates an adequate income, with adequate social protection. It also means sufficient work, in the sense that all should have full access to income-earning opportunities."

In fact, a number of industries are engaged in the EAP and empowerment, either on their own or in partnership with others, through CSR activities. Therefore, it is also important for the social workers to look at the structures and agencies that are responsible for causing and maintaining poverty. It could be argued that the social workers are blinded by the "false consciousness" of the dominant and powerful capitalist structures of Mauritian society.

As this case reflects, although empowerment offers a more positive vision of the productive possibilities of power, this concept can be too imprecise and capable of misuse to be of great practical value (Tew, 2006). In rural areas it is crucial for social workers to consider empowerment as an approach to social justice also, rather than simply a technique enabling people to benefit from programs and services (Adams, 2008). Social justice within social work should centrally focus on the elimination of institutionalized unfairness, domination, and oppression (Mullaly, 2010). Social workers operating within rural communities, therefore, require a clear understanding of the power dynamics that exist within the context and work toward the emancipation of clients to liberate them from various forms of oppression, such as political, social, relational, and economic.

Perhaps this is easier said than done. In social work practice each rural context presents certain challenges that hinder empowerment interventions. Social workers need to identify and deal with these challenges. The following section, therefore, focuses on two main challenges identified in this case study.

Challenges in Empowering Rural Poor Communities

Understanding the Dynamics

To empower the rural poor, social workers need to study and understand poverty dynamics. Poverty is, in many cases, imposed and maintained on a certain group of people. Lack of provision for childcare services, gender-based attitudes, low-paid insecure jobs, and poor health and safety conditions at home and at work are inherent in poverty dynamics. Lack of childcare services and facilities is perhaps a major issue for certain residents of the southeast rural coastal regions. In a number of cases, it was found that women could not join the formal labor market due to a lack of free childcare facilities. For instance, a woman with three children reported that she has never worked because she could not afford childcare and so has had to look after her children. Childcare services cost a minimum of US $300 per month (mostly informal and unregulated by authorities), and for many women this cost is about one-half of the monthly income earned in low paid, insecure jobs. Women are forced by the economic situation to stay at home for childcare and, therefore, become dependent (femininization of poverty) on others—mainly the man, as monoincome earner—for their livelihoods. By not providing childcare services and facilities for parents, authorities are, in some ways, imposing poverty on people. The NEF and their partners from the corporate sectors have started to provide childcare facilities; however, most of these services are located in urban or suburban areas.

Certain poor people (mostly men) from the case study villages also believe that women should not be in the formal job market. Social workers in the region report that patriarchal norms are stronger in the rural communities. Relying on monoincome heightens the financial and economic vulnerability of the whole family. In some cases a whole family collapses into deep poverty after the death or serious injury of the monoincome earner. Within this context, one social worker states:

> Social worker 02: "Rural people are more attached to traditions, e.g., girls get married very young, no matter if she has education or not... it's tradition, and they are not so allowed to attain training programs in community centers, there are cases where they are not allow to go to work."

Those women who manage to go to work find employment in low-paid and insecure seasonal jobs. In the majority of cases, the poor people from these rural areas are employed in sugar cane fields. They usually start at 5:00 a.m. and finish at 11:00 a.m. The daily salary earned from these types of jobs is commonly around RS 150 for women and RS 200 for men. A number of people also report that they have been victims of accidents at work. While probing, it was found that their jobs, as well as their residences, pose health and safety risks. Most of the chronically poor people have low levels of education and little ability to voice concerns regarding health and safety risks and rights at work; therefore, they remain in vulnerable working and living conditions and thus stay within the poverty trap. In a similar manner, Kern and Ritzen (2001, p. 8) state that poverty creates illiteracy, leaving people poorly informed about health risks and "forced" into dangerous jobs that harm their health.

Moreover, when this study was carried out, it was found that high voltage electricity had been provided and installed in a manner that jeopardized the lives of people. In some cases, high voltage wires and main electricity supply boxes were hanging within the reach of small children (see Figure 4). Social workers report that the people construct such houses illegally, and, because of the political pressure during the election campaign, electric supply has been provided to such houses quickly and without planning. Supplying electricity to squatters is mainly done before, during, and

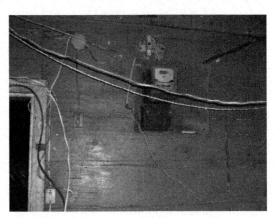

FIGURE 4. High voltage wires and the main electricity supply box in a squatted house.

immediately after the election campaign, as a way to show care and support for poor people—which is one of the commonly used strategies to gain votes by the local politicians. Within this particular context, the National Audit Office (2010) reports:

> Squatting is a social problem. ...Government is also under the pressure to provide the necessary infrastructure to remote areas that are unsuitable for residential development. For instance, the provision of basic amenities, like electricity and water, to sites squatted upon are very often construed by the squatters as the first step to the regularization of their situation and hence, a commitment on the part of Government.

One of the main challenges for social workers engaged in empowering rural communities is to understand the poverty dynamics and inherent oppression within it. Poverty is simultaneously the expression and the consequence of political, economic, ethnic, or gender oppression, and understanding it as oppression is related to the analysis of larger power relations in society (Strier & Binyamin, 2010). In many instances oppression is camouflaged and even normalized. In this connection Mullaly (2010) states that, "Oppression is more effective in achieving its apparent function of maintaining the privileged position of the dominant group when both victims and perpetrators are unaware of the dynamics of oppression."

It is also important to realize that social workers operate within a complex social system. Even though social workers might be aware of the oppressive agencies, structures, and mechanisms and have a high level of determination and willingness for antioppressive practice, the power for making a difference sometimes lies beyond their reach. As previously mentioned, power lies in a continuum with limits, and it is relative in nature. The power dynamics in social work practice depend not only on the personal attributes and capacity of the social worker, but also on the complex interplay between different aspects within the social worker's environment, which play a part in "influencing" interventions (Smith, 2008). Social workers, therefore, have limited power for autonomy in their work. Social workers exercise powers, duties, and responsibilities that do not originate in them, but rather in the political organizations under which they operate (Harris, 2002). In some contexts social workers even risk facing some kind of reprisal, including the job loss, when they challenge a culture of oppression inherent within certain political organizations (Mullaly, 2010). Nevertheless, it is important for social workers to be guided by the principles of social justice in their practice and interventions. The concept of social justice is considered empowering, because it includes the conditions necessary for the development and exercise of individual capacities for physical and social functioning (Mullaly, 2010).

Dealing With Legal and Control Barriers

Many aspects of the lives of the poor might include illegality, although such aspects are not always criminal (Mitlin, 2006). In the SRCVs most chronically poor people live in houses that are illegally built on state land. Over the years a number of people have been squatting on state land and, therefore, do not have the required deed and legal permits for construction. Most illegal constructions do not follow building regulations or the sanitation norms. In some cases, the government has tried to demolish the illegally built houses, and such moves have caused uproar in the press and among certain politicians and NGOs. In certain cases, the Trust Fund for the Integration of Vulnerable Groups has tried to relocate of squatters by offering low-cost housing in other regions, but social workers report that most of these chronically poor people have refused to move out. When asked why the squatters do not opt for the low-cost housing, a typical response was that, because their work was in the sea, the squatters needed to live near it, and that it was their land, where the families had always lived.

In addition, some residents are involved in illegal and informal (nonregistered) income generating activities and businesses. During the field visits a number of chronically poor people were found to be illegal fishers and also nonregistered small business owners doing backyard animal rearing, street vending, unlicensed trading, and so forth. For instance, a number of people have small-scale cattle or poultry rearing businesses (see Figure 5). Most such businesses have no permit and do not meet health and sanitation requirements. According to the social workers, relevant authorities have not allocated those people the permit for animal/poultry production, because (a) the owners do not possess the land deed and (b) the land is too small for such businesses. Thus, the businesses, through which people are trying to better their economic situation, are not legally recognized for empowerment support. Under

FIGURE 5: A backyard poultry raising operation.

such conditions it becomes more challenging for social workers to empower their clients through available financial schemes for microbusinesses and income generating activities.

Social workers employed under the aegis of the NEF are involved in various types of activities for supporting microbusiness initiates, such as technical support for project development, finance and support to microprojects, promoting social entrepreneurship, and promoting networking of micro- and small enterprises (NEF, 2009b). Social workers are also employed in various other government agencies and NGOs to carry out regular field visits to support, advise, and organize referral services for such microbusiness initiatives and promote production for food for self-sufficiency among the poor people.

In addition, the NEF has undertaken a pilot project of creating an integrated village in another rural area, called Bambous. The idea of an integrated approach to empowerment is to create a new village, called the La Valette, with housing to relocate 200 families living in absolute poverty. The model village, with a cost of RS 204 million, has integrated facilities and services, such as for leisure and recreation, training, and microbusinesses (NEF, 2009c). Families are asked to sign a contract whereby agree to respect the environment and social rules imposed by the MSIEE. Social workers are engaged to organize, monitor, and report on various socioeconomic activities for the integrated village. The interesting aspects of this integrated village concept are that services, such as those for life skills, small and medium enterprises, and sports and recreation, are all incorporated within the immediate environment of the families. However, one of the major critiques of such a concept is that all families having somewhat similar social problems have been clustered for better control and oppression by authorities. Recently, the MSIEE decided to evict five families from the La Vallette social housing project because the families did not respect the environmental and social rules laid out in their contracts (The Independent, 2011). In the years to come, it would be interesting to have an integral evaluation of both the providers' and beneficiaries' perspectives of the empowerment program through the integrated village approach to see whether such initiatives should be extended to villages like those in the SRCVs of Mauritius.

As the above discussion shows, social workers must consider a number of challenges in their intervention to empower poor people in rural communities. Each rural context represents a set of challenges that need identification and consideration. In this endeavor, social workers need to think of strategies to ensure that rural poor communities can understand risks, dangers, and ways to obtain protection as

rights. If poor people can actively make sense of the dynamics of their poverty status, make relevant demands, and stand up for their rights, this will help them toward the eradication of their poverty. Poverty needs to be viewed as deprivation of
basic human and social rights (Strier & Binyamin, 2010); therefore, social workers
working toward empowerment should focus more attention on human and social
rights. But this case study also found that poor and oppressed people are not encouraged by policy makers and social workers to be vocal regarding their rights. As
Bradshaw (2006) states,

> A parallel barrier exists with the political system in which the interests and par-
> ticipation of the poor is either impossible or is deceptive. Recent research has
> confirmed the linkage between wealth and power, and has shown how poor peo-
> ple are less involved in political discussions, their interests are more vulnerable
> in the political process, and they are excluded at many levels.

Conclusion

In this chapter, through a case study approach, social work practice related to empowerment of rural poor communities has been discussed. First, it is argued that,
although empowerment is an important concept in rural social work practice, there
is a danger of limiting the conceptualization of the term to enablement. In having
a limited conceptualization of empowerment as enablement, social workers get
trapped in oppressive practices. In particular, it is crucial for social workers who
are engaged in empowering rural poor communities to recognize the oppression
they might create as well as deal with other forms of oppression their clients might
experience. In fact, empowerment in rural social work needs to be seen as emancipation of the rural communities, especially those who are poor and marginalized. In this sense social work practice in rural communities can aspire to social
justice, by engendering power among vulnerable and marginalized communities
(Fook, 2002; Lee, 2001). Through analysis of the case study, two main challenges
associated with empowering rural poor communities have been discussed. First,
each rural context presents its own challenges to empowering the communities.
Second, in rural social work an empowerment intervention needs to enhance the
people's ability to gain freedom from various forms of oppression (social, economic,
political, and so on). In this connection, antioppressive social work practice requires a personal and collective commitment to social justice (Mullaly, 2010).

Finally, it could be said that power remains the central aspect of empowerment. In rural social work practice related to empowerment, social workers need to analyze and deal with several complexities related to power dynamics and direct power for the emancipation of their clients. Enhancing the capabilities of their clients for emancipation is what makes social work a transformative practice. Without a profound analysis of the power dynamics within contexts and a corresponding vision of how it should work in social justice terms, there is a danger that empowerment can simply become a tool to preserve existing power imbalances that oppress the poor and marginalized people in rural areas (Fook, 2002). For empowerment to have an emancipatory effect on people, such as the rural poor communities who are marginalized, strategies must go beyond developmental goals, such as better housing, higher productivity, higher consumption, and higher formal education (Jönsson, 2010). In particular, rural social work for the empowerment of the poor requires the use of critical thinking to work against the social structures, barriers, and power relations that cause oppression by maintaining dependencies and injustices among the poor. Social work is an empowering profession and the principle of social justice is central to empowerment, whether it is for individuals, groups, or communities from rural or urban settings.

References

Adams, R. (2003). *Social work and empowerment*, 3rd ed. Basingstoke, UK: Macmillan.

Adams, R. (2008). *Empowerment, participation and social work*, 4th ed. New York, NY: Palgrave Macmillan.

African Development Bank. (2009). *Appraisal report on competitiveness and public sector efficiency: Mauritius*. Retrieved from http://www.afdb.org

Anderson, J. (1996). 'Yes, but is it empowerment?' Initiation, implementation and outcomes of community action. In B. Humphries (Ed.), *Critical perspectives on empowerment* (p. 105–127). Birmingham, UK: Venture Press.

Askheim, O. P. (2003). Empowerment as guidance for professional social work: An act of balancing on a slack rope. *European Journal of Social Work*, 6(3), 229–240.

Bradshaw, T. K. (2006). Theories of poverty and anti-poverty programs in community development. Rural Poverty Research Center Working Paper No. 06-05.

Central Statistics Office. (2000). *Population census 2000*. Retrieved from www.gov.mu/portal/sites/ncb/cso/report/.../census5/index.htm

Central Statistics Office. (2002). *2000 Housing and population census: Relative Development Index*. Retrieved from www.gov.mu/portal/sites/ncb/cso/ei393/intro.htm

Central Statistics Office. (2010). *Estimated resident population by village council area.* Retrieved from www.gov.mu/portal/goc/cso/hs/demo/t16.xls

Chamberlin, J. (1997). A working definition of empowerment. *Psychiatry and Rehabilitation Journal* 20(4), 43–46.

Chuttoo, R., & Ragoo, J. (2010). *Message of the CTSP on Labour Day.* Retrieved from http://www.lalitmauritius.org/viewnews.php?id=990

Danso, R. (2009). Emancipating and empowering de-valued skilled immigrants: what hope does anti-oppressive social work practice offer? *British Journal of Social Work 39,* 539–555.

Dominelli, L. (2002). *Anti-oppressive social work: theory and practice.* London, UK: Palgrave Macmillan.

DuBois, B. & Miley, K. K. (2011). *Social work: An empowering profession.,* 7th ed. Boston, MA: Pearson.

Eyben, R., Kabeer, N., & Cornwall, A. (2008). *Conceptualising empowerment and the implications for pro poor growth: A paper for the DAC poverty network.* Retrieved from http://preval.org/files/povnet%20draft%2023%20september%202008.pdf

Fook, J. (2002). *Social work: Critical theory and practice.* London, UK: Sage.

Freire, P. (1993). *Pedagogy of the oppressed.* New York, NY: Continuum.

Ginsberg, L. (2005). The overall context of rural practice. In L. Ginsberg (Ed.), *Social work in rural communities.* 4th ed., (pp. 1–15). Alexandria, VA: Council on Social Work Education.

Glaser, B. & Strauss, A. L. (1967). *The discovery of grounded theory: Strategies for qualitative research.* Chicago, IL: Aldine.

Government of Mauritius. (2006). *Social security.* Retrieved from www.gov.mu/portal/goc/mof/files/20052006/social.pdf

Government of Mauritius. (2010). *Provision of Rs 800 m for eligible corporate social responsibility activities.* Retrieved from http://www.gov.mu/portal/site/Mainhomepage /menuitem.a42b24128104d9845dabddd154508a0c/?content_id=1575f7da10934210 VgnVCM1000000a04a8c0RCRD

Harris, R. (2002). Power. In M. Davies (Ed.), *The Blackwell companion to social work* (pp. 29–33). Oxford, UK: Blackwell.

International Federation of Social Workers (IFSW). (2004). *Definition of social work.* Retrieved from http://www.ifsw.org/f38000138.html

International Fund for Agricultural Development (IFAD). (2005). *Republic of Mauritius country strategic opportunities paper.* Retrieved from http://www.ifad.org/gbdocs /eb/86/e/EB-2005-86-R-12.pdf

International Fund for Agricultural Development (IFAD). (2007). *Rural poverty in Mauritius*. Retrieved from http://www.ruralpovertyportal.org/web/guest/country/home/tags/mauritius

International Institute for Democracy & Electoral Assistance. (2006). *Mauritius: Country report based on research and dialogue with political parties*. Retrieved from http://www.idea.int/parties/loader.cfm?url=/commonspot/security/getfile.cfm&PageID =12479

International Labour Organization (ILO). (1999). *Decent work*. Geneva, Switzerland: ILO.

Jönsson, J. H. (2010). Beyond empowerment: Changing local communities. *International Social Work, 53*, 393–406.

Kern, A., & Ritzen, J. (2001). *Dying for change: Poor people's experience of health and ill-health*. Geneva, Switzerland: World Health Organisation, World Bank.

Lee, J. (2001). *The empowerment approach to social work practice: Building the beloved community*. New York, NY: Columbia University Press.

Locke, B. L. & Winship, J. (2005). Social work in rural America: Lessons from the past and trends for the future. In R. A. Lohmann and N. Lohmann (Eds.), *Rural social work practice* (pp. 3–24). New York, NY: Columbia University Press.

Lord, J., & Hutchison, P. (1993). The process of empowerment: Implications for theory and practice. *Canadian Journal of Community Mental Health, 12*, 5–22.

Mauritius Council of Social Services (MACOSS). (2010). *War on extreme poverty*. Retrieved from http://www.macoss.info/ACTION_PLAN_POVERTY.pdf

Ministry of Environment & National Development Unit. (2010). *Mauritius strategy for implementation national assessment report 2010*. Retrieved from http://www.sidsnet.org/msi_5/docs/nars/AIMS/Mauritius-MSI-NAR2010.pdf

Ministry of Finance & Economic Empowerment. (2006). *Poverty analysis: 2001/2002*. Retrieved from www.gov.mu/portal/goc/cso/report/natacc/poverty/poverty.pdf

Ministry of Finance & Economic Empowerment. (2009). *Poverty analysis: 2006/07*. Retrieved from www.gov.mu/portal/goc/cso/report/natacc/poverty/poverty07.pdf

Mitlin, D. (2006). *The role of collective action and urban social movements in reducing chronic urban poverty*. CPRC Working Paper 64. Retrieved from http://www.chronicpoverty.org /uploads/publication_files/WP64%20Mitlin.pdf

Mullaly, B. (2010). *Challenging oppression and confronting privilege*, 2nd ed. New York, NY: Oxford University Press.

National Audit Office. (2010). *Audit statement: Ministry of Housing & Lands*. Retrieved from http://www.gov.mu

National Empowerment Foundation (NEF). (2009a). *Historique*. Retrieved from http://www.nef.mu/historique.php

National Empowerment Foundation (NEF). (2009b). *Programme d'aide à l'entreprenariat*. Retrieved from http://www.nef.mu/services_esp.php

National Empowerment Foundation (NEF). (2009c). *Développement social intégré*. Retrieved from http://www.nef.mu/services_socialdevelopment.php#section2

Payne, M. (2005). *Modern social work theory*, 3rd ed. New York, NY: Palgrave Macmillan.

Pease, B. (2002). Rethinking empowerment: A postmodern reappraisal for emancipatory practice. *British Journal of Social Work, 32*, 135–147.

Perpar, A. (2007). Characteristics of rural areas in Slovenia: Advantages, weaknesses and possibilities for improvement of present situation from viewpoint of sustainable rural development. *Journal of Central European Agriculture, 8*(2), 229–236.

Poverty Observatory Bulletin. (2009). *Being poor in Mauritius*. Retrieved from http://www.mrc.org.mu/Documents/POBulletinVlI1.pdf

Pugh, R., & Cheers, B. (2010). *Rural social work: An international perspective*. Bristol, UK: Policy Press.

Rambaree, K. (2007) Bringing rigour in qualitative social research: The use of a CAQDAS [Special issue]. *University of Mauritius Research Journal, 13A*, 1–16.

Rambaree, K. (2009). The Mauritian employment relations Act 2008 and social justice: A critical discourse analysis. *South African Journal of Labour Relations, 33*(1), 43–62.

Roy, P. (2010). Analyzing empowerment: An ongoing process of building state—civil society relations—the case of Walnut Way in Milwaukee. *Geoforum, 41*, 337–348.

Saltman, J., Gumbert, J., Allen-Kelly, K., & Zubrzycki, J. (2004). Rural social work practice in the United States and Australia: A comparison. *International Social Work, 47*, 515–531.

Sheppard, M. (2006). *Social work and social exclusion: The idea of practice*. Aldershot, UK: Ashgate.

Simon, B. (1990). Rethinking empowerment. *Journal of Progressive Human Services, 1*, 27–39.

Smith, R. (2008). *Social work and power*. Basingstoke, Hampshire, UK: Macmillan Publishers Limited.

Sobhee, S. K. (2004). Economic development, income inequality and environment degradation of fisheries resources in Mauritius. *Environment Management, 34*(1), 150–157.

Sobhee, S. K., Jankee, K., & Rambaree, K. (2007). *Report on the socio-economic status of fishers in Mauritius*. Port Louis, Mauritius: Ministry of Fisheries and Agro-Industry.

Stiglitz, J. (2002). Employment, social justice and societal well-being. *International Labour Review, 141*(1–2), 9–29.

Strier, R., & Binyamin, S. (2010). Developing anti-oppressive services for the poor: a theoretical and organisational rationale. *British Journal of Social Work, 40*, 1908–1926.

Tew, J. (2006). Understanding power and powerlessness: Towards a framework for emancipatory practice in social work. *Journal of Social Work, 6*(1), 33–51.

The Independent. (2011). *Duval warns La Valette families.* Retrieved from http://theindependent.mu/2011/06/08/duval-warns-la-valette-families/

United Nations Development Programme (UNDP). (2001). *Final report: Patterns and trends in the feminisation of poverty in Mauritius.* Port Louis, Mauritius: UNDP.

United Nations Development Programme (UNDP). (2008). *Achieving the MDGS and reducing human poverty.* Retrieved from http://un.intnet.mu/undp/html/mauritius /povertyred.htm

4 Global Access and Rural Inclusion in Information and Communication Technology

KAREN V. HARPER-DORTON

The swift advance of information and communications technology (ICT) reaches throughout global societies, urban and rural alike. This chapter addresses the importance of accessing information technology for the social and economic well-being of rural citizens and communities worldwide. *ICT* is commonly used to refer to all communication technologies and devices, including radio, television, cellular phones, computers, satellite systems, and related software. ICT links all sectors, including economic development, energy, social services, health care, education, and the broad nonprofit service sector in an increasingly global economy. Wireless technology and potentially larger broadband capacities hold great promise for ICT use for communication, education, and businesses in rural areas and distant regions. The growth and sophistication of data, voice, and imaging are far ahead of the challenge of solving ease of access, including availability of hardware for many people in rural areas, particularly remote areas. Some rural areas are challenged by the presence of mountains, others are separated by vast distances and sparse populations, and most lack local providers for various Internet systems. Microwave, fiber, satellite, and wireless supported networks have capacities that can reduce barriers of terrain and distance in deploying information technology to rural people in nations around the world. Although these technologies hold great promise, wireless access for distant and sparsely populated rural areas greatly improves cost and profit analyses for providers. Developments in greater bandwidth availability are reaching more and more areas, making wireless communication available worldwide.

Just as in most other nations, the United States has open spaces of rural land and distant and small communities, where some areas lack ICT access, and where residents may or may not have resources to purchase hardware or software for such. Rural areas stretch across 2.3 billion acres of land in the United States; only 2.6%, or 60 million acres, are identified as urban land. The remainder is a mix of grassland, cropland, wildlife, forests, and parks. Rural residential land is estimated at about 94 million acres; however, identifying rural residential land as separate from surrounding farms, forests, and rangeland confounds findings (Lubowski, Vesterby, Bucholtz, Baez, & Roberts, 2002). Census 2000 reports 20.7% of the U.S. population, or 59,274,456 of 285,230,516 people, lived in rural areas (Federal Highway Administration, 2004). The U.S. population increased to 308,745,538 by 2010, with the estimated rural population being about 62 million people (U.S. Census Bureau, 2011).

Digital Divide in Rural America

National and governmental efforts allocated funding in the 1990s to bring rural America into the information age, at a time when T1 copper lines supported available technologies and served as common carrier for voice and data. Point-to-point installation of these lines presented enormous challenges for wide expanses and mountain ranges in remote and rural areas (National Telecommunications and Information Administration [NTIA], 1995, 1999, 2000). The slow speeds, limited hardware and software, and even more limited access to ICT systems in the 1990s now linger only in remote memory when compared to today's sophisticated ICT resources. Concerns of access at the time of ICT development in the 1990s focused mostly on access within countries, not internationally. Families living in rural areas and small communities in the 1990s were at great risk of technological illiteracy due to lack of ICT access and/or equipment. The gap created by the phenomenon of the "digital divide" is one more link in the chain of rural populations being left behind—in income, education, opportunities, and ICT access.

Identifying the gap in ICT access and capacities for Internet and computer applications, NTIA (2000) funded early projects to reduce the digital divide, the disparity between the "haves" and the "have-nots," or those people and households with access to the Internet versus those without. NTIA's research efforts identified gaps in network capacity and Internet access known to negatively impact small businesses and nonprofit organizations. Furthermore, information and hardware gaps, lack of network capacity, or lack of access jeopardize safety and military preparedness in the event of natural disaster (Oden & Stover, 2002).

Early Action to Reduce Digital Divide in Parts of Appalachia: Project Example

One area of the nation targeted as lacking ICT access is well-known to scholars of Appalachian politics, poverty, and culture. The Appalachian Regional Development Act of 1965 followed the President's Appalachian Regional Commission, which President Kennedy established in 1963. Appalachia, the rural, mountainous region from southern New York to Mississippi and Alabama, became known as the most socioeconomically distressed region in the nation, with 399 counties and a population of 24.8 million people (Couto, 1994). Appalachia now includes a total of 420 counties, as some adjacent counties have been added (Appalachian Regional Commission, 2011). Federal grants and awards flowing into the region as part of the Appalachian Regional Development Act helped establish facilities and employment in a wide range of technology related industries, including pharmaceuticals, chemicals, motor vehicles, communications, and aerospace facilities, some of which currently operate as secure research facilities (Feser, Goldstein, Renski, & Renault, 2002).

The NTIA, U.S. Department of Commerce, contracted with the U.S. Census Bureau in 1994 to gather and analyze data on telephone and computer/modem access. This study included factors of income, race, age, educational attainment, and rural, urban, and central city locations. Low-income households in central cities were found to be the telephone "have-nots," whereas the rural poor were the computer "have-nots" (NTIA, 1995). Taking action in response to their findings, the NTIA created the Telecommunications and Information Infrastructure Assistance Program (TIIAP) to leverage seed money for technology projects to reach underserved populations in rural and central city areas.

This author was principal investigator of one such project, Nonprofit Collaborative to Facilitate Rural Community Networking (NCFRCN), funded in the amount of $678,221from 1999 to 2003 (Harper-Dorton & Yoon, 2002). Essentially, using TI lines, ISDN (integrated services digital network) lines, and distributive training technology, two-way interactive video sites were funded for teleconferencing training along with actual practice at workstations in West Virginia National Guard Sites and public education facilities in rural counties and towns.

Project personnel and graduate students introduced rural consumers to Windows, Word, Excel, the World Wide Web, and e-mail. This project helped extend preparedness and learning readiness via computer-based learning with two-way audio–video communication and technology networks, including electronic mailing lists and Web-based communication. The NCFRCN project served approximately 10,000 people, including middle- and upper-level managers of nonprofit agencies, community-based social service providers, welfare-to-work clients, West Virginia National Guard members and families, and other West Virginia households. Partners involved in accomplishing these tasks included the West Virginia National Guard, the Governor's Office of Technology, a private software company, and several local nonprofit agencies.

The primary purpose of the project was to assist a broad range of nonprofit organizations in building capacities for information and technology access in Appalachian counties and isolated regions (Harper-Dorton & Yoon, 2002). A second function provided hands-on training in keyboarding and basic ICT processes. Additional important outcomes involved skill development for nonprofit agency managers via two-way interactive multimedia technology to use teleconferencing as a means of professional development for agency staff. This effort helped nonprofit organizations by increasing their capacities to lead rural areas and communities in using technology and to participate in changing economic and technological development. Multimedia delivery of information and coursework provided chat rooms and electronic mailing lists for nonprofit agency personnel, welfare-to-work families, and other community consumers.

In retrospect, perhaps the most important outcome of the NCFRCN project is the effect that exposure to technology has in contributing to readiness for lifelong learning, even in such basic and introductory efforts as this early project. For many lower-income households, particularly in rural areas, time for learning is time away from work that is needed just to meet basic needs. Comments from persons enrolled in basic computer training made to the principal investigator of the project offer small windows for understanding consumer interest in gaining ICT access:

"Lady, I have a barn full of antiques that I want to sell. Just retired! Show me the 'on-button.'"

"My husband sent me, so I can teach him."

"I'm unemployed now and need to get a job. Maybe learning how to use a computer will help me find a job."

"I have to learn how to use a computer, because my kids are learning about that at school and will need my help, I think."

"I want to e-mail my kids and grandkids."

However labor intensive this early technology project was, satisfaction was evident in amazed expressions among some who found the "on button" and watched excitedly as the computer screen opened.

Under the umbrella of NTIA from 1994–2004, the Technology Opportunities Program funded more than 600 projects nationwide, all intended to build and promote the use of network technologies across fields of health, community development, and education. Undoubtedly, networking between public and nonprofit sectors increases computer literacy and contributes to economic development in rural and/or underprivileged areas. Under the Department of Commerce, NTIA continues to be the federal point for leading and attesting to just how important ICT access is to all areas of the nation. ICT innovation, deployment, use, and access places the United States as a leader among nations (NTIA, 1999, 2000, 2011).

Moving beyond this earlier development of installing T1 lines and teaching computer literacy to consumers in neighborhoods, libraries, and community centers, the advent of digital technology has occurred. Although ICT continues to develop, globalization of current 3G and 4G technologies brings ICT to people throughout the world. With some remaining gaps in more remote and/or poor regions of the world, each annual update of ICT penetration reports moderate to quite rapid growth in cities, towns, and countrysides (Internet World Stats, 2010a, 2010b, 2010c, 2011a, 2011b, 2011c).

Inequality of Digital Access: A Global Phenomenon of Changing Disparities

Around the world, 1.4 billion people, nearly three fourths of the developing world, live in extreme poverty. Although education and ICT may not be within their reach, their labor is critical to supporting agricultural and world food production (International Fund for Agricultural Development, 2010).

The term *rural* indicates expansive distances and broadly diverse populations, including indigenous populations. Isolated but now wired, according to the World Summit on the Information Society, the Navajo Nation has grown from only about 20% of people having telephones and only about 10% with access to the Internet to much higher access supported by community centers somewhere in their

27,000 square mile remote territory. These community centers offer access to distance education classes with opportunities for employment and connectivity with many other people and places. The report lists numerous nations around the world where ICT capacities need to be accessible to indigenous populations for opportunities that include education, health information, and much more (Tunis, 2005; World Summit on the Information Society, 2003).

Current ICT Development Around the Globe

Europe. Rural development and economic conditions in European contexts vary greatly but reflect many of the same concerns—population density, vast distances, economic infrastructure, and the importance of connecting rural enterprise and making education accessible and affordable. Around the world, Internet usage is lower in rural households than urban households. In 2002 approximately 79% of urban households in Greece had computer and Internet access as compared to 9–11% of rural households (Labrianidis & Thanassis, 2006). The Netherlands had less rural/urban ICT disparity, but only about one third of households with access overall. Not unlike many other countries, European countries have increased ICT availability, computer usage, and Internet access, with some cities being equal to or surpassing those in the United States. ICT growth comes with a cost to individuals who have continuing disparities in access and hardware due to socioeconomic indicators such as income, education, and age. Gender is a limiting factor to ICT access, because many women in developing countries have the burdens of basic food subsistence and problems of child health and child mortality as part of daily life, particularly in rural or remote areas. Despite growing ICT technologies it is evident that adequate information, education, and income are critical factors in the race for ICT access and use globally.

ICT in the European context is as varied and complex as are the nations, cultures, and social and political contexts. Much of Europe has fixed broadband lines and many fewer fiber-based connections than some Asian countries. ICT penetration is slightly less than in the United States. Technologically astute, Europeans enjoy buying and selling goods online and use mobile devices and 3G Internet. Not unlike in the United States, e-commerce, manufacturing, communications, and education throughout Europe uses ICT to grow and participate in digital economies. Germany and Russia, with large populations, lead Europe in number of users and with penetration rates of 65.1% and 59.7%, respectively. Having much smaller populations, Iceland, Norway, and Sweden report penetration rates of

97.0%, 94.4, and 92.4%, respectively (Internet World Stats, 2011c). Iceland, Norway, and Sweden have concentrated population with major shifts to urban living over the last one half century. ICT is more easily distributed to smaller and concentrated populations.

Australia. Australia has vast rural areas with only about 3% of indigenous people in very remote areas having computers and 1% having some sort of Internet access. In general, 28% of indigenous youth, as compared to 75% of nonindigenous youth, have Internet access. Much of Australia's population is clustered and has ICT access. In 2003, 53% of households had Internet access (Willis & Tranter, 2002, 2006). The country's rural and remote areas present challenges of illiteracy among potential end-users, in addition to costs and distances. Data from 2006 indicate that 72% of Australian businesses, including a preponderance of large businesses, use ICT resources (Arnold, 2007). In 2010 as much as 80.1% of Australia's population accessed ICT resources (Miniwatts Marketing Group, 2010).

Based on their work in Australia, Willis and Tranter (2006) point out that Internet diffusion does not happen as a linear process. Changing social conditions vary among nations and regions in social mores, political structures, and lifestyles, all of which are critical factors in technical innovations and their deployment. For rural areas, disparities of deployment affect Internet access and use. For example, some regions that are part of the international coal industry are heavily dependent on ICT for monitoring safety concerns and tracking production and shipping data. It is noted that underground technology is mostly antenna based but sophisticated enough to track movement of individual miners as they work below the earth's surface.

Africa. Africa's widespread poverty and lack of access to ICT, and even to electricity in many regions, are huge burdens for rural areas. In addition to lacking ICT access, many rural dwellers may be far from ever owning a personal computer. Considering remote and sparsely populated areas of Africa, where most rural households are without electricity, the use of solar panels for lighting is increasing. For example, only 1 million of Kenya's 17 million people have electricity. Communication with others is important for many reasons, and about one in three Kenyan adults carries a cell phone that has a solar panel for renewable energy (Basu & Karimi, 2009). The use of technology in health care is increasing for many Kenyans; remote villages now offer self-testing for HIV and seek funding for tents to use as health care stations. It is noted that Africa represents 15% of the world's population, with only 11% of the population having Internet access and representing only 5.7% of the world's ICT users (Internet World Stats, 2011b). "A whopping 99% of the Internet traffic in Kenya is done via mobile operators, meaning 3G, Edge or GPRS" (Hash, 2011). Approximately 22% of Kenya's population has access to Internet resources (Hash, 2011).

Egypt. Egypt leads much of Africa with Internet penetration reaching 15.4% in 2008 (Open Net Initiative, 2009) and 30.05% in 2011 (ArabCrunch, 2011). ICT services are available to about 1 million households, more than half of which share connections with neighbors. Egypt has household access, as well as Internet cafés. Efforts calling for personal identification and sometimes placing restrictions on se-lected media, such as Facebook, are not well-received by the general population and particularly not by young people, who communicate their dissatisfaction in street demonstrations. Recent political unrest brought worldwide attention to the shutdown of Internet access by the Egyptian government. The 5-day shutdown of access demonstrated government control of this important communication medium and was met with a considerable number of demonstrations and other cel-lular communication.

China. China and India are the most populated nations in the world and have large cities, but half or more of their populations live in rural areas. China's popu-lation is approaching 1.4 billion, with a reported 36.2% accessing Internet re-sources. Without counting children under the age of 6, estimates claim 485 million people have Internet access as of 2011. It is noted that older and rural Chinese are much less likely to have access or ICT skills or interest (Kan, 2011). The rural countryside is home to about 51% of China's population and has only 15% Internet penetration. As many as 66% of rural Chinese access ICT resources using mobile devices, a means of communication and information-gathering supported by recent technology and new devices, including cell phones (East-West-Connect, 2011).

India. Determining the level of Internet penetration in India is difficult, and es-timates range from 24 million current Internet users to 100 million by the end of 2011 (Internet World Stats, 2011a; Penn Olson, 2011). This huge nation has 1.21 billion people, with about 72% living in rural areas. Rural India is heavily agrar-ian and is home to about 75% of the nation's poor people. As in many other rural areas, mobile devices have deep penetration in India and continually attract addi-tional providers. Cybercafés and ICT kiosks are extremely popular throughout much of India, including villages and rural areas. Women manage and operate the vast majority of thousands of cybercafés and kiosks and connect their people to the outside world, including some medical care and information delivered online (Internet World Stats, 2011a). China and India are huge markets for ICT growth, including greater personal ownership of hardware. Without a doubt, rural populations use ICT and are populations to be served.

North and South Korea. ICT in North Korea is a politically sanctioned commodity with governmental networks that are not accessible to many citizens. In this isolated and secretive nation, this network is believed to be offered only in Korean. In August 2010 a Twitter account, translated as "our people," opened to people and was followed by the addition of a YouTube channel. Outside the nation a great deal is unclear about the extent of usage and the level of online control in North Korea (Boyd, 2010).

ICT access in South Korea is much different from that in North Korea. In 2004 about 64% of South Koreans had ICT access (Myung, 2004). Investing heavily in ICT over the past decade, 81% of South Koreans are Internet users. Interestingly, there continues to be evidence of the digital divide, because more affluent households, males, and younger people use access more frequently than females and older adults (Internet World Stats, 2010c). It is possible that some women and older adults exercise personal preference and may simply have less interest in frequent use of ICT technologies.

Central America. Central America is another region where ICT is positioned to grow, particularly with wireless technology. In 2010 overall Internet usage in the region was 24.9%, with Costa Rica having the highest usage at 44.3%. Nicaragua, with half its population living in extreme poverty, has the lowest usage at only 10% (Internet World Stats, 2010b).

The Middle East. The Middle East is a composite of 15 diverse countries and territories, with an average of 29.8% Internet penetration in a population of slightly more than 212 million people. Heavily dependent on food importation, the region has vast expanses of deserts, rich valleys, oceans, and some areas that are mostly uninhabitable. Populations cluster in crowded cities and along areas rich in vegetation and rainfall. Nations rich in oil have the highest per capita income of anywhere in the world. Nations that are torn by war and political struggles lack resources. Internet use in the Middle East ranges from 75.9% in the United Arab Emirates, with a population of about 5 million people, to 1.8% in Yemen, with a population of nearly 24 million. Iraq has a population just under 30 million, with only about 1.1% having Internet access (Internet World Stats, 2010b). The United Arab Emirates is predominantly urban, whereas Yemen is mainly rural, with population projections calling for a small decline to 68.7% of the country's population by 2015, and about one third of Iraq's people live in rural areas (Economic and Social Commission for Western Asia, 2008).

Oppression of women in the Middle East has been a topic of many reports, articles, and books. However, findings from a study of women living in more urban and economically strong Middle Eastern countries show that 85% of the 1,250 women surveyed report using the Internet daily and sometimes for up to 10 hours. Interests in networking, socializing, shopping, and education are all motivating forces for Internet use by Middle Eastern women (Media Line, 2010). The report found that the majority of women who responded enjoyed Facebook accounts and spent considerable time in social networking through media, such as Facebook and e-mail.

Reflections on ICT Globalization

Looking at the use and growth of ICT technologies around the world, communication and information demands are priorities for every nation. ICT fuels economies, stores data, delivers entertainment, and is the backbone for distributing education, banking, and health information. No longer is point-to-point technology necessary, as ICT brings global access to Internet resources at increasingly higher speeds and lower costs. New labels and technologies continue to emerge, including the concept of "cloud computing," in which virtual technologies pool, involving public and private networks in which signal and connection redundancy occur somewhere in cyberspace. The ICT revolution has moved through cellular, digital, and data communication and now on to 4G, the fourth generation of wireless communication. Rural households can access ICT technologies easier than ever before, and the ICT revolution is about to further gear-up. Clearly, important in this growth of ICT technologies is the recognition that rural areas are critical in terms of natural resources, labor markets, and agricultural production needed throughout the world. The world simply cannot afford to exclude rural markets from active ICT participation and communication.

United States, 2011: President Obama and 4G

On February 10, 2011, President Obama traveled to Northern Michigan University in Marquette, a town of just under 21,000 people, located on Michigan's Upper Peninsula on the rural shores of Lake Superior. Fishing, hunting, dog sledding, skiing, and outdoor recreation attract many people, despite ample snowfall and subzero winter temperatures.

President Obama spoke of the "interconnected world" and importance of technology in economies of the future (HuffPost Social News, 2011). Of particular note is that Northern Michigan University is recognized as a leader in having developed its own high-speed wireless service, with capacities to provide K–12 education on the rural Upper Peninsula. President Obama's pledge to spend $3 billion for research and development and another $5 billion to extend 4G for ICT access to reach rural areas is a huge commitment, attesting to the importance of rural access for education, communication, information, and economic development in the United States. The president called for bringing ICT access and usage to 98% of Americans, up from about 65% with access at the end of 2010. Such investment and increased access are huge steps in connecting the nation and the world. The presidential message delivered at Northern Michigan University is another step in rural America's growth beyond the important 2009 legislation, the American Recovery and Reinvestment Act of 2009 (ARRA).

The appropriation of $2.5 billion, called for by ARRA, targets infrastructure and economic development in rural America. There is extensive assistance in broadband infrastructure, biofuels research, and assistance in farm disasters. Growing more ICTs with expansions from 3G to 4G brings wireless broadband with much faster speed and consistent video streaming. Wireless access makes the concept of the "global village" possible, as cyberspace becomes the next social environment with accessibility for communication among people anywhere in the world; no longer will rural areas lack access. The act provides funding for supplemental nutrition, clean water, and wastewater systems in rural areas as part of economic development.

Sharp Learning Curve Ahead: Rural and Urban Alike

New concepts in the world of ICT advances, and even familiar information with new labels, all require changing practices and present avenues for learning. The challenge of access is much greater in rural areas, but information and use of ICT in the global context raise numerous concerns so that, as technology advances, information and resources can be used to build and support civil societies and human well-being. Although there are many economic opportunities and social concerns to attend to as ICT progresses, some areas to pay attention to are already on the horizon: interoperability, telehealthspheres, practices in child welfare, and education.

Interoperability

One such term on the horizon of ICTs is that of *interoperability*. In human services, *interoperability* refers to data sharing and management and planning among agencies with related missions and/or serving similar populations. For instance, public health and human services have similar missions and, in rural areas, the same consumers of services. At an upper level such data management could benefit participating organizations and serve consumers in both rural and urban environments. However, Schoech (2010) raises concerns that, as linking and sharing reach global levels with electronic exchanges of data being possible, concerns of ownership arise in terms of management and responsibility. Such concerns of ownership and confidentiality raise even more questions about the risk of compromising security and privacy. Of course, if health data were to overlap with public and mental health data, the aggregated data would provide a much more accurate and comprehensive report about health and mental health of a population or nation. Concerns about confidentiality and privacy raise ethical issues for human services and health care professions. Without a doubt, much remains to be learned as organizational change and governance grow in relation to growth and use of ICT resources and capacities.

Telehealthspheres

There are huge opportunities in providing high-quality health care to every American and in every city, town, and rural area. The Patient Protection and Affordable Care Act of 2010 calls for efficient initiatives to improve health outcomes; gathering data to address and report gaps in care; providing care in situations of high-cost chronic illnesses and disease; reducing health disparities by income, geographic areas, and other factors; and providing improved research and information (MacKinney, Lundblad, Coburn, McBride, & Mueller, 2010). Interestingly, territorial debates continue as to whether telemedicine, telepsychiatry, or telementalhealth should identify health or mental health practices (Surface, 2007). Although *telehealth* is a tempting label, in 2001 the term included behavioral health but was used to target underserved, rural, and developing countries (Stamm, 1998), and, if used in the future, it would need to be broadened. Considering the involvement of the social work profession in health and rural health care, *telehealthspheres* could become the term appropriate to include physical, mental, emotional, and social health.

Limitations and/or changes in language call for social work professionals to take action, demand changes, and celebrate the presence of the profession in all realms of human care. Delivery of rural health and mental health care through cyberspace is particularly open to social workers. Advocacy, community development, support for local health clinics, and assistance in developing and implementing funded projects under legislation such as ARRA or other relevant funding opportunities fall within the expertise of social workers.

Practices in Child Welfare

A great deal of information about the state of children in the United States and the world is available and easily accessed through ICT. The plight of children living in poverty in rural areas is well-known. Reports and articles are numerous and address topics such as child health, disabilities, abuse, neglect, abandonment, child endangerment, and human trafficking increases in the last decade. As a field of practice, child welfare has strong researchers and large databases with updated information on the state of children annually. However, considering service delivery to children and families in their homes and communities and in view of requirements for security and confidentiality, it is likely that the child welfare field is somewhat behind in using ICT to report and/or store data in this sensitive field of practice. Many rural child welfare agencies lack funding and need better ICT access, equipment, and training to upgrade capacities. The time lag between incidences affecting children and any sort of intervention is one area for greater applicability of ICT in the child welfare arena, because expedited protective services, foster care, custody, and other interventions could save lives. Although not replacing practitioners in the field, ICT is indeed another level of information exchange that can be helpful in determining outcomes for children (Nguyen, 2007).

The cyberspace environment calls for protection of children on many levels. The report titled "End Child Prostitution, Child Pornography and Trafficking of Children for Sexual Purposes" makes important contributions to a larger study, the United Nations Secretary-General's study *Violence Against Children* (Muir, 2005). In their technical and social environments children are at risk of receiving or distributing pornography, child sexual abuse, and cyber bullying, stalking, and solicitation. Psychological harm from various age-inappropriate information can result in self-harm, blurred boundaries of self and others, and emotional disorders. Emotional, physical, and sexual abuses during childhood place children at greater risk for a wide array of dysfunctional behaviors, including violence, truancy, and school failures. Children exposed to the sexual acts of others or to inappropriate information may engage in acts of sexual perpetration, perhaps beginning dysfunctional or even criminal behaviors that can become lifelong problems.

Healthy development of children and youths is critical to success in the adult years and to lifelong well-being.

Nair (2006) raises the need to balance protecting children from harm with also protecting their rights to information and freedom of speech, which are now linked to ICT communications. Not all children have mobile phones, Internet access, or their own computer, but many do. Generally, households with adequate incomes to provide children with wireless devices do so. Children carry mobile phones at early ages, learn to use computerized toys, and enjoy Internet access well before entering public education. Nair (2006) notes that one study in the United Kingdom found that about 50% of children ages 7–16 had their own mobile phones in 2001 (BBC News, 2001).

Mobile phones come with GPS tracking systems, cameras, texting, and searching capacities, all of which may present both hazards and access to safety. Children have rights, but adults have rights and responsibilities. Educating families and children about safety and determining what regulations provide both protection and access are needed. Interestingly, most children in rural areas either do or will soon have access to ICT with higher speeds and capabilities that can be managed somewhat by the sophistication of their mobile phones. Advancing ICT technologies are reducing rural isolation for children and families outside of urban areas.

The social work profession functions at the helm of child welfare nationally and internationally. Shaping ethical practices and developing policies to protect children are critically important in protecting children in all societies from harm by others and from harmful communication in the Internet environment (Tregeagle & Darcy, 2008).

Education: Linked-In

ICT technologies are changing education for teachers and students and increasingly depend on information sharing, networking, and communication. Entire degree programs can be accessed by a click of the mouse. Master's and bachelor of social work degree programs and other programs in health and social services can be accessed online. Professional education and postdegree courses are plentiful, cover numerous topics, and are offered in many countries with culturally appropriate language, learning objectives, and assignments. Colleges and universities are growing more and more online offerings, including professional development and other training opportunities for professionals in a variety of industries and service arenas. Online education is widely available although difficult to access by "dial-up" Internet service systems.

ICT technologies support a variety of technological deliveries. Social interactions on Facebook and Twitter are convenient means for communicating and networking. Website browsing accesses news publications, sports notices, shopping, libraries, the New York Stock Exchange, investment firms, and information centers for companies, universities, and individuals. Audio books, movies, television, and music offer online entertainment. Travel opportunities offer ticketing sites, GPS locaters, and pages by travel agents. User-created opportunities include podcasts, blogs, and more. In other words, opportunities to seek, find, and give information abound. Educating and supporting populations to make intelligent uses and rational choices in ICT environments is perhaps the greatest challenge of the first half of the 21st century.

Social Work: Linked-In to Challenges and Opportunities

Cyberspace is here and links the world for most practical purposes. ICT has capacities to bring cultures together, bridging differences in diversity and supporting communication that may help mend unnecessary divides for generations and for diverse populations. With wireless access in place, distance is so much easier to bridge for future generations. The broad range of ICT applications paints a new, interconnected world in which rural areas can participate.

Social Work and the Human Side of ICT for Rural Access

Looking at concerns of rural access, unfamiliar service delivery applications, and gaps in policies and infrastructure, Wasko (2005) raised the question of "whether (or not) the profession can change quickly enough to truly help rural people in the struggles that lie ahead" (p. 62). Social work is the profession most equipped to organize rural communities and households in collective efforts to gain access and develop skills necessary to maintain civil societies alongside membership as active cyberspace citizens. The social work profession has a huge role in advocating for ethical practices, legislative rules, and laws that protect privacy, assure accountability, and prevent invasive or unethical use of cyberspace technologies.

The first decade of the third millennium holds much information and many things, including war, civil unrest, advances in science, growth toward 4G, and globalization of ICT. At this point of globalization, ICT is quite uneven, both in access and necessary hardware. The explosion of various ICT and wireless devices increasingly supports exchange of information and communication necessary for rural equality; however, realizing equality is another uphill struggle for many rural dwellers who experience challenges of poverty, isolation, and lack of information or equipment for ICT participation.

Advocacy, community action, and community development are charges for social workers throughout small towns and rural areas globally. Social work is the profession foremost in government, nonprofit, and for-profit agency administration and service delivery. Social work education and professional licensure are gatekeepers for practice with individuals, families, groups, organizations, and communities. The work of social workers complements professional fields, such as psychology, law, public health, medicine, pharmacy, nursing, public administration, and more. There are numerous roles for social work involvement for rural populations in response to the emerging themes discussed previously: interoperability, telehealthspheres, practices in child welfare, and education. Direct practice and organizational/community social work practice continue to expand in diverse human and social service settings globally. In addition to promoting access for rural populations, opportunities for future involvement for social work are broad, especially within policy and ethical concerns related to ICT innovations in the ever-growing cyberspace.

References

Appalachian Regional Commission. (2011). *The Appalachian region.* Retrieved from http://www.arc.gov/appalachian_region/TheAppalachianRegion.asp

ArabCrunch. (2011, April 28). *Egypt's MCIT: Egypt has 23.51 million Internet users, 71.46 million mobile subscribers & 3972 ICT companies.* Retrieved from http://arabcrunch.com/2011/04/egypts-mcit-egypt-has-23-51-million-internet-users-71-46-million-mobile-subscribers-3972-ict-companies.html

Arnold, B. (2007). *Digital divides in Australia. Caslon Analytics Digital Divides.* Retrieved from http://www.caslon.com.au/dividesprofile6.htm

Basu, M., & Karimi, F. (2009). *Solar cell phones take off in developing nations. CNN.Com/technology.* Retrieved from http://edition.cnn.com/2009/TECH/08/21/solar.cellphone/index.html

BBC News. (2001) *Half UK children own mobiles.* Retrieved from http://news.bbc.co.uk/2/hi/uk_news/1142033.stm

Boyd, C. (2010). *North Korea creates Twitter and YouTube presence.* Retrieved from http://www.bbc.co.uk/news/world-us-canada-11007825

Couto, R. A. (1994). Appalachia. In R. A. Couto, N. K. Simpson, & G. Harris (Eds.), *Sowing seeds in the mountains: Community-based coalitions for cancer prevention and control* (pp. 14–28). [NIH Publication No. 94-3779]. Bethesda, MD: National Cancer Institute.

East-West-Connect. (2011). *China's digital divide—differences in urban and rural Chinese Internet users.* Retrieved from http://www.east-west-connect.com/urban-vs-rural -chinese-internet-users-2010

Economic and Social Commission for Western Asia. (2008). *The demographic profile of Arab countries ageing of rural populations.* Retrieved from http://www.escwa.un.org/information /publications/edit/upload/sdd-07-bk1-rev1-e.pdf

Federal Highway Administration. (2004). *Census 2000 population statistics: U. S. population living in urban vs. rural areas.* Retrieved from http://www.fhwa.dot.gov/planning/census/cps2k.htm

Feser, E., Goldstein, H., Renski, H., & Renault, C. (2002). *Regional technology assets and opportunities: The geographic clustering of high-tech industry, science and innovation in Appalachia.* Chapel Hill, NC: University of North Carolina at Chapel Hill.

GigaOM Pro. (2010). *Who will profit from broadband innovation?* Retrieved from http://pro.gigaom.com/2010/03/who-will-profit-from-broadband-innovation

Górniak, K. (1996). The computer revolution and the problem of global ethics. *Science and Engineering Ethics, 2*(2), 177–190.

Harper-Dorton, K. V., & Yoon, D. P. (2002). Information technology in rural nonprofit agencies: Local concerns and global potentials. *New Technology in the Human Services, 14*(3-4), 24–33.

Hash. (2011). *Kenya's mobile & Internet, by the numbers (Q4 2010).* Retrieved from http://whiteafrican.com/2011/02/18/kenyas-mobile-internet-by-the-numbers-q4-2010/

HuffPost Social News. (2011, February 12). *Obama speaks at Northern Michigan University.* Retrieved from http://www.huffingtonpost.com/2011/02/10/obama-speaks-at -northern-_n_821468.html

International Fund for Agricultural Development. (2010). *Rural poverty report.* Retrieved from http://www.ifad.org/rpr2011/index.html

Internet World Stats. (2010a). *Internet usage and population in Central America.* Retrieved from http://www.internetworldstats.com/stats12.htm

Internet World Stats. (2010b). *Internet usage in the Middle East.* Retrieved from http://www.internetworldstats.com/stats5.htm

Internet World Stats. (2010c). *Korea Internet usage, broadband, and telecommunications reports.* Retrieved from http://www.internetworldstats.com/asia/kr.htm

Internet World Stats. (2011a). *India Internet usage statistics and telecommunications.* Retrieved from http://www.internetworldstats.com/asia/in.htm

Internet World Stats. (2011b). *Internet usage statistics for Africa.* Retrieved from http://www.internetworldstats.com/stats1.htm

Internet World Stats. (2011c). *Internet usage statistics for Europe.* Retrieved from http://www.internetworldstats.com/stats4.htm

Kan, M. (2011). *China reaches 485 million Internet users as growth slows.* Retrieved from http://www.itworld.com/

Labrianidis, L., & Kalogeressis, T. (2006). The digital divide in Europe's rural enterprises. *European Planning Studies, 14*(1), 23–39

Lubowski, R. N., Vesterby, M., Bucholtz, D. S., Baez, A., & Roberts, M. J. (2002). *Major uses of land in the United States, 2002.* [Economic Research Service/USDA EIB-14]. Retrieved from http://www.ers.usda.gov/Publications/EIB14/

MacKinney, A. C., Lundblad, J. P., Coburn, A. F., McBride, T. D., & Mueller, K. J. (2010). *Securing high quality health care in rural America: The impetus for change in the affordable care act.* Federal Office of Rural Health policy, Health Resources and Services Administration, U S Department of Health and Human Services. Retrieved from http://www.rupri.org/Forms/HealthPanel_ACA_Dec2010.pdf

Miniwatts Marketing Group. (2010). *Australia Internet usage stats and telecommunications reports.* Retrieved from www.internetworldstats.com/sp/au.htm

Muir, D. (2005). *Violence against children in cyberspace.* Bangkok, Thailand: End Child Prostitution, Child Pornography and Trafficking of Children for Sexual Purposes.

Myung, S. E. (2004). *South Koreans face digital divide.* Retrieved from http://news.cnet.com/South-Koreans-face-digital-divide/2100-1025_3-5305190.html

Nair, A. (2006). Mobile phones and the Internet: Legal issues in the protection of children. *International Review of Law Computers & Technology, 20*(1-2), 177–185.

National Telecommunications and Information Administration (NTIA). (1995). *Falling through the net: A survey of the "have nots" in rural and urban America.* Retrieved from http://www.ntia.doc.gov/ntiahome/falingthru.html

National Telecommunications and Information Administration (NTIA). (1999). *Falling through the net: Defining the digital divide.* Retrieved from http://www.ntia.doc.gov/ntiahome/fttn99/acknowledgements.html

National Telecommunications and Information Administration (NTIA). (2000). *Falling through the net: Toward digital inclusion.* Retrieved from http://www.ntia.doc.gov/ntiahome/fttn00/contents00.html

National Telecommunications and Information Administration (NTIA). (2011). *Digital nation: expanding Internet usage.* Retrieved from http://www.scribd.com/doc/52464660/NTIA-Internet-Use-2011

Nguyen, L. H. (2007). Child welfare informatics: A new definition for an established practice. *Social Work, 52*(4), 361–363.

Oden, M., & Strover, S. (2002). *Links to the future: The role of information and telecommunications technology in Appalachian economic development.* Retrieved from www.utexas.edu/research/.../research/finalarctelecomupdatereportjune23.pdf

Open Net Initiative. (2009, August 6). *Egypt.* Retrieved from http://opennet.net/research/profiles/egypt

Penn Olson. (2011. April 15). *India to hit 24 million rural Internet users in 2011.* Retrieved from http://www.penn-olson.com/2011/04/15/india-rural-internet-users/

Schoech, D. (2010). Interoperability and the future of human services. *Journal of Technology in Human Services, 28*(1), 7–22.

Stamm, B. H. (1998). Clinical applications of telehealth in mental health care. *Professional Psychology: Research and Practice, 29,* 536–542.

Surface, D. (2007). Country comfort—mental health telemedicine in rural America. *Social Work Today, 7*(1), 28.

The Media Line. (2010, June 14). *Arab women show digital prowess.* Retrieved from http://www.jpost.com/MiddleEast/Article.aspx?id=178412

Tregeagle, S., & Darcy, M. (2008). Child welfare and information and communication technology: Today's challenge. *British Journal of Social Work. 38,* 1481–1498.

U. S. Census Bureau. (2011). *Comparing the official census counts to others ways of estimating the population size.* Retrieved from http://blogs.census.gov/2010census/2011/02/comparing-the-official-census-counts-to-other-ways-of-estimating-the-population-size.html

Wasko, N. (2005). Wired for the future? The Impact of information and telecommunications technology on rural social work. In N. Lohmann & R. A. Lohmann (Eds.), *Rural social work practice* (pp. 41–72). New York, NY: Columbia University Press.

Willis, S., & Tranter, B. (2002). *Beyond the "digital divide": Socio-economic dimensions of Internet diffusion in Australia.* Retrieved from http://www.sisr.net/events/docs/0208willis.pdf

Willis, S., & Tranter, B. (2006). Beyond the digital divide: Internet diffusion and inequality in Australia. *Journal of Sociology, 42*(1), 43–59.

World Summit on the Information Society. (2005). *Navajo Nation ICT based on Indigenous Traditions Project, Project ID 1201789071.* Retrieved from http://www.itu.int/wsis/stocktaking/plugin/documents2.asp?project=1201789071&lang=en&email=&userid=-1

5   Technology in Rural Social Work Practice

GLENN STONE

In 1986 I wrote a grant to fund a case management program for at-risk youths and their families. One of the unusual requests in the budget was for a desktop computer. Not many social service agencies in our rural area had computers, nor had actually even seen a desktop computer. However, just a few years later Macarov (1991) wrote a book in which he made predictions about the future of social work practice. Macarov speculated about the potential for technology to have a profound effect on social work practice. Specifically, Macarov believed there would be a significant increase in the use of computers in the areas of agency management, policy planning, research, and service to clients. He also noted that there would be challenges connected with this new technology. He noted that this type of technology could lead to greater levels of scrutiny of workers and shifting power relationships between and within agencies. Macarov foresaw that the electronic recordkeeping systems could lead to concerns regarding confidentiality. As Vernon (2005) points out, "these forecasts have been remarkably accurate" (p. 91). It is now widely accepted that technology is more than just a tool, as it actually begins to shape the manner in which we provide services.

This chapter provides an overview of some of the ways technology is used now in social work practice and social service agencies, explores some emerging uses, and outlines some of the current challenges social workers face when using technology. A special emphasis is given to how these technology trends affect rural social work

87

practice. Of course, as with anything to do with technology, what is written about it today could appear prehistoric by the time it is read. This is also true in regard to buying any sort of technological device. We accept that today's new technological gadget will be next week's dinosaur. With this in mind, I will "jump in" and begin writing about the present situation, with hopes that what is written here holds some value in the future.

It is difficult to determine the most current trends in technology use in rural social work practice, because it is a challenge to determine how technology is used in social service agencies in general. Fortunately, Blatt and Duggan (2009) completed an analysis for IBM Global Business Services of emerging trends in technology that are changing how social services operate worldwide. They identified six technological advances that are having immediate impact on rural and urban social services and also seem to be part of the future functioning of social services agencies: (1) decision support systems, (2) assistive technology, (3) sensors and home health monitoring, (4) collaboration tools, (5) intelligent processing, and (6) intelligent identity. The most relevant four of these six areas are subsequently examined, and their application to social work practice in rural settings is discussed.

Decision Support Systems

Anyone who has worked in a busy rural social service setting can attest to the difficulty of attempting to make difficult decisions about the efficacy of agency programs, budgeting, staffing patterns, resource allocation, individual client interventions, and numerous other agency practices. These issues share the common feature of challenging staff to sort through large amounts of data to make "informed" decisions. Is the agency-based welfare-to-work program actually leading to meaningful employment for participants? Should the social worker meeting with a suicidal client press for hospitalization? Is the agency spending too much money on maintaining its outdated computer system? Making the correct decisions in these various situations is often based on the quality of data collected and the ability to transform that data into useful information. "Decision Support Systems provide a way to model and understand complex data and make quality decisions based upon that data" (Blatt & Duggan, 2009, p. 5).

Social work agencies have a history of using decision support systems (herein abbreviated DSS—not to be confused with Department of Social Services) in a wide range of areas, and research has explored the effectiveness of their use. A recent study by Monnickendam, Savaya, and Waysman (2005) explored the thinking processes in the use of DSSs by social workers in a human services agency to determine whether the workers used the system to improve their case reasoning. The findings from the study were mixed. Workers indicated that for "routine" cases the DSS information was not that helpful. However, workers noted that the DSS information was very useful for cases that were seen as "atypical." This is helpful for rural agencies, which often operate on tight budgets. DSS information might prove best reserved specifically for unusual cases that defy common responses.

Blatt and Duggan (2009) suggest there is significant need for DSS in the future and suggest the following uses.

- Reducing fraud and abuse by actively highlighting abnormal claims

- Minimizing audit risk by identifying clients who are not compliant with service rules

- Improving the use of outcome measurements that enable the elimination of ineffective programs

- Allocating financial resources effectively based on accurate, timely, and easily accessible information

- Holding managers and staff accountable for operating goals by tracking key performance indicators and making that information available in real time

- Providing stakeholders with relevant data on program effectiveness, customer satisfaction, and financial measures with balanced scorecard reports (p. 5).

Blatt and Duggan (2009) note that agencies are currently using DSS to engage in these tasks, but contend that there is fragmentation in how data is collected and used. For example, data collected on individuals in one department of an agency might not be shared with another department within the same agency. From Blatt and Duggan's (2009) perspective, future use of DSS will involve finding ways to integrate the information to better serve clients. In their words, "clients will be viewed holistically across all of the benefits and services they are receiving and decisions will be made by caseworkers based on that view" (Blatt & Duggan, 2009, p. 5). In theory this should allow for the smooth integration of information and case management systems. If this is the case, clients should also begin to see the benefits of DSS usage for their lives. Benefits that clients might derive include

- decisions about services for clients that contain fewer errors;

- organizational "wisdom" generated through expert input into the DSS model that would improve decisions about services to clients; and

- resources to clients that can be used in a more efficient manner, thus providing more services for those in need.

Of course, DSS models are useful only if workers access the available information to make critical decisions. Studies have noted barriers to the adoption of these types of technology by social service workers, such as workers not seeing the added value of technology (Damodaran & Olphert, 2000); time limitations; the effort necessary to learn a new technology (Chen et al., 2004; Mukoyama, 2004); and low comfort with technology (Mukoyama, 2004). Other researchers have identified such issues as lack of user friendliness; slow system response time; inadequate user support and training; and cultural, policy, and practice issues (Damodaran & Olphert, 2000). And some studies also note the difficulty finding information, encountering outdated information (Chen et al., 2004), and a preference for reading information on paper rather than on computer screens (McAlearney, Schweikhart, & Medow, 2004).

Although the barriers to adoption may be numerous, it is vital that rural social service agencies realize that the growing demand for accountability has created the need for improved outcome measurement in social services. Blatt and Duggan (2009) suggest that "in the end, technology can only support humans in understanding data, developing usable hypotheses, and executing strategies" (p. 6). It seems most likely that DSS will not be going away anytime soon and that, quite the contrary, their role in social service decision making will only increase. Rural social service agencies need the information that the DSS can provide to improve client outcomes and demonstrate program effectiveness.

Assistive Technology

Assistive technology (AT) can be defined as "an umbrella term for any device or system that allows an individual to perform a task they would otherwise be unable to do or increases the ease and safety with which the task can be performed" (Cowan & Turner-Smith, 1999, p. 154). It is most often associated with providing additional care to older adults, children with special needs, and individuals with disabilities. It seems obvious that AT will become increasingly relevant, given the growth in number of people living longer. As of 2011 the estimated 371 million elderly people in the world constitute about 5% of the world's population. It is projected that by 2050 the world's population will grow to about 9.37 billion. Older adults will make up approximately 15% of that number—1.4 billion people (Blatt & Duggan, 2009). It is a bit more difficult to obtain accurate data on the number of people who have a disability. Part of this difficulty stems from the fact that there are various definitions of what is considered a disability. However, the United Nations Convention on Rights of Persons with Disabilities has made an effort to look at the issue on a worldwide basis. According to their study, disabilities affect about 15–20% of every country's population (UN Convention on the Rights of Persons with Disabilities [CRPD], 2008). If we extrapolate from these percentages, we can estimate that there are about 650 million people with disabilities worldwide. It should also be noted that this figure may increase, as there is a connection between growing older and developing various disabilities.

One obvious form of AT is the ability to access the Internet to search for answers about health issues. It is well-known that use of the Internet continues to grow across all age groups in the United States. Fox (2004) reports that, overall, 77% of 18- to 29-year-olds, 75% of 30- to 49-year-olds, 58% of 50- to 64-year-olds, and 22% of adults 65 and older have access to the Internet. Furthermore, Fox and Fallows (2003) report that more than 80% of adult users (or 93 million) have searched the Internet for health related information. However, of that 93 million, only 5 million adults age 65 and older have used the Internet to retrieve and use information about health care. Although the difference in Internet use among age groups decreases each year, a large gap exists between seniors who regularly use the Internet to find information about health care and those who do not use the Internet for such purposes.

Campbell and Nolfi (2005) suggest that one way to close this age gap is to teach seniors to use the Internet to search for health care information. They believe that this type of education will result in (1) increased willingness in seniors to use computers and increased motivation to use the Internet to find health care information and (2) increased willingness in seniors to use external health care information to handle their own health care. The results of the Campbell and Nolfi study showed that participants experienced an increased willingness to use computers to locate health information. However, participants were not more likely to use information from the Internet to become more involved in their personal health care or to use this information to make health care decisions. Although the educational program did not make changes in how Internet-accessed information was used, it did demonstrate that at least there are effective ways to get seniors to become familiar with the Internet. It is possible that, with time, seniors' use of the Internet may lead to integrating that information into their health decisions.

Implications for Rural Social Work Practice

The findings on Internet use as linked to health care are beneficial for rural social workers to keep in mind as they attempt to help rural seniors become comfortable with and access the various health resources available on the Internet. Workers need to remember the importance of helping senior clients understand the value of using this health information to be more involved with health decisions in their lives.

Of course, AT is not limited to the Internet and computers. Rural social service agencies also need to think of ways they can use technology in an assistive manner in broader terms. For example, rural agencies need to ensure that their mainstream public services are accessible for people with disabilities and older adults. This may mean installing automatic doors or other assistive technologies. Rural agencies also need to communicate to their clientele in a manner that is accessible. How accessible is information for those who are blind or deaf? Technology may provide mechanisms to facilitate these types of communication.

Technology has been, and can continue to be, a "game changer" for the way that rural social services provide benefits and services. Although it may be helpful to get our clients to access the Internet and to feel comfortable in doing so, the real "assistive" element of this technology occurs when clients can use the Internet as a tool for getting the services and information they need. Blatt and Duggan (2009) suggest that "universal design" is an important element of moving forward in creating more accessible forms of technology. In "traditional" design, the focus has commonly been on the characteristics of the average user. However, when companies design for the average user, they may create unintentional barriers to full accessibility that even AT cannot overcome. Proponents of universal design contend that designs should not systematically exclude people who have physical or cognitive challenges, or cultural or gender differences, simply because the design team did not consider these variables. Rather, diversity issues should be taken into consideration in such a manner as to eliminate discrimination. For example, when designing computer systems for use with older adults, it might be helpful to design keyboard enhancement utilities for seniors who have trouble typing and controlling a mouse, provide on-screen keyboards for seniors who are unable to use a standard keyboard, or design effective screen magnifiers that, like a magnifying glass, help seniors enlarge items on the screen (Blatt & Duggan, 2009).

Rural social workers can play a unique advocacy role for clients who have special needs that are not addressed by traditional design. This could include advocating with funding agencies to request that they be more receptive to allocating resources for unique adaptive technological aids.

Sensors and Home Health Monitoring

The growing population of older adults will most likely mean that there will be an increase in the number of older adults who wish to stay in their own homes or in the homes of their families. This trend toward in-home care, in fact, is already occurring (Blatt & Duggan, 2009). It is already putting a great deal of pressure on people and, with the world's elderly population increasing, this pressure will increase significantly. It is estimated that one out of four U.S. workers is currently caring for a parent or other relative (National Alliance for Caregiving, 2009). Seventy percent of caregivers report making changes, such as cutting back on working hours, changing jobs, stopping work entirely, taking a leave of absence, or other such changes as a result of their caregiving role. It seems clear that caregiving has a substantial impact on the lives of the caregivers and society as a whole. Elderly people in rural areas have higher rates of poverty than elderly urbanites, and rural areas tend to have a higher percentage of elderly in their total population than their urban counterparts (Cawthorne, 2008); therefore, it seems especially important that rural social service agencies become better acquainted with these technological aids.

Blatt and Duggan (2009) assert that, given these increasing trends in home health care, it is clear that "health care and social services have to move into the home in order to enable elders to 'age in place' and remain in their homes for longer periods while allowing caregivers to succeed at work" (p.12). These types of home health care aids seem particularly important to rural agencies. Given the sometimes expansive geographic area that a rural agency may cover, the adjunctive use of home monitoring units would seem ideal. By using this technology, rural social service agencies could work to ensure the safety and well-being of the older adult, while also reducing the stress on the caregiver.

Assurance Systems

Currently there are technologies that can facilitate home health care through monitoring the elder in the home. First, there are assurance systems that are designed to track behavior and provide up-to-date information to the caregiver, providing status reports by phone or e-mail. Systems can also be designed to alert caregivers to risky behaviors by the elder in the home. For example, a sensor system might alert the caregiver when a door has been opened to the outside, thus alerting the caregiver when an elderly person with cognitive impairments has left the home (Blatt & Duggan, 2009). Other systems exist that contain an assortment of sensors that are constantly monitored to detect changes in common patterns of behaviors. Lack of movement near a kitchen or medicine cabinet may indicate a failure to take medication. The absence of motion above a certain height may be a sign that someone has fallen. These sensors could then alert the caregiver to potential problems that may necessitate intervention. If rural caregivers work closely with local rural social service providers in the use of such sensing devices, it might be possible to construct a viable and efficient safety net for elderly clients.

Compensation Systems

The second form of AT are referred to as compensation systems. Whereas assurance systems simply monitor behaviors, compensation systems can intervene to assist an individual trying to complete an activity. They can compensate for impairments and help with navigation issues, scheduling, locating objects, and facial recognition. A schedule management system can remind people to eat, take medications, take care of their hygiene, or check in with a caregiver.

One specific example of a compensation system is termed *navigational support*. Various systems have been developed to help older adults find their way around their environments. Most of these systems aim to assist people who can no longer safely find their way around, either because of either sensory difficulties, such as diminished vision, or mobility impairments that make walking difficult. A major goal of these systems is obstacle avoidance. One example of such a system is the Intelligent Mobility Platform (IMP; Morris et al., 2003). IMP consists of a standard commercial walker, augmented with a laser range finder, a handheld computer with a touchscreen interface for the user, an active drive mechanism, and intelligent navigation software. The IMP can help a potentially confused user find his or her way around a setting (e.g., a large assisted-living facility) without becoming lost. Such technology could prove very valuable for social work staff in rural nursing home settings where reduced staffing patterns may pose a challenge.

A second type of compensation system is schedule management. It helps users who have suffered from memory loss that makes them more prone to forget routine daily activities. For example, schedule-management systems have been used to remind people when to take their medicine, eat meals, take care of personal hygiene, or check in with their adult children. An example of this system is the Autominder, which maintains an accurate and up-to-date model of its user's daily plan, monitors the execution of that plan, and issues reminders accordingly (McCarthy & Pollack, 2002). The system could provide increased autonomy for the client and reduce the demands on the family and caseworker.

Assessment Systems

Finally, researchers are also looking at the use of assessment systems that can provide recurrent, naturalistic assessment of an individual's cognitive status. Cognitive assessments are rarely completed in clinical settings when a person visits the doctor (Lee & Dey, 2004). Even if the assessment is completed, it may not be very useful if the person is having an unusually good or bad day. In contrast, assessment systems provide ongoing feedback on cognitive functioning. Dishman (2004) describes this type of assessment as consisting of sensing systems that continuously collect data on functional abilities to promote healthy behaviors, detect diseases, and facilitate informal caregiving. In a recent study by Lee and Dey (2004), an effort was made to determine the effectiveness of this type of assessment system to assist elderly clients, their families, and health care workers in making better health-related decisions. Their findings suggested that assessment technology can be used to monitor how well elders perform activities of daily living. The researchers found that information about task effort, errors, and accuracy provided early indicators of decline before actual failures in task completion began to occur in participants. They also reported that participants found the information from assessment systems very valuable in providing increased awareness for elders and their family caregivers and facilitating clinical judgment for workers. Once again, it is easy to see how the use of this type of technology could serve as a vital addition to the care of older adults or disabled people in rural settings. Clients could be miles from the nearest service facility, yet ongoing data could be collected and assessed regarding their current cognitive status.

Implications for Rural Social Work Practice.

It seems clear how these various forms of sensors and home health monitoring could be used by rural social workers in their practices. Finding ways to monitor the health and well-being of rural residents through home sensors could address the pressing issues of rural communities (i.e., there is a greater proportion of elders in rural areas, the higher rate of disabilities related to traffic and farming accidents, and the geographic isolation, combined with lack of public transportation). These technology aids provide a way to monitor and assist older adults and disabled people in their own homes, meaning that transportation issues also are addressed. Consumers will not need to struggle to find ways to make it to a provider's office, because technology sensors will be gathering data on the consumer's condition on a daily, if not hourly, basis to send to the provider.

Collaboration Tools

It is clear that a vital mission of social service agencies in rural areas is to increase levels of collaboration within their work domains. This means better collaborative relationships within the agency itself, between agencies, with the community, and with clients. Blatt and Duggan (2009) contend that, more than ever before, consumers of social benefits and programs want to be active participants rather than passive recipients of services and benefits. Clients want to have input into which benefits and services they receive; they want to participate in the selection of service providers; and they want a choice in where and when they will receive those services. Community members also want to voice opinions about the quality of social service programs and benefits. Many social service organizations are aware of the merit of such collaborative relationships and are putting the requisite mechanisms in place to make them possible. Stakeholder collaboration will become a more frequent feature of social service agencies. It is conceivable that stakeholders will collaborate on policy, service delivery, training, and the general sharing of ideas. But tools for active collaboration are needed to make this happen. Two such tools are subsequently discussed.

Web 2.0

The first tool is Web 2.0. A simple way to think of Web 2.0 is to view it as "a rich social networking environment that provides secure and integrated collaboration tools which allow people to harness the total knowledge of the extended enterprise" (Blatt & Duggan, 2009, p. 15). The term also is used to describe a second generation of the World Wide Web, focused on the capacity for people to collaborate and share information online. Web 2.0 basically refers to the transition from static HTML websites to a more dynamic Web that is more organized and is based on serving Web applications to users (Webopedia, 2011). Web 2.0 software has emerged to facilitate new online activities, many of which could not have been achieved previously. Online social interaction has been enriched through the use of wikis, blogs, and podcasts (Beldarrain, 2006). Web 2.0 encourages a more human approach to interactivity on the Web, better supports group interaction, and fosters a greater sense of community in a potentially impersonal social environment (Wallace, 1999). As Abram (2005) notes, the social Web is about conversations, interpersonal networking, personalization, and individualism. Robinson (2005) refers to it as the "People-centric Web." As Web 2.0 has emerged, numerous tools have been developed to better use the interactive nature of the environment.

Internet Wikis

Wikis are good examples of "social writing" software within Web 2.0. A wiki is a collaborative software that allows users to add content but also allows that content to be edited by anybody (Sharp, 2006). Wikis can be used for sharing knowledge, such as an encyclopedia-style wiki (e.g., Wiki Surgery at http://www.wikisurgery.com), social policy monitoring (e.g., OpenCongress.org at http://www.opencongress.org/wiki /Equal_access_to_services_policies), and/or running community projects. A good example of the latter is the World Help Training Center wiki (http://www.appropedia.org/WHTC_Technology_Plan), which serves as a central knowledge point for disseminating information and tracking the progress of a "convertible community" project in Georgia. Convertible communities have efficiently designed space to allow the greatest use and most flexibility for inhabitants.

The utility of wikis for rural social service agencies is in their ability to provide information contributed or edited by local professionals and thus more relevant to local experience. Wikis could also be a valuable means for rural agencies to disseminate information about new programs in a manner to allow feedback and suggestions from the community. This information could prove very valuable for program development and evaluation.

Internet Blogs

Blogs are simple content management tools enabling nonexperts to build easily updatable Web diaries or online journals (Sharp, 2006). They are published chronologically, with links and commentary on various issues of interest. Frequently, blogs are networked between several users who post thoughts that often focus on a common theme (Barsky, 2006). Although most blogs are currently focused on news, relationships, and politics, many are medical/health related (e.g., the DrugScope DrugData Updated blog http://drugscope.blogspot.com, the TRIP Database blog http://tripdatabase.blogspot.com) and mental health related (e.g., such as the National Alliance on Mental Illness [NAMI] at http://blog.nami.org). The NAMI blog site provides useful information about mental illness from the perspective of the consumer and would certainly be an asset to rural mental health agencies and their clients. Often, social isolation is a problem for rural clients who suffer from a mental illness, and it could be helpful to connect them with the advocacy-based NAMI organization. The blogs on the NAMI site are informative and written in a manner that most readers could understand and find a connection with.

Podcasting and Streaming Video Services

Podcasts are time and location independent digital files. Free software enables computer users to subscribe to regular podcast sources, download them automatically, and then transfer them to a portable device such as an Apple iPod or MP3/MP4 player for later playback. Individuals may also choose to listen to or watch them on any laptop or desktop computer equipped with speakers and supported by media software, such as Windows Media Player (Barsky, 2006). Researchers are beginning to explore the usefulness of podcasts in health and mental health settings. For example, the results of a recent study by Turner-McGrievy (2010) suggested that a well-designed, theory-based podcast may be an effective way to promote healthy weight loss, which could prove valuable for rural workers seeking to provide cost-effective ways to intervene with clients experiencing weight problems. It is also possible that, if podcasting was helpful with a weight loss program, it might also be helpful with other health and mental health issues (Turner-McGrievy, 2010) that rural social workers deal with on a daily basis.

Social Networking Services

Social networking services are online group-forming applications that connect people through shared information interests. They allow users to locate links with people through mutual friends or acquaintances, build profiles, and update address books. Moreover, sites such as Meetup (http://www.meetup.com/) and Facebook (http://www.facebook.com) provide social tools to build communities of practice with the purpose of facilitating face-to-face meetings across cities all over the world.

Increasingly, social networking capacities are being used for more than simply making friends or keeping in touch with family. They are being used to help connect people with health-related issues. Medical and health-related examples of social networking services include the LibraryThingMedicine group (http://www.librarything.com/groups/medicine), a library social network site promoting social interactions, book recommendations, self-classification, and monitoring of new books; and the Facebook Cure Type 1 Diabetes page (http://www.facebook.com/pages/Cure-Type-1-Diabetes/286459145148), which is run by patients and supporters. Some social networking services combine several Web 2.0 tools/features, such as instant messaging (e.g., Facebook), social bookmarking, blogs, and podcasts. Examples of these services include the Mental Health Social Network (http://social.realmentalhealth.com/) and the IJS portal (http://www.theijs.com/), a global community portal centered on the *International Journal of Surgery*.

Researchers are just beginning to explore the impact of social networking on those who use the services. In a recent study Walz (2009) examined whether college students can achieve a greater sense of belonging through the use of computer-mediated forms of social networking, such as social networking websites. Results revealed that college students' sense of belonging was positively correlated with the number of hours per day they reported using social networking sites and with the total number of friends they reported having on the sites. These findings suggest that the use of social networking sites may benefit college students by increasing their sense of belonging. Although this study focused on college students, it seems possible that the findings may hold true for other populations as well.

Implications for rural social work practice. Rural social workers may find it helpful to encourage isolated rural clients to engage in positive forms of social networking to increase the clients' sense of belongingness as well. As noted throughout this chapter, rural social workers are constantly dealing with issues related to older adults and disabled people because of the demographics of rural America. Social networking services can help these populations feel less isolated and gain a sense of connectedness with others despite their geographic isolation.

Virtual Worlds

An online virtual world is "an interactive computer simulation which allows participants to see, hear, use, and modify simulated objects in a computer-created world" (Hughes & Moshel, 1997, p. 145). Virtual worlds can be designed for single participants; simultaneous participants; or multiple groups of users, referred to as a "virtual community" (Boulos, Hetherington, & Wheeler, 2007). An example of one such virtual world that is accessible through the Internet is Second Life, which permits users to interact with each other in much the same way they might in real life. It is not clear how many people regularly use Second Life, but it has almost 2 million registered users (Blatt & Duggan, 2009). Increasingly, companies and organizations have found it useful to advertise through Second Life or at least have a presence within the virtual world. It is even being used to support social service programs. One example is Virtual Ability Island (http://slurl.com/secondlife/Virtual%20Ability/69/175/23), which was created to support people with disabilities and chronic illnesses. Virtual Ability Island is managed by Virtual Ability, Inc., a nonprofit 501(c)(3) corporation based in Colorado. Its mission is to enable people with a wide range of disabilities to enter into virtual worlds like Second Life and provide them with a supportive environment experience. The group offers members information, encouragement, training, companionship, referrals to other online resources and groups, ways to contribute back to the community, and entertainment. People with disabilities can do things in Second Life like everyone else can in real life and do not have to be socially isolated—readily finding peer support and information important to understanding their situations (Zielke, Roome, & Krueger, 2009).

Implications for social work practice. Although there is still only scant research on the full extent of the usefulness of virtual worlds such as Second Life for social work practice, the initial findings suggest that virtual worlds can serve as an important adjunctive tool in assisting certain populations to enjoy a range of experiences that could prove beneficial to their overall well-being (Zielke et al., 2009). Once again, it is possible that rural social workers might find ways to use this technological advancement to assist them in their work. For example, workers might introduce their clients with a disability to the supportive aspects of Virtual Ability Island on Second Life to improve the client's sense of community with other individuals experiencing some form of disability. Rural life can have its isolating features because of the geographical distances between individuals, and giving clients with disabilities the chance to interact with like-minded individuals could be very beneficial to their well-being.

Additional Trends

Although Blatt and Duggan (2009) provide a commendable overview of some of the major trends affecting social service agencies, there are still some trends that should be mentioned regarding the ways technology is affecting rural social work practice.

Basic Agency Computerization and High Speed Internet Access

Many outside the field of rural social work may not realize that innumerable rural areas are still in the process of computerizing social service agencies. Although most business organizations are well into this process, it is still common to see articles in social work journals about worker resistance to the computerization of their agency (see Weaver, 2002; Zhang & Gutierrez, 2007). What some research has determined is that reluctance to use the technology is not entirely based on a negative attitude, but rather on a lack of knowledge and skills in the use of the technology. For example, a study by Carrilio (2005) found that skill and experience with computers accounted for a large part of the variance in whether workers used the information systems in their agencies. This does not seem surprising considering the large variety of programs and software that agencies may expect workers to use in their daily schedules.

In addition to the challenge of providing computers in social service agencies, there is also the problem of accessing high-speed Internet in rural locations. According to a study by the Pew Internet & American Life Project (2008), only 38% of rural American households have access to high-speed Internet connections. That is an improvement from 15% in 2005, but it pales in comparison with 57% and 60% for city and suburb dwellers, respectively. The project also notes that this lack of fast Web access is helping create a country of broadband haves and have-nots—a division that not only makes it harder for businesses to get work done, but also impedes workers' efforts to find jobs, puts students at a disadvantage, and leaves a wide swath of the country less connected to the growing storehouse of information on the Web, from health sites to news magazines to up-to-date information on presidential candidates. The project further notes that broadband is a distance killer, which can especially help rural Americans. It can be said that broadband is "not just an information source for news and civic matters, but it is also a pathway to participation" (Pew Internet & American Life Project, 2008, p. 12). Social workers in rural settings may need to find ways to advocate for increased Internet access for their agencies and for their clients.

For rural agencies, there is the added dimension of the affordability of technology. Computers obviously cost money, as does the software to run them. In addition, there is the expense to maintain the technology. These problems may be compounded by a potential shortage of professionals to provide training in the requisite knowledge and skills to operate the programs used within an agency.

Telework/Telecommuting

Telecommuting and telework are terms often used interchangeably. They refer to a system whereby employees periodically, regularly, or exclusively perform work for their employers from home or another remote location equipped with the appropriate computer-based technology to transfer work to the central organization (Nilles, 1994; WorldatWork, 2009). An exploration of research on this topic for social work did not turn up many studies on this area. However, it is clear that there are social service agencies experimenting with this type of work option. For example, the Child Welfare League of America (CWLA) discusses a telework program that has been initiated in Harris County in Texas. The Harris County teleworking program began as a pilot project, Delivering Accountable Services from Home (DASH), in 1999, after the local Child Protective Services (CPS) office sustained severe storm damage. By the time building repairs were complete, however, teleworking had become more than just a temporary solution to the loss of office space, but rather a way to increase job satisfaction and flexibility by allowing caseworkers to work from home. CPS staff was then given the option of working from home or remaining in the office. Those who participated in DASH received a combination phone/fax/printer, a laptop computer, and training in maintaining a secure, functional home office. Teleworking caseworkers access information from home via computer, just as they would in the office. They also can use a telecenter at the Harris County Department of Social Services, with desks, phone lines, computer ports, and space for meetings, conferences, supervision, and messages.

Evaluation showed DASH was associated with greater stability and job satisfaction. Job turnover for caseworkers decreased from 25% to 9% during the pilot, job satisfaction increased from 38% to 76%, and caseworkers said they were better able to balance their work and personal lives. The initial evaluation of the pilot program primarily addressed job satisfaction and peer support. CWLA reports that the Harris County Department of Social Services is now evaluating the effect on client outcomes. Based on the DASH evaluation's positive findings, the agency replicated the teleworking model in its Adult Protective Services and Child Care Licensing sections in 2001. The newer programs are under evaluation, and the agency predicts positive results.

A handful of rural agencies use either 100% telework or hybrid models, which combine some work in the office with work at home. For many of workers, their vehicle becomes their office on wheels. The advent of Internet capable smartphones and laptops tethered through these phones to access the Internet has allowed these workers to be highly mobile.

Telework may be especially relevant to rural areas, because workers may have to cover many miles in a day between home visits, appointments, and other work-related meetings. The ability to communicate via technology could allow workers more freedom to work from home and/or commute from one appointment to the next without the need to return to the office to update information on their clients.

Concurrent Documentation

Essentially, concurrent documentation means that providers work with their clients during assessment, service planning, and intervention sessions to complete as much related documentation as possible and appropriate. Technology is at least partially responsible for this trend, because workers are able to enter responses to interview questions directly into the computer. This information could simply remain on the worker's computer, or it could be part of a central database of information collected on each client by the agency. Some view this trend as a positive change for the profession. Proponents of concurrent documentation cite a number of benefits:

- enhancing client and family involvement in the therapeutic/rehabilitative process,

- improving the quality of life for staff by eliminating documentation backlogs and the feeling of "never catching up" by drastically reducing documentation time to direct service ratios,

- helping staff more easily attain performance standards and have time for other useful activities, and

- focusing and improving the quality of documentation content (Rosenberg, 2009).

These possible benefits would seem to make concurrent documentation an interesting alternative for rural social workers. As previously noted, rural social workers often have particularly limited resources. If this type of documentation could help free up time for other client-related tasks, then it seems worth investigating. Wilkerson (as cited in Grantham, 2010) states that the key to concurrent documentation is the ability to document information with the client. Wilkerson contends that most clinicians complete notes at the end of a session, summarizing what was discussed and learned and what the client will be working on. In approaching clinicians to consider using concurrent documentation, Wilkerson suggests saying to the worker, "You're going to do [the notes] as you learned, but now, you're going to enter them in the computer at the same time that you give them to the patient" (as cited in Grantham, 2010, p. 39).

Of course, there are some who contend that concurrent documentation is not such a helpful tool. As one clinician shared, "How am I supposed to be building a relationship with a client when I am working on the computer?" It has also been noted that this type of technological advance may end up increasing workers' already heavy workloads. One clinician shared how she now spends much more time completing paperwork that, in the past, would have been handled by support staff. In this clinician's view concurrent documentation symbolized the growing demand that workers engage in work that is "clerical" in nature.

In addition, the cost of concurrent documentation may prove prohibitive for rural social service agencies. For example, if a large number of workers are making home visits as a regular part of their work, they will need laptop computers to conduct concurrent documentation. Many rural social service agencies may lack the financial resources to provide laptops. Additional research may be needed to fully understand the ramifications of concurrent documentation on the workload of the rural social worker and the effect it could have on client outcomes.

Webinars

A webinar is "a live online educational presentation during which participating viewers can submit questions and comments," combining the terms "Web + seminar" (merriam-webster.com). Webinars use the Internet as a real-time presentation format along with audio channels (via Web or telephone) that allow participants to listen and possibly interact with the session. Webinars allow people to participate in information or training sessions from anywhere with available Internet and audio access. A simple Web search on the term *webinar* provides a sampling of the wide range of topics available for consumers interested in using the Internet as a source of educational opportunities. Topics for social work included such areas as empowerment, grant writing, workforce development, mental health practice, training nonprofit board members, nonprofit management, and even how to conduct a webinar.

This vast array of educational opportunities could prove very useful to the rural social worker in need of additional training in areas of practice that may not be readily available in a rural location. Webinars could also assist licensed rural social workers to obtain required continuing education credits in topics of interest to them. One caveat: little research has been conducted on the effectiveness of webinars in providing quality educational opportunities. Rural social workers might choose to experiment with the format to see if it meets their needs.

Future Challenges

Before concluding this review of technology in rural social work practice, it seems imperative to discuss some of the challenges and concerns related to the use of technology in rural practice. It would be helpful to review some of the following areas.

Cost

First and foremost among the challenges for rural agencies is the issue of cost— the cost of the technology itself, the cost of training employees how to use the technology, and the cost to maintain the technology. These expenses are particularly challenging in an economic downturn, such as the one the world experienced starting in the late summer of 2008, when both urban and rural social services agencies found themselves in an unusual bind. At a time when government budgets were severely cut and staff members were laid off, many organizations found that they were providing services to more people than ever before. One response to such an economic reality is to continue doing everything the same way. Blatt and Duggan (2009) assert that an organization may be able to slide by for a short period with increased caseloads combined with fewer staff and smaller budgets, but in a protracted economic decline this approach may not work. They suggest that, in an economic atmosphere in which many organizations hope to simply carry on, forward-looking administrators find ways to flourish. Blatt and Duggan see technology as a tool for finding new ways to get the most value from current programs, as well as finding new ways to meet the needs of staff and clients.

Digital Divide

There has been much talk about the digital divide between rural and urban America (see also Chapter 4 in the current volume). The Pew Internet & American Life Project's 2003 national sample survey of Internet use in rural areas provides some of the most up-to-date and inclusive findings available regarding Internet use in rural America. Findings from this survey show that, although Internet use is becoming an increasingly popular activity in rural America, it is still less prevalent than in urban and suburban America (Bell, Reddy, & Rainie, 2004). For example, urban and suburban residents have nearly a 15% lead over rural residents in Internet use. Broadband Internet users make up a larger percentage of urban and suburban users than rural users. This study also found that rural residents are more likely than urban and suburban residents to depend on having an Internet connection outside of the home. The report in which these results are published points to both lack of Internet infrastructure and demographic factors—especially age and income—to explain these disparities in Internet use.

Why are there fewer Internet users in rural areas than in urban areas? Researchers addressing this question focus on the lack of Internet infrastructure and demographic factors in rural areas. Rural areas often lack affordable Internet connectivity and contain relatively high numbers of people who are unlikely to adopt Internet connections at home—specifically older adults and those without a postsecondary education (Boase, 2010).

Worker Autonomy

In a recent study of workers and the introduction of hand-held computers in a working team in home-help services (Hjalmarsson, 2009), workers expressed the view that the new technology was a form of subordination. From the workers' perspective, the new technology was not a tool for supporting their efforts, but rather was an instrument of registration and control by management. The workers felt they were being controlled and that the power differential between employer and employee created the opportunity for and the acceptance of this control. In essence, the new technology reduced worker autonomy and, at times, increased the level of micromanagement by supervisors because of the activity tracking abilities of the new technology. More studies are needed to see how widespread this belief may be among workers.

Ethical Challenges

A recent article by Reamer (2011) notes that social workers need to keep an eye on the ethical issues that arise when using interactive technology tools. Reamer was primarily concerned about the emerging use of "cybertherapy," in which clients use a computer-designed avatar to represent themselves in a virtual world. The avatar is a visual image the client creates as a character or a persona that he or she presents to others on an Internet-based therapy site. Avatar-based cybertherapy enables clients to use chat room technology with relative anonymity to engage in a virtual approximation of traditional face-to-face therapy. Reamer's concern is that, in cybertherapy, there is the potential loss of the human factor that he believes is vital to clinical encounters. In his view clinicians and clients who interact electronically lose the opportunity to connect in person and experience visual and vocal cues, which may lead to clinically relevant misunderstandings.

Reamer also indicates concern regarding the issue of privacy and confidentiality in such virtual clinical encounters. The concern is that a social worker who works with a client sitting at a computer hundreds of miles away may not be able to control who has access to the client's computer screen. As Reamer notes, there is always the possibility that the privacy of electronic communications can be breached by hackers or others who illegally access a client's or social worker's computer account. Reamer's concerns are worth noting, and rural social workers should take every precaution to address these ethical issues.

Conclusion

Despite the challenges, the future for the use of technology in rural social work practice is bright, or at least inevitable. The potential for incorporating such technologies as decision support systems, sensors and home health monitoring, assistive technologies, and assessment systems into rural practice seems to hold promise for improved practice and better outcomes for rural clients. Such issues as alienation and solitude for clients could be lessened through use of social networking activities and other interactive technological tools. Rural practitioners might be better educated and better connected through webinars and professional social networking blogs, virtual worlds, and other related interactive sites. Hopefully, these connections will assist the rural social worker to provide better services to clients.

References

Abram, S. (2005). Web 2.0—huh? Library 2.0, librarian 2.0. *Information Outlook, 9*, 44–5.

Barsky, E. (2006). Introducing Web 2.0: Weblogs and podcasting for health librarians. *Journal of Canadian Health Library Association, 27*, 33–34.

Beldarrain, Y. (2006). Distance education trends: Integrating new technologies to foster student interaction and collaboration. *Distance Education, 27*, 139–153.

Bell, P., Reddy, P., & Rainie, L. (2004). *Rural areas and the Internet*. Washington, DC: Pew Internet & American Life Project.

Blatt, R., & Duggan, M. (2009). Six technologies that are changing social services and social security worldwide. Armonk, NY: IBM Corp.

Boase, J. (2010). The consequences of personal networks for Internet use in rural areas. American Behavioral Scientist, 53, 1257–1267.

Boulos, M., Hetherington L., & Wheeler, S. (2007). Second life: An overview of the potential of 3-D virtual worlds in medical and health education. Health Information Library Journal, 24, 233–245.

Campbell, R.J. & Nolfi, D.A. (2005). Teaching elderly adults to use the Internet to access health care information: Before- after study. Journal of Medical Internet Resources, 7(2), e19.

Carrilio, T. (2005). Using client information systems in practice settings: Factors affecting social workers' use of information systems. Computers in Human Services, 25(4), 41–62.

Cawthorne, A. (2008). Elderly poverty: The challenge before us. Center for American Progress. Retrieved from http://www.americanprogress.org/issues/2008/07 /pdf/elderly_poverty.pdf

Chen, E. S., Mendonça, E. A., McKnight, L. K., Stetson, P. D., Lei, J., & Cimino, J. J. (2004). PalmCIS: A wireless handheld application for satisfying clinician information needs. Journal of the American Medical Informatics Association, 11(1), 19–28.

Cowan, D., & Turner-Smith, A. (1999). The role of assistive technology in alternative models of care for older people. In Royal Commission on Long Term Care, With respect to old age (pp. 2325–2346). London, UK: Her Majesty's Stationery Office.

Damodaran, L., & Olphert, W. (2000). Barriers and facilitators to the use of knowledge management systems. Behaviour & Information Technology, 19, 405–413.

Dishman, E. (2004). Inventing wellness systems for aging in place. Computer, 37, 34–41.

Fox, S. (2004). Older Americans and the Internet. Washington, DC: Pew Internet & American Life Project.

Fox, S., & Fallows, D. (2003). Health Internet resources. Washington, DC: Pew Internet & American Life Project.

Grantham, D. (2010). Concurrent documentation wins trifecta. Behavioral Healthcare, 30(8), 32–37.

Hjalmarsson, M. (2009). New technology in home help services: A tool for support or an instrument of subordination? Gender, Work and Organization, 16, 368–384.

Hughes C. E., & Moshell J. M. (1997). Shared virtual worlds for education: The ExploreNet experiment. ACM Multimedia, 5, 145–154.

Lee, M., & Dey, A. (2004). Embedded assessment of aging adults: A concept validation with stakeholders. Pittsburgh, PA: Human-Computer Interaction Institute, Carnegie Mellon University.

Macarov, D. (1991). *Certain change: Social work practice in the future.* Silver Spring, MD: NASW Press.

McAlearney, A. S., Schweikhart, S. B., & Medow, M. A. (2004). Doctors' experience with handheld computers in clinical practice: Qualitative study. *British Journal of Medicine, 328,* 1162–1166.

McCarthy, C. E., & Pollack, M. E. 2002. A plan-based personalized cognitive orthotic. *Proceedings of the 6th International Conference on AI Planning and Scheduling,* 213–222.

Monnickendam, M., Savaya, R., & Waysman, M. (2005).Thinking processes in social workers' use of a clinical decision support system: A qualitative study. *Social Work Research, 29,* 21–23.

Morris, A., Donamukkala, R., Kapuria, A., Steinfeld, A., Matthews, J., Dunbar-Jacobs, J., & Thrun, S. (2003, Sept.). *A robotic walker that provides guidance.* Paper presented at the IEEE International Conference on Robotics and Automation, Taipei, Tawain.

Mukoyama, T. (2004). Diffusion and innovation of new technologies under skill heterogeneity. *Journal of Economic Growth, 9,* 451–479.

National Alliance for Caregiving. (2009). *Caregiving in the U.S.* Retrieved from http://www.caregiving.org/data/Caregiving_in_the_US_2009_full_report.pdf

Nilles, J. (1994). *Making telecommuting happen.* New York, NY: Van Nostrand Reinhold.

Pew Internet & American Life Project (2008). *Home broadband adoption: 2008.* Retrieved from http://www.pewinternet.org/~/media//Files/Reports/2008/PIP_Broadband_2008.pdf

Reamer, F. (2011). *Eye on ethics: The expanding use of computer-based services in clinical social work.* Retrieved from http://www.socialworktoday.com/news/eoe_111210.shtml

Robinson, K. (2005).*Web 2.0? Why should we care?* Retrieved from http://www.publish.com/article2/0,1759,1860653, 00.asp

Rosenberg, L. (2009). *Concurrent documentation for treating patients with mental illness.* Retrieved from http://www.articlesbase.com/mental-health-articles/concurrent-documentation-for-treating-patients-with-mental-illness-1424942.html

Sharp, D. (2006). *Smart Internet 2010—Social networks.* Melbourne, Australia: Swinburne University of Technology/Smart Internet Technology CRC Pty Ltd. Retrieved from http://smartinternet.com.au/ArticleDocuments/121/Social-Networks-2010.pdf.aspx

Turner-McGrievy, G. (2010). Pounds off digitally (POD): An examination of the use of podcasting to promote weight loss. *Dissertation Abstracts International: Section B: The Sciences and Engineering, 70*(7-B), 4097.

United Nations Convention on the Rights of Persons with Disabilities. (2008). *Electronic citation.* Retrieved from http://www.un.org/disabilities/default.asp?navid=14&pid=150

Vernon, R. (2005). Technology convergence and social work: When case management meets geographic information. *Advances in Social Work, 6*(1), 91–96.

Wallace, P. (1999). *The psychology of the Internet.* Cambridge, UK: Cambridge University Press.

Walz, L. (2009). The relationship between college students' use of social networking sites and their sense of belonging. *Dissertation Abstracts International: Section B: The Sciences and Engineering, 70*(5-B), 3192.

Weaver, R. (2002). Resistance to computer innovation: Knowledge coupling in clinical practice. *Computers and Society, 6,* 16–21.

Webopedia. (2011). Retrieved from http://www.webopedia.com/TERM/W/Web_2 _point_0.html

WorldatWork. 2009. *Telework trendlines 2009.* Retreived from http://www.worldatwork.org /waw/adimLink?id=31115

Zhang, W., & Gutierrez, O. (2007). Information technology acceptance in the social services sector context: An exploration. *Social Work, 52,* 221–231.

Zielke, M., Roome, T., & Krueger, A. (2009). A composite adult learning model for virtual world residents with disabilities: A case study of the virtual ability Second Life Island. *Journal of Virtual Worlds Research, 2,* 3–21.

6   Dual Relationships in Rural Areas

Lois A. Bosch and Laura S. Boisen

A school social worker meets a client on the street in the small town where she works and lives. She is unsure whether she should approach or avoid the client. A social worker needs his car fixed in a small town where there is only one mechanic. The mechanic happens to be his client. A social worker discovers that her new client is a neighbor. A social worker belongs to a book group that includes a former client. In all of these situations, social workers face decisions about how to handle dual relationships. This chapter presents a literature review on dual relationships in rural areas, particularly as it applies to working cross-culturally. The chapter also presents practice principles drawn from the evidence.

The NASW Code of Ethics refers to dual relationships as occurring when "social workers relate to clients in more than one relationship, whether professional, social, or business" [NASW, 2008; Standard 1.06 (c)]. This relationship can occur before, during, or after the professional relationship and may be defined by state licensing statute. Standard 1.06 of the NASW Code of Ethics goes on to state that "social workers should not engage in dual or multiple relationships with clients or former clients in which there is a risk of exploitation or potential harm to the client" (NASW, 2008). The concept of dual relationships in social work is an outgrowth of the "developing industrial or institutional model" for urban social work practice (Watkins, 2004, p. 67). Increasing urbanization reduced the personal interaction between the social worker and client, created a focus on depersonalized service delivery, and focused on a desire for equity and efficiency of service. In this vision of the emergent professionalism of social work, the prescribed role of the social worker requires a heightened awareness of confidentiality and boundaries between clients and workers. Professionals are discouraged from having dual roles that equalize or confuse the power dynamic between client and social worker.

Various writers have reviewed the perceived dangers of dual relationships, with some advocating that they must be avoided (Kagle & Gibelhausen, 1994) to protect the client from the risk of exploitation by the worker. Indeed, the Code of Ethics also stipulates that the social worker is "responsible for setting clear, appropriate, and culturally sensitive boundaries" (NASW, 2008; Standard 1.06 [c]). Barker (2003) identifies dual relationships as "the unethical practice of assuming a second role with the client," suggesting that these relationships "have long-term negative consequences" for clients (p. 131). Because of the fiduciary nature of the social work relationship, there is an inherent power imbalance that must be judiciously guarded to prevent exploitation of clients (Dietz & Thompson, 2004). Dual relationships that potentially exploit clients include sexual, social, or business relationships.

Other writers describe the harmful potential for dual relationships to put the worker at risk when too much information is given about the social worker to his or her clients (Pugh, 2007). Such a harmful dual relationship might arise if the social worker shares personal stories or his or her home phone number and address with the client or if the worker and client share the same doctor, school, or neighborhood. A harmful dual relationship might transpire if social worker and client become friends. In these instances, sharing personal information might confuse the client about the nature of the relationship with his or her social worker.

Reamer (2006) suggests that there is a continuum of dual relationships that ranges from not necessarily harmful (incidental meeting in public places) to "clearly problematic" (p. 49) interactions that include intimate or otherwise potentially harmful relationships with the client. Galbreath (2005) has categorized dual relationships as "boundary violations" (when something unethical has occurred) or "boundary crossings" (when the roles of worker–client are blurred by another relationship; p. 107). Viewing dual relationships using a continuum differentiates the myriad of ways that clients and social workers may interact. A boundary crossing may be unavoidable and not necessarily harmful. An example of a boundary crossing could be a chance meeting of a client in the grocery store or at a sporting event. No long-term personal relationship develops from this incidental contact and, therefore, little harm can come to the client or worker. A boundary violation, conversely, is more serious and potentially troublesome. It includes a range of client–worker relationship possibilities from establishing a social friendship with a client to the most egregious violation, establishing a sexual relationship with a client. These more serious violations of boundaries are the basis for many of the ethics complaints reported by state licensing boards. Strom-Gottfried (1999) reports that 29% of ethics complaints included boundary violations; the most frequently cited involved sexual violations.

Both Reamer's (2003) and Galbreath's (2005) categorizations of dual relationships suggest there are variations, such as the purpose, intent, and outcome of those relationships. The reasons for the dual relationship include benefit to the client or worker, such as friendship or business opportunities. Indeed, social workers make decisions regarding whether to engage in dual relationships based on the degree of present and future risk to the client and the worker (Boisen & Bosch, 2005). These social workers were aware that any community member is a potential client.

The concerns about dual relationships include risk management by the agency and worker—that is, to be sure that there is no impropriety that might expose the agency to risk. Furthermore, a prohibition against dual relationships guards against potential exploitation of the client for financial or personal gain, as in the case of the social worker who borrows money from a client or hires the client for work. Finally, a prohibition against dual relationships prevents confusion about the power and roles of the client and social worker—who and what the relationship signifies (Ringstad, 2008). Although many social workers find an absolute prohibition of all dual relationships unrealistic, it is the potential for these concerns that has contributed to the consensus that dual relationships should be avoided, if possible (Barker, 2003; Kagle & Giebelhausen, 1994), and considered carefully in any event (Reamer, 2006).

Absolute prohibitions against dual relationships present unique challenges to social workers in rural areas (Boisen & Bosch, 2005; Miller, 1998; Pugh, 2003, 2007; Ringstad, 2008). The National Rural Social Work Caucus has urged a more balanced understanding of dual relationships, favoring a more nuanced approach, because dual relationships are unavoidable and essential in rural practice (Boland-Prom & Anderson, 2005). Moreover, there might be a lack of opportunity to collaborate or consult with other social workers or a shortage of supervisors to guide the worker. In these instances, although the likelihood of dual relationships may increase, the opportunities for feedback about those relationships may decrease.

From the literature, three areas surface that are of particular challenge to rural social workers: (1) expectation of authentic membership, (2) geographic isolation,
and (3) scrutiny of the public persona of the social worker. For example, a challenge
to avoiding dual relationships in rural areas is the perception of a decreased power
differential within the "influence of the community context" (Mellow, 2005, p. 54)
prevalent in rural areas. There is the expectation that all community members will
participate authentically. Rural communities may hold a perception that professionals who do not interact in a friendly or casual way with other community members are arrogant or insincere. Moreover, professionals who live in the community
may be expected to join boards, serve as Scout leaders, or otherwise participate in
dual roles. A social worker who does not participate in community life may be perceived as haughty, which can be a challenge to the authentic role of the professional.
Pugh (2007) refers to this as compromising the perceived trust of the professional.

Another challenge to avoiding dual relationships is geographic isolation, which
can keep the number of human service professionals low and limit available resources (Mellow, 2005, p. 54). Although it may be advisable to refer close friends,
relatives, or neighbors to another helping professional, in remote rural environments there may not be another school social worker or mental health worker
within a reasonable distance. The social worker must weigh the implications of
serving the client in a dual relationship against not serving the client at all.
Similarly, another social worker might have difficulty finding a car mechanic, if
the only shop in town is managed by a client. In each of these situations the rural
social worker must decide how to serve clients appropriately when there are no
other options for service.

Finally, social workers in rural areas may deal with scrutiny of their total persona, rather than their professional face alone (Pugh, 2007). This could prove bur-
densome to social workers with problems or family lifestyles that deviate from the
accepted norm. For example, a social worker in a rural environment might find that
she or he shares the same mental health professional with a client. Another social
worker might have grown up in the same community where she or he is currently
employed. In these instances and others community members may judge the quality of professional practice based on how professionals conduct their personal lives.
School social workers in our study referred to the need to be consistently congru-
ent in their professional and personal practice, since "anyone you visit with in the
community could be a client the next day" (Boisen & Bosch, 2005, p. 199). This
necessitates less anonymity and higher social visibility (Pugh, 2007) and holds the

social worker up to a more rigorous standard of behavior. Another social worker may find it difficult to socialize, knowing that actions are measured against professional demeanor. Rural social workers describe this as a fishbowl effect and find that as a social worker you may need to "go outside of the community to let your hair down" (Boisen & Bosch, 2005, p. 199).

Cross-Cultural Relationships in Rural Social Work

Although much has been written about same-race dual relationships in rural areas, little has been written about cross-cultural dual relationships in social work—either in metropolitan or rural communities. This is despite an influx of individuals and families with diverse backgrounds into small-town communities and rural areas. During the past 2 decades, many U.S.-bound immigrants and refugees from African nations, Mexico, Latin American countries, Southeast Asia, Russia, and Eastern European countries have begun their lives in the United States in larger cities only to relocate to more rural communities (Teixeira & Li, 2009) for a better standard of living and job opportunities (Shandy & Fennelly, 2006).

Without the migration of these groups to rural communities, many of these areas would experience a declining population (Parra & Pfeffer, 2006). However, these new residents have received a mixed welcome. Although the immigrants' and refugees' discretionary spending and tax dollars can be an economic asset to a rural community, long-time rural residents can hold anti-immigrant sentiments (Helbok, Marinelli, & Walls, 2006; Shandy & Fennelly, 2006), because some view immigrants' presence as an economic burden to the community (Schmitz, Jacobus, Stakeman, Valenzuela, & Sprankel, 2003). Hokenstad and Midgley (1997) found that refugees can and do help themselves and support each other economically. However, the effects of immigrants and their successful adjustment extend beyond economics into the cultural aspects of community life. This includes relationships with helping professionals.

Newcomers to rural areas might experience stress that requires professional attention, and so may long-time residents. Many researchers have delineated the inherent tension of immigrants, refugees of color, and gay and lesbian families moving to rural communities. Although persons living in rural communities tend to avoid conflict, they also might "have limited tolerance for diversity" (Helbok et al., 2006, p. 36) and deep religious ties (Cook, Copans, & Schetcky, 1998; Helbok et al., 2006; Stockman, 1990). For a century the dominant culture of many rural areas has been that of White, U.S.-born, middle-class, Christian individuals and families. Coupled with the loss of young people (Carr & Kefalas, 2009), this recent immigration pattern is literally changing the face of these small rural communities and can be unsettling for long-time residents (Parra & Pfeffer, 2006).

The influx of more diverse residents and neighbors can be an opportunity for rural social workers to incorporate their cross-cultural expertise. It also presents some specific dilemmas related to dual relationships and cultural expectations of the helping relationship. For example, resident members of an extended family will often meet newly arriving refugees or immigrants at the airport as they take their first steps in the United States. It is not uncommon for social workers engaged with the resident family to be invited to ride to the airport with the family, join in the welcome, and celebrate the immigrant's appearance with a postarrival party at a private residence—activities that last several hours in nonprofessional settings. Does participation in these activities violate boundaries or blur the lines of professionalism? Is participation in some or all of these activities necessary to engage and successfully intervene with non-Western cultures? In essence, are there different appropriate boundaries when working cross-culturally?

Peterson (1992) defined boundaries as "the limits that allow for a safe connection based on the client's needs" (p.74). Are these limits that allow for connection different cross-culturally? Cheers (1992) says that multiple roles can create a humanizing effect on the helping relationship, thereby improving the overall outcome for clients. Nandan (2005) recommends nontraditional approaches with Asian Indian immigrants. Scopelliti and colleagues (2004) advocate for boundary crossings because they increase understanding, familiarity, and connectivity, which enhances the likelihood for success.

Hall (1976), an anthropologist, discussed how culture impacts ways of thinking and the meaning associated with behaviors. He delineated the "linear, step-by-step, compartmentalized way of thinking" (Hall, 1976, p. 12) that he said dominates the United States. Hall (1976) contrasted low- and high-context communication systems, offering ample examples of how individuals socialized in the United States communicate via explicit messages, whereas information in high-context societies is internalized either in the wider context or in the person. Thus, in high-context cultures actions are "rooted in the past, slow to change, and highly stable" (Hall, 1976, p. 93). Hall concluded that because of the internalized messages, communication in high-context cultures is more economical, efficient, satisfying, and unifying. However, to understand the nuance of communication and participate in the unifying nature of a high-context culture, one must devote time to learning high-context patterns and meanings. Pedersen, Crethar, and Carlson (2008) elaborated on low- and high-context systems specific to the counseling process. They believe that recognition by the practitioner of the differences between low- and high-context individuals and groups can lead to greater empathy and success in the counseling relationship. Their work suggests that, because of the value of "inclusion, approval, and association" (Pedersen et al., 2008, p. 26), more fluid boundaries might be necessary. These high-context communication patterns may apply to the rural community as well as to the cross-cultural community.

Other authors also have written about cross-cultural adjustments in practice. In the early 1990s Parson (1993) spoke of the practitioner's willingness to judiciously self-disclose in cross-cultural relationships as a mechanism to more securely build a working alliance. Dyche and Zayas (2001) asserted that the power differential is so great in cross-cultural therapy that practitioners must work in an "untraditional open style" (p. 253). Finally, Owen and English (2005) shared their experience with cross-cultural supervision of paraprofessionals and the crucial role of more fluid boundaries (i.e., the importance of joint participation and sharing of social and cultural rituals and an open exchange of personal experiences.)

Thus, long-time rural community members may not be the only population to value authenticity and mistrust professional distance in the social work relationship. Indeed, Jacobson (2001), in her discussion of reorienting the helping relationship, decries the clinical focus (i.e., assessment based on expertise rather than need) of many social work students–even those interning at settlement houses. She suggests attitudinal adjustments that would result in cocreation of the process (Jacobson, 2001). We suggest that professional boundaries that have represented professional social work practice for decades may need to be different when it comes to cross-cultural practice.

However, how do fully embracing high-context communication patterns and cross-cultural mores intersect with other social work ethical guidance relative to boundaries and dual relationships? For instance, how does a social worker reconcile the NASW Code of Ethics guidance related to practitioner and client boundaries with cross-cultural patterns of interaction, if the two conflict in terms of boundaries? What boundaries make sense given the literature related to cross-cultural practice?

Practice Principles for Navigating Dual Relationships

This chapter highlights the role of dual relationships in rural social work practice. Dual relationships pose challenges for social work practice. Diverse population groups may have different expectations regarding boundaries between the social worker and the client. There is no simple solution for cross-cultural dual relationships, because these relationships are diverse in their purposes and meanings. It is important, however, to reinforce that undertaking any dual relationship must be done with intentionality and clear reflection. The following practice principles are suggested.

Normalize

Expect dual relationships. Dyche and Zayas (2001) hold that "judicious self-disclosure can be interpersonal glue that bonds the therapist and client in a working alliance." (p. 247). Glibly suggesting that social workers "just say no" is not effective advice or an effective way to practice. It also may be addressing the wrong question—rather than saying "Should social workers engage in dual relationships?" perhaps we should ask "When should social workers engage in dual relationships, and in what ways are they useful?" This acknowledges the inevitability of dual relationships while normalizing the concept (Boisen & Bosch, 2005) and responding to the demands of cross-cultural practice. It allows professional social workers and their clients space within which to work. In some respects "we wonder whether we as practitioners, in our attempts to protect ourselves and our profession, have enacted barriers that separate us from our clients to their potential detriment" (Dietz & Thompson, 2004, p. 6).

Professional Preparation

Address dual relationships and boundary issues in professional preparation. Many social workers complain that they are not prepared for practice in rural environments (Boisen & Bosch, 2005) and feel inadequate to practice cross-culturally. This is consistent with social workers' lack of preparation for rural practice in general (Kelly & Clark, 2009) and "is a concern that must be addressed" (p. 299). Social workers need tools and strategies for effective rural practice. It is impossible to understand the nuances of every culture. Some suggest that the key to cultural responsiveness or effective cross-cultural practice is the ability to elicit clients' narrative and foster the working alliance (Shibusawa & Chung, 2009). Others recommend even more self-disclosure and a more informal, personal clinical style (Lu, Organista, Manzo, Wong, & Phung, 2001). This might suggest that dual relationships are an important component of the helping alliance; we must train professionals to handle them responsibly and effectively.

Supervision

NASW suggests that

> social workers practicing in rural areas must have advanced understanding of
> ethical responsibilities, not only because dual or multiple relationships are un-
> avoidable, but also because the setting may require that dual or multiple rela-
> tionships be used and managed as an appropriate method of social work practice.
> (Kelly & Clark, 2009, p. 300)

With more fluid boundaries, supervision becomes imperative.

Proactive supervision can provide guidance for social workers attempting to
navigate dual relationships. First, the supervisor must explicitly focus on dual relationships as a matter of course. This is followed by a careful definition, description, and cross-cultural rationale for dual relationships. Every supervision session
could begin with the question, "What is your experience with dual relationships
in your practice?" This question could encourage social workers to identify and examine their interactions with clients on all levels. Second, the supervisor could
help the social worker examine the dual relationship for costs and benefits to the
client, the practitioner, and the agency. The benefits of the relationship should not
only outweigh the costs but also be culturally responsive. Finally, the supervisor
should provide a documentation plan that includes the clarification of costs/ben-
efits to key constituents, ethical and cultural considerations, and a plan for future
review.

Regarding dual relationships, the supervisor must make it clear that it is the social worker's responsibility to set appropriate parameters for any relationship with
a client. Reamer (2001) suggests criteria that detail steps for evaluation of dual relationships, including assessing the amount of power the social worker has over the
client, determining how long the relationship has lasted or will last, having clear
conditions for terminating the relationship, having a clear conception of the client's
clinical profile, and observing professional ethical standards.

In environments where there is little or no supervision the profession must develop creative ways to provide consultation or supervision. Consultation for rural
social workers can take advantage of new technology, including online video communication such as Skype, chat rooms, and other forms of communication.

Although access to supervision may be problematic, there are possible solutions even in the most remote of environments.

Transparency

Discuss the relationship with the client. In the social worker's discussion with the client, outline the possible perils of this relationship. Although some boundary crossings are unavoidable and pose minimal risk, others are more precarious. In discussing these potential dual relationships social workers must be alert to community considerations to avoid offending cultural norms. In certain cases the use of a bicultural paraprofessional (Owen & English, 2005) or a cultural guide would be useful.

An important caveat: The social worker must realize that an actions he or she takes may be broadcast to the wider community. If the community perceives that the social worker acts selfishly (e.g., uses professional opportunities to parlay a favorable business transaction) the social worker's dual relationship has harmed not only his or her relationship with the client, but with future clients as well. Therefore, the social worker in rural and cross-cultural communities must always consider what message he or she is transmitting. Does the message imply that the social worker is being fair and equitable in treatment of clients or that the dual relationship is unfairly balanced toward favoring the social worker?

Authenticity

Galbreath (2005) describes the need for consistency in relationships, that "professionals cannot afford to be accepting and nurturing in the office and unapproachable in the community" (p. 120). This aspiration for authenticity was also reported by rural school social workers (Boisen & Bosch, 2005) who perceived avoiding dual relationships would hinder the social worker's credibility in the community.

As discussed previously, social workers must consider other cultural norms and mores. Do members of other cultural communities, including those in rural areas, have greater expectations of dual relationships with their social workers? Will a prohibition against dual relationships (e.g., sharing a meal, accepting gifts, or attending social events) mark the social worker as arrogant or inaccessible? The literature is clear: Developing more fluid worker–client relationships and using nontraditional approaches, including dual relationships, enhances the helping alliance and provides a better result (Nandan, 2005; Scopelliti et al., 2004;

Shibusawa & Chung, 2009; Lu et al., 2001). Social workers must choose their roles carefully, and how to manage dual relationships is one such decision.

Support Further Research

The profession would benefit from further investigation into how the changing demographics of rural populations are changing the face of rural social work practice. It is not enough to ask whether rural social workers are affected by dual relationships; rather, we need to further investigate how social workers intervene with a broader array of clients that reflect the changing demographics in rural areas. Perhaps more important, future research should focus on how social workers in rural areas cope with dual relationships to preserve the workers' authenticity, cultural responsiveness, and professional sensibilities, while maintaining the safety of the client, worker, and agency.

References

Barker, R. (2003). *The social work dictionary* (5th ed.). Washington, DC: NASW Press.

Boisen, L., & Bosch, L. (2005). Dual relationships and rural social work: Is there a rural code? In L. Ginsberg (Ed.), *Social work in rural communities* (4th ed.; pp. 189–203). Alexandria, VA: Council on Social Work Education.

Boland-Prom, K., & Anderson, S. (2005). Teaching ethical decision making using dual relationship principles as a case example. *Journal of Social Work Education, 41*, 495–510.

Carr, P., & Kefalas, M. (2009). The rural brain drain. *Chronicle of Higher Education.* Retrieved from http://chronicle.com/article/The-Rural-Brain-Drain/48425

Cheers, B. (1992). Rural social work and social welfare in the Australian context. *Australian Social Work, 45*(2), 11–21.

Cook, A. D., Copans, S. A., & Schetky, D. H. (1998). Psychiatric treatment of children and adolescents in rural communities. *Child and Adolescent Psychiatric Clinics of North America, 7,* 673–690.

Dietz, C., & Thompson, J. (2004). Rethinking boundaries: Ethical dilemmas in the social worker-client relationship. *Journal of Progressive Human Services, 15*(2), 1–24.

Dyche, L., & Zayas, L. H. (2001). Cross-cultural empathy and training the contemporary psychotherapist. *Clinical Social Work Journal, 29,* 245–258.

Galbreath, W. (2005). Dual relationships in rural communities. In N. Lohmann & R. Lohmann (Eds.), *Rural social work practice.* New York, NY: Columbia University Press.

Graham, J. R., Bradshaw, C., & Trew, J. L. (2009). Addressing cultural barriers with Muslim clients: An agency perspective. *Administration in Social Work, 33,* 387–406.

Graham, S., & Liddle, B. (2009). Multiple relationships encountered by lesbian and bisexual psychotherapists: How close is too close? *Professional Psychology: Research and Practice, 40*(1), 15–21.

Hall, E. T. (1976). *Beyond culture.* Garden City, NY: Anchor Press/Doubleday.

Helbok, C. M., Marinelli, R. P., & Walls, R. T. (2006). National survey of ethical practices across rural and urban communities. *Professional Psychology: Research and Practice, 37*(1), 36–44.

Hokenstad, M. C., & Midgley, J. (1997). *Issues in international social work: Global challenges for a new century.* Washington, DC: NASW Press.

Jacobson, W. (2001). Beyond therapy: Bringing social work back to human services reform. *Social Work, 46,* 51–61.

Kagle, J., & Giebelhausen, P. (1994). Dual relationships and professional boundaries. *Social Work, 39,* 213–220.

Kelly, J., & Clark, E. (2009). Rural social work. In *Social work speaks: NASW policy statements* (8th ed.; pp. 297–302). Washington, DC: NASW Press.

Lu, Y. E., Organista, K. C., Manzo, S., Wong, L., & Phung, J. (2001). Exploring dimensions of culturally sensitive clinical styles with Latinos. *Journal of Ethnic & Culturally Diversity in Social Work, 10*(2), 45–66.

Mellow, M. (2005). The work of rural professionals: Doing the Gemeinschaft-Gesellschaft gavotte. *Rural Sociology, 70*(1), 50–69.

Miller, P. (1998). Dual relationships and rural practice: A dilemma of ethics and culture. In L. H. Ginsberg (Ed.), *Social work in rural communities* (3rd ed.; pp. 55–62). Alexandria, VA: Council on Social Work Education.

Nandan, M. (2005). Adaptation to American culture: Voices of Asian Indian immigrants. *Journal of Gerontological Social Work, 44*(3/4), 175–203.

National Association of Social Workers (NASW). (2008). *Code of ethics.* Washington, DC: NASW Press.

Owen, C. L., & English, M. (2005). Working together as culture brokers by building trusting alliances with bilingal and bicultural newcomer paraprofessionals. *Child Welfare, 84,* 669–688.

Parra, P. A., & Pfeffer, M. J. (2006). New immigrants in rural communities: The challenges of integration. *Social Text, 24*(3), 81–98.

Parson, E. R. (1993). Ethnotherapeutic empathy—Part II: Techniques in interpersonal cognition and vicarious experiencing across cultures. *Journal of Contemporary Psychotherapy, 23,* 171–182.

Pedersen, P. B., Crethar, H. C., & Carlson, J. (2008). *Inclusive cultural empathy: Making relationships central in counseling and psychotherapy.* Washington, DC: American Psychological Association.

Peterson, M. R. (1992). *At personal risk: Boundary violations in professional-client relationships.* New York, NY: W.W. Norton.

Pugh, R. (2003). Considering the countryside: Is there a case for rural social work? *British Journal of Social Work, 33,* 67–85.

Pugh, R. (2007). Dual relationships: Personal and professional boundaries in rural social work. *British Journal of Social Work, 37,* 1405–1423.

Reamer, F. (2001). *Tangled relationships: Managing boundary issues in the human services.* New York, NY: Columbia University Press.

Reamer, F. (2003). Boundary issues in social work: Managing dual relationships. *Social Work, 48,* 121–133.

Reamer, F. (2006). *Ethical standards in social work: A review of the NASW Code of Ethics* (2nd ed.). Washington, DC: NASW Press.

Ringstad, R. (2008).The ethics of dual relationships: Beliefs and behaviors of clinical practitioners. *Families in Society: The Journal of Contemporary Social Services, 89,* 69–77.

Schmitz, C. L., Jacobus, M. V., Stakeman, C., Valenzuela, G. A., & Sprankel, J. (2003). Immigrant and refugee communities: Resiliency, trauma, policy, and practice. *Social Thought, 22*(2/3), 135–158.

Scopelliti, J., Judd, F., Grigg, M., Hodgins, G., Fraser, C., Hulbert, C., ... Wood, A. (2004). Dual relationships in mental health practice: Issues for clinicians in rural settings. *Australian and New Zealand Journal of Psychiatry, 38,* 953–959.

Shandy, D. J., & Fennelly, K. (2006). A comparison of the integration experiences of two African immigrant populations in a rural community. *Journal of Religion & Spirituality in Social Work, 25*(1), 23–45.

Shibusawa, T., & Chung, I. W. (2009). Wrapping and unwrapping emotions: Clinical practice with East Asian immigrant elders. *Journal of Clinical Social Work, 37,* 312–319.

Stockman, A. F. (1990). Dual relationships in rural mental health practice: An ethical dilemma. *Journal of Rural Community Psychology, 11,* 31–45.

Strom-Gottfried, K. (1999). Professional boundaries: An analysis of violations by social workers. *Families in Society, 80,* 439–448.

Teixeira, C., & Li, W. (2009). Immigrant and refugee experiences in North American cities. *Journal of Immigrant and Refugee Studies, 7,* 221–227.

Watkins, T. (2004). Natural helping networks: Assets for rural communities. In T. Scales & C. Streeter (Eds.). *Rural social work: Building and sustaining community assets* (pp. 65–76). Belmont, CA: Brooks/Cole/Thomsen Learning.

7 Educating for Rural Competence: *Curriculum Concepts, Models, and Course Content*

Michael R. Daley and Barbara Pierce

Rural social work is a unique field of practice that requires context-based educational preparation in cultural competence, rural cultures, diversity, ethics, and practice skills (National Association of Social Workers [NASW], 2009). Yet there remain critical shortages of professional social workers in rural areas (NASW, 2009) to meet the needs of the 21% of the population who live in these communities (Ginsberg, 2005). Daley and Avant (1999) and NASW (2009) argue that social work education has a responsibility to address the preparation of social workers for rural practice both in terms of more programs offering rural content and enhanced rural content in the curriculum. If social work is to address the needs of this significant, and often invisible, minority of Americans, it is important for social work education to tackle this challenge.

Although the literature exhorts social work education to take action, individual programs are given little guidance other than a general list of important topics regarding the best ways in which to incorporate rural content in the curriculum. As a result, social work educational programs often struggle with the best way to define the rural community and how to most effectively deliver content such as generalist practice, social work ethics, and rural culture to best prepare graduates for rural practice. This is a significant issue for education programs in social work, because 44% of the BSW programs and 17.4% of the MSW programs are located in rural settings (Council on Social Work Education, 2007). Many social work graduates enter the workforce with little preparation for rural practice, even though they may eventually practice in rural communities.

This chapter addresses these concerns by discussing the important elements in developing rural social work content in the curriculum. The crucial issues to consider in this development are (a) defining rural in terms of the multiple, and sometimes conflicting or confusing, definitions in the literature; (b) curriculum delivery models for rural content; (c) rural social work as cultural diversity; (d) generalist practice in a rural context; (e) social work ethics in a rural context; and (f) rural concepts for the curriculum. Using this information as building blocks may help assist social work programs interested in rural issues in developing a stronger curriculum.

Defining What is Rural

Rural social work education typically occurs in schools located in rural areas. However, even schools of social work in urban areas may serve rural communities in some states. The basic questions that social work educators must ask then are: Do residents of the service area think of themselves as rural and possess rural attributes and behaviors? Do the communities have rural characteristics? If the answer is yes, then the program should consider incorporating rurality into its mission statement and rural content into the program in a meaningful way.

One of the first challenges that faces social work programs and educators is getting a satisfactory answer to the question: Are we rural? In trying to answer this question, a person is immediately plunged into the multiple and complex definitions of how rurality is determined in the United States, which can be a major conceptual hurdle.

An absolute approach, or using an arbitrary number of residents, is the most common method for identifying a community as rural. Yet there are at least three absolute population figures in use for determining the rurality of a community. This tends to be confusing for programs trying to determine whether their service area is rural. For example, the common way of determining whether a geographic area is rural is based on population figures as determined by the U.S. Census Bureau. One definition is that urban areas are those with populations under 2,500 and nonadjacent to urban areas. A second definition is that used by the Office of Management and Budget, which identifies communities with less than 50,000 as nonmetropolitan. A third definition used in the 2000 Census characterizes rural areas, urban areas, and urban clusters (Olaveson, Conway, & Shaver, 2004).

The Census and the Office of Management and Budget have their own reasons for using an absolute definition for rural, but these definitions are only marginally useful for a social work program trying to define its service area and function. The reality is that social workers often find the social, structural, and cultural characteristics of rurality of more importance than its geographic components. For example, the distinction between a community of 48,500, classified as nonmetropolitan, and a metropolitan community of 53,000 may not be particularly meaningful for determining rurality for the purposes of educational program identity. If the residents of both communities view themselves as rural, drawing arbitrary distinctions is indeed arbitrary.

The concept of "rurality," or being rural, has been in use by sociologists since at least the mid-1960s and refers to communities having rural characteristics (Bealer, Willitis, & Kuvlesky, 1965). This conceptualization defines communities using structural terms such as occupations, ecology, and sociocultural elements. This structural and functional definition of rurality (Bealer et al., 1965) is more compatible with defining rural in terms of the systems and issues that confront social workers in both education and practice.

The literature in the field of rural social work has numerous examples of rural characteristics found in communities that appear common and somewhat independent of population size. These distinctive features include residents' attachment to the land or place, emphasis on a personal style of social interaction, conservatism, importance of faith, use of natural helping networks, and a close knit community where peoples' lives are enmeshed, often referred to as a "fishbowl" (Daley & Avant, 2004a; Ginsberg, 2005). All of these have an important effect on human behavior and the delivery of social work services.

Identifying rural social work based on community characteristics and the cultural and behavioral norms of the people is recommended by both Daley and Avant (2004a, 2004b) and Ginsberg (2005) and is a more practical approach than population size, at least for social work purposes. According to Daley and Avant (2004a), "Rural social work should be viewed as work with rural people as well as practice in and with rural communities." Essentially, rural social work occurs where a person finds a rural community, be it in a small town or a pocket of rural people in an urban environment. All of this argues that, where the social work program is concerned, population figures should be secondary to consideration in determining the rurality of a service area.

It is more productive for the social work program and educator to base the definition of rurality on community characteristics, because the environment served is more complex than a simple either/or definition of rurality based on population size. Social work education programs typically serve multiple communities in a region, and those communities represent a mix of characteristics and community types. Rural pockets are found in areas officially defined as urban, and over time urban areas encroach on rural communities, yet the residents remain fundamentally rural.

Curriculum Models for Rural Social Work

When social work programs have successfully addressed their own definition of rurality in relation to their missions and service areas, a conceptual challenge arises: how to structure this content most effectively within the existing curriculum. There is no "one size fits all" model, because each program has its own unique curriculum, faculty, and context with which to contend.

Social work programs have created different approaches to educate students about rural issues. Little appears to have been published about the models used to deliver rural content in the curriculum, but an examination of social work curricula shows at least four basic approaches to the presentation of content emerge. Clearly, each program should choose an approach that best suits its needs. The educational models for delivering rural content include (a) rurality as diversity, (b) rurality as stand-alone content, (c) infusion of rural content, and (d) a mix of types.

Some educators choose to educate for rural cultural competence in human behavior in the social environment (HBSE), approaching rural as one type of diversity in classes. Although the literature is clear that social workers need to be culturally competent regarding rural people and contexts (Allen, 2005; Daley & Avant, 2004a; Lohmann & Lohmann, 2005; NASW, 2009), social work education often views rural social work as simply another field of practice. The cultural competence approach gives students an overall perspective that rurality is an important component behavior of all social systems and is not community-bound. The drawback is that rural social work involves more than just cultural competence. The rich themes of rural poverty, rural strengths, and the nuances of values and ethics could be lost as rural people become one more diverse group about which students must learn. This method is certainly one way to ensure that at least some information is presented to students, yet seems oversimplified and inadequate for practice in rural communities.

Other social work programs have developed stand-alone courses either as required or elective content in rural social work. This is a good way to present in-depth information to students who are interested in rural social work, because an entire semester can be devoted to a variety of practice, policy, and diversity issues related to rural people and places. This method allows for the presentation of advanced generalist content related to rural practice (Daley & Avant, 2004a). It also allows for an in-depth, term length project related to rural social work.

A good stand-alone course in rural social work should include several key elements. These include definitions of rurality (Daley & Avant, 2004b; Ginsberg, 2005; Olavson et al., 2004), the context of rural practice (Ginsberg, 2005; Lohmann & Lohmann, 2005; Scales & Streeter, 2004), social work ethics in rural practice, rural social policy, and challenges of rural social work in various fields of practice. The course should also have one or more assignments that increase the sensitivity of students to the rural environment, whether physical or social, and its effects on problems, practice, and issues. The advantage of a stand-alone course is that students develop increased knowledge and skill through intensive study. The limitation is that students may see rurality as content divorced from the rest of the curriculum. If the course is presented as an elective, many students may receive little or no content in rurality at all, even though they may need the information for practice. Finally, having one more course to fit into an already crowded curriculum may limit the number of programs offering this course even as an elective.

Rural information can also be infused in many different courses or across the curriculum. If the program considers rural content extremely important, this is one mechanism to delivery it integrated with other required social work aspects of the curriculum. For example, the Council on Social Work Education (CSWE) has recognized that some content is important to all courses, so that diversity, research, and values and ethics cut across all courses in the curriculum (CSWE, 2008). Allen (2005) also discusses the importance of infusing the curriculum with rural content, specifically about rural women's behavioral health needs. From the gerontology education literature, infusion has been demonstrated to increase knowledge, skill, and practice on pretest to posttest scores, and all students in the study were exposed to the content, rather than just the few who would take an elective course (Lee & Waites, 2006).

Infused rural content can be presented where it would most naturally fit in the curriculum. For example, when the class grapples with boundary issues in general, they can examine specific boundary issues commonly experienced in rural practice settings. Or a policy class can examine the effect of poverty on rural versus urban settings. The strengths of this form of education are that all students are exposed to the content, it is consistent with generalist practice, and educators can tailor the content to each course. The limitations are that it is time-consuming to ensure so many topics are represented in each course, the material presented is certainly not as intensive as if it were presented in a stand-alone course, and it is possible that the importance of the rural context could get lost.

The final option is for a mixed model of content delivery. The mixed model combines any or all of the elements of the previous models. Thus, the program may choose to offer a stand-alone course and infuse rural content simultaneously. For example, students may take a freestanding required or elective course in rurality while rural content also is infused in other areas of the curriculum, such as social policy or practice methods through readings and assignments. At the same time, rurality may be presented as diversity in an HBSE course. In many ways this offers the advantages of the various models while minimizing the drawbacks. The drawback that remains is that this takes a great deal of planning in design and execution to prevent needless repetition.

Rural Social Work as Cultural Diversity

Recent literature on rural social work has highlighted the importance of understanding rural culture as distinct and representing a form of diversity that should be recognized (Daley & Avant, 2004a; Ginsberg, 2005; NASW, 2009). Indeed, rural culture often provides a useful perspective from which problems and solutions can be developed.

On one level rural social work "is, ideally, simply good social work that reflects and considers the environment" (Ginsberg, 2005, pp. 4). Daley and Avant (2004a) expand on this idea and indicate that rural social work is not entirely confined to rural communities. They suggest a more inclusive view that rural social work is work with rural populations, wherever they are found. This incorporates the idea that rural social skills and approaches are needed for working with rural people who may live in communities that are not geographically rural. This method is useful for understanding and working with rural pockets that develop within urban areas.

Although rural people often move to urban areas in search of better economic opportunities or to be near family, they may not abandon their rural culture and strategies for coping with life. They may not even have to move, as urban areas are rapidly encroaching on some rural communities and absorbing the inhabitants. So, although rural people are found in rural communities, which are abundant in many states in the United States (Lohmann & Lohmann, 2005), communities are rarely entirely homogeneous, and elements of rural communities often exist in urban areas and vice versa (Mellow, 2005).

Social workers, then, can find people and even communities who identify themselves as rural and exhibit rural culture, norms, and behaviors in many places. Although there have been changes in location or environment, rural people still approach life and seek help from a rural perspective. The important point for social work education is that students require the development of cultural competence in their educational preparation to recognize and respond appropriately to the needs of clients and communities. The development of this competence should be an important priority, especially in programs that have rural communities as an important part of their service areas.

Generalist Practice in a Rural Context

One of the early proponents of generalist practice for rural social work was the Southern Regional Education Board (1993). The Board's position was that, because formal resources were often unavailable in rural communities, the social worker often had to respond as a generalist. Ginsberg (2005) supports this idea from a slightly different perspective. He suggests that, although social work specialists are important in rural communities, social workers are often required to find resources and develop and operate programs, and these are skills best suited to the generalist. Daley and Avant (1999) point out that social work specialists are not as numerous in rural areas, and therefore social workers are more apt to fill multiple roles. All of these perspectives support the need for generalist preparation and competency for rural social workers.

A number of authors have suggested that rural social work should be primarily community-focused in its approach (Belanger, 2005; Jacobsen, 1980; Martinez-Brawley, 1993; White & Marks, 1999), and at one time this was the predominant view of rural social work. Unfortunately, although a community-based focus is an important consideration in rural social work, community-based practice often offers little specific guidance to social workers engaged in direct practice with individuals, families, and groups. Indeed, more of a generalist orientation in practice allows for both community- and direct practice-based methods that are appropriate for rural practice.

The NASW (2009) Rural Social Work policy statement supports the idea that generalist practice is the appropriate educational preparation for rural practice. However, to best prepare for rural social work, some enhancement of the generalist approach may be helpful. For example, Daley and Avant (2004a) present a generalist model of rural social work based on a systems-based strengths perspective that incorporates social exchange theory. *Gemeinschaft* and *gessellschaft* are important theoretical concepts that help explain the functional differences between rural and urban communities. These concepts help explain the more personal relationships and interactions of rural communities, compared to the formal relationships that often characterize urban environments. Social systems provide the framework for understanding problems and developing strategies for addressing them (Daley & Avant, 2004a). Social exchange theory provides a basis for understanding the dynamics, interactions, and behavior within and between systems. The strengths perspective adds an overall approach for using and building strengths in rural systems that are too often viewed as deficient or dysfunctional. The model is broad based, gives a framework for direct and indirect practice, and appears consistent with the generalist model of social work.

Traditionally, generalist social work is closely identified with undergraduate education, whereas graduate education is more closely identified with specialization. In the past this perception has limited preparation for rural practice at the graduate level. The growth in the number and diversity of advanced generalist programs in recent years is an encouraging development, especially for rural practice. NASW (2009) and Daley and Avant (1999) indicate that advanced generalist education at the graduate level is important for building the rural social work labor force, where social workers at all levels are needed.

A number of models for advanced generalist practice in social work have been developed. For example, Roy and Vecchiolla (2004) discuss six models of advanced generalist education, whereas Daley and Avant (2004b) present an advanced generalist model specific to rural practice. Advanced generalist preparation for rural practice can help fill the critical need for social workers with the skills to engage in advanced practice, supervision, and administration in rural areas.

Ethics in Rural Social Work

A common beginning for discussions about the unique nature of rural social work practice often centers on ethical dilemmas, specifically those of dual relationships and confidentiality. Clearly the foundation of social work is the Code of Ethics, and, indeed, this is reflected in social work education because the first competency included by CSWE educational policy and accreditation standards is to "apply social work ethical principles to guide professional practice" (CSWE, 2008).

Much has been written about applying social work ethical principles in rural settings, specifically as it relates to maintaining confidentiality in the rural setting (Burkemper, 2005; Daley & Doughty, 2006; Galambos, Watt, Anderson, & Danis, 2005; Green, 2003; Gumpert & Black, 2005; Strom-Gottfried, 2005) and the inevitability of dual relationships in small towns and close-knit rural communities (Boisen & Bosch, 2005; Burkemper, 2005; Daley & Doughty, 2006; Galambos et al., 2005; Galbreath, 2005; Green, 2003; Gumpert & Black, 2005; Miller, 1998; Strom-Gottfried, 2005; Watkins, 2004). These are significant issues for rural practice, and the task for educators is to explain the nuances of the Code of Ethics and practice strategies for handling issues that may arise.

Quite frankly, these are issues that tend to unfold differently in rural communities than in urban communities because of the close and personal relationships of rural people. Confidentiality tends to be a greater concern in rural communities, because people are more easily recognized and more widely known than would be typical in a larger community. Dual relationships are also more likely in a rural setting because of the multiple contexts in which people interact. Dual relationships are not specifically prohibited by the NASW Code of Ethics and, thus, the curriculum competency must center on how to recognize and manage dual relationships appropriately.

The discussion of ethical issues specific to rural communities has expanded considerably in recent years and broadened to include more aspects of the Code of Ethics (Daley & Hickman, 2011). One of these issues is poor practice boundaries, or practicing outside the scope of one's practice skills (Burkemper, 2005; Croxton, Jayratne, & Mattison, 2002; Daley & Doughty, 2006; Strom-Gottfried, 2005). That is important, because the social worker in a rural community often is called to intervene in situations beyond his or her expertise. Consequently, it is important for students to learn their scope of practice and how to manage situations outside their expertise. Securing outside supervision and consultation, as well as finding resources to meet these needs, are recommended strategies. In addition, since rural communities may not have another social worker in town, the generalist must cultivate supervisory relationships via telephone or Internet.

Another ethical dilemma for rural practice concerns self-disclosure (Strom-Gottfried, 2005) and personal presentation (Ginsberg, 1998; Martinez-Brawley, 2000) that affect rural practice. The "fishbowl" nature of life in rural communities suggests that programs should prepare students to consider the implications of personal actions and disclosures that might have adverse effects on their practice.

Finally, rural contexts provide ethical risks for social workers with respect to colleague relationships, which themselves may be multiple and overlapping (Daley & Hickman, 2011). Just as with client relationships, dual relationships with colleagues require ethical skill, and it is important to learn how to recognize and address these issues.

Important Rural Competency Areas

The literature on rural social work is a rich source of information on the content and skills necessary for practice, yet this information generally is not found in a centralized source in the literature. This makes it difficult for educational programs developing rural content because it almost forces an exhaustive review of the literature. A summary of the general themes that emerge is useful in providing direction about measuring rural practice competency.

It is clear from the literature that the generalist method of social work is the most appropriate model for rural practice (Allen, 2005; Davenport & Davenport, 1995; Ginsberg, 2005; Lohmann & Lohman, 2005; Reibschleger, 2007). In the undergraduate social work curriculum CSWE mandates the generalist perspective (CSWE, 2008). However, in the graduate curriculum, although some schools choose to offer an advanced generalist track, they are not required to do so (CSWE, 2008, pp. 8; Daley & Avant, 2004a). As Ginsberg (2005) discusses, some disagreement exists, especially in relation to the provision of mental health services in rural areas. Because of the higher chance of being the only practitioner with little or no supervision or support, some argue that the MSW should be trained as a specialist. Ginsberg (2005), however, argues that rural social workers often collaborate with the few other social workers in their communities and must fill-in in many areas of practice. Generalist skills allow for the full range of practice that may be necessary in a rural area.

Other important competency areas include the following abilities.

- *Understanding the pace of change in rural communities and gaining acceptance* (Nooe & Bolitho, 1982). This includes developing an understanding that rural communities are often resistant to change and distrustful of those considered outsiders. Thus, skills in establishing a relationship are very important, as is understanding how to influence community change in rural areas.

- *Using informal networks* (Gumpert, Saltman, & Sauer-Jones, 2000; Hovestadt, Fennell, & Canfield, 2002). All too often the formal resources needed to address client and community issues are not present, and the skills for creatively assembling or developing resources from informal networks are critical.

- *Providing on-going community assessment* (Reibschleger, 2007). Rural social workers must be sensitive to the needs and norms of the community to deliver and develop appropriate services.

- *Engaging in culturally responsive practice* (Allen, 2005; Daley & Avant, 2004a, 2004b; Lohmann & Lohmann, 2005; NASW, 2009). One size does not fit all, even for rural communities, so it is important to understand the cultural norms and traditions that affect behavior. The rural emphasis on a close family, fierce independence, and attachment to the land may make service delivery more difficult. Yet they are part of the local culture and ultimately may be strengths in terms of developing practice-based solutions.

- *Understanding social justice issues, especially issues of rural poverty* (Blakely & Locke, 2005; NASW, 2009). Poverty rates are higher, and the economy is less diverse than in urban areas. This can result in more widespread economic distress, which leads to individual stress and community disruption.

- *Negotiating professional practice issues, such as access to supervision, relationships with colleagues, and managing intersecting roles in the community* (Ginsberg, 1998; Riebschleger, 2007). Social workers in rural communities tend to be more isolated professionally. They have fewer opportunities for continuing education, peer supervision, and supervisory contact. This, coupled with the multiple roles they must fill in the community, requires creativity in developing strategies for meeting continued learning and professional development. The ability to obtain online training for continuing education is an important development for rural practitioners.

Riebschleger (2007) found evidence of support for these rural themes in her research with rural social work practitioners. She conducted focus groups and asked practitioners, "What are your suggestions for engaging in effective social work practice in rural areas?" and found that the previously mentioned themes were, in fact, identified by the practitioners. These practitioners also made suggestions for social work educators. They suggested five areas for strengthening the rural curriculum:

(1) increase the curriculum on rural practice,
(2) include rural/urban context and the person-in-environment perspective,
(3) define rural people as a diverse group,
(4) discuss the impact of social welfare policy on rural areas, and
(5) provide field placements in rural areas (Riebschleger, 2007).

Given the increased emphasis on competency-based education in social work (CSWE, 2008), the real challenge for social work education is to translate the teaching and learning of rural competence within the curriculum. Using the previously mentioned competency areas, programs can tailor the educational policy and accreditation standards (CSWE, 2008) competencies for rural or urban practice. However, unless this challenge is met, it will be difficult, if not impossible, to determine whether program graduates have the basic competence necessary to be professional social workers with rural populations.

Conclusion

Rural social work is an important field of practice that serves a significant and often forgotten minority. Yet, given the social work profession's traditional urban roots, rural social work and rural social workers have often been overlooked by social work education. In the last 20 years a significant amount of literature has accrued, addressing key areas of social work practice with rural populations and communities that can be used in building curriculum content to aid in the development of rural social work.

This chapter identifies key conceptual and content issues that can be used to support the development of the idea of rurality in the education of social workers. The issues of rural definition, curriculum models, generalist practice, diversity, professional ethics, and key competency areas are explored. Hopefully, this information can lead to the strengthening of rural themes in the social work curriculum and assist in the professional development of social workers who are best able to meet the need of rural clients and communities.

References

Allen, E. V. (2005). Teaching generalist practice in a rural context. In L. H. Ginsberg (Ed.), *Social work in rural communities*, 4th ed. (pp. 451). Alexandria, VA: Council on Social Work Education.

Bealer, R. C., Willitis, F. K., & Kuvlesky, W. P. (1965). The meaning of "rurality." *Rural Sociology, 30*(3), 255–266.

Belanger, K. (2005). In search of a theory to guide rural practice: The case for social capital. In L. H. Ginsberg (Ed.), *Social work in rural communities* (4th ed.). (pp. 4–7). Alexandria, VA: Council on Social Work Education.

Blakely, E. H., & Locke, B. L. (2005). Rural poverty and welfare reform. In N. Lohmann, & R. A. Lohmann (Eds.), *Rural social work practice* (pp. 25–40). New York, NY: Columbia University Press.

Boisen, L. S., & Bosh, L. A. (2005). Dual relationships and rural social work: Is there a rural code? In L. H. Ginsberg (Ed.), *Social work in rural communities*, 4rd ed. (pp. 189–203). Alexandria, VA: Council on Social Work Education.

Burkemper, E. M. (2005). Ethical mental health social work practice in the small community. In L. H. Ginsberg (Ed.), *Social work in rural communities*, 4th ed. (pp. 175–188). Alexandria, VA: Council on Social Work Education.

Council on Social Work Education (CSWE). (2007). *Top findings on baccalaureate social work education: from the 2007 annual survey of social work programs*. Retrieved from http://www.cswe.org/File.aspx?id=25657

Council on Social Work Education (CSWE). (2008). *Educational policy and accreditation standards*. Alexandria, VA: Council on Social Work Education. Retrieved from http://www.cswe.org/File.aspx?id=13780

Croxton, T. A., Jayaratne, S., & Mattison, D. (2002). Social work practice behaviors and beliefs: rural–urban differences. *Advances in Social Work, 3*(2), 117–132.

Daley, M. R., & Avant, F. (1999). Attracting and retaining professionals for social work practice in rural areas: An example from East Texas. In I. B. Carlton-La Ney, R. Edwards, & P. N. Reid (Eds.), *Preserving and strengthening small towns and rural communities* (pp. 335–345). Washington, DC: NASW Press.

Daley, M. & Avant, F. (2004a). Reconceptualizing rural social work. In T. L. Scales, C. L. Streeter (Eds.), *Asset building to sustain rural communities* (pp. 34–42). Belmont, CA: Thomson.

Daley, M. & Avant, F. (2004b). Model three: Stephen F. Austin State University: Advanced generalist social work for rural practice. In A. W. Roy, & F. J. Vecchiolla (Eds.), *Thoughts on an advanced generalist education* (pp. 37–58). Peosta, IA: Eddie Bowers.

Daley, M. R., & Doughty, M. O. (2006). Ethics complaints in social work practice: A rural–urban comparison. *Journal of Social Work Values and Ethics*, 3(1). Retrieved from http://www.socialworker.com/jswve/content/blogcategory/12/44/

Daley, M. R., & Hickman, S. (2011). Dual relations and beyond: Understanding and addressing ethical challenges for rural social work. *Journal of Social Work Values and Ethics*, 8(1). Retrieved from http://www.socialworker.com/jswve/spr11 /spr11daleyhickman.pdf

Davenport, J. A., & Davenport, J., III. (1995). Rural social work overview. In R. L. Edwards (Ed.), *Encyclopedia of social work*, 19th ed. (pp. 2076–2085). Washington, DC: NASW Press.

Galambos, C., Watt, J. W, Anderson, K., & Danis, F. (2005). Ethics forum: Rural social work practice: Maintaining confidentiality in the face of dual relationships. *Journal of Social Work Values and Ethics*, 2(2). Retrieved from http://www.socialworker.com/jswve/content/blogcategory/11/37/

Galbreath, W. B. (2005). Dual relationships in rural communities. In N. Lohman, & R. Lohman (Eds.), *Rural social work practice* (pp. 107). New York, NY: Columbia University Press.

Ginsberg, L. H. (1998). Introduction: An overview of rural social work. In L. H. Ginsberg (Ed.), *Social work in rural communities*, 3rd ed. (pp. 12–13). Alexandria, VA: Council on Social Work Education.

Ginsberg, L. H. (2005). The overall context of rural practice. In L. H. Ginsberg (Ed.), *Social work in rural communities*, 4rd ed. (pp. 4–7). Alexandria, VA: Council on Social Work Education.

Green, R. (2003). Social work in rural areas: A personal and professional challenge. *Australian Social Work*, 56(3), 209–219.

Gumpert, J., & Black, P. N. (2005). Walking the tightrope between cultural competence and ethical practice: the dilemma of the rural practitioner. In L. H. Ginsberg (Ed.), *Social work in rural communities*, 4th ed. (pp. 157–174). Alexandria, VA: Council on Social Work Education.

Gumpert, J., Saltman, J. E., & Sauer-Jones, D. (2000). Toward identifying the unique characteristics of social work practice in rural areas: From the voice of practitioners. *Journal of Baccalaureate Social Work*, 6(1), 16–35.

Hovestadt, A. J., Fennell, D. L., & Canfield, B. S. (2002). Characteristics of effective providers of marital and family therapy in rural mental health settings. *Journal of Marital and Family Therapy*, 28(2), 225–231.

Jacobsen, G. M. (1980). Rural communities and community development. In H. W. Johnson (Ed.), *Rural human services* (pp. 196–202). Itasca, IL: Peacock Publishers.

Lee, E. O., & Waites, C. E. (2006). Infusing aging content across the curriculum: Innovations in baccalaureate social work education. *Journal of Social Work Education,* 42, 49–66.

Lohmann, N., & Lohmann, R. A. (2005). Introduction. In N. Lohmann, & R. A. Lohmann (Eds.), *Rural social work practice* (pp. 3–24). New York, NY: Columbia University Press.

Martinez-Brawley, E. (1993). Community oriented rural practice. In L. H. Ginsberg (Ed.), *Social work in rural communities*, 2nd ed. (pp. 67–81). Alexandria, VA: Council on Social Work Education.

Martinez-Brawley, E. (2000). *Close to home: Human services in the small community.* Washington, DC: NASW Press.

Mellow, M. (2005). The work of rural professionals: Doing the gemeinschaft-gesselschaft gavotte. *Rural Sociology, 70*(1), 50–69.

Miller, P. J. (1998). Dual relationships and rural practice: A dilemma of practice and culture. In L. H. Ginsberg (Ed.), *Social work in rural communities* (3rd ed.). (pp. 55–62). Alexandria, VA: Council on Social Work Education.

National Association of Social Workers (NASW). (2009). Rural social work. In *Social work speaks: National Association of Social Workers policy statements.* (pp. 297–302). Washington, DC: NASW Press.

Nooe, R. M., & Bolitho, F. H. (1982). An examination of rural social work literature. *Human Services in the Rural Environment, 7*(3), 10–17.

Olaveson, J., Conway, P., & Shaver, C. (2004). Defining rural for social work practice and research. In T. L. Scales, & C. L. Streeter (Eds.), *Asset building to sustain rural communities* (pp. 9–20). Belmont, CA: Thomson.

Riebschleger, J. (2007). Social workers suggestions for effective rural practice. *Families in Society, 88*(2), 203–213.

Roy, A. W., & Vecchiolla, F. J. (2004). Thoughts on an advanced generalist education. In A. W. Roy, & F. J. Vecchiolla (Eds.), *Thoughts on an advanced generalist education.* (pp. 1–116). Peosta, IA: Eddie Bowers.

Scales, T. L., & Streeter, C. L. (2004). *Introduction: Asset building to sustain rural communities.* In T. L. Scales, & C. L. Streeter (Eds.), *Asset building to sustain rural communities.* (pp. 1–5). Belmont, CA: Thomson.

Southern Regional Education Board. (1993). Educational assumptions for rural social work. In L. H. Ginsberg (Ed.), *Social work in rural communities*, 2nd ed. (pp. 20). Alexandria, VA: Council on Social Work Education.

Strom-Gottfried, K. (2005). Ethical practice in rural environments. In L. H.Ginsberg (Ed.), *Social work in rural communities,* 4th ed. (pp. 141–155), Alexandria, VA: Council on Social Work Education.

Watkins, T. R. (2004). Natural helping networks. In T. L. Scales & C. L. Streeter (Eds.), *Rural social work building and sustaining community assets* (pp. 70). Belmont, CA: Thomson/Brooks Cole.

White, C., & Marks, K. (1999).A strengths-based approach to rural sustainable development. In I. B. Carlton-LaNey, R. Edwards & P. N. Reid, (Eds.), *Preserving and strengthening small towns and rural communities* (pp. 27–42). Washington, DC: NASW Press.

8   Rural Social Work Recruitment and Retention Challenges: *Why Is it Difficult to Fill Rural Social Work Positions?*

PAUL FORCE-EMERY MACKIE

One might think that rural-based social service agencies and programs should have no problem hiring skilled, competent, and qualified staff. What is not to like about living and working in rural areas? These are the places Garrison Keillor celebrates on his National Public Radio show, *A Prairie Home Companion*, where he famously finishes his news from Minnesota's fictional town of Lake Wobegon by summing up this rural community as a place "where the women are strong, the men are good looking, and all of the children are above average" (Prairie Home Productions, 2011). In fact, it is not uncommon to find rural places represented as serene and pleasing areas (Cashwell, 2008). Idyllic rural metaphors abound: snowcapped mountain vistas, vast seas of grass, historic farms, fields of grain spanning the horizon, towering forests, seemingly endless coastlines. These are the visual images we often hold as a rural reality. But there is another reality—one in which, too often, it is difficult for social service providers to recruit, hire, and retain qualified staff across rural areas. Empirical, as well as anecdotal, evidence shows that there is a social service and mental health labor force shortage across rural America (Hundall-Stamm, 2003; Mackie & Lips, 2010). Sadly, this is not just a contemporary problem. History tells us that this challenge has been chronic and persistent. This is not a new problem, but an old one in need of new approaches, strategies, and solutions.

This chapter reviews what is currently known about recruiting, hiring, and retaining rural social service providers. Based on the evidence available, we know that this is a real problem, but this information also allows us to draw some conclusions and, perhaps, offer suggestions to improve the situation. Before we delve into this question specifically, however, it is important to review the history of rural social work and ask how this history influences and affects rural social work today. In addition, topics such as how we define and identify what *rural* means (and what it does not), why these definitions differ from each other, how we personally and collectively perceive what is rural, and how these definitions may affect the labor force are important to address as well.

Defining *Rural*

At the most basic statistical level, the Economic Research Service of the U.S. Department of Agriculture (ERS/USDA, 2008) estimates the rural population in the United States at about 59 million people, or about 20% of the total population. How does one draw this conclusion? A calculation of the total rural population of the United States is based on multiple sources of measurement, and there is no single way to define the population. Although many definitions of *rural* currently exist in the literature (Ciarlo & Zelarney, 2000), at this time there are three principal definitions in broad use by the federal government. The first is from the U.S. Bureau of Census (BOC), the second comes from the U.S. Office of Budget and Management (OBM), and the third was developed by ERS/USDA. Each has unique qualities, as well as challenges.

BOC defines rural areas based on three basic criteria: (1) population density, (2) proximity to urban centers, and (3) population size of a region. This definition is, essentially, an inverted one, in that BOC defines what is rural by defining what is considered "not urban." According to BOC, an urbanized area includes a population center or urban nucleus (e.g., a city and the immediate surrounding areas) with a population consisting of at least 50,000 people. The city in and of itself does not have to contain the entire population of 50,000, but the regional area (referred to as an Urbanized Area) must meet this minimum population criteria. In addition, the density of the population is expected to exceed 1,000 people per square mile within what is called a Metropolitan Statistical Area (MSA) and may contain adjacent territory with at least 500 people per square mile and towns or centralized communities with populations exceeding 2,500 people. Based on this definition, rural areas are defined as those spaces that do not fit within this urban definition. More simply stated, *rural* is defined as the places that do not contain a regionalized population of 50,000 or more people and open land space with population settlements containing fewer than 2,500 people (BOC, 2010a).

The federal Office of Management and Budget (OMB) defines *rural* somewhat differently. OMB focuses on MSAs as counties with at least one urbanized area and outlying areas, which may include portions of other counties that are economically tied to the core county. Outlying areas are included in the MSA if at least 25% of workers living in the outlying area commute to the centralized urban area for employment. Thus, nonmetropolitan counties are those falling outside the boundaries of the MSA. These areas are further subdivided into two separate groups. Micro-Politian Statistical Areas (MicroSAs) are nonmetropolitan areas with an urban cluster of at least 10,000 people and to which at least 25% of the workers from the outlying area commute. Areas that do not fit within these definitions are referred to as noncore counties, or the most "rural" of the designations (USDA, 2008).

The third definition comes from ERS/USDA. This approach to defining *rural* is often considered more accurate and robust than the previous two, due to the careful consideration of more detailed population data on which the formula is based. It uses census tract classifications and focuses on the Rural-Urban Commuting Area (RUCA) systems. This more complex approach considers the BOC definition and combines it with different MSAs by size and proximity to other MSAs, as well as by zip code. It also considers different degrees of urbanization on a continuum (USDA, 2008). Defining *rural* using this approach is by far the most complex discussed here, but probably the most accurate for many different reasons. For example, the definition developed by BOC is limiting in that there are many "regional" or "centralized" communities across the prairie states that do not exceed a population of 50,000; however, these communities are the "urban" hub or center of the region, due to the vast and less populated outlying areas. Conversely, the many eastern states, such as those in New England or on the Atlantic seashore, may not be considered rural because there are large county populations adjacent to the core counties where many people work but do not actually live. Situations such as these increase the complexity of defining *rural*.

Developing a better understanding of what is and what is not rural may be best described with a few examples. I once drove from New York City to Poughkeepsie (NY), which takes about 2 hours. Having started the trip from the very urban Manhattan Island, I travelled north and, after about 30 minutes, felt like I was in a rural area. Trees lined the highway, the distance between houses stretched farther, and there were even some farms across the landscape. But, at the same time, it was also evident that there were sustained populations of people along the way—it was not too rural, but had rural attributes. As I approached Poughkeepsie (population

30,050), I felt as if I were somewhere in Middle America, not a short 2 hours from the largest city in the United States. Although the area may have appeared rural based on the landscape, by definition I had never actually left an "urban" place— each county I passed through was considered an MSA or Urban Area, depending on the definition applied. In a sense, I held a perception that I was in a "rural" landscape, based on the lack of recognizable urban features, but never actually entered one that is identified statistically as "rural."

In another example, I once visited Scotts Bluff, NE, in the western panhandle of that state. This is a city of approximately 15,000 people, and the county (Scotts Bluff) it is located in has a population of about 37,000 residents. Due to the centralized nature of the community, it is considered a regional center for health care, entertainment, and commerce. In association with the nearby town of Gering, it is the seventh largest urban area in Nebraska and is considered by the U.S. Census Bureau as a MicroSA. This community is the population hub in an otherwise sparsely populated geographic region, and, by any formal definition, rural. Although most residents of Scotts Bluff would agree that they are indeed in a rural place, they might also argue that it is city where a person may obtain certain amenities (i.e., health care, entertainment, and commerce) not otherwise available across the broader regional landscape. Driving through the town, I interpreted the community as more urban-like, given the stark rural nature of the landscape around it.

A final example can be found in the unique case of St. Louis County, MN. According to BOC (2010b), this county contains a land mass area of 6,225 square miles, slightly more than the states of Connecticut and Rhode Island combined. It is the second largest county by land mass east of the Mississippi River. The population of St. Louis County in 2009 totaled 197,767 people, of which 84,167 lived in the city of Duluth proper, with several well-populated communities adjacent to that city (BOC, 2010). This is a big county that stretches from the southern tip of Lake Superior north to the Canadian border. However, the county population center (Duluth) is hardly centered at all, being located at the southeastern-most section of the county. Based on the population of the greater Duluth MSA, the county is defined as urban, as well as adjoining Douglas County, WI. However, drive north from Duluth only a few miles, and you can make the same observations found between New York City and Poughkeepsie—the local population becomes sparser, and geographically the land looks more rural. Unlike the area north of New York City, however, St. Louis County is very rural north of Duluth but is identified as urban by most official definitions.

The central point of these examples is to show that, although rural and urban areas can be quantitatively defined, the reality is that the perception or interpretation of what is considered rural or urban can contain local interpretations. Scotts Bluff, NE, is not urban, but it is designated as a MicroSA by definition due to the community's regional centeredness and population density, compared to outlying areas. The space between New York City and Poughkeepsie is not defined as rural, but it may look as if it is. St. Louis County, MN, is by all accounts very rural, but, due to the containment of a large community at its southern tip, it is officially defined as urban.

A final rural definition in need of address is that of the "frontier rural" status—those that contain fewer than seven persons per square mile (Ciarlo & Zelarney, 2000; Popper, 1986). These are the most rural of rural areas and contain less than 1% of the total population of the United States (Ciarlo & Zelarney, 2000; Popper, 1986). It would be difficult to find anyone of the opinion that these places, based on the level of remoteness and isolation, are anything other than rural.

Defining what is and is not rural can be accomplished formally, through the application of specific definitions from government entities, as well as informally based on sociocultural perceptions and individual or group interpretations. This is an important yet seldom addressed issue when a person needs to understand the complexities of recruiting, hiring, and retaining social workers in rural areas. How people interpret and perceive rurality is an important factor to the overall understanding of who is more likely to become a successful rural practitioner. For example, a social worker from New York City may perceive Poughkeepsie as rural, or at least a place with rural attributes. Conversely, a social worker from western Nebraska may view a community the size of Poughkeepsie as quite urban, given its size and proximity to more populated cities. Over time, these questions have been discussed to varying degrees with different interpretations and outcomes. Perhaps a conclusion about what is and is not rural, in relation to recruiting and retaining social workers in isolated areas, is best understood as a question of individual and group perception and less one of quantifiable, statistically based designations. At the same time, statistically grounded designations also serve to provide clarity, specificity, and borders. In short, understanding the complexities of defining rurality are grounded in formal and informal interpretations. Delving deeper into an understanding around these issues, a review of the history of rural social work and how the discipline has attempted to interpret these perceptions in the past may be beneficial.

History of Rural Social Services

The historical timeline of rural social work and social services is difficult to establish. The act of formally and informally helping others has a long, rich tradition across societies, including rural societies in the United States. In rural areas communities have a history of coming together in times of crisis where resources are often shared, and, at least on a stereotypical level, "neighbors watch out for each other." Although these may be examples of informal helping systems, Vidich and Bensman's seminal work *Small Town in Mass Society* (1960) describes how something perceived as informal by some may be, in fact, formal to others, simply less formally defined. This is an interesting observation in that, once again, the question of perception arises. What may be perceived as informal helping systems among urban dwellers may actually be very formal in a rural environment. For example, according to Vildich and Bensman (1960), rural residents are more likely to check in on each other, provide food, shelter, and other social services to those in need, and otherwise be more highly engaged in and attentive to the lives of others. Although it may be difficult to determine the nuances between formal and informal systems, there are a few known points in time when rural social work as a formal definition is addressed as a needed, wanted, and, otherwise, recognized, societal entity.

Swanson (1972) conducted a review of early professional social work in rural areas and identified interesting findings from this research. Beginning with information from after the turn of the 20th century, Swanson investigated questions about the development of social work in rural areas. Initially, social workers in rural areas primarily focused on improvements in farm management, health care, social welfare, education, leadership skills, and general social well-being of residents. Bailey (1908, as cited in Swanson, 1972) shared that social work problems found in urban areas clearly existed in rural areas as well, but, too often, the social needs of rural residents were overlooked because of the excessively urban focus of the social work field. According to Swanson (1972), this is where the apex of a debate that continues today can be identified: Are we practicing "social work in rural areas" or "rural social work?" Swanson (1972) argued that, historically, professional social work has vacillated between being viewed as "social work in rural areas" and the more professionally defined, and articulated, subdiscipline "rural social work." Social work in rural areas was defined as the field's philosophy and by interventions-based treatments and techniques grounded in urban social work practice methods.

Conversely, rural social work emerged as a defined subdiscipline within the field that identifies unique qualities with special focus on rural-specific concerns not otherwise adequately addressed from a more urban perspective. For example, a demand for rural-focused social work grew from pressure applied by the Red Cross Home Service after World War I to support the needs of rural residents suffering from the loss of wage earners to the war effort (Swanson, 1972). During this timeframe many rural states sought to develop rural social work programs, with varying degrees of success. Iowa, Minnesota, and North Carolina worked to integrate social workers into rural areas by placing them in lower population-dense locations. North Carolina was especially attentive to this movement, requiring each county to establish a welfare board and place a social worker on staff. These social workers were responsible for monitoring and assisting with educational expectations, probation, parole, and family and child welfare concerns. By the early 1930s the concept of rural social work was well-established and recognized. By the early 1940s, however, the concept began to wane and slip back into the domain categorized as social work in rural areas, as schools of social work returned to a focus on treatments and interventions mostly developed and tested in urban areas and away from rural populations. Swanson (1972) concluded that "rural social work disappeared because the profession quit identifying significant distinctions in rural work" (p. 526). If this is accurate, one might conclude that the rural social work concept passed away due to benign neglect.

Beginning in the mid-1960s Ginsberg (2006) began to "invent" rural social work education. Over time it became apparent that, although some educational programs purported to be rural-focused, the curricula did not reflect this claim. A clear definition of what rural social work education was (and was not) had not yet been developed. As the director of the Division of Social Work at West Virginia University, Ginsberg started the work necessary to change that. Rural-based field placements were developed, a new curriculum was proposed, and a move toward integrating knowledge about rural culture and lifestyle began with the goal of using this unique knowledge and transferring it into practitioners' skills. Later, rural-focused training sessions to improve rural practice also were created. Either explicitly or implicitly, Ginsberg's goal was to recast the nature of rural social work practice—to redefine this area of practice and scholarship from "social work in rural areas" back to "rural social work." This was accomplished through the venue of higher education, schools, programs, and departments of social work and through the growth and development of rural-specific scholarship. It becomes clear that, if we truly want to address the rural social work labor force problems, we may benefit from educating social work students on the more valuable aspects of rural practice. Ginsberg's work has been influential and continues today, largely lead by the National Rural Social Work Caucus (2011). This organization supports a journal that focuses on disseminating rural social work concerns, advocates for the advancement of rural social work issues, and holds regular conferences and professional meetings to disseminate pertinent findings.

The distinction between rural social work and social work in rural areas has become convoluted and blurred over time, with some evidence that the focus on social work in rural areas remains. Matthews (1927) discussed the question of whether practicing social work in rural areas was indeed different from that practiced in urban environments and asked "[can] a case worker who has always been on duty in a city come to a rural neighborhood and work without making very definite changes in her methods?" (p. 67). Matthews (1927) concluded that, although the objectives of the position are similar, rural social workers often need to adapt their practice methods and be more cognizant of their role as generalist practitioners, compared to their urban counterparts who could be, and often were, more specialty focused. Additionally, Matthews (1927) discussed the importance of understanding the culture of rural life, the social worker's place in the greater fabric of small communities, how social workers fit into the community, and the need to understand unique rural concerns, such as are associated with agriculture, mining, and lumbering. Essentially, Matthews (1927) concluded that practice methods applied in rural areas may not immediately appear much different from those applied in urban areas but that, for them to be successful, the rural social worker needed a very different knowledge base about culture and lifestyle than what would be expected among urban-based social workers.

Much later, York, Denton, and Moran (1989) studied the differences in practice approaches across rural areas and concluded that there are no real differences—social work practice methods and techniques in rural areas look essentially the same as those applied in urban areas. In response, Green (2003) argued that, due to the complex nature of rural communities and unique socioeconomic and cultural differences among those who live there, practicing social work in rural areas does indeed differ from practicing in more urbanized environments. This position is echoed by Riebschleger (2007), who conducted a qualitative analysis of what social workers felt differentiated rural from urban practice. Findings show that rural social workers regularly consider the structures of communities and personal and professional connections and connectedness between social work and residents, as well as maintain an ability to practice from a generalist perspective and hold a broad understanding of diversity and how it intersects with the wider community. These elements were all considered critical to effectively practicing in rural areas. Are there other elements, or do social workers in rural areas, essentially, practice the same as their urban counterparts? Perhaps the difference between practicing social work in rural areas is less about specific treatment modalities and approaches and more about understanding the complexities of culture and ways of life found in rural communities and the unique challenges presented.

Recruiting, Hiring, and Retaining Rural Social Workers

I have discussed differences in how rural areas are defined and how individual perceptions and attitudes may differ from more quantitative methods of definition. I also have briefly reviewed the history of social work in rural areas and how theoretical paradigm shifts have occurred over time and affected rural practice. Now we turn to problems associated with hiring rural social workers, difficulties associated with maintaining a sufficient labor force across remote places, and the challenges of providing social and mental health services in rural areas.

State and federal entities have attempted to address the lack of mental health and social service practitioners in rural areas as a serious problem and developed policy strategies aimed at addressing this concern. Perhaps the best known policy-based response to this problem focuses on student loan repayment programs and scholarships for those willing to practice in rural areas. The National Health Service Corps (2010) within the Health Resources and Services Administration of the U.S. Department of Health and Human Services administers programs focused on placing professional health care workers in rural and underrepresented regions. Recognizing the complications of providing adequate health and mental health care in isolated and underrepresented regions, these programs contain an array of federally funded opportunities that focus on staffing health care systems with providers such as physicians, psychiatrists, midwives, nurse practitioners, dentists, supporting allied health service workers, and clinical social workers. Loan repayment programs and scholarships exist to aid in the redistribution of workers across rural America. Although considered by many an effective approach, a large number of open positions continue to go unfilled. Among those that are filled, too often the positions become a "revolving door problem"—as soon as the provider's time obligation is satisfied, he or she leaves.

Recognizing the problem with staffing professionals in rural areas, the President's New Freedom Commission on Mental Health report, *Achieving the Promise: Transforming Mental Health Care in America* (2003), stated that "although the support of well-trained mental health professionals is inadequate in most areas of the country, rural areas are especially hard hit" (p. 70). This report provided several suggestions to address the problem and improve the quality of care for consumers in rural areas. The report's authors recommended increased research in this area, supported a more collaborative focus on rural mental health needs, and encouraged increasing the use of midlevel and alternative providers of mental health services in rural and remote areas. Clearly, the federal government recognizes that delivering appropriate mental health services in rural areas is essential to the positive growth and well-being of rural communities. What is less clear is why there continues to be a lack of providers across the rural landscape.

Problems with hiring and retaining a professional skilled labor force in rural regions are neither new nor unique to social work. Researchers across the fields of education (Murphy & Angelski, 1996), nursing (Bushy & Leipert, 2005), medicine (Somers, Trasser, & Jolly, 2007), and psychology (Benson, 2003) have worked to identify predictors among those more or less likely to pursue professional careers in rural areas. Regardless of the profession, a general consensus across disciplines emerges: It can be difficult to find and retain professional workers in rural areas. Like others professions, social work continues to struggle with this (Daley & Avant, 1999; Lohmann & Lohmann, 2005; Ricketts, 1999).

Student Perceptions About Rural Practice

Beginning with the education of social workers, Mackie and Simpson (2007) investigated factors influencing undergraduate social work students' perceptions about practicing in rural areas. Although they identified no differences between class levels (i.e., freshman through senior), they did find significant differences between those who were raised in rural areas, compared to those who grew up in more urban environments. Students who grew up in rural areas claimed they were more likely to consider practicing in a rural area after graduation compared to their urban counterparts. Based on their responses, rural-raised students appeared to perceive working in rural places as more acceptable, interesting, and likely than those raised in urban areas. This evidence suggests that, even at the undergraduate level, there may be a natural tendency among developing social workers to gravitate back to familiar geographic areas, based on where a person was raised. In the same study Mackie and Simpson (2007) also investigated more qualitative questions regarding what respondents considered positive and negative factors associated with working in rural areas. Mackie and Simpson (2007) found that rural-raised students were more likely to focus on the positive aspects of working in rural areas, compared to urban-raised students, who were more likely to focus on the more negative aspects.

Among positive factors identified, the dominant theme to emerge was that of personal familiarity with rural places. Students reported that they wanted to return to where they grew up to be closer to family, raise their children in the rural lifestyle, and felt they understood rural life ways and culture. Respondents also shared that they preferred rural life to urban life because of a lower cost of living, fewer complications with travel and commuting, a general feeling that life is simply better in small communities, and the safety associated with living in rural communities. These findings suggest that the students perceive the rural lifestyle as healthier and more affordable, providing an overall higher quality of life when compared to living in an urban space. Students also reported that they preferred the professional opportunities available in rural areas. Here, a passion for working with rural populations emerged. Rural-raised respondents' argued that rural areas are in need of social service assistance no differently than urban places, and, based on their background, they are uniquely qualified to provide these services. Others responded that based on their experiences of living in small communities they understand the problems associated with rural residents. Many shared a desire to give back to the communities with which they felt personal and emotional ties.

Although many positive factors were identified, negative factors emerged as well. The most dominant theme was that of professional challenges. Many urban-raised students felt that working in rural areas meant having to accept lower incomes compared to salaries found in urban areas, the need to address challenges associated with travel and geographic distance between provider and consumer, and a lack of professional support. The second theme focused on consumer-based concerns. Both groups expressed apprehension about dual relationships, an often cited concern among rural-based professionals. For example, students worried about lack of privacy in communities where often "everyone knows everyone" (Mackie & Simpson, 2007, p. 14)

The third and final theme to emerge was personal concerns. Students expressed apprehension about the potential for closed-mindedness among rural community members and the lack of diversity across rural regions. Respondents worried that residents of close-knit communities can be resistant and unwilling to accept social change, narrow-minded, and even discriminatory or racist. This may be an example of misinformation among students and serves as an example of how perceptions can perpetuate social problems.

Evidence from this study displays some of the complexities involved with the preference of some to work in rural areas, compared to those less interested in doing so. What ultimately appears to emerge is that this is a statement of perception. Some perceive living and working in a rural area as positive and see it as comfortable, warm, and embracing. Others focus on negative aspects, such as closed- and narrow-mindedness of community members, personal and professional isolation, and less attractive salaries.

Educational Factors in Attraction, Hiring, and Retaining Rural Social Workers

In related research Mackie (2007) sought to develop a better understanding of educational and demographic differences between rural and urban social workers. Using a nationwide sample of social workers already working in the field, some in rural and others in urban areas, Mackie (2007) found that those working in rural areas were more likely to have grown up in similar areas, completed either an undergraduate or graduate practicum in a rural setting, or had been exposed to "rural content" during their undergraduate or graduate studies. These findings suggest that, although the less malleable influences of one's personal background such as growing up in a rural area are important, the effects of more easily manipulated factors such as where students are placed in practicum and the level of rural-specific content also affect the choice of practice location.

These findings have interesting implications. Social work education can have a significant effect on staffing in rural areas through the processes of selective recruiting, directed curriculum, and targeted field placements. Although a complex proposition, horizontal and vertical inclusion of these concepts throughout a social work curriculum could net positive results. For example, more aggressive and targeted recruiting practices might increase the number of students who eventually become rural social workers. The infusion of rural-specific material across content could increase interest in and understanding of rural social work, as well as dispel myths and address concerns regarding rural practices.

Education programs committed to addressing the rural social work labor force problem may also need to be more flexible in field placements, allowing students to complete their practicum in a location geographically further from the home institution than in the past. One challenge cited regarding monitoring the progress of distantly placed students in field education is just that—distance. Social work faculty members regularly conduct seminars and site visits to connect the field experience with student learning. Placing students far from the home institution, however, can create complications. In response to this concern, Taylor, Mensinga, Casey, and Caldwell (2008) found that implementing a multifaceted approach to training, monitoring, and evaluating student performance through the use of technology was effective in bridging the geographic divide between student and field coordinator. Applying teletechnology to reach across large geographic areas is not a new concept, but rather one that has taken time to fully mature. For example, LaMendola (2000a, 2000b) and Hudnall Stamm (2003) discussed how the use of telemental health services can link consumers and providers with needed resources and services. However, the application of the technology at that time was often limited because of the need for special equipment and additional resources. This has changed significantly. Today teleconferencing technology is available to nearly everyone through the use of reasonably priced software and standard personal computers. What was once a significant technological challenge is now a lesser concern, because this technology continues to evolve and become more user-friendly.

Mackie and Lips (2010) conducted research in which social service supervisors across rural Minnesota were surveyed and asked about the challenges hiring and retaining their work force. This investigation found that when bachelor level practitioners were sought, rural-based social service supervisors overwhelmingly (86% of the time) preferred to hire baccalaureate-prepared social workers, compared to candidates with related undergraduate degrees such as psychology, sociology, or general human service degrees. However, supervisors also reported that they were only able to hire social work-prepared workers about one-half the time, leaving them to hire outside of this specific degree. This study also found a positive relationship between distance from MSAs and the difficultly in hiring social workers for rural areas. The investigators found that for every 10 miles a person moved away from an MSA, the difficulty of filling a social service position increased by 3%. For example, if an agency is located 25 miles from an MSA, the difficulty of hiring a provider increases to 7.5%. If the agency is located 75 miles from an MSA, the difficulty increases to 22.5%. Across sparsely populated rural areas such as those found in Minnesota, it is not uncommon to identify counties and communities that are 75–100 miles from the nearest MSA. These findings provide two important points of information. First, the farther a person moves from larger population centers the more difficult it is to even hire staff, regardless of the degree earned. Second, although supervisors strongly prefer to hire workers with social work-specific backgrounds, too often they cannot do so and instead hire the workers they can find, not necessarily the workers they want, to fill positions.

Indications of Successful Strategies for Hiring and Retaining Workers

Mackie and Lips (2010) study also included a qualitative analysis based on general questions around "successes" and "challenges" of hiring and retaining rural workers. Several main themes emerged regarding successful strategies employed by rural supervisors: familiarity, meeting worker personal needs, meeting worker professional needs, and salaries and benefits. Within the familiarity theme, three subthemes emerged: roots in rural areas, hiring interns, and employee referral. Findings from the first subtheme show that supervisors believed one successful strategy for hiring and retaining staff was to locate individuals with roots in the rural community, such as those who grew up or had family there. In support of this finding supervisors stated that they preferred to hire applicants who explicitly expressed interest in living in a rural area and believed these applicants would often emerge as more competent and successful social workers compared to those less interested in living in a rural location. Regarding the second subtheme, supervisors shared that applicants can build ties to a rural area through a practicum experience, and, when this occurred, social workers were more likely to remain over time and be more committed to the agency and the region. These findings show that supervisors identify and value hiring individuals with local connections, either from personal experience or developed through an internship, a finding also supported in related research (Daley & Avant, 1999). The third subtheme shows that supervisors place value on employee referrals. Supervisors reported that being referred as a potential candidate for a rural social work position by a current employee is a positive predictor for future success in the position.

Supervisors also discussed the importance of meeting workers' personal needs. Supervisors claim that they successfully recruit and retain workers by fostering a work–home balance. They discussed the importance of offering flexible schedules, showing employees that they are valued as an important part of the purpose and mission of the agency, even providing private rooms for nursing mothers. Supervisors felt that valuing their staff promoted excellence in the workplace and reduced work–home scheduling conflicts. The end result is a more contented and highly motivated workforce. Another theme to emerge focused on meeting workers' professional needs. Supervisors stated that they believed it was imperative to provide opportunities to complete continuing education requirements, provide clinical and licensure supervision, and allow workers to share in decision-making processes.

Salaries and benefits were also considered important to hiring and retaining a quality workforce. Interestingly, however, this theme fell under both "successes" and "challenges." As a success, employers stated that they are often able to offer competitive salaries and benefits, which increases the likelihood that workers will not leave their positions. But it was clear that not all employers have this experience. Others stated that the lack of salary and benefits is one reason workers often leave. There is some disagreement in this particular area, largely based on the funding sources of individual agencies. Those working for state or county municipalities were more highly compensated compared to those working for private nonprofit providers.

Main Challenges of Hiring Rural Social Workers

Among the many challenges cited in the Mackie and Lips (2010) study, supervisors reported four main themes: lack of applicants, salaries and benefits, the "stepping-stone" problem, and employee burnout. The lack of qualified applicants emerged as the single most noted challenge to hiring workers. Supervisors found that, too often, applicants may initially state they are interested in working in rural areas but later either accept positions in more populated communities, accept a rural position then soon exit, or refuse a position offered in a rural area.

The next challenge was briefly discussed previously—the lack of competitive salaries and benefits. Although some state and county-based positions pay well and provide good benefits, many private nonprofit providers and counties with smaller budgets are challenged to provide attractive compensation. Supervisors affiliated with smaller agencies often found that their agencies were used as starting points, and employees eventually gravitated to higher paying agencies within the same geographic area.

The stepping-stone problem reverberated throughout the findings from this study. This refers to young, inexperienced workers accepting positions in rural areas, gaining experience, and then shifting to positions in more populated areas. Supervisors stated that they are often frustrated with the process of hiring, training, and otherwise preparing workers for the complexities of rural work only to later lose them to urban locations. For example, respondents stated that they are unable to compete with salaries, benefits, and amenities more likely found in urban centers and, thus, rural agencies often become social work training grounds.

Professional burnout was also cited as a reason rural social workers leave their positions over time. Burnout is a common theme across the general social service literature (LeCroy & Rank, 1987; Maslach, 1986, 2003) and, specifically, literature focused on rural social service practice (DeStefano, Clark, & Potter, 2005; Mackie, 2008a, 2008b; Poulin & Walter, 1993; Soderfeldt, Soderfeldt, & Warg, 1995). Supervisors stated that newly graduated and inexperienced social workers soon felt the effects of high and complicated caseloads, leading to burnout, which eventually results in workers leaving the workforce prematurely. Practice areas of greatest concern are concentrated around child welfare and mental health—critical areas of practice desperately needed in rural social services.

An example of this is found in research conducted by Mackie and Berg (2005), who studied what rural social workers identified as joys and challenges of working in geographically remote environments. Not surprisingly, burnout emerged as a common challenge among rural workers. The study found that rural social workers identified problems such as conflicts between coworkers, personal and professional isolation, and conflicts with consumers, especially in the area of dual relationships. Workers shared that they often felt unable to fully disengage from their work because the possibility of interacting with a consumer outside of work is very common.

The term "dual relationships" refers to the potential for interactions between care provider and care receiver outside of the professional realm (Schank & Skovholt, 2006; see also Chapter 6 of the current volume). This is a common concern discussed across the literature. Schank and Skovholt (2006) identified this problem among rural psychologists, and Sidell (2007), DeStefano et al. (2005), and Mackie (2008a) investigated these concerns among rural social workers. A review of these works shows that complications related to dual relationships are complex and create a stress on rural practitioners who are challenged to maintain professional and personal boundaries in rural places where such boundaries are often more fluid and less defined. Although rural areas may be geographically large, populations tend to be small, and populations congregate or otherwise interact in familiar places such as sporting events, restaurants, grocery stores, schools, county fairs, and parades.

Based on the information provided in this chapter, it becomes clear that several factors are involved in the problems of hiring and retaining social workers in rural communities. Too often, rural social workers feel the challenges of keeping personal and professional lives separate, due to the dual nature of their relationship between themselves, consumers, and the community. Rural social workers may be concerned that there are not enough professional development opportunities for them. They worry that salaries are too low. Some are concerned that rural residents are narrow-minded, conservative, and resistant to change. Based on the research, these are all legitimate concerns, if for no other reason than they are what individuals perceive as problems—problems that create barriers and negatively influence decisions about working in rural areas.

Rural areas can be places of familiarity and comfort, especially for those who have lived there, because rural culture and ways of life differ from urban places in both stark and subtle ways. The remoteness of some rural areas provides opportunities for greater community involvement, closer relationships, and opportunities to truly be a generalist practitioner. These are also places often defined as beautiful, serene, quiet, and slower paced. Is rural America accurately portrayed as Garrison Keillor's iconic and idyllic Lake Wobegon? That may depend more on who is answering the question. However, there is one certainty—rural areas need social workers. The social problems found in urban areas are found in rural areas as well. The populations in need of services exist in rural areas just as they do across urban communities. Perhaps the real question one must ask, before considering whether to become a rural social worker, is: What is your perception of rural?

Conclusion

There is much that can be done to address the lack of social service providers in rural places. Enhancing recruitment efforts and focusing on educational strategies that encourage practice in rural areas might well be effective strategies to successfully increasing the rural labor force. Workers who consider working in rural areas are often people who grew up in such areas and are interested in returning. They cite being close to family, raising their families, and being a part of rural culture as important. Evidence suggests that social workers already working in rural locations are more likely to have grown up in a rural area, completed a rural practicum, or been exposed to a rural lifestyle as social work students. This implies that there is value in either arriving with a familiarity with rural areas, developing it through purposeful placement such as a practicum, or by finding an interest via careful design among higher education programs that emphasize and promote rural practice. Supervisors stated that they preferred to hire individuals who had rural backgrounds or otherwise appeared to have an understanding of rural lifestyles, people, and culture. They have found that people with ties to rural areas are more likely to be retained and less likely to use a rural agency as a stepping-stone to another job.

Addressing the lack of social workers in rural areas is also a question of perception: How do potential social workers perceive rural areas? Do they view these areas as places of opportunity or challenge? Do they feel that they can "fit in," or is there concern that they are, and perhaps will remain, "outsiders"? What biases might they hold about rural areas? Finally, how might social work education address these very real concerns sometimes held by social work students? Based on the available research, it appears that those who grow up in more urban areas have very different perceptions about living and working in rural areas, compared to those who grew up in rural environments. Although this can be a challenge, it can be addressed through educational processes focused on increasing understanding, reducing misunderstandings, and addressing myths about rural America.

References

Benson, E. (2003). Beyond "urbancentrism." *The Rural Psychologist, 34*(6), 54.

Bushy, A., & Leipert, B. (2005). Factors that influence students in choosing rural nursing practice: A pilot study. *Rural and Remote Health, 5,* 1–12.

Cashwell, S. T. (2008). Rural social work practice. In D. M. DiNitto, & C. A. McNeese (Eds.), *Social work issues and opportunities in a challenging profession* (pp. 333–356). Chicago, IL: Lyceum Books.

Ciarlo, J. A., & Zelarney, P. T. (2000). Focusing on "frontier": Isolated rural America. *Journal of the Washington Academy of Sciences, 86*(3), 1–24.

Daley, M., & Avant, F. (1999). Attracting and retaining professionals for social work practice in rural areas: An example from east Texas. In I. B. Carlton-Laney, R. L. Edwards, & P. N. Reid (Eds.), *Preserving and strengthening small towns and rural communities* (pp. 335–345). Washington DC: NASW Press.

DeStefano, T., Clark, H., & Potter, T. (2005). The assessment of burnout among rural mental health staff. *Journal of Rural Mental Health, 30*(1), 18–24.

Ginsberg, L. (2006). "Inventing" rural social work. *Reflections: Narratives of Professional Helping, 12*(4), 33–42.

Green, R. (2003). Social work in rural areas: A personal and professional challenge. *Australian Social Work, 56*(3), 209–219.

Hudnall Stamm, B. (2003). *Rural behavioral health care: An interdisciplinary guide.* Washington, DC: American Psychological Association.

LaMendola, W. F. (2000a). Telemental health services in U.S. frontier areas. *Journal of the Washington Academy of Sciences, 86*(3), 189–196.

LaMendola, W. F. (2000b). Telemental health services in US frontier areas: Provider and consumer perspectives. *Journal of the Washington Academy of Sciences, 86*(3), 197–203.

LeCroy, C. W., & Rank, M. R. (1987). Factors associated with burnout in the social services: An exploratory study. *Journal of Social Service Research, 10,* 23–39.

Lohmann, N., & Lohmann, R.A. (Eds). (2005). *Rural social work practice.* New York, NY: Columbia University Press.

Mackie, P. F. E. (2007). Understanding educational and demographic differences between rural and urban social workers. *Journal of Baccalaureate Social Work, 12*(3), 114-128.

Mackie, P. F. E. (2008a). *Burnout and job satisfaction among rural and urban social workers: An investigation of differences between groups.* Saarbrücken, Germany: VDM Verlag Dr. Müller Aktiengesellschaft & Co.

Mackie, P. F. E. (2008b). Are social workers really burned out? An analysis between rural and urban social workers. *Journal of Rural Mental Health, 32*(2), 3–18.

Mackie, P. F. E., & Berg, T. (2005). Burnout and satisfaction between rural and urban social workers: A qualitative analysis. *Journal of Rural Mental Health, 30*(3), 9–14.

Mackie, P.F.E. & Lips, R.A. (2010). Is there really a problem with hiring rural social service staff? An exploratory study among social service supervisors in rural Minnesota. *Families in Society, 91*(4), 433-439.

Mackie, P. F. E., & Simpson, C. L. (2007). Factors influencing undergraduate social work students' perceptions about rural-based practice: A pilot study. *Journal of Rural Mental Health, 31*(2), 5–21.

Maslach, C. (1986). Burnout research in the social sciences: A critique. *Journal of Social Service Research, 10,* 95–105.

Maslach, C. (2003). Job burnout: New directions in research and intervention. *Current Directions in Psychological Science, 12,* 189–193.

Matthews, H. J. (1927). Special problems of rural social work. *Social Forces, 6*(1), 67–73.

Murphy, P. J., & Angelski, K. (1996). Rural teacher mobility: A report from British Columbia. *Rural Educator, 18*(2), 5–11.

National Health Service Corps. (2010). *About the NHSC.* Retrieved December 28, 2010, from http://nhsc.hrsa.gov/about/

National Rural Social Work Caucus. (2011). *Homepage.* Retrieved July 6, 2011 from http://www.ruralsocialwork.org/

New Freedom Commission on Mental Health. (2003). *Achieving the promise: Transforming mental health care in America.* [DHHS Pub. No. SMA-03-3832]. Rockville, MD: U.S. Department of Health and Human Services.

Popper, F. (1986). The strange case of the contemporary American frontier. *Yale Review, 76,* 101–121.

Poulin, J. E., & Walter, C. A. (1993). Retention plans and job satisfaction of Gerontological social workers. *Journal of Gerontological Social Work, 19,* 99–114.

Prairie Home Productions. (2011). *A prairie home companion with Garrison Keillor.* Retrieved from http://prairiehome.publicradio.org

Ricketts, T. C., (1999). *Rural health in the United States.* New York, NY: Oxford University Press.

Riebschleger, J. (2007). Social workers suggestions for effective rural practice. *Families in Society, 88*(2), 203–213.

Schank, J. A., & Skovholt, T. M. (2006). *Ethical practice in small communities: Challenges and rewards for psychologists.* Washington, DC: American Psychological Association.

Sidell, N. L. (2007). An exploration of nonsexual dual relationships in rural public child welfare settings. *Journal of Public Child Welfare, 1*(4), 91–104.

Soderfeldt, M., Soderfeldt, B., & Warg, L. E. (1995). Burnout in social work. *Social Work, 40*(5), 638–646.

Somers, G. T., Strasser, R., & Jolly, B. (2007). What does it take? The influence of rural upbringing and sense of rural background on medical students' intention to work in a rural environment. *Rural and Remote Health, 7,* 1–11.

Swanson, M. (1972). Professional social work in America. *Agricultural History, 66,* 515–527.

Taylor, S., Mensinga, J., Casey, J., & Caldwell, B. (2008). Implementing and evaluating and alternative model for training field work educators: A pilot study in Central Queensland. *Journal of Practice Teaching and Learning, 8*(1), 51–73.

U.S. Census Bureau (BOC). (2010a). *Census 2000 urban and rural classification.* Retrieved from http://www.census.gov/geo/www/ua/ua_2k.html

U.S. Census Bureau (BOC) (2010b). *Locating urbanized area and urban cluster boundaries.* Retrieved from http://www.census.gov/geo/www/ua/uaucbndy.html

U.S. Department of Agriculture (USDA). (2008). *What is rural?* Retrieved from http://www.nal.usda.gov/ric/ricpubs/what_is_rural.shtml.

Vidich, A. J., & Bensman, J. (1960). *Small town in mass society.* Garden City, NY: Doubleday & Company/Anchor Books.

York, R. O., Denton, R. T., & Moran, J. R. (1989). Rural and urban social work practice: Is there a difference? *Social Casework, 70*(4), 201–209.

9   Rural Settlements: *Rural Social Work at the Forks of Troublesome Creek*

Vanda Galen and Dexter Alexander

This chapter describes the work of two unsung foremothers of social work, the founders of rural settlements that developed simultaneously with the urban settlement programs heralded in social work literature. The researchers examined archives of these exemplary rural settlement programs, reviewed literature related to their educational, cultural, and craft programs, and attended continuing programs at the settlements to reclaim these women as social work pioneers and recognize their contributions to social work.

In 1902 Katherine Pettit and May Stone established Hindman Settlement School at the forks of Troublesome Creek in the coal regions of southeastern Kentucky. Their program was inspired by the settlement house movement, counted in an early census of national and international settlement programs (College Settlement Associations, 1905), and represented in a 1908 gathering of settlement programs at Harvard University. Hindman Settlement School and Pine Mountain Settlement School, founded by Pettit in 1913, were cataloged as two of the three Kentucky independent nonsectarian schools in a 1921 census of 193 Southern Highland schools. (Campbell, 1921). Both institutions still exist to serve rural Appalachia.

The rich history of these programs has been ignored in social work literature. This chapter argues for expanding the history of the settlement movement to include the programs that were developed in rural areas and for celebrating their founders as contributors to the development of social work. The successes and failures of these founders can be instructive for rural social work today. The founding women, as well as their motivations, sacrifices, and accomplishments, should be noted in the history of rural social work. Further research on these successful rural models may lead to helpful lessons for initiating social service and educational programs in underdeveloped, rural and international settings.

Social work histories discuss the importance of the Settlement House movement. Modeled on Toynbee Hall, established in London in 1884, settlement houses became neighborhood centers in impoverished areas, with a particular focus on serving new immigrants. The Neighborhood Guild of New York City was established in 1887. Jane Addams established Hull House in Chicago in 1889, and Lillian Wald established New York's Henry Street Settlement in 1893. Settlement workers lived in the neighborhoods and sought to improve housing, health, and living conditions.

The Settlement Houses provided education, recreation centers, health services, and kindergartens. Immigrants received help to learn English and prepare for citizenship. The settlements sought to provide a neighborhood focal point in a time of rapid change. Neighborhood residents were supported in the transition from their known culture to the new unknown, and efforts were made to preserve the former. Many settlements engaged in social action. Hull House developed surveys of housing and other social conditions in the neighborhood, as a prelude to seeking regulation, enforcement of codes, or new legislation (Jansson, 2009).

Leaders in the settlement movement, like Jane Addams, were usually young, well-off, upper-middle class graduates of the new women's colleges. These young women sought ways to do meaningful work in a society that restricted their access to careers. They expanded their assigned female roles by undertaking the care of others in a broader sense and extending their "housekeeping" duties into "cleaning up" societal problems.

Although any standard social work or social welfare history text includes information on the Settlement House movement, the wide reach of the movement is neglected. Zastrow (2004) is typical of other authors who confine their discussion of the settlement movement to urban areas. "In 1884 Toynbee Hall became the first settlement house in London. Many others were soon formed in larger U.S. cities" (Zastrow, 2004, p. 45). Similarly, Axinn and Stern (2005) report, "Located in large cities, these settlement houses emphasized neighborhood services and community development" (p. 112). DuBois and Miley (2008) include a discussion of Black settlement workers, but still confine the focus to cities. Neither early 1967 nor current 2008 editions of the *Encyclopedia of Social Work* mention the rural programs in the discussion of settlements.

The rural settlements were established for similar reasons to those of urban settlements and arose contemporaneously with the city-based programs, and the Settlement House model was adapted to rural areas. Writing in *The Commons*, Gavit (1899) suggested:

> There is the same occasion (1) to exemplify higher family and intellectual ideals; the same opportunity (2) to unify a community reft with schisms, social, racial, religious; the same crying absence of (3) a force to mediate the advantages of education and world-knowledge to those whose ill- paid labor has placed to their credit against society a large obligation; the same absence to fill (4) of initiative to social action for the betterment of local and general conditions. (p. 5)

At the turn of the 20th century Southern Appalachia, particularly southeast Kentucky, was experiencing rapid change. Industrialization was coming to the mountains, as railroads were entering (or encroaching) to haul away the resources of coal and timber. Like the new immigrants to the cities of New England and the Midwest, the long-term residents of Southern Appalachia were moving from the known to the unknown, as the economy and environment changed around them (see Shockel, 1916 for a contemporary account of the changing conditions).

The Appalachian area and the emerging needs had come to the attention of the broader society in several ways. Local colorists like James Lane Allen (1892) painted romantic versions of the mountaineer, and John Fox, Jr., in *Hell Fer Sartain* (1897) and *The Kentuckians* (1898), was beginning to develop the themes of his later popular novels *The Trail of the Lonesome Pine* (1908) and *Little Shepherd of Kingdom Come* (1903), which contrasted and linked the native Kentucky mountaineer and the cultured Bluegrass gentleman. *The New York Times* reported on lawlessness, inbreeding, feuding, and vigilantism in southeastern Kentucky, with headlines like "Courthouse and Jail Burned," May 29, 1892; "Kentucky Factions at War," June 17, 1885; "Men Athirst for Blood," March 30, 1889; and "Woman Repulses Regulators," March 17, 1897. Sociologists described the area as "a retarded frontier" and justified outside intervention (Vincent, 1898). The area was portrayed as a paradox: it was both uncivilized and the uncorrupted home of "our contemporary ancestors" (Frost, 1899).

According to Eller (2008),

Discovered, or more accurately, created by urban journalists in the years following the Civil War, the idea of Appalachia provided a counterpoint to emerging definitions of progress at the turn of the twentieth century. Those writers
who disliked modernity saw in the region a remnant of frontier life, the reflection of a simpler, less complicated time that ought to be preserved and protected.
Those who found advancement in the growth of material production, consumption, and technology decried what they considered the isolation and back-
wardness of the place and sought to uplift the mountain people through
education and industrialization. (p. 1)

Progressive Era Women Respond to Rural Needs

Choosing education and social settlement work as the path for uplift, Katherine
Pettit, 34, and May Stone, 35, residents of the Bluegrass region of Kentucky,
founded the Hindman Settlement School in the Appalachian Mountains of southeastern Kentucky in 1902. The Settlement was a carefully considered undertaking.
Katherine Pettit had explored southeastern Kentucky on several previous trips.
Stone and Pettit had visited Hull House, Tuskegee Institute, and other institutions
that had adopted the progressive education ideas of John Dewey to study their
programs. The women and four companions had conducted a summer camp in
Hazard, Kentucky, in 1899, and returned for two consecutive summers to host
camps in more remote areas. From their festively decorated tents, they provided
reading materials and taught cooking, sewing, and reading to the residents who
were attracted to their encampment. The last encampment in Sassafras, Kentucky,
lasted 3 months (Stoddart, 1997).

Establishing the camps was not an easy or safe task. It was difficult to reach the
encampment sites. Railroads stopped at Jackson, Kentucky, 40 miles from Hazard.
Wagon travel along creek beds and sometimes through quicksand took the six
women slowly to their destination. A 20-year feud between the French and
Eversole families, which claimed 50 lives and led to a 2-day pitched battle in the
streets of Hazard, had not been long ended (Pettit, 1899).

When Stone and May set off to Hazard, they were responding to an invitation
sent by a Methodist minister to the meeting of the General Federation of Women's
Clubs:

Cannot the State Federation send us a woman, a gentle, womanly woman, a dear old fashioned woman, young or old, who can win woman's true rights in that conquest, that in itself is simply being a woman? What do I want of a woman? I want her a few weeks of the coming summer to assist in the conduct of meetings of wives, mothers, housekeepers, young ladies and little girls. Lectures and lessons in cooking and home-making should be made particularly enthusiastic and then the intellectual and moral features can be made interesting. (quoted in Stoddart, 1997, p. 59)

The women who answered the call went far beyond the minister's description of "dear old fashioned women" and began a process on behalf of mountain women much greater than he envisioned. The camps quickly drew curious onlookers and eager participants.

Stone and Pettit found many compelling needs in the mountain region. Trachoma, a potentially blinding infection called "sore eyes" by the mountaineers, was endemic in the region. Schools met for only a few months each year and teachers were rarely trained. Illiteracy in the encampment counties ranged from 40 to 49% (Ruggles et al., 2010). Sanitation was lacking. Cleanliness was not possible. Ninety percent of the population was afflicted with hookworm (Schockel, 1916).

The women began to plan for a permanent program in the mountains and launched fundraising tours in the Bluegrass and the Northeast to establish their program. In fundraising literature, Pettit described the world of the mountaineer. She echoed the portrayal of the mountaineers as pure Anglo-Saxons, our "contemporary ancestors," left out of the finer elements of the modern culture.

We find they are English, Scotch Irish, French Huguenot, some Welsh and some Scotch. The English and Scotch-Irish predominate. [A line in an earlier draft noting that "There is a good strong strain of German blood" was deleted.] In Kentucky scarcely twenty miles from such thriving towns as Middlesboro, Richmond, or Berea, there are people living who have never seen a town, who have never left the little farms on which they were born, who have never been out of a hollow. ... They go barefoot; they sleep in the same clothes they wear in the day time; the one room of their log cabin is the common bedroom for all the members of the family and any visitors. [Pettit also edited out the next descriptor of shared sleeping quarters for "male and female, old and young, married and single" perhaps as being too negative a representation.] The effect of a century of such living as here indicated has left its injurious impress upon the people of the mountains. (Pettit, 1899)

Pettit commented on the health, nutrition, and behavior of the mountaineer:

The idea which commonly prevails in regard to the fine physical development of the simple dwellers in the hills is indeed a mistake. They are thin and un-healthful in appearance, instead of being the strong vigorous individuals we are taught to believe them; and this physical condition is said to be due to the poor cooking and the excessive use of tobacco. (Pettit, 1899)

The fundraising itinerary emphasized women's colleges, and the plight of women in the mountains was underscored:

It is the deplorable condition of the women that appeals so strongly to me. Their condition is truly wretched. The domestic life of the mountaineer is crude. They know absolutely nothing of decent living. How can they when the women who should be fitted for housekeepers and homemakers are doing the work of the men, who think their duty consists in hunting, fishing, and sitting on the fence talking politics. While the women hurriedly cook their meals and spend the rest of the time in cultivating crops, building fences and milking the cows. Often these women, after a day of toil in the fields…must hunt over the mountain side for the cows; and I have known of them spending several hours at night in such a search. Can you wonder at the depravity of these homes when such a condi-tion for women exists. The men consider labor a disgrace. (Pettit, 1899)

Schockel (1916) later remarked similarly on the status of eastern Kentucky women. "Woman is inferior to man in number and position…Not only is she a household drudge, but a field hand as well.…The Modern Woman Movement has hardly penetrated into the hills, and when it does it will meet orthodox opposition" (Schockel, 1916, p. 128.)

The fundraising appeal ended with a request to contribute to the opening of a settlement program under the sponsorship of the Women's Christian Temperance Union (WCTU).

So the W.C.T.U. seeing the urgent need of regular, systematic and continuous effort along all educational and religious lines propose to start a Christian social settlement. We hope to have a regular school, with kindergarten, normal and industrial departments. We want to have thirty or forty acres of land, have a garden; have trees, have a place where all the neighbors can come and see these things cultivate, where the children can be trained to cultivate bulbs, seeds and plants and to watch these wonderful things in their development. (Pettit, 1899)

The future hopes for the settlement were reemphasized before the request for funding was made:

This will be a land of letters some day. The poverty of the soil will drive the young to the cultivation of their fertile minds as did the stony lands of New England. Schools will flourish here in the future, and their feuds will be written up in the Story Song by the Scotts that shall spring from these highland fastnesses. (Pettit, 1899)

"It will take $3000 to place this work on a sure foundation," Pettit wrote, "and this privilege belongs preeminently to the large hearted men and women whose lives have been lived amid the highest civilization that all the ages have produced" (Pettit, 1899).

In her fundraising efforts, Pettit needed to walk a careful line. She wanted to portray the needs of the region without blaming the mountaineers for their condition or making their problems seem intractable. Contemporary and current readers may object to some elements of her portrayal, and, in later years, Pettit carefully monitored all public writing and even the postcards of settlement workers to be sure nothing injurious to mountain pride would be published.

Pettit and Stone's fundraising was successful, as was the call for teachers and settlement workers. Women from the eastern colleges came into the mountains to pursue education and settlement work.

The women who came to work and teach at institutions like Hindman...were mostly young, educated females with a sense of mission and an optimistic commitment to the improvement of the region. They viewed Appalachia as a remote, almost foreign land, and they saw their experiences in the rugged hinterland as a great adventure, perhaps *the* most important adventure of their lives. (Forderhase, 1987, p. 244)

According to the Settlement's promotional literature, the location of a permanent facility in Hindman was prompted by the entreaties of 80-year-old Sol Everidge, who reportedly walked 22 miles barefooted into the summer camps to plead for the establishment of a school where his "greats and grands" could be educated. Although there is obvious myth-making about "Uncle Sol," whose portrait is now displayed in the main Settlement building, there were several reasons to locate at Hindman. The site had the advantages of being in the county seat of the recently created Knott County, on a hillside above Troublesome Creek. Although the location was even more remote and difficult to reach than Hazard, these factors appealed to Pettit, who recognized the cultural changes that would accompany the roads and railroads that were being built farther into the mountains.

Education was the major emphasis of the Settlement School, but the programs had a clear connection to the settlement movement and the founders described their work as settlement work. In addition to the visit to Hull House, they had worked at Louisville's Neighborhood house, an urban settlement, to gain experience. The founders were connected to one of the key figures at Hull House, Sophonisba Breckinridge, a Lexington native and, like Stone, a Wellesley alumna. Breckinridge, holding a master's degree, a doctoral degree, and a law degree, held the position of dean at the Chicago School of Civics and Philanthropy from 1907 to 1920. When the school was incorporated into the University of Chicago in 1920 as the Graduate School of Social Service Administration, Breckinridge was a professor and dean of Social Service Students. Breckinridge's sister, Curry Breckinridge, accompanied the founders to Hindman. Their brother, Desha Breckinridge, owner of the major newspaper of the Bluegrass region, publicized their efforts, and their sister-in-law was developing another rural settlement at the same time.

The Hindman Settlement School opened in 1902 with 192 students. The programs that developed at Hindman followed those at Hull House. Both had kindergartens, clubs for youth and adults, classes in proper diet, drama and singing groups, and courses in cooking, dressmaking, child care, and manual arts. "Where Hindman and Hull House diverged rested more on the difference between urban and rural needs than on any difference in philosophy" (Stoddart, 1997, p. 42)

By 1916

there were fourteen buildings, including a powerhouse and a hospital, and three hundred students, one hundred of whom boarded. By 1927, the plant comprised 345 acres of land and twenty buildings, including dormitories and offices, a workshop, a hospital, a twenty-eight room settlement house, a library, and a powerhouse that supplied electricity for both the school and the town of Hindman using coal from a mine located on school property. The institution's annual budget was nearly seventy thousand dollars, and its net worth was more than double that amount. (Whisnant, 1983, p. 29)

The medical services and outreach from the school had reduced trachoma, which had blinded a considerable portion of the population (Stucky, 1913). With foresight, the founders had established an endowment for the school in 1906.

The mission of the school was to provide an educational opportunity for the youth of the mountains and keep them mindful of their heritage (Stoddart, 2002). The founders knew the transformative effects of education but hoped to educate the students back to their homes not away from the region. In response to questions regarding their purposes for coming into the mountains, Pettit replied that they hoped to "learn all we can and teach all we can" (Whisnant, 1983). Two areas of mountain culture, music and crafts, were particularly intriguing to Pettit. On her first trip for the encampment at Hazard, she heard lumbermen singing ballads. She began transcribing these ballads, and Hindman Settlement School became a center for "songcatchers" who came to study mountain music (Campbell & Sharp, 1917; Pettit, 1907; Wyman & Brockway, 1916). Some of the ballads had Elizabethan roots. Others had local origins. The first ballad that captured Pettit's attention was "Barbara Allen," the tale of a hard-hearted woman who would not visit the swain who was dying for love of her. Barbara soon repented and took to her own death bed. Many versions exist. Pettit transcribed this last verse:

Out of his grave, there grew a rose
Out of hers a brier;
They lapped and tied in a true love-knot,
A rose around the brier. ("Camp Industrial at Hindman, Knott County Kentucky," 1900)

Olive Dame Campbell was similarly impressed by this ballad, when she heard it sung several years later by a Hindman student (Campbell & Sharp, 1917).

The Settlement also promoted the basketry and weaving of the mountain women. Pettit and Stone found commercial outlets for the handiwork, and the sale of these items augmented meager household budgets. Craft industries provided some support to the settlement. Whereas Pettit hoped to retain the purity of the mountain arts, the women artisans were not willing to continue the laborious process of making homemade dyes from madder root and indigo plants when manufactured dyes were easily obtained (Baugh, 2005; Kahn, 2003).

Legacy of the Hindman Settlement School

The Hindman Settlement School has continued for 109 years. The Settlement had a budget of $1,273,129 for 2009–2010. There were 18 employees, including the director, the development officer, cultural workers, teachers, and campus staff. An endowment provided nearly $500 thousand, program revenue was $269,700, and donations filled the rest of the budget. The Daughters of the American Revolution, which has supported the Settlement since 1921, contributed 10% of the donations (Hindman Settlement School [HSS], 2009a). Programs have changed over the years, but the mission still reflects its founders' goals: "to provide education and service opportunities for people of the mountains, while keeping them mindful of their heritage" (HSS, 2009b). Programs developed at the Settlement moved to the public school system, as the system matured and strengthened. Most recently, the Settlement moved its innovative dyslexia program into the school system, supporting the program through finances and training. The Settlement pays the salary of a cultural educator who provides enrichment courses in traditional music, dance, and art to public school students and community residents.

The Settlement maintains the Marie Stewart Craft Store, selling products for local artisans. The campus facilities are available for community meetings and regional conferences. Two key programs, Family Folk Week and The Writers Workshop, continue the cultural preservation work of the founders.

Key Cultural Programs at Hindman Settlement School

Family Folk Week

A legacy of the Settlement is Family Folk Week, which celebrated its 34th year in 2011. "Family" receives as much emphasis as "Folk" in this event, with some families attending every year. The intergenerational program has something to offer all age groups. One young man has celebrated all of his 20 birthdays at Folk Week.

Participants stay on the Settlement campus. Their day starts with an ample breakfast, served in the dining room of the May Stone building. Morning singing follows, led by a different staff member or group each day. Traditional folk songs, rounds, and hymns are featured. After singing, children are dismissed to activities. Adults may choose from Appalachian seminars or adult folk dance classes. After lunch, a variety of classes is offered. Crafts may be pursued through quilting, doll making (corn shuck or cloth), basket weaving, wood carving, or chair making. Traditional mountain musical instruments can be studied: guitar, banjo, harmonica, fiddle, bass fiddle, mandolin, or the lap or mountain dulcimer at beginning, intermediate, or advanced levels. Several levels of clogging classes are available. Shape note singing, based on the Sacred Harp hymnals, has been offered for several years. Although traditional mountain music and crafts are the emphasis of the school, the programs are not stagnant. Classes have been added in blues guitar and harmonica.

The topics of Appalachian seminars vary. Recent classes have addressed the musical careers of traditional performers, Appalachian literature, and environmental concerns, such as Mountain Top Removal. Each day ends with a musical performance by staff members, culminating with an evening of squares, reels, sets, waltzes, and contra dances.

Music is the centerpiece of Folk Week activities. Participants practice under campus trees, and the porch of the May Stone building fills with informal jam sessions. Playing continues late into night in the wood shop, fortuitously located off official campus property, so the prohibitions against alcohol consumption on the campus can be skirted.

Traditional songs are preserved through Folk Week, and the creativity and culture of the mountain musicians is respected. A strong "ethic of attribution" is evident. Performers do not claim the songs as their own, but proclaim the history of the music played. Each rendition is usually preceded with a story of where the song was first heard, who was performing it, and any variations that have been made in the original version.

In 2010 Jean Ritchie, 86—singer, composer, dulcimer player, and acknowledged matriarch of Folk Week—missed her first Folk Week, due to a stroke. Ms. Ritchie traditionally opened the group singing, performed in midweek, and taught dulcimer for several years. She was confined to a hospital on Long Island, New York, where she has made her home for over 60 years. Folk Week at Hindman, however, provided a second home. Fittingly, Ritchie is a descendant of "Uncle Sol," the legendary patriarch who sought education for his "greats and grands" at the Settlement. She trained as a social worker and began her career at the Henry Street Settlement. Many staff members are drawn from the Appalachian area or from Kentucky's universities, where they have fashioned academic careers connected to mountain heritage, but a popular couple from the Northeast are performers and instructors, having found an affinity for the music of Appalachia.

Kentucky has the largest representation of participants, but attendees in 2010 came from Maine, Minnesota, Texas, Missouri, North Carolina, Wisconsin, and Alabama. Most are from university towns, where many participants are employed. Although education inevitably altered students and may have led them away from their birthplace, the Settlement School has, perhaps, succeeded in educating "back to their homes," by providing an idealized home place that participants may have never had in fact, but to which they have aspired.

Appalachian Writers Workshop

Another continuing program of the Hindman Settlement School, the Appalachian Writers Workshop, is also described by participants as a homecoming (Lyon, Miller, & Gurney, 1993). Founded by poet and writer Albert Stewart (the youngest boarder ever at Hindman, who came to the school in 1919, when he was 5 years old), the Writers Workshop is in its 33rd year. The workshop brings together experienced authors and aspiring writers. In the dedication of *Clay's Quilt*, emerging Appalachian author Silas House acknowledges the Hindman Writer's Workshop for encouraging his talents (House, 2005).

The Writer's Workshop exerts some power, albeit informally, over whose work may be considered Appalachian and which writers benefit from the networking opportunities and critiques available at the workshop. In the choice of instructors and the competitive review of manuscripts, the workshop continues to define and redefine representations of Appalachian culture.

The workshop builds on a literary tradition at Hindman. Ann Cobb, one of the first teachers to come to the school was a poet. Lucy Furman, who worked and taught at the Settlement School from 1907 to 1927, described in her obituary as a social worker, publicized the school through her novels, *Mothering on Perilous* (1913), *Sight to the Blind* (1914), *The Quare Women* (1923), *The Glass Window* (1925), and the *The Lonesome Road* (1927). James Still (*River of Earth*, 1940) was a writer in residence and is buried at the Settlement School. A workshop participant wrote,

> The culture of the Appalachian Writers Workshop is at once thoroughly Appalachian and deeply literary. There is probably more respect for literature as a serious human endeavor here than at any other institution I've known. I think the reason is that Appalachians know that reading and storytelling and writing

and speaking are all about the essential, deep, intimate connection created by human voices calling to one another across space and time through the spoken and written word. (Kendrick & Lyon, 2002, p. 4)

Although the Settlement School has been criticized for not undertaking advocacy efforts (Whisnant, 1983), the Writer's Workshop has facilitated social action. In recent years an airplane trip was arranged for writers to view the effects of mountain top removal and write their reactions. *Something's Rising* (House & Howard, 2009) is a collection of oral histories and observations of writers and environmental activists protesting this destruction of the land and culture. A *Something's Rising* jacket blurb, written by Studs Terkel shortly before his death, says,

This revelatory work is a challenging tocsin shouting out the effects of poverty and exploitation of the Appalachian people by strip miners and other corporate pirates. I am reminded of the fighting spirit of the Eastern Kentuckians when I visited these embattled pioneers in their hills and hollers. Here, Jean Ritchie and others speak out in the fighting tradition of the 1930s and 1960s. It is oral history at its best. (House & Howard, 2000)

By providing a place for "gathering at the forks" (a reference to the location on Troublesome Creek) and a focal point for Appalachian and regional concerns, the Settlement has facilitated the social action efforts of its participants and visitors. It has also served to continue to define Appalachian culture by the recognition and support provided to writers who are chosen to attend.

Pine Mountain Settlement School: 1913–Present

Katherine Pettit left Hindman in 1913. Along with Ethel DeLong, she founded the Pine Mountain Settlement School in a remote section of Harlan County, Kentucky, some 40 miles from Hindman. Pine Mountain followed a similar history to Hindman, although the school was operated as a private, rather than a public, school. Like Hindman, Pine Mountain emphasized preservation of mountain music and crafts. The School also developed service programs and medical clinics. Its buildings, designed by architect Mary Rockwell Hook, are now on the National Historic Register.

The Pine Mountain Settlement School has continued for 97 years. The Settlement had a budget of $941,304 for 2008–2009. There were 27 employees, including the director, assistant director, program directors and instructors, and campus staff. According to information filed with the Internal Revenue Service, endowment funds and an investment portfolio provided nearly $500 thousand, program revenue was $309,511, and donations and sales filled out the rest of the budget. The Alpha Sigma Tau National Foundation has supported Pine Mountain Settlement School since 1945. In recent years the Foundation has provided funds for building expansion and renovation, acquisition of a 15 passenger vans, and, most recently, established an endowment that provides funds for the Settlement School's Intervention Program, which pays the costs of two teachers to give remedial math and reading instruction to elementary students. Other major donors and grantors include the Berea College Appalachian Fund and the AmeriCorps*VISTA program (Pine Mountain News, 2010). Campus facilities are available for community meetings and regional conferences and workshops.

Pine Mountain Settlement closed its schools in 1972 and shifted its focus to the solution of other problems in Kentucky's southeastern mountain region. Today, Pine Mountain Settlement "provides instruction in environmental education, Appalachian culture, and crafts to students and adults."(Pine Mountain Settlement School, 2010)

The Settlement School's environmental mission has four goals:

- To present environmental education as an integral part of all subjects

- To provide an accurate interpretation of the natural environment and mountain culture through hands-on experiences and use of historical materials

- To offer opportunities to study and understand the special nature of the Appalachian region

- To promote responsible stewardship of natural lands and waterways. (Pine Mountain Settlement School, 2010)

The school's nearly 800-acre campus includes the 348 acre James E. Bickford State Nature Preserve. The school's natural environment classes are articulated with the Kentucky Department of Education's Core Content areas and include forest and stream ecology; tree and wildflower identification; edible and medicinal plants; and observation and classification of mammals, amphibians, and reptiles. Public and private schools sponsor their students for environmental education at Pine Mountain. Program participants can apply their newly acquired knowledge of Pine Mountain's geology, flora, and fauna during a hike to the summit of Pine Mountain, visit two small sandstone caves on Pine Mountain's summit, and learn how to measure a tree. The environmental curriculum includes sustainability classes and classes about the region's cultural environment. The cultural environment curriculum includes an examination of the history of the region's Native Americans and the early settlers. Traditional mountain crafts, country folk dances, and Appalachian region music and storytelling complete the environmental curriculum.

The school's community outreach includes serving as an educational and social center. The Pine Mountain Settlement School offers children's activities, programs for adults, and family-oriented social events. The school sponsors an intervention program in local schools to help children meet expected achievement levels in reading and math.

The Settlement School offers internship opportunities in environmental education and in its sustainability initiative. AmeriCorps*VISTA positions are also available on the school's campus.

The Pine Mountain Settlement School's mission changed with the changing social and economic needs of its service region. The constant factor that ties today's Pine Mountain Settlement School together with its years as a boarding and day school, agricultural and home economics demonstration project, and its service as a community center is the school's determination to continue improving the rural southern highlander's quality of life (PMSS, 2010).

Council of the Southern Mountains, Inc.

In addition to the enduring institutions, Stone and Pettit were part of establishing and maintaining the Conference of Southern Mountain Workers. This organization of mountain workers, renamed the Council of Southern Mountain Workers in 1944 and the Council of the Southern Mountains in 1954, continued for 77 years. In 1912, John C. Campbell, a researcher of the southern mountain social and economic conditions and the newly appointed director of the Southern Highland Division of the Russell Sage Foundation, issued a call to the southern highlands social workers to meet in Atlanta to discuss the formation of an organization that would provide "frequent conference and interchange of ideas...between those outside the mountains who are attempting a new line of rural work...and those within the mountains who are striving to adapt their work to meet local needs" (Campbell,

1969). The Hindman Settlement School sent its principal to the first organizational meeting. Katherine Pettit, already at Pine Mountain, was one of two women named to the executive committee at the inaugural 1913 conference (Council of the Southern Mountains Records, 1912–1917). By 1915 and the Council's third annual conference, both May Stone and Katherine Pettit were members of the executive committee (Council of the Southern Mountains Records, 1912–1917). The conference issued a report on mountain workers' perceptions about the needs of the region and the desired qualifications for workers. Pettit and Stone were thanked for their contributions (Blackwell, 1998, p. 185). Concerning the qualifications needed for mountain workers, there were varied responses. One writer remarked that "the person who works among the mountaineers must possess the essential qualities of a social worker anywhere," including flexibility, understanding, "intelligent sympathy" for mountain people, thrift, diligence, patience, a sense of humor, and physical strength" (Blackwell 1998, p. 186).

Olive Dame Campbell, John Campbell's widow and his successor as executive secretary for the Council of the Southern Mountains, wrote a retrospective of the agency's first 16 years in the Council's journal, *Mountain Life and Work*. At the first meeting, Campbell noted, the conferees "met as strangers. ...We had no conception of the similarity of many of our problems nor the extent of such problems" (Campbell, 1928). Few realized they were dealing with "acute rural situations" that could be found either inside or outside the southern highlands (Campbell, 1928, p. 1–4).

The Conference of Southern Mountain Workers made possible the identification and communication of existing and new solutions to common problems. Through this organization, these pioneering women contributed not only to the communities of Hindman and Pine Mountain, but also to building community among mountain social workers.

Conclusion

Pettit and Stone deserve recognition as founding mothers of rural social work. The programs they developed should be acknowledged as exemplars of rural development work. Their ties to the settlement movement were strong and indisputable. In 1975, Elizabeth Watts, who came to Hindman Settlement School in 1909 and served in various capacities ranging from teacher, principal, assistant director, and director until her retirement in 1956, reflected on the connections to the urban settlement movement:

I do not know whether they (Stone and Pettit) went together or separately, but both of them visited Hull House and talked over their plans with Jane Addams who was very much interested in their project. She agreed with them that a boarding and day school, where the regular public school courses were taught, would be greatly enriched by the same sort of classes and club work involving the people of the community that were carried on at Hull House.

I do not know when Miss Pettit and Miss Stone first became familiar with the Henry Street Settlement, but I do know they stayed there in the very early days of the work at Hindman while they were raising money for the Settlement School at Hindman. The relation with them, as well as Hull House, was very cooperative and cordial. That friendly relationship continued at least as long as Jane Addams lived at Hull House, and equally long at Henry Street, for I had the pleasure of staying in both Settlement Houses. Another Hindman staff member and I had the honor of being Jane Addams' guests for several days and had an opportunity to talk with her and feel the charm of the place and its importance in the community. (Bertrand, 1975, pp. 68–69)

Pettit and Stone transplanted the Settlement House model into one of the most needy and isolated rural areas. Although urban areas held challenges, rural Appalachia presented many obstacles to social service work. Pettit and Stone and the women who joined them left comfortable homes to accept the risks of mountain life at the turn of the 20th century. They endured fleas, lice, typhoid, jolt wagons, irascible mules, gunfire, and sporadic mail service to come to an area where they were clearly the "furrinn," "fotched-on," "quare wimmen."

Although they may have had initial misconceptions, they soon recognized the importance of valuing the mountain culture. They did not impose, but rather responded to the invitation and the investment of the local people in building settlement institutions. They proved able administrators and fund raisers; they used the popular media to their advantage; and they kept their commitment to the people's cause. May Stone was the director at Hindman until 1946. Katherine Pettit remained at Pine Mountain until her retirement in 1930.

These founders and the women who joined them left a wealth of historical materials: reports, records, letters, and diaries. Original materials are available at Hindman Settlement School. Berea College houses copies of the Hindman materials and maintains an archive of similar materials from other southern settlements. The materials have informed several dissertations focusing on education, crafts, and music. The journal records of the camps have been published as the *Quare Women's Journals* (Stoddart, 1997), and Stoddart (2002), a historian, Hindman Settlement School board member, and daughter and niece of Settlement School graduates, has published a history. Whisnant (1983) wrote chapters on Hindman Settlement and Pine Mountain Settlement Schools, setting off debates whether the settlement workers had intruded and altered the mountain culture (Robie, 1991; Deaton, 1991). Whisnant (1983), ironically, simultaneously faults Pettit and Stone for intervening in the culture and for failing to stop the industrialization that would further alter the mountain existence.

Unfortunately, the social work profession and, particularly, rural social work has neglected this history. Perhaps this silence in social work literature is because Pine Mountain and Hindman were both settlements and schools. This combination was a strength for the programs. The settlements modeled integrated services, combining community development with education (Jurgens & West, 1996). The settlement programs expanded the infrastructure of the community. They were involved in building roads and acquiring electricity. Their fireside industry programs provided employment and income. Agricultural extension programs trained farmers in new cultivation techniques and land preservation. Recreational facilities and activities contributed to the community's social structure.

The lessons that Pettit and Stone taught and learned could still inform rural workers who enter areas in transition. Their history would be particularly relevant for social workers in developing regions like Central America, where modern pressures are impacting more traditional societies. Pettit and Stone's experiences attest to the multiple roles required of rural workers and the need for generalist preparation. Alternately, they were teachers, group leaders, community organizers, fund raisers, and publicists. They "followed the demands of the client task" from building fences to preparing a dead toddler for burial, while comforting the grieving mother (Stoddart, 1997).

Pettit and Stone were skilled administrators, succeeding where others failed. Their techniques for recruiting and training staff, working with the local community, developing indigenous leaders, and managing public relations could add valuable insight for community workers. They blazed a trail for other service workers who came into the mountains. Similar programs developed in the area, including the Caney Creek Community Center, established in 1915 by a Radcliffe graduate, which continues today as Alice Lloyd College. Pettit and Stone also developed the human capital of the region, where many of their graduates returned after completing professional programs. Lula Hale, a graduate of Hindman, established The Homeplace Settlement in an adjoining county.

These Settlement Schools did not pursue social reform the same way that some urban settlements did. Their programs did, however, help foster pride in the mountain culture and build a common identity among individualistic mountaineers, prerequisites for social action.

Pettit's and Stone's careers can also shed light on the roles of women at the turn of the 20th century. They were able to expand the sphere of women's work; they took on the manual labor, as well as the intellectual labor, of building their institutions. Their relationships with mountain women could suggest ways to negotiate the issues and tensions facing the predominantly female social work profession as it relates to a predominantly female clientele.

There were class differences between the founders and many in the mountain community, and the founders bridged the gaps. The ways they built a sense of community could also inform the social work profession. In many aspects, the founders were "ahead of their time." Pettit, particularly, might be studied as an early ecofeminist, concerned with preserving and protecting the natural environment.

The early organizers of the Hindman and, later, Pine Mountain Settlement Schools were not perfect. An examination of their work reveals missteps and mistakes, but they remained committed to their goals to "learn all we can and teach all we can" (Whisnant, 1983). They may still teach about the importance of relations, resources, and resiliency in rural social work.

Pettit and Stone succeeded in the goal to educate the population "'back to their homes,'" by developing enduring institutions that serve as a focal point for Appalachian culture. Perhaps the best metaphor for their work is the Barbara Allen ballad that Katherine Pettit heard during that first night of travel to the initial encampment: Although briars may be found intertwined with the roses, they support the beauty of the flowers.

References

Allen, J. L. (1892). *The blue-grass region of Kentucky and other Kentucky articles.* New York, NY: Harper & Row.

Axinn. J., & Stern, M. J. (2005). *Social welfare: A history of the American response to need,* 6th ed. Boston, MA: Pearson.

Baugh, C. T. (2005). *To teach and to learn: Settlement and missionary school fireside industry programs in eastern Kentucky, 1900–1930* (Doctoral dissertation). Miami University, Miami, FL.

Bertrand, J. (1975). *The Appalachian settlement schools: The rural response to an urban concept* (Master's thesis). Bryn Mawr College, Bryn Mawr, PA.

Blackwell, D. L. (1998). *The ability "to do much larger work:" Gender and reform in Appalachia. 1890–1935* (Doctoral dissertation). University of Kentucky, Lexington.

Camp Industrial at Hindman, Knott County, Kentucky (1900). Hindman Settlement School Records, 1899–1979, Hindman, KY.

Campbell, J. C. (1969). *The Southern highlander & his homeland.* Lexington, KY: University Press of Kentucky.

Campbell, O. D. (1921). *Southern highland schools maintained by denominational and independent agencies.* New York, NY: Russell Sage.

Campbell, O. D. (1928). Editorial. *Mountain life and work, 4*(2), 1–4.

Campbell, O. D., & Sharp, C. (1917). *English folk songs from the Southern Appalachians.* New York, NY: Knickerbocker Press.

Chambers, V. A. (1970). *Music in four Kentucky mountain settlement schools.* (Doctoral dissertation). University of Michigan, Ann Arbor.

College Settlements Association. (1905). *Bibliography of settlements,* 5th ed. Chicago, IL: Blakely Press.

Council of the Southern Mountains Records. (1912–1917). *The Council of Southern Mountains Records.* Southern Appalachian Archives, Berea College Special Collections and Archives.

Deaton, J. H., Flannery-Dess, V. S., & Hobgood, J. B. (1991). Those settlement schools: Harmful or benign? Three responses to Robie. *Appalachian Heritage, 19*(3), 45–52.

DuBois, B. L., & Miley, K. K. (2008). *Social work: An empowering profession.* Boston: Pearson.

Eller, R. D. (2008). *Uneven ground: Appalachia since 1945.* Lexington, KY: University of Kentucky Press.

Forderhase, N. K. (1987). Eve returns to the garden: Women reformers in Appalachia in the early twentieth century. *Register of the Kentucky Historical Society, 85,* 237–261.

Fox, J. (1897). *Hell fer sartain: And other stories.* New York, NY: Harper.

Fox, J. (1903). *The little shepherd of kingdom come.* New York, NY: Grosset & Dunlap.

Fox, J., & Smedley, W. T. (1898). *The Kentuckians.* New York, NY: Harper & Brothers.

Fox, J., & Yohn, F. C. (1908). *The trail of the lonesome pine.* New York, NY: Charles Scribner's Sons.

Frost, W. G. (1899). Our contemporary ancestors in the Southern mountains. *Atlantic Monthly, 83,* 311–319.

Furman, L. (1913). *Mothering on Perilous.* New York, NY: Macmillan.

Furman, L. (1914). *Sight to the blind.* New York, NY: Macmillan.

Furman, L. (1923). *The quare women.* New York, NY: Macmillan.

Furman, L. S. (1925). *The glass window: A story of the quare women.* Boston, MA: Little, Brown.

Furman, L. S. (1927). *The lonesome road.* Boston, MA: Little, Brown.

Gavit, J. P. (1899, May). Rural social settlements. *The Commons,* 5–6.

Hindman Settlement School (HSS). (2009a). Donor report. Hindman, KY: Hindman Settlement School.

House, S. (2001). *Clay's quilt.* New York, NY: Ballantine Books.

House, S., & Howard, J. (2009). *Something's rising: Appalachians fighting mountaintop removal.* Lexington, KY: University of Kentucky Press.

Jansson, B. (2009). *The reluctant welfare state.* Belmont, CA: Brooks/Cole.

Jurgens, E., & West, R. (1996). *Southern Appalachian settlement schools as early initiators of integrated services.* Paper presented at the Annual Conference of the Mid-South Educational Research Association, Tuscaloosa, AL. Retrieved from the ERIC database. (ED404097)

Kahn, P. H. (2003). *How the social reform movement impacted handiwork at Hindman Settlement School in Hindman, Kentucky, during 1902–1920.* [Unpublished doctoral dissertation]. Ohio State University, Columbus, OH.

Kendrick, L., & Lyon, G. E. (2002). *Crossing Troublesome: Twenty-five years of the Appalachian Writers Workshop.* Nicholasville, KY: Wind Publications.

Lyon, G. E., Miller, J. W., & Gurney, N. (Eds.). (1993). *A gathering at the forks: Fifteen years of the Hindman Settlement School Appalachian Writers Workshop.* Wise, VA: Vision Books.

Pettit, K. (1899). *Kentucky mountain folk.* [Unpublished typescript]. Hindman Settlement School Archives, Hindman, KY.

Pettit, K. (1907). Ballads and rhymes of the Kentucky mountains. *Journal of American Folklore, 20,* 251–276.

Pine Mountain News. (2010). Environmental education. Retrieved from http://www.pinemountainsettlementschool.com/uploads/notes/20100804149905.pdf

Pine Mountain Settlement School (PMSS). (2010). *Pine Mountain Settlement School.* Retrieved from http://www.pinemountainsettlementschool.com/

Robie, H. (1991). Resolved: That on balance the settlement schools were harmful to the culture of the Southern mountains. *Appalachian Heritage, 19*(1), 6–10.

Ruggles, S., Alexander, J. T., Genadek, K., Goeken, R., Schroeder, M. B., & Sobek, M. (2010). *Integrated Public Use Microdata Series: Version 5.0*. [Machine-readable database]. University of Minnesota, Minneapolis, MN.

Schockel, B. H. (1916). Changing conditions in the Kentucky mountains. *Scientific Monthly, 3*, 105–113.

Still, J. (1940). *River of earth*. New York, NY: Viking Press.

Stoddart, J. (Ed.). (1997). *The quare women's journals: May Stone and Katherine Pettit's summers in the Kentucky mountains and the founding of the Hindman Settlement School*. Ashland, KY: Jesse Stuart Foundation Press.

Stoddart, J. (2002). *Challenge and change in Appalachia: The story of the Hindman Settlement School*. Lexington, KY: University of Kentucky Press.

Stucky, J. A. (1913). Trachoma among the natives of the mountains of Eastern Kentucky. *Journal of the American Medical Association, 61*, 1116–1124.

Vincent, G. (1898). A retarded frontier. *American Journal of Sociology, 4*, 1–20.

Whisnant, D. (1983). *All that is native and fine: The politics of culture in an American region*. Chapel Hill, NC: University of North Carolina Press.

Woods, R. A., & Kennedy, A. (Eds.). (1911). *Handbook of settlements*. New York, NY: Russell Sage Foundation.

Wyman, L., & Brockway, H. (1916). *Lonesome tunes: Folk songs from the Kentucky mountains*. New York, NY: H.W. Gray.

Zastrow, C. (2004). *Introduction to social work and social welfare*. Belmont, CA: Brooks/Cole.

PART II

Social Work with Special Rural Populations

The second part of this book deals with special rural populations, a persistent subject in rural social work literature. Those who study or practice social work in rural communities have long known that rural populations are, in some ways, different from their urban and metropolitan counterparts. As mentioned in Chapter 1, the 1960s study about "the people left behind" highlighted some of the differences between rural and urban residents. Some of those "left behind" were essentially people who remained rural residents after the sweeping rural-to-urban migration that accompanied World War II and the years that followed. A special kind of migration, that began even earlier, was the movement of rural African American people from the small towns of the South to the urban North, which some call the largest single population dislocation in history. That migration is chronicled in Isabel Wilkerson's 2010 book, *The Warmth of Other Suns: The Epic Story of America's Great Migration*.

Some rural residents are disadvantaged and thus of special interest to social workers. They include older adults; marginally employed or unemployed members of minority groups, such as the remaining African American rural population; Latinos; Native Americans and Alaska Natives; people with disabilities; and children.

Of course, not all rural residents are disadvantaged. Small town America has a share of America's wealthiest people, especially those who own large agriculture and mineral extraction or mining enterprises, as well as land owners. Small town bankers and business people may also be relatively well-off financially, as is also mentioned in Chapter 1. The resurgence of American agriculture has changed the nature of rural employment and income.

In Chapter 10 Suzanne Pritzker and Aaron Metzger conceptualize the preparation of youth in rural communities to participate in civic activities.

Larry Kreuger provides Chapter 11, a discussion of working with children in rural areas after natural disasters. This is an update from the previous edition of this book.

Prisoners and correctional facilities are an important part of the landscape in many rural communities. Historically, states, as well as the U.S. government, have often located their corrections institutions far from metropolitan centers. Prisoners may be from rural communities, especially with the advent of rural substance abuse crimes and production of drugs such as methamphetamines, and may seek to reenter such communities after their prison sentences are completed. Chapter 12, coauthored by Paul Duong Tran, Abigail Kristen Nelson, and Heather Ann Dodson, deals with community reentry issues posed for this special population.

Although American Indians are increasingly an urban and metropolitan population in the United States, many continue living in rural areas both on reservations and in small nonreservation communities. Pat Conway, Dolores S. BigFoot, and Elana Premack Sandler write about resiliency and behavioral health challenges among American Indians and Alaska Natives in rural communities in Chapter 13.

Rural America also has a large religious involvement—rural Christian churches, both Protestant and Roman Catholic, are often the most active rural community institutions. And some special rural populations, such as the Amish, are distinctive groups. Social work and social services for the Amish are discussed in Gretchen Waltman's Chapter 14.

Shawn King's Chapter 15 is about the rural gay, lesbian, bisexual, and transgender community, a new subject for this book.

10 Facilitating Civic Engagement Among Rural Youth: *A Role for Social Workers*

SUZANNE PRITZKER AND AARON METZGER

Civic engagement commonly refers to individuals' involvement and connections with their local communities and with the broader society at large. It is defined by community-focused helping behaviors, organized prosocial activities, involvement in the social or political sphere, and related knowledge, skills, attitudes, and beliefs (McBride, 2008; McBride, Sherraden, & Pritzker, 2006; Sherrod, Torney-Purta, & Flanagan, 2010). In terms of knowledge and skills, civic engagement may entail familiarity with local organizations or the ability to identify local community and political leaders. Attitudes indicative of civic engagement might include efficacy, the belief that one can make a difference through his or her actions, or some degree of trust in local organizations or officials. Behaviors related to community involvement and public benefit are wide-ranging, including providing informal help to neighbors, volunteering, donating funds or goods to charitable organizations, communicating with public officials, and voting in local, state, or national elections.

Research has focused on the civic activities and civic development of youth, in part, because identity development, including the development of a civic identity, is a key task of early and middle adolescence (Erikson, 1968; Sherrod, 2006; Youniss & Yates, 1997). How youth connect with their communities can have both long-lasting effects on how they understand and act relative to the broader society (Flanagan, 2003; Youniss, McLellan, & Yates, 1997) and short-term effects, including reductions in problem behavior and illicit substance use (Duncan, Duncan, Strycker, & Chaumeton, 2002; Eccles, Barber, Stone, & Hunt, 2003).

However, those who are socially or economically disadvantaged and those who lack time, civic resources, such as civic skills or access to civic opportunities, or money are particularly unlikely to participate in civic affairs (Atkins & Hart, 2003; Verba, Schlozman, & Brady, 1995), leaving them outside the sphere of civic influence and potentially exacerbating the experiences and effects of disadvantage. Research has consistently found strong associations between adolescent volunteering and civic activity and the economic status of the neighborhoods in which they reside (Verba et al., 1995). Adolescents from higher socioeconomic status families tend to be more involved civically (Hart, Atkins, & Ford, 1998), including volunteering and club membership. Low levels of civic participation among disadvantaged populations may result in the "unequal engagement of minority groups with misunderstood political needs, or worse, silenced political voices" (Schur, Shields, & Schriner, 2003, p. 120). Unequal civic participation raises significant social justice concerns about whose voices, interests, and needs are heard by people in power (Levinson, 2010).

Research also suggests that where children and adolescents live may substantially affect how they connect with and become involved with their communities (Ginsberg, 2005; Lay, 2003, 2006). Local civic and community institutions exist within a specific geographic and demographic context, and these contextual elements may serve to either facilitate or inhibit youth involvement (Levinson, 2010). Although civic activity can be national or even global in nature, a large percentage of youth civic activity takes place close to home, through local community organizations. Constraints that some rural communities face, such as high unemployment, low educational attainment, poverty, and the longer distance and time needed to travel to connect with community organizations or institutions, may limit civic engagement among youth in rural areas. For rural youth, however, the character of social relations and social interactions may make rural areas the "best environments for political [and presumably civic] learning" (Lay, 2006), in ways that differ substantially from urban and suburban areas (Elder & Conger, 2000), shaping the civic and political identity of rural youth in a distinctly rural manner.

Social workers have an important role to play in helping facilitate rural youth civic development. Social workers are uniquely situated to serve as a bridge between rural youth and civic opportunities, due to their front-line experience and broad awareness of community resources. The following section outlines why developing civic engagement is integral to the social work profession. Literature is then presented on the current state of knowledge about rural youth civic engage-ment, including facilitators and challenges to engagement. A brief case study of rural youth engagement and examination of the civic behaviors of youth in a rural Appalachian town with little agricultural activity are also discussed. Finally, the chapter concludes with an overview of program models that social workers can implement to facilitate civic development among youth in rural areas.

Social Work and Civic Engagement

"A historic and defining feature of social work is the profession's focus on well-being in a social context and the well-being of society" (National Association of Social Workers [NASW], 1999).

With regard to young people, social workers often focus on their care, whereas it is much less common to focus on empowering youth to connect with and serve their community (Checkoway & Gutiérrez, 2006). Yet, a commitment to promot-ing civic and community participation among vulnerable populations is central to the profession. Social work's civic mission is integrated into the Ethical Principles laid out within the NASW Code of Ethics, which call on social workers to "pursue social change," not just on behalf of vulnerable populations, but also "with" them. Social workers are expected to "strengthen relationships among people," helping to develop interpersonal relationships that benefit not only individuals, but also or-ganizations and communities. Furthermore, social workers are expected to ensure "meaningful participation in decision making for all people," by supporting vul-nerable populations to become meaningfully involved in community and organi-zational decision making (NASW, 1999).

The fact that individuals who are disadvantaged socially or economically are less likely to be civically engaged than their peers should be an important concern for social workers, who possess an ethical obligation to empower disadvantaged persons. Social workers must identify ways to empower willing and interested in-dividuals and strengthen access to civic engagement opportunities (McBride, 2008). Organizing and engaging vulnerable populations in strengthening societal well-being has been an important role for social workers throughout the profes-sion's history (McBride, 2008). Jane Addams and her fellow Settlement House movement reformers exemplified this commitment, as they organized neighbor-hood residents to improve their communities through social change efforts.

More recently, this commitment has been reflected within social work's em-powerment perspective, particularly from a macro definition of empowerment "as the process of increasing collective political power" (Gutiérrez, 1990, p. 149–150). Empowerment emphasizes the capacity and rights of individuals to be active participants in affecting the decisions and policies that affect them (Staples, 1990). Individuals who lack access—or perceive a lack of access—to institutions in their communities may experience powerlessness, which they then internalize as feelings of helplessness and alienation (Parsons, 1991). When we empower youth and adults to become involved in their communities and to affect community structures, we enable them to develop and utilize tools that enable them to regain a sense of control and self-esteem and to strengthen their own well-being. We equip them with the knowledge and skills to improve their communities and to help bring about social justice both locally and more broadly.

Youth Civic Engagement in a Rural Context

Rural Youth Civic Involvement

Much adolescent civic involvement research has focused on the civic and community behavior of poor youth living in urban contexts (Hart & Atkins, 2002; Hart & Fegley, 1995), whereas substantially less research has examined rural youth involvement (Bobek, Zaff, Li, & Lerner, 2009; Elder & Conger, 2000; King, Elder, & Whitbeck, 1997). One seminal study used a qualitative methodology to explore multiple dimensions of the lives of rural Iowa youth in grades 7–12 (Elder & Conger, 2000). This study focused primarily on the positive benefits of farming for youth, including close work with positive parental role models and other adults who echo principles and standards for behavior taught at home, due to the homogeneous nature of the communities under study. The authors theorized that the consistency of these value-laden messages helps protect these youth from problem behavior. They also documented rural youth organized activity involvement in religious groups and community groups or clubs, such as 4-H, Boy/Girl Scouts, and extracurricular activities. Organized activities enabled youth to come together with community members, to meaningfully contribute, and to develop wider social contacts important for rural youth who may be geographically isolated from community institutions. Organized activity involvement is positively and longitudinally associated with youth academic performance (Elder & Conger, 2000).

In a more recent study, Ludden (2009) also examined the civic involvement of youth residing in a Midwestern agricultural community. A central goal of this study was to examine whether distinct categories of organized activity and civic involvement were associated with a variety of indicators of psychological well-being. One-half of the eighth and ninth grade adolescents in the study indicated involvement in at least one community, school, or religious activity. Most commonly, 32% of the sample indicated involvement in a religious activity, with Future Farmers of America (FFA) the most popular school group and 4-H the most popular community civic activity. Similar to Elder and Conger's (2000) findings, Ludden (2009) found that adolescents who participated in religious activities engaged in less problem behavior and obtained higher grades than uninvolved youth, whereas adolescents who engaged in community-based and school-based civic activities reported more academic engagement.

A key limitation of existing research on rural youth civic behavior is the lack of a consistent or formal definition of *rural*. Individuals living in rural areas may vary in how close/far they are from major cities and small towns, which may offer youth greater civic opportunities. Rural youth civic research has focused solely on agricultural communities, which may differ from other rural areas where farming is less prevalent. Research tells us little about what spurs youth involvement in rural communities, where the economy is instead focused on coal mining, textiles, or other industries. In rural areas of Appalachia, for example, coal mining is a primary source of employment, potentially providing youth with different civic opportunities than agriculturally centered communities.

Facilitators of Rural Civic Engagement

Although there is a scarcity of research examining rural youth's civic behavior, the small extant literature points to some consistent findings about what aspects of rural life may facilitate civic engagement. A key community asset is the presence and involvement of supportive adults working beside the youth. When adults are involved with youth, providing role models of civic and community citizenship, as well as directly assisting children's involvement by providing transportation to events, youth membership in multiple civic and community groups is promoted (Elder & Conger, 2000). This form of social capital—being supported by and connected with adults—is critical for high-quality youth engagement.

Organized opportunities to involve youth in their communities may also facilitate civic development in a distinctly rural way. One example is 4-H, a positive youth development organization administered through the U.S. Department of Agriculture, which focuses on developing citizenship, leadership, and life skills through experiential learning. Although 4-H is available to suburban and urban youth, it is most popular among rural youth. Historically, 4-H has had a substantial agricultural learning focus, although it also integrates learning through science, engineering, and technology. The opportunity to develop community connections and relationships, while honing skills specific to a rural lifestyle, may make 4-H participation an ideal activity for facilitating a rural civic identity in agricultural areas (Elder & Conger, 2000). 4-H participation has been consistently linked to multiple aspects of positive youth development. A large, longitudinal study found 4-H involvement to be associated with decreased problem behaviors and increased character development (Lerner, Phelps, Forman, & Bowers, 2009; Lerner, Von Eye, Lerner, & Lewin-Bizan, 2009), as well as with outcomes specific to adult civic participation, such as increased civic participation, adult social connection, and beliefs about civic duty (Bobek et al., 2009). In-school civic engagement opportunities focused on agriculture, such as Future Farmers for America, also reflect a distinctly rural type of extracurricular involvement. Such activities may be less prevalent in rural areas, where agriculture plays a more minor role, such as in coal mining communities in rural West Virginia. Although 4-H is available in such communities, far less is known about other organizations and activities that may facilitate youth civic engagement. Other institutions, such as schools, may take on larger roles, as they often provide a centralized location for extracurricular and civic activities for students from a wide area, further fostering connections to the broader community. Community churches continue to serve as powerful organizational forces in the lives of individuals in rural communities, and individuals in rural settings are more likely to report regular church attendance than individuals in urban settings (Chalfant & Heller, 1991). Thus, organized religious activity is a key community asset through which rural youth connect with a broader community (King et al., 1997). Religious youth groups provide rural youth with a significant way to spend time with like-minded peers, and youth who are actively engaged in religious activity are less prone to engage in problem behavior (Bryk, Lee, & Hollard, 1993). Adolescent religious involvement has been theorized to facilitate the development of additional forms of community and even political involvement in adulthood (Youniss, McLellan, & Yates, 1999), meaning the preponderance of rural youth involvement in religious groups may have both short- and long-term effects on their civic development.

Challenges to Rural Civic Engagement

Several characteristics of rural settings serve to facilitate youth civic involvement; however, several potential challenges also exist. The dramatic economic change, stemming from the Farm Crisis of the 1980s that rural America has undergone for approximately 35 years, has significantly increased the prevalence of individuals living in poverty (Conger, 1997). This was exacerbated by the economic downturn during the early 21st century. Furthermore, the downturn has been linked directly to increased rural adolescent and young adult substance use (Lambert, Gale, & Hartley, 2008); if youth are lured away from community groups by more deviant peers, civic involvement may be effected. Additionally, a lack of job opportunities in economically depressed rural areas has led many rural young people to move to cities, leading to an "aging rural America." Young adults who do remain in their rural community may be less educated and less civically-involved than their peers who leave, reducing the availability of positive civic role models for rural adolescents (Johnson, 2006).

Although these authors endorse the value of diverse civic experiences for youth, the sparse and spread out population of rural areas means rural adolescents may have to travel long distances to reach more populated towns or urban areas with varied civic opportunities. Such travel may be especially difficult for teenagers, who have limited means and access to transportation, especially among the increasing number of rural teens living in poverty. The availability of diverse civic engagement opportunities may also be limited to a small number of community groups or service activities, as rural areas may not be able to support multiple civic organizations. 4-H groups and churches provide strong civic opportunities; however, it is highly likely that these groups are fairly homogenous both in their demographic characteristics (socioeconomic status, ethnicity), as well as in the shared values of group members. This stands in contrast to the importance of "heterogeneous engagement" in a range of activities stressed by civic theorists (Flanagan, Gill, & Gallay, 2005). Participation in a variety of groups and organizations exposes adolescents to diverse political and moral vantages considered key for the development of civic attributes, such as social trust and democratic values (Flanagan, 2004).

A Case Study of Adolescent Civic Involvement in a Rural Mining Community

This section addresses a key limitation of rural civic engagement research, by examining the civic behaviors and influences on one group of rural youth attending school in a rural Applachian town characterized by coal mining as a primary source of employment. The town was specifically chosen, due to its rural location, at least

1 hour by car (60 miles) from a city of at least 25,000 people and more than 4 hours by car from a city with a population of at least 200,000. The schools draw students from across the county; thus, the sample of 284 students from a middle-school (n=101, Mean age=12.16, SD=1.12) and high-school (n=183, mean age=15.94, SD =1.22) all live in a small, "rural" community, with some students living in more secluded areas surrounding the town. All students at the middle school and one-half of the students at the high school were recruited; however, participants were those students who returned parent permission forms (21% of the middle school and 48% of eligible high school students).

Demographically, 58% of the sample is female. Similar to other rural Appalachian communities, 92% are White; however, how adolescents engage civically may differ in rural communities with a different racial and ethnic makeup. According to school report card data, 39.3% of the middle-school students and nearly 27.9% of the high-school students are eligible for free lunch, suggesting a moderate level of poverty in this sample. Nearly one-half of the sample reported that their parents have a high school degree or less (mothers=45%, fathers=45.5%), approximately 30% of parents have a college degree (mothers=30.1%, fathers=27.4%), and a small portion of parents have graduate degrees (mothers=14.4%, fathers=10.1%). Remaining participants reported "don't know or unsure" for their parents' education (mothers=10.6%, fathers=17%).

To understand how these rural adolescents are civically engaged, we measured their current civic activity involvement, using the Youth Civic Behavior Questionnaire (Metzger & Smetana, 2009), a 25-item Likert scale adapted from measures used in previous research (Eccles et al., 2003; Smetana & Metzger, 2005; Youniss et al., 1997). The items represented current involvement in five categories, including four community service activities (e.g., volunteer to help poor, sick, or disabled people in your community), four community group activities (e.g., take part in a community group or club, such as Boy/Girl Scouts or YMCA), six school or community political activities (e.g., take part in a political rally or protest), four school involvement/extracurricular activities (e.g., take part in a school art, music, or drama group), and three religious activities (e.g., attend religious services). Four additional items, based on previous research and tailored specifically to a rural sample, were added and analyzed separately, including an item assessing involvement with 4-H and an item assessing working to "help your neighbors out on projects at their home/farm for no pay." Adolescents were asked to both rate their level of involvement over an average month from 1 (never) to 5 (very often) and report the total number of hours they participate in each activity on a monthly basis. The subscales all had adequate internal reliability (α =.69–.92).

Findings suggest that youth are most highly engaged in religious activities. Only 25% of adolescents in the case study reported that they "never" attend church, consistent with previous research, which has found that churches play an important role in rural community organization. Adolescents are also actively engaged in school involvement/extracurricular activities; such involvement has consistently been linked with a host of positive developmental outcomes, including increased voting in young adulthood (Eccles et al., 2003). For instance, 45% of adolescents reported participating in a school sports team "quite often" or "very often." In contrast to school activity involvement, only 7% reported participating in a community group activity "quite often" or "very often." The sprawling population of rural areas may make consistent community group involvement difficult for rural youth, whereas schools and religious institutions may provide a more centralized way for rural adolescents to become involved.

Although previous research has pointed to high levels of 4-H involvement among rural youth, the current study found much lower levels of participation. Seventy-nine percent of the youth stated that they "never" participate, and only 7% reported they are involved with 4-H "quite often" or "very often." This low level of involvement could stem from the unique coal-mining dependent economic structure of the mountainous Appalachian region from which the current data were taken. 4-H's primary focus on agricultural skills may not be as relevant to youth in rural areas where farming is less common. This finding highlights the importance of considering specific dimensions of different types of rural areas and how they may promote or thwart adolescent civic engagement.

In terms of involvement directly tied to the broader community or political activities, many of the youth in the sample are involved in community service in some form. Only 11% of youth stated they "never" participate in community service. Youth are even more involved in service close to home, as 95% of the youth reported some engagement in activities aimed at helping family, extended family, or neighbors. In contrast, much fewer of the adolescents in this sample engage in political activities, with 33% of the adolescents having reported "quite often" or "very often" knowing what is going on in the news or about political events, and just 7% reported participating in an organization focused around a political or social cause. Adolescents, regardless of community, tend to be less engaged in political activities than adults, but this level of political involvement is significantly lower than that of suburban adolescents (Metzger & Smetana, 2009). Similar to arguments by sociologists that individuals in marginalized groups tend to view civic commitments in terms of service to their community, rather than to broader civic and political institutions (Sanchez-Jankowski, 2002), these data suggest that rural youth may feel isolated and disconnected from national political issues and, instead, may focus their civic energy on helping their own neighbors and families.

Prior research has not examined whether diversity in demographic variables, such as degree of "ruralness" or socioeconomic status, influences youth civic engagement. In the current study, 65% of the participants reported living in a town of any size, with the remaining 35% living up to 40 miles from the small rural town in which they go to school. Thus, even within this rural sample, youth vary in their degree of "ruralness." Our findings suggest that living further from a town may be associated with lower levels of community group involvement and higher chances of 4-H involvement. This finding points to the importance of examining heterogeneity within the rural contexts, when considering rural youth civic engagement. Although rural areas may provide youth with limited opportunities for civic engagement, the lengthy travel distances for youth living in the most secluded areas of rural districts may make participation in civic groups even more inaccessible. For these more isolated youth, 4-H is a source of civic activity, consistent with previous research on rural youth.

Socioeconomic status may also be a relevant factor in understanding rural adolescent civic behaviors. In the current study, wealthier students, as measured by higher parental education, are more involved in community group, political, and community service activities, but not religious, school involvement/extracurricular activities, or 4-H activities. Although involvement in many extracurricular, civic, and community activities may be more difficult for poorer rural youth to access, perhaps due to time and transportation demands, rural institutions, such as churches and schools, appear more accessible and offer opportunities for engagement, regardless of socioeconomic status. Although the current case study utilized concurrent, self-reported data and may not be generalizable to other nonagricultural rural settings, the findings do point to potential processes underlying civic involvement in a sample of rural youth.

Facilitating Rural Youth Civic Engagement

Although this case study suggests broad rural adolescent involvement in some forms of civic activity, it also points to possible key gaps in civic involvement, both in terms of involvement type, such as political activity, and in terms of the sub-populations involved, with poorer and more "rural" youth engaging at lower rates. How can social workers act to expand civic participation across all groups of rural youth and empower them to become more meaningful community participants? Research suggests that civic engagement increases when individuals are specifically presented with opportunities to become involved or are directly asked to participate (McBride, 2008; Rosenstone & Hansen, 1993). School and community-based social workers in rural communities are well-situated to build on civic development models implemented across the United States to provide youth with specific opportunities to participate in civic activities that can help expand their civic involvement. Four program models that may be well-suited to a rural setting are subsequently discussed: community service, service-learning, participatory action research, and youth participation in community development and governance.

Community Service

Supporting opportunities for youth to engage in community service is the most common program model to build youth's engagement with their communities. Through community service programs, youth are connected with opportunities to volunteer, typically within their local communities. Currently, community service opportunities are offered by over two-thirds of U.S. public schools (mostly high schools), although less than one-half of the students in these schools participate in service (Scales & Roehlkepartain, 2004; Spring, Grimm, & Dietz, 2008). A higher percentage of rural schools arrange community service opportunities than their urban or suburban counterparts (Spring et al., 2008). However, low-income youth participate in community service opportunities at substantially lower rates than other groups of youth. For instance, higher-income schools provide more community service opportunities (61%) than schools serving primarily low-income families (54%; Spring et al., 2008).

Structured community service opportunities can be designed and facilitated by social workers working within both school and community-based settings. Given the active involvement in religious activities indicated in the case study, religious institutions may offer a particularly important venue for community service opportunities (Ludden, 2010). Community groups or clubs, such as 4-H and Boy/Girl Scouts, are well-tailored to implement community service opportunities; however, it is equally important to identify activities that can engage rural youth who may not be involved with these organizations, as with the 79% of students in this case study who reported never participating in 4-H. Depending on the context, community service programs may be voluntary, offered to youth expressing interest in community involvement, or mandatory, such as when schools require students to complete a specified number of hours of service for a specific class or for graduation. Metz and Youniss (2005) indicate that mandatory and voluntary community service may be equally effective in strengthening students' attitudes towards civic engagement.

Specific types of community service activities vary widely but often address local social, educational, or environmental issues. For example, youth may volunteer to serve food regularly to community members in poverty or spend time with elderly nursing home residents. Older youth may tutor younger students at the county elementary school, or youth may help clean up local rivers or parks. Although some community service programs recruit students to help with minor administrative tasks or to serve in a role, such as hall monitor at school, research suggests that students benefit most when they find their service meaningful. Meaningful service activities that address local community needs or enable direct client contact help youth gain more positive views of their communities and a stronger belief in their ability to affect the communities (Metz, McLellan, & Youniss, 2003; Nesbit & Brudney, 2010; Reinders & Youniss, 2006). They also become more likely to engage in continued volunteer activity and seek out community involvement in other ways (Lakin & Mahoney, 2006; Melchior, 1999; Melchior & Bailis, 2002; Metz & Youniss, 2003, 2005; Perry & Katula, 2001).

Effective community service programs also enable youth to have an active and participatory "voice" in making choices about the type of service in which they engage and planning how that service is structured (Lakin & Mahoney, 2006; Mitra, 2009). Designing service opportunities that take place over a longer period of time, requiring a degree of commitment, helps youth develop connections with their community and a desire for continued participation (Denault & Poulin, 2009; Lakin & Mahoney, 2006).

Service-learning.

Like community service programs, service-learning enables youth to engage in volunteerism. However, in service-learning programs, the service is typically planned and structured in a more intentional manner. The service youth provide is directly linked to educational content, based on an explicit connection between the service and what the youth are being taught. A key component of service-learning programs is systematic reflection by youth on their service experience. This reflection can be in writing, such as through essays on the youths' service experiences, or verbally in a group setting, or both. By connecting volunteer activity to a curriculum, service-learning provides youth with the opportunity to reflect on their experiences and to better understand the larger societal factors that may have contributed to the social problem they are addressing.

In social work education, when we think of service-learning, field instruction often comes to mind. Despite substantial similarities between the two, as social work students engage in providing service as a key component of their curricula, some scholars argue that field instruction should be clearly differentiated from service-learning for three primary reasons. First, the knowledge and skills that students are expected to learn in field instruction are determined primarily by curricula and student interests, whereas the knowledge and skills students learn through service-learning are expected to be determined by the needs of the community (Lemieux & Allen, 2007). Second, service-learning participants are expected to engage in service as community members, not as agency employees or service providers (Phillips, 2007). Finally, service-learning requires critical reflection to a greater degree than may commonly be seen in field instruction (Phillips, 2007). These differences—roles determined by the needs of the community, serving as a community member, and critical reflection on the service—may be welcome in social work field instruction, but are essential to effective service-learning.

Service-learning is offered by slightly under one-fourth of public schools in the United States (Scales & Roehlkepartain, 2004; Spring et al., 2008). Approximately 35% of secondary schools, 25% of middle schools, and 20% of elementary schools offer service-learning activities. At schools with service-learning, 36% of students, on average, and 32% of teachers are involved, resulting in about 10% of U.S. K–12 public school students participating in service-learning opportunities (Scales & Roehlkepartain, 2004; Spring et al., 2008). A smaller percentage of rural schools (22%) offer service-learning, compared to their urban and suburban counterparts (CNCS, 2006; Nesbit & Brudney, 2010; Spring et al., 2008). Furthermore, more higher-income schools (27%) offer service-learning programs and activities, as compared to 20% of low-income schools. Just 31% of disadvantaged youth reported participation in either school-based community service or service-learning (CNCS, 2007).

Although more than one-half of elementary school principals believe their students are too young for service-learning (Spring et al., 2008), social workers can play a crucial role in creating and facilitating developmentally appropriate service-learning opportunities both for younger children and for adolescents. By working with teachers to identify, develop, and sustain relationships with community organizations and business partners, social workers can help facilitate such service-learning activities as collecting recyclable materials and counting them as part of a math lesson, creating audio recordings of children's books for blind children as part of a reading or language arts lesson, or teaching community members about an important local environmental issue as part of a science lesson. In one rural Texas community, for example, a creative service-learning model engages high school students learning about youth development in service-learning through teaching and mentoring fifth grade students. The fifth grade students, in turn, integrate these lessons into a year-long environmental service-learning project to create community awareness about the integral nature of playa lakes to community sustainability.

Although less common, service-learning programs may also take place in a community-based setting (Bailis, 2003; Durlak et al., 2007). For example, a national teen pregnancy prevention program model, Teen Outreach Program, incorporates service-learning in both school and community-based settings throughout the country; in this case, the service is linked to educational content about leadership, community involvement, and reduction of risk behaviors (Allen & Philliber, 2001; Capaldi, 2009). For agricultural communities, a service-learning program outside a classroom might include providing and reflecting on agricultural support to struggling farmers, while simultaneously learning about agricultural science through a Future Farmers of America or 4-H group. Youth in other rural communities might work with a county museum to collect and present artifacts of the community's history, while simultaneously learning about local history.

When high-quality service-learning is implemented, service-learning has important effects on youth's civic engagement (Billig, Root, & Jesse, 2005; Eyler & Giles, 1997; McKay, 2010; Melchior & Bailis, 2002; Moore & Sandholtz, 1999; Morgan & Streb, 2001; Nesbit & Brudney, 2010) . Unfortunately, many programs termed "service-learning" are not of high quality and, instead, have minimal service requirements, are tenuously connected to classroom learning, or lack substantive reflection on the youth's service (Eyler, 2002; Moore & Sandholtz, 1999; Nesbit & Brudney, 2010). Such programs have been found unlikely to substantially affect youth civic development. Based on research evidence, social workers should strive to facilitate high quality service-learning that meets the following standards:

- Meaningful Service: Service-learning actively engages participants in meaningful and personally relevant service activities.

- Link to Curriculum: Service-learning is intentionally used as an instructional strategy to meet learning goals and/or content standards.

- Reflection: Service-learning incorporates multiple challenging reflection activities that are ongoing and prompt deep thinking and analysis about oneself and one's relationship to society.

- Diversity: Service-learning promotes understanding of diversity and mutual respect among all participants.

- Youth Voice: Service-learning provides youth with a strong voice in planning, implementing, and evaluating service-learning experiences with guidance from adults.

- Partnerships: Service-learning partnerships are collaborative, mutually beneficial, and address community needs.

- Progress Monitoring: Service-learning engages participants in an ongoing process to assess the quality of implementation and progress toward meeting specified goals and uses results for improvement and sustainability.

- Duration and Intensity: Service-learning has sufficient duration and intensity to address community needs and meet specified outcomes. (Billig & Weah, 2008)

Participatory Action Research

Participatory action research (PAR) enables youth to conduct their own community research, develop and present their own community change proposals, and participate in community action related to the proposals. Deriving, in large part, from Pablo Freire's work, participants are taught to question and analyze what they learn through the research process, to develop critical consciousness, and to challenge oppression in society (Foster-Fishman, Law, Lichty, & Aoun, 2010). PAR models have traditionally been used to empower people around the globe and are increasingly used with marginalized youth (Gant et al., 2009; Strack, Magill, & McDonagh, 2004; Wang, 2006). They also offer potential for youth in rural communities, particularly given the prevalence of supportive partnerships between rural youth and adults (Elder & Conger, 2000; Spatig, Gaines, MacDowell, & Sias, 2009), and may be well-suited for implementation by community-based or religious organizations, or even school-based extracurricular activities.

Likely due to the intense commitment required of youth and adult facilitators, PAR programs are much less common than community service and service-learning models. In PAR, youth become researchers. They make decisions about the research process and how the findings will be interpreted and used to strengthen their communities. Despite the extensive involvement required, this model has been initiated worldwide in multiple programs with children and youth as young as 8 years old, researching and designing community change projects in rural and urban communities alike (Chawla, 1997; Driskell, Bannerjee, & Chawla, 2001; Hussain, 2010).

One model of PAR increasingly implemented with youth in community organizations or school settings is "photovoice" (Wang, 2006; Wang & Redwood-Jones, 2001). Youth research and assess their community through photography, as part of a structured curriculum (Gant et al., 2009). Participants are guided through a process of critical reflection and then put the photographs together in an exhibit for policy-makers and other influential community members, in an effort to influence policy. For example, photographs exhibiting poverty in town or of shuttered businesses, side-by-side with photographs of a church picnic, can spur youth to reflect and develop creative recommendations on how to strengthen community institutions to better meet the needs of their poor or unemployed neighbors.

Such PAR models can bring youth and adults together, both in conducting research and working side by side to strengthen their communities. Although empirical research on the effects of PAR models on youth civic engagement is scant, case studies suggest that PAR promotes community participation and youth empowerment, as well as positively affects for the community under study (Chawla, 1997; Driskell et al., 2001; Strack et al., 2004; Wang, 2006; Wang & Redwood-Jones, 2001).

Youth Participation in Community Development and Governance

Social workers may also design, implement, or facilitate programs that enable rural youth to play a role in community decision-making. Typically, societal institutions offer youth few opportunities to participate in making community decisions (Camino & Zeldin, 2002; Mitra, 2009); however, enabling youth to make real decisions that affect their communities may simultaneously enhance the civic development of youth and the community contexts in which they live. Social workers can identify ways that youth can directly engage in community development projects that affect their lives in an immediate way (Lakin & Mahoney, 2006; O'Donoghue, Kirshner, & McLaughlin, 2002). For example, youth could be integrated into decision-making around creating youth employment opportunities, developing a town playground and basketball court, or disseminating small grants for community change projects (O'Donoghue, 2006).

Social workers can encourage the invitation of youth to take leadership roles in agency or local town boards and councils. Although models of engaging youth in community governance are more common outside of the United States, this is relevant and feasible in communities across the United States as well. Youth positions on town councils, boards of directors, or advisory groups for community organizations can be created (Golombek, 2006). For example, a youth budget council might be responsible for deciding how to use a portion of a town's or county's budget dedicated for children and youth's programming (Cabannes, 2005; Guerra, 2002). Children and youth can be involved in local governance, although the nature of the experiences and responsibilities may need to vary based on their developmental levels (Bartlett, 1999 as cited in Frank, 2006; Golombek, 2006).

Rural social workers can build upon rural community strengths, refocusing already-existing supportive relationships and partnerships between rural youth and adults (Elder & Conger, 2000) to focus on achieving community improvement goals together. In what Zeldin, Camino, and Mook (2005) term "youth/adult partnerships for community change," programs provide youth with opportunities to take on visible and challenging decision-making roles in conjunction with adults to address community issues (Mitra, 2009; Pittman, 2002; Zeldin et al., 2005). It is expected that youth and adults will teach and learn from each other (Camino, 2000; Mitra, 2009), with shared power expected to result in an increased sense of community among youth (Lakin & Mahoney, 2006; Zeldin et al., 2005).

Youth participation roles across these different civic and community engagement models range from consultative to direct involvement in planning and implementing projects (Alparone & Rissotto, 2001). However, youth engagement programs are most effective, when the role of youth participants goes beyond consultation and, instead, includes youth in the "real" decision-making process (Checkoway, 1998; Mitra, 2009). The quality and degree of youth participation is key; accordingly, social workers who seek to expand youth involvement in governance need to pay particular attention to how youth involvement is initiated, how the process of engaging youth is managed, and how achievements are communicated to participating youth. A risk with this type of program model is that poor mechanisms for ensuring meaningful youth participation may harm more than help youth civic engagement (Checkoway, 2011; Matthews, 2001; Matthews, Limb, & Taylor, 1999); positive effects are most likely to accrue, when participation is both meaningful and authentic and involves partnerships with adults (Mitra, 2009; Nesbit & Brudney, 2010; Zeldin, Camino, & Calvert, 2003).

Overall, there is little empirical research on the effects of this type of program model, but case studies indicate that engaging youth in community development and/or governance can strengthen the civic knowledge, skills, social connectedness, and community participation of youth, while also leading to improved organizational capacity and healthier communities (Checkoway, 2005, 2011; Checkoway & Gutiérrez, 2006; Pittman, 1996; Sherrod, 2006). However, some forms of youth participation in community development and governance are more far-reaching than others, in terms of how many youth may participate. Due to the low numbers of youth that may be involved in any particular board setting, for example, inclusiveness of diverse rural youth may be limited.

Conclusion

Social workers bring a unique commitment and ethical obligation to empowering people, particularly vulnerable populations, and to developing engagement with community and political institutions. Given the growing poverty in rural communities and the outmigration of younger residents from rural areas, rural settings provide an important context for social workers to integrate this commitment into their work, by facilitating programs that promote resident empowerment and a commitment to rural community development.

Much youth civic engagement research has focused on urban or suburban contexts, with little attention to youth in rural settings. As a result, research tells us little about the role that rural environments play in shaping how youth connect with and become involved in their communities. What little research exists suggests that rural youth face substantial challenges to civic engagement, including increased poverty and unemployment, an aging population, the homogeneity of available civic opportunities, and the long distances many rural adolescents must travel to reach civic opportunities. Due to these barriers, youth in rural communities may be less involved in specific types of civic activities, such as political engagement. Poorer rural youth and those that live in more distant, isolated areas may also be less able to participate in multiple civic activities than wealthier youth or those living more proximate to town.

At the same time, rural communities possess substantial community assets that encourage civic engagement, including the nature of social interactions, supportive adults that provide civic role models, high levels of religious activity, and distinctly rural organized opportunities for youth. These community assets provide a platform for social workers to build upon to overcome the challenges to rural civic participation. Such program models as community service, service-learning, participatory action research, and involvement in community governance can help develop rural youth engagement. Creating and supporting opportunities for civic participation can empower rural youth and support them in developing civic knowledge and skills, potentially leading to life-long habits of civic involvement.

References

Allen, J. P., & Philliber, S. (2001). Who benefits most from a broadly targeted prevention program? Differential efficacy across populations in the Teen Outreach Program. *Journal of Community Psychology, 29*(6), 637–655.

Alparone, F. R., & Rissotto, A. (2001). Children's citizenship and participation models: Participation in planning urban spaces and children's councils. *Journal of Community & Applied Social Psychology, 11*, 421–434.

Atkins, R., & Hart, D. (2003). Neighborhoods, adults, and the development of civic identity in urban youth. *Applied Developmental Science, 7*(3), 156–164.

Bailis, L. N. (2003). Overview of what is known about the scope of community-based service-learning in the United States. *Generator, 21*(3), 17–19.

Billig, S. H., Root, S., & Jesse, D. (2005). The relationship between quality indicators of service-learning and student outcomes: Testing professional wisdom. In S. Root, J. Callahan & S. H. Billig (Eds.), *Advances in service-learning research: Vol. 5. Improving service-learning practice: Research on models to enhance impacts* (pp. 97–115). Greenwich, CT: Information Age.

Billig, S. H., & Weah, W. (2008). K-12 service-learning standards for quality practice. In N. Y. L. Council (Ed.), *Growing to greatness 2008* (pp. 8–15). Saint Paul, MN: National Youth Leadership Council.

Bobek, D. L., Zaff, J., Li, Y., & Lerner, R. M. (2009). Cognitive, emotional, and behavioral components of civic action: Towards an integrated measure of civic engagement. *Journal of Applied Developmental Psychology, 30*, 615–627.

Bryk, A. S., Lee, V. E., & Hollard, P. B. (1993). *Catholic schools and the common good.* Cambridge, MA: Harvard University Press.

Cabannes, Y. (2005). Children and young people build participatory democracy in Latin American cities. *Children, Youth and Environments, 15*(2), 185–210.

Camino, L. (2000). Youth-adult partnerships: Entering new territory in community work and research. *Applied Developmental Science, 4*(Suppl. 1), 11–20.

Camino, L., & Zeldin, S. (2002). From periphery to center: Pathways for youth civic engagement in the day-to-day life of communities. *Applied Developmental Science, 6*(4), 213–220.

Capaldi, D. M. (2009). Youth after-school programs: Time to involve the parents and community? *Criminol Public Policy, 8*(2), 413–422.

Chalfant, H. P., & Heller, P. L. (1991). Rural/urban versus regional differences in religiosity. *Review of Religious Research, 33*, 76–86.

Chawla, L. (1997). Growing up in cities: A report on research underway. *Environment & Urbanization, 9*(2), 247–252.

Checkoway, B. (1998). Involving young people in neighborhood development. *Children and Youth Services Review, 20*(9/10), 765–795.

Checkoway, B. (2005). Forward: Youth participation as social justice. *Community Youth Development Journal*, (Fall), 15–17.

Checkoway, B. (2011). What is youth participation. *Children and Youth Services Review, 33*, 340–345.

Checkoway, B., & Gutiérrez, L. (2006). Youth participation and community change: An introduction. *Journal of Community Practice, 14*(1/2), 1–9.

Conger, R. D. (1997). The special nature of rural America. In E. Robertson, Z. Slobododa, G. Boyd, L. Beatty & N. Kozel (Eds.), *Rural substance abuse: State of knowledge and issues* (pp. 1–5). Rockville, MD: U.S. Department of Health and Human Services, National Institute of Health, National Institute on Drug Abuse.

Corporation for National and Community Service (CNCS). (2006). Educating for active citizenship: Service-learning, school-based service, and civic engagement *Youth Helping America Series* (Vol. Brief 2). Washington, DC.

Corporation for National and Community Service (CNCS). (2007). Leveling the path to participation: volunteering and civic engagement among youth from disadvantaged circumstances. Washington, DC: Corporation for National and Community Service.

Denault, A.-S., & Poulin, F. (2009). Intensity and breadth of participation in organized activities during the adolescent years: Multiple associations with youth outcomes. *J Youth Adolescence, 38*, 1199–1213.

Driskell, D., Bannerjee, K., & Chawla, L. (2001). Rhetoric, reality and resilience: Overcoming obstacles to young people's participation in development. *Environment & Urbanization, 13*(1), 77–89.

Duncan, S. C., Duncan, T. E., Strycker, L. A., & Chaumeton, N. R. (2002). Relations between youth antisocial and prosocial activities. *Journal of Behavioral Medicine, 25,* 425–438.

Durlak, J. A., Taylor, R. D., Kawashima, K., Pachan, M. K., DuPre, E. P., Celio, C. I., ... Weissberg, R. P. (2007). Effects of positive youth development programs on school, family, and community systems. *American Journal of Community Psychology, 39,* 269–286.

Eccles, J., Barber, B., Stone, M., & Hunt, J. (2003). Extracurricular activities and adolescent development. *Journal of Social Issues, 59,* 865–889.

Elder, G. H., & Conger, R. D. (2000). *Children of the land: Adversity and success in rural America.* Chicago, IL: University of Chicago Press.

Erikson, E. (1968). *Identity, youth, and crisis.* New York: W.W. Norton.

Eyler, J. (2002). Reflection: Linking service and learning—Linking students and communities. *Journal of Social Issues, 58*(3), 517–534.

Eyler, J., & Giles, D. (1997). The importance of program quality in service-learning. In A. S. Waterman (Ed.), *Service-learning: Applications from the research* (pp. 57–76). Mahwah, NJ: Lawrence Erlbaum Associates.

Flanagan, C. (2003). Trust, identity, and civic hope. *Applied Developmental Science, 7*(3), 165–171.

Flanagan, C. (2004). Institutional support for morality. In T. A. Thorkildsen & H. J. Walberg (Eds.), *Nurturing morality* (pp. 173–183). New York: Kluwer Academic/Plenum Publishers.

Flanagan, C., Gill, S., & Gallay, L. (2005). Social participation and social trust: The importance of heterogenous encounters. In A. Omato (Ed.), *Processes of community change and action* (pp. 149–166). Mahwah, NJ: Erlbaum.

Foster-Fishman, P. G., Law, K. M., Lichty, L. F., & Aoun, C. (2010). Youth ReACT for social change: A method for youth participatory action research. *American Journal of Community Psychology, 46,* 67–83.

Frank, K. I. (2006). The potential of youth participation in planning. *Journal of Planning Literature, 20*(4), 351–371.

Gant, L. M., Shimshock, K., Allen-Meares, P., Smith, L., Miller, P., Hollingsworth, L. A., & Shanks, T. (2009). Effects of photovoice: Civic engagement among older youth in urban communities. *Journal of Community Practice, 17*(4), 358–376.

Ginsberg, L. H. (2005). Introduction: The overall context of rural practice. In L. H. Ginsberg (Ed.), *Social work in rural communities* (4th ed.). (pp. 1–13), Alexandria, VA: Council on Social Work Education.

Golombek, S. B. (2006). Children as citizens. *Journal of Community Practice, 14*(1/2), 11–30.

Guerra, E. (2002). Citizenship knows no age: children's participation in the governance and municipal budget of Barra Mansa, Brazil. *Environment & Urbanization, 14*(2), 71–84.

Gutiérrez, L. M. (1990). Working with women of color: An empowerment perspective. *Social Work, 35*(2), 149–150.

Hart, D., & Atkins, R. (2002). Civic competence in urban youth. *Applied Developmental Science, 6*(4), 227–236.

Hart, D., Atkins, R., & Ford, D. (1998). Urban America as a context for the development of moral identity in adolescence. *Journal of Social Issues, 54*(3), 513.

Hart, D., & Fegley, S. (1995). Prosocial behavior and caring in adolescence: Relations to self-understanding and social judgement. *Child Development, 66*(5), 1346–1359.

Hussain, S. (2010). Empowering marginalised children in developing countries through participatory design processes. *CoDesign, 6*(2), 99–117.

Johnson, K. (2006). *Demographic trends in rural and small town America.* Durham, NH: University of New Hampshire, Carsey Institute.

King, V., Elder, G. H., & Whitbeck, L. B. (1997). Religious involvement among rural youth: An ecological and life-course perspective. *Journal of Research on Adolescence, 7,* 431–456.

Lakin, R., & Mahoney, A. (2006). Empowering youth to change their world: Identifying key components of a community service program to promote positive development. *Journal of School Psychology, 44,* 513–531.

Lambert, D., Gale, J. A., & Hartley, D. (2008). Substance use by youth and young adults in rural America. *The Journal of Rural Health, 24,* 221–228.

Lay, J. C. (2003). *Civic engagement in poor communities: Differences between urban and rural poverty.* Paper prepared for presentation at the Annual Midwest Political Science Association Meeting, Chicago, IL.

Lay, J. C. (2006). Learning about politics in low-income communities: Poverty and political knowledge. *American Politics Research, 34,* 319–340.

Lemieux, C. M. & Allen, P. D. (2007). Service-learning in social work education: The state of knowledge, pedagogical practicalities, and practice conundrums. *Journal of Social Work Education, 43,* 309–325.

Lerner, J. V., Phelps, E., Forman, Y. E., & Bowers, E. (2009). Positive youth development. In R. M. Lerner & L. Steinberg (Eds.), *Handbook of adolescent psychology.* (pp. 524–558). Hoboken, NJ: John Wiley & Sons.

Lerner, R. M., Von Eye, A., Lerner, J. V., & Lewin-Bizan, S. (2009). Exploring the foundations and functions of adolescent thriving within the 4-H study of positive youth development: A view of the issues. *Journal of Applied Developmental Psychology, 30,* 567–570.

Levinson, M. (2010). The civic empowerment gap: Defining the problem and locating solutions. In L. R. Sherrod, J. Torney-Purta & C. Flanagan (Eds.), *Handbook of civic engagement in youth* (pp. 331–361). Hoboken, NJ: John Wiley and Sons, Inc.

Ludden, A. B. (2009). The effects of religion and gender on well-being, substance use, and academic engagement among rural adolescents. *Youth & Society, 40,* 311–335.

Ludden, A. B. (2010). Engagement in school and community civic activities among rural adolecsents. *Journal of Youth and Adolescence,* 1–17. doi: DOI: 10.1007/s10964-010-9536-3.

Matthews, H. (2001). Citizenship, youth councils and young people's participation. *Journal of Youth Studies, 4*(3), 299–318.

Matthews, H., Limb, M., & Taylor, M. (1999). Young people's participation and representation in society. *Geoforum, 30,* 135–144.

McBride, A. M. (2008). *Civic engagement encyclopedia of social work* 20th ed. New York: Oxford University Press.

McBride, A. M., Sherraden, M., & Pritzker, S. (2006). Civic engagement among low-income and low-wealth families: In their words. *Family Relations, 55,* 152–162.

McKay, C. (2010). Critical service learning: A school social work intervention. *Children & Schools, 32*(1), 5–13.

Melchior, A. (1999). *Summary report: National evaluation of learn and serve American school and community based programs.* Waltham, MA: Brandeis University, Center for Human Resources.

Melchior, A., & Bailis, L. N. (2002). Impact of service-learning on civic attitudes and behaviors of middle and high school youth: Findings from three national evaluations. In A. Furco & S. H. Billig (Eds.), *Advances in service-learning research: Vol. 1. Service-learning: The essence of the pedagogy* (pp. 201–222). Greenwich, CT: Information Age Publishing.

Metz, E., McLellan, J., & Youniss, J. (2003). Types of voluntary service and adolescents' civic development. *Journal of Adolescent Research, 18*(2), 188–203.

Metz, E., & Youniss, J. (2003). A demonstration that school-based required service does not deter—but heightens—volunteerism. *PS Political Science & Politics, 36,* 281–286.

Metz, E., & Youniss, J. (2005). Longitudinal gains in civic development through school-based required service. *Political Psychology, 26*(3), 413–437.

Metzger, A., & Smetana, J. (2009). Adolescent civic and political engagement: Associations between domain-specific judgements and behavior. *Child Development, 80*(2), 433–441.

Mitra, D. L. (2009). Strengthening student voice initiatives in high schools. *Youth & Society, 40*(3), 311–335.

Moore, K. M., & Sandholtz, J. H. (1999). Designing successful service learning projects for urban schools. *Urban Education, 34*(4), 480–498.

Morgan, W., & Streb, M. (2001). Building citizenship: How student voice in service-learning develops civic values. *Social Science Quarterly, 82*(1), 154–169.

National Association of Social Workers (NASW). (1999). Code of ethics of the National Association of Social Workers. Washington, DC: National Association of Social Workers.

Nesbit, R., & Brudney, J. L. (2010). At your service? Volunteering and national service in 2020. *Public Administration Review* (December), S107–S113.

O'Donoghue, J. L. (2006). "Taking their own power": Urban youth, community-based youth organizations, and public efficacy. In S. Ginwright, P. Noguera & J. Cammarota (Eds.), *Beyond resistance! Youth activism and community change* (pp. 229–245). New York: Routledge.

O'Donoghue, J. L., Kirshner, B. R., & McLaughlin, M. (2002). Introduction: Moving youth participation forward. *New Directions for Youth Development,* 96(Winter), 15–26.

Parsons, R. (1991). Empowerment: Purpose and practice principle in social work. *Social Work with Groups, 14*(2), 7–21.

Perry, J. L., & Katula, M. C. (2001). Does service affect citizenship? *Administration & Society, 33*(3), 330–365.

Phillips, A. (2007). Service learning and social work education: A natural but tenuous connection. In M. Nadel, V. Majewski. & M. Sulivan (Eds.), *Social work and service learning: Partnerships for social justice* (pp. 3–20). Lanham, MD: Rowman and Littlefeld.

Pittman, K. (1996). Community, youth, development: Three goals in search of connection. *New Designs for Youth Development,* (Winter), 4–8.

Pittman, K. (2002). Balancing the equation: Communities supporting youth, youth supporting communities. *Community Youth Development Journal,* (Spring/Summer), 19–24.

Reinders, H., & Youniss, J. (2006). School-based required community service and civic development in adolescents. *Applied Developmental Science, 10*(1), 2–12.

Rosenstone, S. J., & Hansen, J. M. (1993). *Mobilization, participation, and democracy in America.* New York: Macmillan.

Sanchez-Jankowski, M. (2002). Minority youth and civic engagement: The impact of group relations. *Applied Developmental Science, 6*(4), 237–245.

Scales, P. C., & Roehlkepartain, E. C. (2004). *Community service and service-learning in U.S. public schools, 2004: Findings from a national survey.* St. Paul, MN: National Youth Leadership Council.

Schur, L., Shields, T., & Schriner, K. (2003). Can I make a difference? Efficacy, employment, and disability. *Political Psychology, 24*(1), 119–149.

Sherrod, L. R. (2006). Promoting citizenship and activism in today's youth. In S. Ginwright, P. Noguera & J. Cammarato (Eds.), *Beyond resistance! Youth activism and community change* (pp. 287–299). New York: Routledge.

Sherrod, L. R., Torney-Purta, J., & Flanagan, C. (Eds.). (2010). *Handbook of research on civic engagement in youth.* Hoboken, NJ: John Wiley and Sons, Inc.

Smetana, J. G., & Metzger, A. (2005). Family and religious antecedents of civic involvement in middle class African American late adolescents. *Journal of Research on Adolescence, 15*(3), 325–352.

Spatig, L., Gaines, S., MacDowell, R., & Sias, B. (2009). Like a mountain: Performing collaborative research with youth in rural Appalachia. *Collaborative Anthropologies, 2,* 177–212.

Spring, K., Grimm, R., & Dietz, N. (2008). Community service and service-learning in America's schools. In Office of Research and Policy Development (Ed.), *Community srevice and service-learning in America's schools* (pp. 1–41). Washington, DC: Corporation for National and Community Service.

Staples, L. (1990). Powerful ideas about empowerment. *Administration in Social Work, 14*(2), 29–42.

Strack, R. W., Magill, C., & McDonagh, K. (2004). Engaging youth through photovoice. *Health Promotion Practice, 5*(1), 49–58.

Verba, S., Schlozman, K. L., & Brady, H. (1995). *Voice and equality: Civic voluntarism in American politics.* Cambridge, MA: Harvard University Press.

Wang, C. (2006). Youth participation in photovoice as a strategy for community change. *Journal of Community Practice, 14*(1/2), 147–161.

Wang, C., & Redwood-Jones, Y. (2001). Photovoice ethics: Perspectives from Flint photovoice. *Heath Education & Behavior, 28*(5), 560–572.

Youniss, J., McLellan, J., & Yates, M. (1997). What we know about engendering civic identity. (Social Capital, Civil Society and Contemporary Democracy). *American Behavioral Scientist, 40*(5), 620–631.

Youniss, J., McLellan, J., & Yates, M. (1999). Religion, community service, and identity in American youth. *Journal of Adolescence, 22,* 243–253.

Youniss, J., & Yates, M. (1997). *Community service and social responsibility in youth.* Chicago: University of Chicago Press.

Zeldin, S., Camino, L., & Calvert, M. (2003). Toward an understanding of youth in community governance: Policy priorities and research directions. *Social Policy Report, 27*(3), 3–20.

Zeldin, S., Camino, L., & Mook, C. (2005). The adoption of innovation in youth organizations: Creating the conditions for youth-adult partnerships. *Journal of Community Psychology, 33*(1), 121–135.

11 Serving Rural Children After a Natural Disaster

Larry W. Kreuger

This chapter discusses how social workers have learned to assess the special emotional vulnerabilities and intervention needs of child and adolescent rural disaster victims. The chapter illustrates how social workers were involved in the assessment of need for services following a natural disaster, by examining data from a project aimed at helping the child and adolescent victims of the 500-Year Great Midwestern Flood. An outline is offered for a disaster impact model that further specifies how and where social service workers helping families and children in rural disaster areas can best direct their intervention efforts.

Although the short-term effects of disasters have become better understood (Doostgharin, 2009; Ronan et al., 2008), the longer-term effects are not as well identified for either children or adults (Dean, 2006; Rohrbach, Grana, Vernberg, Sussman, & Sun, 2009; Rosenfield, Caye, Ayalong, & Lahad, 2005; Seroka, Knapp, Knight, Siemon, & Starbuck, 1986; Williams & Ell, 1998). Conditions in rural areas that improve or worsen the effects of natural disasters on children and families are also not well-known (Sahin, Batigun, & Yilmaz, 2007). At the outset, it is important to recognize that people who live in rural areas are more likely than their urban contemporaries to depend on the natural environment for economic survival and a range of family activities.

Additionally, cultures in rural communities often include firmly held beliefs about individual autonomy, self-reliance, and distrust of outsiders (Coleman &

Coleman, 2004). These predilections have been reported to interfere with disaster and postdisaster-related recovery and rebuilding phases (Karim, 1997; Stretch, Kreuger, & Hennicke, 1998; Villaba & Lewis, 2007). As Wagenfeld, Murray, Mohatt, and DeBruyn (1997) indicate, providing help that works in rural areas may be a matter of timing. Outreach workers and crisis counselors need to be sensitive (Poulin & Soliman, 1999; Soliman, Rasquinha, Burkett, & Shelton, 2001) to seasonal variations in seeding, ground preparation, and harvesting that may influence accessibility and consistency in the quantity and quality of services (Robertson, 1997). In addition, farmers' sense of pride may prevent them from applying for help, they may have underestimated their own losses, and they may believe that others are more in need of help.

Children in rural areas, the focus of this chapter, can be difficult to assess following a natural disaster because their activity levels may disguise their risks. In addition, disasters disrupt rural children in ways that are not always apparent to those unfamiliar with rural culture (Burnham, 2009; Caruna, 2010; Ell & Aisenbert, 1998). Harm to family, pets, livestock, farm equipment and outbuildings, roads, schools, friends, and neighbors may be difficult to detect. Children whose family business is farming are often required by necessity to assume responsibility for a number of farm chores. After a disaster, there is likely an expectation that children will assist with farm-related clean-up and other more adult responsibilities, leading to absences from school. Rural children, therefore, may need special attention to be identified and then provided with longer-term supportive counseling, if warranted.

Special Vulnerabilities of Rural Communities When Disaster Strikes

Today, according to the U.S. Census Bureau, rural areas encompass 2,288 counties that account for 83% of the total land mass. Rural locales, according to the U.S. Census Bureau, are defined as places with fewer than 2,500 people, including wilderness and frontier territories, farming and ranching regions, small towns, and peripheral locations adjacent to larger urban communities. Economies in many rural areas are based on self-employed or corporate farming, mining, or oil and gas field work. Rural areas offer a unique way of life for those willing to undertake what many see as relative hardships, including geographic isolation, economic vulnerability, difficulties in transportation and communication, and often inadequate resources in health and human services. The very circumstances that make rural life so attractive to some, however, also portend problems when disaster strikes (Duncan, 1992).

Even without natural or human-made disasters, rural areas often have easily disrupted economic bases, and many are suffering from out-migration and economic activities that further diminish their already precarious institutional bases (Robertson, 1997). Many rural Americans are below poverty levels and suffer from high incidence and prevalence rates of mental illness, substance abuse, emotional disturbance, and developmental disability equal to or greater than their urban counterparts. Table 1 summarizes major rural conditions and the disaster-related vulnerabilities associated with them.

TABLE 1   Rural Conditions and Disaster Related Vulnerabilities

Rural Condition	Disaster-Related Vulnerability
Geographic dispersion	Communication and transportation problems, isolation
Availability of nearby natural resources	Disruption/destruction of natural (leisure) environment, such as fields, lakes and forests with attendant wildlife
Farm/home as business	Economic disruption/destruction of the (productive) built environment, such as farming and grazing land, homes and outbuildings
Seasonal cycles	Seeding/planting, harvesting interrupted and delivery to markets delayed
Culture of individualism	Difficulty asking for or accepting assistance, downplaying personal needs, underestimating family need
Caregiver location	Scarcity in crisis-serving capacities of available providers
Caregiver counseling	Familiarity and lack of proximal alternatives may jeopardize confidentiality

Issues in the Determination of Longer-Term Disaster-Related Need in Rural Areas

As previously stated, because of the seasonal nature of the economy in agricultural communities, the effects of disasters in rural areas can be considerably extended in calendar time beyond what might ordinarily have unfolded. One of the key questions facing social workers many months after a disaster in a rural area is the extent to which there are children or families in a community, region, or catchment area who are still in need of services but have not been receiving them. Needs assessment is one way to gather information to help social workers answer this question. Kuh (1982) lists five general reasons social workers might want to evaluate a rural community via a needs assessment after a disaster: to determine whether needs have been met, to assess satisfaction with services, to monitor perceptions of various issues that can guide the development of new programs or policies, to justify existing policies and programs, and to select the most desirable program or policy from several alternatives.

Determining need in rural areas after a disaster requires social workers to think about how needs are defined to begin with. Lenning (1980) defined *met needs* as necessary or desirable conditions that already exist in actuality in a community. As this chapter subsequently shows, in rural areas following a disaster there may well be a sizeable population whose needs have been met, and they are likely to be individuals and families at very low risk. *Unmet needs*, conversely, were defined by Lenning as arising when there is a discrepancy between desirable conditions and current actuality. In a similar vein, Witkin and Altschuld (1995) saw "need" as a discrepancy or gap between what is (the present state of affairs) and what should be (the desired state of affairs).

Bradshaw (1972) identified four ways social workers may wish to ascertain need. First, a normative need is a circumstance, condition, or situation that is identified by a social worker, key informant, or other community expert who has been able to determine there is a gap in existing services relative to some subpopulation's need. For example, a community organizer may know that, by examining information from a central clearinghouse on services to disaster families in rural areas, there are far more families with children who need educational resources than there are children from these areas who are enrolled in community schools. The social worker might recommend that increased transportation services be made available to ensure that children residing in these communities receive support.

A second definition of *need*, according to Bradshaw (1972), is felt need, which involves the traditional notion of ascertaining need by examining actual cases. Much of the literature on needs assessment provides methodological strategies to conceptualize and gather data pertaining to the opinions and beliefs (felt need) of those residing in a particular community. The problem of reaching out in rural areas, however, can be much more difficult.

Bradshaw (1972) called the demand for services *expressed need*. Expressed needs refer to those actual or potential individuals or families who have applied for services or those who have already received services. Such needs might refer to those on a waiting list. The final need identified by Bradshaw (1972) is called *comparative need*. This need is an estimation of the amount of need that may be ascertained by finding out characteristics of those who have already obtained services and then determining how many of those in the larger region are likely to share the same characteristics and, hence, be likely to benefit from service.

Who Should Be Involved in Longer-Term Natural Disaster Needs Assessment In Rural Areas?

Needs assessments in rural areas can be conducted by social workers gathering information about gaps between real and ideal conditions, the reasons these gaps exist, and what can be done about them, all within the context of the beliefs of the community and available resources. Traditionally, social workers have used three sources for this information. The first source is the catchment group or population (i.e., cases, potential clients), the very individuals whose needs the social worker wishes to assess. However, hard-to-reach groups and individuals in rural areas may not be accustomed to having their needs assessed and may lack the verbal or other skills needed to express needs. A second group consists of community leaders, service providers who serve as key informants. These may be opportunely connected individuals with a knowledge of and ability to report on community needs. In rural areas county extension agents, ministers, minority group leaders, newspaper editors, and reporters will likely have broader knowledge of community affairs in extended regions covering a large geographic area. However, there is always a danger is that such key informants may overestimate a target population's interest in a program and overestimate the felt need for change in a rural community or region.

Targeted community members (in this case, children and adolescents themselves) comprise the third group. They consist of all the residents of the entire community, which includes members of the target population, as well as individuals and their families, who will be found to be unaffected by a disaster. Approaching every child or adolescent in a particular catchment area for information has the advantage of potentially learning how broadly based needs are, rather than assuming the needs are restricted to those in close proximity to an actual disaster occurrence. A problem, however, is that an entire population may not be aware of the extent of the needs of more distant members of the outlying region.

Methods for Assesssing Longer-Term Disaster-Related Needs in Children and Adolescents in Rural Areas

Surveys and standardized needs assessment measures are cross sectional, special purpose questionnaires (mailed or distributed, telephone) that gather primarily quantitative data. The key questions for social workers in rural areas include deciding who to survey; selecting a sampling method; determining the content of items to be asked; choosing what type of questionnaire to use (open-ended, multiple choice, scaled with respect to extent of agreement); and selecting a method of distribution (mail, telephone, in-person, in-organization).

Surveys about natural disasters are relatively inexpensive, because a considerable amount of data can be collected at a low cost. Disadvantages include lack of flexibility of surveys regarding the types of information respondents can offer and possibly not hearing the needs of less expressive respondents. Specialized instruments (e.g., an instrument measuring the needs of children) use knowledge developed by clinicians and clients to categories of gaps in needs in an easily coded, self-administered instrument. The main disadvantage, however, may be the lack of locality relevance when instruments that were developed and tested elsewhere miss local contextual information about rural natural disasters.

The use of existing records, statistics, and secondary information sometimes available from service providers, agency files, libraries, and government offices may save social workers time in gathering primary (new) data. A disadvantage is that secondary sources may limit the kinds of information to the preexisting categories, offering insights of limited help. Also, existing information may reflect political decisions or compromises of prior administrations for which current social work practitioners might have little insight or understanding. According to Payne (1999), there are several questions to ask when using existing information. The first is, which geographical areas are covered? Often public and private agencies and providers have different boundaries and coverage areas, when capacities to respond to disasters may be spread over considerable distances. Have existing boundaries changed? Often information may not be comparable over time, as boundaries and catchment area definitions may change due, in part, to differing political parties in power. How old is the information? Is it up to date? Many calculations are based on data from censuses that may be as many as 10 years old. Often information gathered between the decennial censuses is more up-to-date information but likely from estimates using samples. If so, how accurate are the estimates? Have definitions changed over time? Are there any common or disparate elements in definitions that vary? Is the information complete? If information is categorical, how much specificity may have been lost due to grouping of data? If averages are reported, are they appropriate? For example, is using the mean most appropriate, perhaps the median or mode would be a better measure of central tendency?

Researchers reporting on average incomes often use the median, instead of the mean, because one or two very large (or very small) incomes will skew a distribution, if the mean is calculated. What information is missing? Quite often there may be gaps in data gathered in the past. A look at the literature of those also working in an area may provide insights as to what is missing.

Face-to-face and telephone interviews can provide more in-depth information to rural social workers about a range of human needs, primarily because of the social worker's ability to elicit information through follow-up and probe questions. Good rapport between social worker and respondent can provide extremely valid and reliable data. Focus groups are relatively unstructured exercises with small groups (8–12 participants). Membership in focus groups is usually homogeneous, in that members share a particular experience or interest. Sessions usually last 1–2 hours (Morgan, 1988). Initially, members hear a general statement of the purpose of the session and are given a question pertinent to eliciting information about their postdisaster needs. Participants often are asked to write down their ideas or thoughts and share these with the rest of the group. The leader usually tracks ideas, composes summaries, and makes sure there is agreement as to what is being recorded. The advantage (that individuals may offer ideas they would not ordinarily have thought of) can also be a disadvantage (they may not feel comfortable saying what the actually feel; Krueger & Casey, 2000).

Rural community forums are large, open, public meetings or community gatherings and can be used to obtain information about diverse individuals who make up a community. They are similar to town hall meetings, lasting several hours, with large numbers of participants, and special leadership skills are needed to manage gathering information in these settings. One key disadvantage is that there is no assurance of representativeness of various participants, and often those who are most vocal are well-represented, whereas those less verbal may be left behind.

Social workers and other rural human service providers have found that it is very helpful in understanding a community affected by a disaster to both study and create maps of the region, neighborhood, or area of interest. This can be done by selecting geographic maps from state agencies, libraries, or online map-making services and then drawing boundaries around areas of interest. Another method is called "cognitive mapping." This can be a very useful source of information in and of itself, in that it asks local residents to draw a map on a blank piece of paper. One might ask children to draw a map of where they ride a bus to get to school or how they get to a store and how access may have been altered by a natural disaster. One might ask adolescents to draw a map of their farm, neighborhood, and where they play or meet friends. Such freehand maps are often very helpful in stimulating ideas and information that might not otherwise come to mind, especially when rural residents are responding to questions about unmet needs related to a disaster.

Another handy source of information on disasters is the rural newspaper. Newspaper publishers almost always retain copies of their various publications, either stored away as hard copy or in electronic format. Depending on the size of the newspaper and community in question, it may be possible to gather information not otherwise available from newspaper files. Newspaper reporters and editors can also be quite valuable sources of information not only about historical events, but also about ongoing issues and controversies pertaining to disaster recovery. Other helpful sources include librarians, local school teachers, county extension agents, members of the clergy, museum staff, local college personnel, and long-time residents. Another strategy to gathering information on a community is to photograph it or examine photographs taken by others. Again, newspapers; libraries; schools; churches, temples, and synagogues; museums; and historical associations are likely to be excellent sources for this kind of information. Asking residents to photograph locations such as parks or wilderness areas, roads, ponds or streams, and schools and playgrounds is helpful. Additionally, a wealth of information can be transmitted by the use of photographs, which reveal how a rural community copes with a natural disaster.

A Case Example from the Great Flood of 1993–1995

Research has shown that victims ordinarily respond to the natural disaster as it unfolds and also to the various preventive and containment strategies, which may engage rural families on a number of levels (Ursano, McCaughey, & Fulllerton, 1994). Child and adolescent rural flood victims run a gamut from those maximally affected by direct exposure to the event (Kreuger & Stretch 1995; Stretch & Kreuger, 1996), such as by destruction of farm buildings or water on the premises, to those who were peripherally involved, such as by schools closed or classes changed, unusually long commute times, or missed time from work. The rural disaster severity assessment instrument developed by the authors operationalized elements from their own and other models in assessing level of damage from the natural disaster, self-reported amount of harm, and level of recovery from any aspect of the event, whether from the effect or response side.

The project presented here focuses on assessments beginning 3 months postevent, whereas Bradburn (1991) looked at effects 6 months postdisaster, and

Burke, Moccia, Borus, and Burns (1986) examined effects on children 10 months following a disaster. Using the Revised Children's Manifest Anxiety Scale (RCMAS), Lonigan, Shannon, Finch, Daugherty, and Taylor (1991) found, 3 months after a hurricane, that increased disaster exposure was correlated with increased anxiety and was more likely elevated among females. Riad and Norris (1996) reported higher levels of stress in children 6 months following a disaster, whereas Prinstein, LaGreca, Vernbery, and Silverman (1996), in a study of 506 elementary-age children, reported that coping assistance from adults helped reduce symptoms and a considerable amount of posttraumatic stress disorder (PTSD) 10 months after hurricane Andrew, as did Swenson and colleagues (1996) 14 months after a disaster and Shaw, Appelgate, and Schorr (1996) 21 months postevent. Goenjian and colleagues (1997) reported improvement in PTSD but not depression among treated, compared to untreated, groups of children some months following a natural disaster. Finally, Azarian and Skriptechenko-Gregarian (1998) found correlations between stress and age and developmental stage in children and adolescents 6 months after extensive earthquakes.

Method

This project developed a self-report survey instrument, which contained 10 disaster impact items aimed at assessing magnitude and severity of the disaster. The protocol also included questions about harm to self, family, friends, and neighbors; amount of recovery; and limited demographic items, such as gender, age, and family size. The self-report technique used here has several advantages. First, it can gather immediate, relevant information from the individual child who is directly involved. Second, these measures assess respondent subjective feelings. For example, fear, intrusive thoughts, and overwhelming feelings of anxiety and depression related to a natural disaster may be experienced by a child privately, although not disclosed or demonstrated to others on ordinary occasions. Last, from a practical point of view, self-report measures are inexpensive to obtain. Conversely, Carlson (1996) reported that young children may not understand some or all of the questions. Other disadvantages of self-reporting and the difficulties associated with assessing the effect of trauma on children have been examined elsewhere in detail by Putnam (1991) and Wilson and Keane (1999).

Two standardized measures of longer-term risk were also administered: RCMAS (Reynolds & Richmond, 1978) and the Children's Depression Inventory (CDI; Kovacs, 1981). RCMAS has three subscales, which were also tallied, as anxiety was further specified to include (1) worry, (2) physiological manifestations, and (3) concerns about social occasions. Classroom teachers administered these instruments in grades 4–12 in parochial schools. Scores were weighted for disaster impact, and eligibility for treatment screen was employed by Catholic Family Services to assess disaster-related risk. Any child in grades K–3 reporting failure of the family to fully recover was automatically deemed eligible for service, and those in grades 4–12 scoring above the cutoff for RCMAS or CDI (plus any flood effects) were deemed high-risk.

Data were collected in 17 parishes in seven counties where extensive flooding occurred along the Missouri River, which traverses the state from the northwest corner south to Platte County, then east to the southern edge of Boone County, eventually reaching the Mississippi River in St. Charles County, near St. Louis, MO. The Mississippi River also flooded along its borders that form the eastern boundary of Missouri from Clark County in the northeast to the boot heel region in the extreme southeast.

Screening for disaster impacts. Our project screened 3,876 children and adolescents; 30% of these (1,167) were in grades K–3, and the remaining 70% (2,719) were in grades 4–12. The children in grades K–3 were given the Children and Adolescents Protocol on Flood Impact instrument only, and 97 (9%) reported sufficient failure to recover, such that they were included in the referral group. Of the older children and adolescents in grades 4–12, 813 (30%) reported failure to recover, other forms of harm, and disaster effects (regardless of magnitude) and thus were eligible for services according to the protocol established by Catholic Family Services. This group was further stratified according to scores on the RCMAS (anxiety) and CDI (depression) instruments. Of this group (N=813), 59% (n=544) of the 4–12 graders were within normal limits on both instruments, 32% (n=199) showed elevated anxiety on the RCMAS, and 9% (n = 70) were elevated on the CDI showing depression (with overlap on these two indicators of risk). This yielded a total pool eligible for services of 366, amounting to approximately 9% of the total screened.

The accumulated percentages of rural children and adolescents indicating a positive response to any of the 10 basic measures of severity of the disaster was less than 20%. In most cases, fewer than 10% of the children reported any effect at all. Another dimension of disaster severity is amount of self-reported recovery. Most children (approximately 80%) were not affected at all. Another 20% reported effects but also that their family had completely recovered. Finally, approximately

6.4% reported that their families had either mostly recovered or not recovered at all, as of the date of the screening.

Key questions for social workers screening for emotional risk is the assessment of the severity of the disaster and whether it is associated with increased anxiety or depression or both. Also tested was proximity to the disaster, as measured by whether water from the flood was reported in the family farm or residence, whether families had to evacuate the farm or residence, amount of self-reported harm, and whether families had yet to recover. Table 2 shows that those who report any effects from a flood are more likely to show evidence of risk, as measured by either elevated anxiety or depression. Those who report harm to family, whether or not they had to evacuate their farms or residences, and children who reported their families had not completely recovered were all significant predictors of risk at the .001 level. As noted, the presence of water in the residence did not predict risk.

TABLE 2   Disaster Severity and Long Term Need

Predictors of Disaster Severity	Risk[a] (%)	n	No Risk (%)	n	Statistic
Any disaster impact at all?		269/813	26.2	500/1,906	$\chi_2 = 13.1, df = 1, p<.001$
Harm to family?	34.9	290/803	25.5	489/1,916	$\chi_2 = 24.4, df = 1, p<.001$
Flood water on farm?	30.2	95/314	28.0	674/2,405	$\chi_2 = .681, df = 1, ns$
Evacuated farm?	38.5	114/296	27.0	665/2,423	$\chi_2 = 17.1, df= 1, p<.001$
Recovered yet?	37.5	57/152	27.7	712/2,567	$\chi_2 = 17.1, df = 1, p<.001$

[a] Evidenced by elevated scores for the Revised Manifest Anxiety Scale, or depression on the Children's Depression Index.

Social work practice concerns about the evacuation. Particularly important to human service providers planning interventions in rural areas are recovery problems associated with those who have evacuated their places of residence. To test for the effects of evacuating the family residence on the key outcome variable of long-term risk, 100 cases were randomly selected of which children reported their family had evacuated their residence and 100 who reported being able to remain at home. Examined next was whether those who had to evacuate were less likely to recover from the disaster. There was a statistically significant difference (chi square=29.4, df=1, p<.001); 28% of those who had to evacuate reported not recovering, compared to 1% of those who did not evacuate.

Next tested was evacuation of residence and the two measures of risk (RCMAS and CDI), further specifying the three subscales that comprise the RCMAS anxiety scale: worry, physiological manifestations of anxiety, and concern about social occasions. Note that in Table 3, among the randomly selected 200 cases, the overall anxiety score was greater for those who had to evacuate (11.1 compared to 9.1). However, it is noted that the physiological manifestation anxiety score was the only subscale on the RCMAS to show a significant difference, as neither worry nor concern about social occasions was related to evacuation of residence. Finally, note that the depression measure of risk (CDI) was not significantly related to evacuating place of residence.

TABLE 3   Evacuation of Residence and Long-Term Need for Service

	Stayed on Farm or Residence (Mean)	SD	Evacuated Farm or Residence (Mean)	SD	Statistic
Total Anxiety Score	9.1	6.1	11.1	6.8	$t = 2.18$, $df=198$, $p<.05$
Subscales					
Worry	4.14	3.20	4.63	3.33	$t = 1.06$, $df=198$, ns
Physiology	2.81	2.31	3.80	2.31	$t = 2.68$, $df=198$, $p<.05$
Social Concerns	2.14	1.91	2.67	2.02	$t = 1.91$, $df=198$, ns
Depression Score	2.6	3.4	2.8	4.1	$t = .351$ df=198, ns

Implications

In the literature, the conceptualization of longer-term emotional risk to rural children and the operationalization of its components had not yet been tied directly to measurement of the magnitude of the disastrous rural event. In this project some of the logic regarding how much a rural flooding disaster affected child and adolescent victims (severity), as it might be inferred from measures of self-reported harm in the near rural environment and larger region (magnitude), was examined. Next reviewed was how these were informed by two selected measures of risk in children and adolescents (anxiety and depression) and what interventions may be appropriate.

The following model for predicting risk and recommendations regarding appropriate interventions are based solely on experience in the Great Midwestern Flood of 1993–1995 project. A framework was developed for rural disaster magnitude at five levels, as noted in Table 4. Magnitude 1 occurs when the disaster presents no perceived harm in the near environment. The near environment refers to territories of the self that immediately surround the individual child and are relevant to self-awareness, such as the *Umwelt* (immediate physical space surrounding the body), family, neighborhood, and school (Goffman, 1963). Magnitude 1 also initially involves no disruptions in the larger regional environment and no real or perceived risk. Interventions would be aimed at general disaster preparedness.

Magnitude 2 involves minor flooding in the region that may cause disruptions in service for utilities and public transportation. Fewer cases of risk are predicted at this magnitude. Interventions involve mainly information dissemination from the media about various disruptions and rerouting.

Magnitude 3 involves much more inundation in both near and far environments, with disruptions that immediately affect children and adolescents (school schedules change, buses are late). More risk is evident, and interventions need to involve rural school programs at this point.

TABLE 4   A Basic Model Rural Disaster Magnitude, Harm, Risk, and Interventions

Impact Level	Conditions	Harm in Near Environment?	Harm in Region?	Risk?	Interventions
1	Flooding over large area, little inundation locally	No harm	No disruptions	None	Disaster preparedness
2	Minor flooding in region	No harm locally	Minor disruptions in service	One or two cases	Media advice re: damages
3	Some flooding in region, minor local flooding	Some harm to friends	School and work schedules disrupted	Several risk cases evident	Initiate school programs
4	Major local flooding	Sandbagging, evacuations, some water in residence	School cancelled, parents miss work, some damage to crops & livestock	Moderate & severe risk	Outreach & screenings at school
5	Major massive inundation	Evacuation	Residence damaged or lost	Severe & long term	Clinical counseling

Magnitude 4 involves serious harm to the near environment, with sandbagging, water in the residence, and major disruptions in daily rounds. In rural areas there is often major damage to crops and livestock, parents may miss time from work, and moderate to severe longer-term risk will be evident. Human services at this magnitude need to engage outreach and screening for critical services. Finally, at magnitude 5, inundation is so extreme that residences can no longer be safely maintained. Many homes are totally flooded or literally swept away in what is seen as a major disaster. Severe and long-term emotional risk is evident, and a host of direct clinical services are likely required. Counseling and mental health services are also likely required.

For the record, of the entire population of 2,719 children and adolescents in grades 4–12, there were 2,253 (83%) located in the lowest flood impact magnitudes of levels 1 and 2; 170 (6.3%) were in level 3; there were 152 (5.6%) in level 4; and the remaining 144 (5.3%) were in level 5, the highest magnitude of flood impact. As noted from the data reported here, evacuation of residence was a major predictor of emotional risk, and water in the residence (without evacuation) was less well-correlated to emotional risk. The ordering of relationships is difficult to specify exactly, without longitudinal data and associated statistical modeling.

Rural schools are positioned to provide an excellent mediating structure for larger state and federal governments and nonprofit organizations to deliver services, including crisis counseling, to children affected by a disaster. A package of services designed to address and serve the needs of rural schools, their students, and faculty and staff is critical. Rural schools in disaster affected areas have different levels of need for services and, at times, different perceptions of need. Hence, a one-size-fits-all model of crisis counseling will not work. Any given rural social worker might use whole school assemblies, small groups, one-on-one counseling, peer counseling, consultation, or training as effective approaches.

References

Armsworth, M., & Holaday, M. (1993). The effects of psychological trauma on children and adolescents. *Journal of Counseling and Development, 72,* 499–457.

Azarian, A., & Skriptechenko-Gregarian, V. (1998). Traumatization and stress in child and adolescent victims of natural disasters. In T. Miller (Ed.), *Children of trauma: Stressful life events and their effects on children and adolescents* (pp. 77–118). Madison, CT: International Universities Press.

Bradburn, I. S. (1991). After the earth shook: Children's stress symptoms 6–8 months after a disaster. *Advances in Behavior Research and Therapy, 13,* 173–170.

Bradshaw, J. (1972). A taxonomy of social need. In G. McIachlan (Ed.), *Problems and progress in medical care* (pp. 214–234). Oxford, UK: Nuffield Provincial Hospital Trust.

Burke, J. D., Moccia, P., Borus, B., & Burns, B. J. (1986). Emotional distress in fifth-grade children ten months after a natural disaster. *Journal of the American Academy of Child Psychiatry, 25,* 536–541.

Burnham, J. J. (2009). Comtemporary fears of children and adolescents: Coping and resiliency in the 21st century. *Journal of Counseling & Development, 87*(1), 28–35.

Carlson, E. (Ed.). (1996). *Trauma research methodology.* Luthersville, MD: Sidran.

Caruana, C. (2010). Picking up the pieces. *Family Matters, 84,* 79–88.

Colman, R., & Colman, A. (2004). Rural & isolated. *Youth Studies Australia, 23*(1), 12.

Dean, B. M. T. (2006). *The long-term psychosocial effects of trauma on survivors of human-caused extreme stress situations.* Miami, FL: Barry University.

Doostgharin, T. (2009). Children affected by earthquakes and their immediate emotional needs. *International Social Work, 52*(1), 96–106.

Duncan, C. (1992). *Rural poverty in America.* New York, NY: Auburn House.

Ell, K., & Aisenberg, E. (Eds). (1998). Stress-related disorders. In J. Williams & K. Ell (Eds.), *Advances in mental health research: Implications for practice.* Washington, DC: NASW Press.

Goenjian, A., Karaya, I., Pynoose, R., & Minassian, D. (1997). Outcome of psychotherapy among early adolescents after trauma. *Journal of Psychiatry, 154,* 536–542.

Goffman, E. (1963). *Behavior in public places: Notes on the social organization of gatherings.* New York, NY: The Free Press.

Karim, G. (1997). In living context: An interdisciplinary approach to rethinking rural prevention. In E. Robertson (Ed.), *Rural substance abuse: State of knowledge and issues* (pp. 398–412). [NIDA Research Monograph 168]. Rockville, MD: U.S. Department of Health and Human Services.

Kovacs, M. (1981). Rating scales to assess depression in school-age children. *Acta Paedopsychiatrica, 46,* 305–315.

Kreuger, L., & Stretch, J. (1995, April). *A model helping adolescent disaster victims.* Paper presented to the Annual Program Meeting of the National Conference on Social Work Research, Washington, DC,

Krueger, R., & Casey, M. (2000). *Focus groups: A practical guide for applied research.* Newbury Park, CA: Sage.

Kuh., G. (1995). Purposes and principles for needs assessment in student affairs. *Journal of College Student Personnel, 23,* 203–209.

Lenning, O. (1980). Assessment and evaluation. In U. Delworth & G. Hanson (Eds.), *Student services: A handbook for the profession* (pp. 232–266). San Francisco, CA: Josey-Bass.

Lonigan, C. Y., Shannon, M. P., Finch, A. J., Daugherty, T. K., & Taylor, C. M. (1991). Children's reactions to a natural disaster: Symptom severity and degree of exposure. *Advances in Behavior Research and Therapy, 13*, 135–154.

Morgan, D. (1988). *Focus groups as qualitative research.* Newbury Park, CA: Sage.

Payne, J. (1999). *Researching health needs.* Thousand Oaks, CA: Sage.

Pereira, M. S. (2000). Teaching disaster management: Addressing complexities of social work practice. *The Indian Journal of Social Work, 61*, 693–701.

Peters, R. J., Jr., Meschack, A., Amos, C., Scott-Gurnell, K., Savage, C., & Ford, K. (2010). The association of drug use and post-traumatic stress reactions due to hurricane Ike among fifth ward Houstanian youth. *Journal of Ethnicity in Substance Abuse, 9*(2), 143–151.

Peterson, K., Prout, M., & Schwarz, R. (1991). *Post-traumatic stress disorder: A clinician's guide.* New York, NY: Plenum Press.

Poulin, J., & Soliman, H. H. (1999). Disaster outreach service provision: The development of an index. *Journal of Social Service Research, 25*(4), 77–92.

Prinstein, M., LaGreca, A., Vernbery E., & Silverman, W. (1996). Children's coping assistance: How parents, teachers and friends help children cope after a natural disaster. *Journal of Child Psychiatry, 25*, 463–476.

Putnam, F. (1991). Special methods for trauma research with children. In Carlson, E. (Ed.), *Trauma research methodology.* Luthersville, MD: Sidran.

Reynolds, C., & Richmond, B. (1978). What I think and feel: A revised measured of children's manifest anxiety. *Journal of Abnormal Child Psychology, 6*(2), 271–280.

Riad, J., & Norris, F. (1996). The influence of relocation on environmental, social, and psychological stress experienced by disaster victims. *Environment and Behavior, 28*(2), 163–183.

Robertson, E., Sloboda, Z., Boyd, G. & Kozel, N. (Eds.). (1997). *Rural substance abuse: State of knowledge and issues.* [NIDA Research Monograph 168]. Rockville, MD: U.S. Department of Health and Human Services.

Rohrbach, L. A., Grana, R., Vernberg, E., Sussman, S., & Sun, P. (2009). Impact of Hurricane Rita on adolescent substance abuse use. *Psychiatry-Interpersonal and biological Processes, 72*(3), 222–237.

Ronan, K. R., Crellin, K., Johnston, D. M., Finnis, K., Paton, D., & Becker, J. (2008). Promoting child and family resilience to disasters: Effects, inteventions, and prevention effectiveness. *Children, Youth & Environments 18*(1), 332–353.

Rosenfeld, L. B., Caye, J. S., Ayalon, O., & Lahad, M. (2005). *When their world falls apart: Helping families and children manage the effects of disasters*. Washington, DC: NASW Press.

Sahin, N. H., Batigun, A. D., & Yilmaz, B. (2007). Psychological symptoms of Turkish children and adolescents after the 1999 earthquake: Exposure, gender, location, and time duration. *Journal of Traumatic Stress, 20*, 335–345.

Seroka, C. M., Knapp, C., Knight, S., Siemon, C. R., & Starbuck, S. (1986). A comprehensive program for postdisaster counseling. *Social Casework, 67*, 37–44.

Shaw, J., Appelgate, B., & Schorr, C. (1996). Twenty-one month follow up study of school age children exposed to Hurricane Andrew. *Journal of the Academy of Child and Adolescent Psychiatry, 35*, 359–365.

Soliman, H. H., Rasquinha, S., Burkett, A., & Shelton, S. (2001). Counselor's satisfaction with disaster training: The development of an index. *Journal of Social Service Research, 27*(4), 61–78.

Stretch, J., & Kreuger, L. (1996, February). *Screening and serving long term disaster victims*. Paper presented to the Annual Program Meeting of the National Association of Welfare Research and Statistics, San Francisco, CA.

Stretch, J., Kreuger, L., & Hennicke, R. (1998, September). *Empowerment: Disaster responses show the way to helping flood victims*. Paper presented to the Annual Program Meeting of Catholic Charities USA, Houston, TX.

Swenson, C., Saylor, C., Powell, M., Stokes, S., Foster, K., & Belter, R. (1996). Impact of a natural disaster on preschool children: adjustment 14 months after a hurricane. *American Journal of Orthopsychiatry, 66*(1), 122–131.

Ursano, R., McCaughey, B., & Fulllerton, C. (1994). *Individual and community responses to trauma and disaster: The structure of human chaos*. London, UK: Cambridge University Press.

Villalba, J. A., & Lewis, L. D. (2007). Children, adolescents, and isolated traumatic events: Counseling considerations for couples and family counselors. *Family Journal, 15*(1), 30–35.

Wagenfeld, M. O., Murray, J. D., Mohat, D. F., & DeBruyn, J. C. (1997). Mental health service delivery in rural areas: Organizational and clinical issues. *NIDA Research Monograph, 168*. 418–437.

Williams, J., & Ell, K. (1998). *Advances in mental health research: Implications for practice*. Washington, DC: NASW Press.

Wilson, J., & Keane, T. (Eds.). (1999). Assessing psychological trauma and PTSD. New York, NY: Guilford Press.

Witkin, R., & Altschuld, J. (1995). Planning and conducting needs assessments. Thousand Oaks, CA: Sage.

Wolfe, V., Gentile, C., Michienzi, T., Sas, L., & Wolfe, D. (1991). The Children's Impact of Traumatic Events Scale: A measure of post-sexual abuse PTSD symptoms. *Behavioral Assessment, 13*, 359–383.

Yule, W., & Canterbury, R. (1995). The treatment of post traumatic stress disorder in children and adolescents. *International Review of Psychiatry, 6*(2), 141–151.

Yule, W., & Udwin, O. (1991). Screening child survivors for post-traumatic disorders: Experiences from the "Jupiter" sinking. *British Journal of Clinical Psychology, 30*, 131–138.

12 Strengths and Barriers to Successful Reentry in Rural Communities

PAUL DUONGTRAN, ABIGAIL KRISTEN NELSON, AND HEATHER ANN DODSON

This chapter presents a qualitative study that explores the complex problem of postincarceration (reentry) life adjustment and the quality of life of paroled persons living in the rural communities or states, such as Wyoming, with limited health and social services. The Bureau of Justice defines parole as a

> period of conditional supervised release in the community following a prison term, including prisoners released to parole either by a parole board decision (discretionary parole) or according to provisions of a statute (mandatory parole). These data include adults under the jurisdiction of a parole agency, regardless of supervision status (i.e., active supervision, inactive supervision, financial conditions only, absconder status, or supervised out of state).

Furthermore, strict procedures and regulations on reentry are required, and any violation of the conditions of parole results in revocation and reimprisonment. The sampling of paroled persons for this study was guided by convenience in logistics, because they were living in a transitional residence in Cheyenne, the state capitol, under the supervision of the Wyoming Department of Corrections.

Prison and Reentry Challenges in Rural and Frontier Wyoming

Incarceration and reentry of former prisoners present challenging problems for society that require massive financial supports at the local and state levels, along with community acceptance and political will. Reentry into a rural community or state is further complicated by nearly nonexistent social service, educational, economic, and job infrastructures. The two most populous cities in Wyoming, Cheyenne and Casper, have approximately 60,000 and 50,000 residents, respectively.

The state of Wyoming is rural according to federal classification. Being geographically the ninth largest state in the country (surface area of 97,632 square miles), Wyoming has the smallest population—563,626 residents—among the 50 states and District of Columbia. Reentry for a former prisoner in Wyoming is challenging because of the daunting environmental, physical, and social gaps in its rural and frontier setting.

Based on figures from the 2000 U.S. Census, approximately nine million people live in frontier counties, where 812 frontier counties are located in 38 states. Although the percentage of people who live in frontier counties is small, only about 3% of the U.S. population, the area on which they live is large. Frontier counties comprise approximately 56% of the land area and contain 49% of the water area in the United States, a total of 2,125,413 square miles.

A key determiner of frontier life is distance. Accordingly, areas with population density as high as 20 people per square mile could be considered frontier, if the community were located at a great distance or travel time from the closest significant service center or market. The Frontier Education Center (1998) adopted a consensus definition of frontier, which is based on a matrix that includes population density and distance in miles and travel time in minutes from a market-service area. This consensus definition has been formally adopted by both the National Rural Health Association and The Western Governors Association.

Wyoming represents the classic characteristics of large space between villages, towns, or cities, as measured by driving distance. According to Wyoming-Maps.org (2008), Wyoming is derived from

a Delaware Indian word, meaning "alternating mountains and valleys." Eastern Wyoming's terrain features high plains and rolling grasslands which are well-suited to ranching and cattle raising operations. In central and western Wyoming, the high plateau is broken by several mountain ranges. The Big Horn and Laramie Mountains run through northern and southern central Wyoming, respectively, while the Absaroka and Wind River Mountains are located in northwestern Wyoming.

The state topography presents immense physical challenges in elevation. The town of Laramie is 7,277 feet, or 1.40 miles, above sea level. Cheyenne, the capitol and largest city, is at 6,067 feet above sea level, or 1.15 miles. Winter temperatures average below 32° F, with frequent fluctuations between –5° and 5° F. Cheyenne is the only Wyoming city with a public bus system, although it has limited daily and weekend service hours. Traveling in the city or anywhere in this rural-frontier state is a severe physical limitation for a former prisoner. Traveling in an automobile in poor working condition across frozen mountain passes can be life threatening. Bicycling across towns to services or job sites can be hindered in the winter months, beginning in late October and going through early May.

Rural and frontier cultures differ in social behaviors, traditions, and norms. Firearms advocates in Arizona seek constitutional protection under the Second Amendment. Firearms in rural and frontier states such as Wyoming are used to obtain food and nutrients for families throughout the year. The removal of rights to firearms poses a social and nutrition barrier to former prisoners who grew up hunting for family meals in Wyoming (Nelson & Dodson, personal communication, July 13, 2011). Another distinctive frontier characteristic of residents is the staunch resistance to migrate outside their environment (e.g., to towns or out of state). Facing severe social, service, and job limitations, many former prisoners would not consider relocating to other cities or states, because they do not have family or social traditions or networks (Nelson & Dodson, personal communication, July 13, 2011).

Reentry and Legal Barriers

The Bureau of Justice Statistics (2008) estimates that more than two thirds of the individuals released from prison will be rearrested within 3 years. Every year, nearly 700,000 people will leave prison, and another nine million will leave local jails. The ability to facilitate success in reentry for paroled persons is a critical prevention and a positive contribution to society. The challenges of reentry for incarcerated persons are complex and extensive, including housing, employment, financial assistance, family reunification, educational needs, mental health care, and overcoming social stigma. A felony conviction and incarceration invariably strip a prisoner of some constitutional rights, such as the right to vote. Although a reentering person is not persona non grata, his or her life challenges are real. Reentry is not only about the former inmates; the profound effects on the community, families, children, coworkers, neighbors, and society are equally remarkable.

The United States has a high incarceration rate. Some studies show that Russia is higher (Walmsley, 2009). The U.S. incarceration rate on June 30, 2009, was 748 inmates per 100,000 U.S. residents, or 0.75%. According to U.S. Bureau of Justice (2009) statistics, 7,225,800 people at the end of 2009 were on probation, in jail or prison, or on parole—about 3.1% of adults in the U.S. resident population, or one in every 32 adults. A 2002 study survey showed that, among nearly 275,000 prisoners released in 1994, 67.5% were rearrested within 3 years of release, and 51.8% were back in prison (Langan & Levin, 2002).

As noted previously, the challenges of reentry for incarcerated persons are complex and extensive, including housing, employment, financial assistance, family reunification, educational needs, mental health care, and social stigma. The felony conviction is a permanent record only removed through an act of clemency or pardon by a state governor or the president of the United States. Persons released from prisons experience a "resocialization" to pursue effective social integration, despite visible and invisible barriers. On reentry, immediate tasks involve finding housing, gaining employment, dealing with untreated health or mental health diagnoses, reconnecting with family, and fulfilling the lawful obligations of the parole. Ultimately, reentering persons face short timelines to succeed among severe and prohibitive social stigma and nearly nonexistent personal and social resources.

State laws vary on the extension of rights and privileges to former prisoners. In many parts of the United States a convicted felon can face long-term legal consequences, persisting after the end of imprisonment. Felons may be able to apply for restoration of some rights after a certain period of time has passed. Nonetheless, some major prohibitions by federal law include   exclusion from obtaining certain permits and licenses; exclusion from purchase and possession of firearms, ammunition, and body armor; ineligibility to serve on a jury; and deportation, if the criminal is not a citizen. Other legal prohibitions include the denial of federal financial aid for students convicted of a drug offense (Higher Education Act of 1998, amended). It is estimated that more than 128,000 students applying for federal financial aid have been denied assistance. Additionally, most job applications ask about felony history, and answering dishonestly can be grounds for rejecting the application or termination, if the lie is discovered after hire. Many bonding companies will not issue bonds to convicted felons, effectively barring them from certain jobs. Many banks will not lend to convicted felons. Some states also consider a felony conviction to be grounds for an uncontested divorce. Table 1 illustrates the social and legal rights and privileges denied to nearly all reentry prisoners when they seek social integration.

TABLE 1   Normative Assets, Privileges, and Rights of Nonconvicted or Convicted Persons

	Nonconvicted Person	Formerly Convicted Person
High-school or college education	●	
Vocational skills	●	
Employment history	●	
Vocational skills	●	
Bank accounts	●	
Credit cards	●	
Job references	●	
Rent references	●	
Consumer credit rating	●	
Driver's license	●	
Right to vote	●	
Family support	●	
Social support	●	
Health insurance	●	
Mental health needs		●
Health needs		●

Rurality

Rural America is home to a fifth of of the U.S. population, comprises more than 2,000 counties, and accounts for 75% of the nation's land (Kusmin & Hertz, 2010). Being released into a rural community has its unique challenges. In the United States today, for instance, there are more prisoners than farmers (Huling, 2002). Although most prisoners in America are from urban communities, most prisons are now in rural areas. Due to low population density, geographical distance from large metropolitan areas, inclement weather, geographic barriers, lack of transportation, and for other reasons, many rural nonfelon residents are isolated from health and social services. In addition, the culture of rural areas, including a history of self-sufficiency and lack of anonymity, inhibits rural residents from accessing available assistance (Woodhal, 2006).

Since 1980 most new prisons built to accommodate the expanding U.S. prison population have been placed in nonmetropolitan areas, resulting in the majority of prisoners being housed in rural America. By contrast, prior to 1980 only 36% of prisons were located in rural communities and small towns. Calvin Beale (1996), a senior demographer with the Economic Research Service of the U.S. Department of Agriculture, reports that, throughout the 1960s and 1970s, an average of four new prisons had been built in rural areas each year. During the 1980s that figure increased to an annual average of 16, and, in the 1990s, it jumped to 25 new prisons annually (Beale, 1996). Between 1990 and 1999, 245 prisons were built in rural and small town communities—with a prison opening somewhere in rural America every 15 days (Huling, 2002). The new rural prisons of the 1990s had about 235,000 inmates and employed 75,000 workers at the end of the decade—averaging 30 employees for every 100 prisoners. Approximately 350 rural counties have acquired new prisons since the start-up of the prison boom began in 1980, and more than half of all rural counties added prison work to their available employment mix during the final two decades of the 20th century (Huling, 2002). In this prison-building and economic-revitalization boom in rural America, another form of institutional racism has been produced. Racial hatred behind and beyond prison walls is another deeply troubling consequence of the increasing dependence of rural communities on prisons. Although racism is not a new feature of the U.S. prison system, efforts to address the problem are undermined by the trend toward building prisons in rural areas, where the workforce is predominantly White and prisoners are predominantly people of color (Chesney-Lind, 2002).

For the current study we explored and assessed the knowledge, attitude, and perception of paroled persons on reentry and differences among the sample subgroups. The following research questions guided our research:

- What are the perceived fears, barriers, efficacy, or control to facilitate positive reentry for paroled persons?

- What are the knowledge, attitude, and perception differences among the paroled persons, parole officers, administrators, and social work students?

Method

Participants

In designing the study we chose four groups of people we considered most pertinent to the process and experience of prisoner reentry after release from prisons: parolees (*n*=8), parole officers (*n*=2), correction administrators (*n*=2), and social work students (*n*=9). Parole officers have the most intimate knowledge of the personal needs, legal requirements, and social difficulties in securing stable housing, employment, and substance-use controls throughout the parole period. Corrections administrators have a direct knowledge of policy implementation and resource allocation important to reentry effectiveness. In this study we were also interested in assessing the knowledge and attitudes of social work students enrolled in the MSW program at the University of Wyoming to gauge their awareness and academic and professional interests to engage professionally in the problems of incarceration and reentry.

The research study met the human-protection guidelines, as approved by the Institutional Review Board at the University of Wyoming for 2007 and 2008.

Recruitment. The research project was presented to and approved by the corrections administrators of the Wyoming Department of Corrections in Cheyenne, WY. Assistance was provided in arranging a meeting with the parolees who were residents of the Transitional House in Cheyenne.

The inclusion criteria for selection included that parolees have a minimum of 5 years in prison and currently be paroled or on probation. Selection excluded any sex-offense felony. Parolees were registered on parole and living in Wyoming. They were males who had averaged 5–23 years in prison and were 3–8 months on parole at the time of the study.

Parole officers included one male and one female, both employees of the Wyoming Department of Corrections. Similarly, the corrections administrators were one male and one female and also were employees at the Department of Corrections in Cheyenne, WY. The administrators supervised the state reentry program and the half-way houses for the state of Wyoming. Lastly, social work students were recruited from the MSW program at the University of Wyoming in Laramie. Two male and seven female students were enrolled in their first academic year of MSW study and were native residents of Wyoming.

Measurement and procedure. Using various methods, data were collected from parolees (one-time focus group), from corrections administrators (telephone interviews), from parole officers (face-to-face interviews), and from social work students (focus group). The interview questions focused on five thematic areas the researchers considered important in the responses and reaction to reentry for a paroled person: personal fear, social resources, family, work, and technology.

Prior to data collection the research team had discussions with two former prisoners, who did not participate in the final data collection, to explore the typical emotions, perceptions, and expectations in preparing for reentry. Social resources, family support, and work are normative expectations for successful reentry. The two additional themes are surprising and contradictory: personal fear and technological apprehension. The public images of former prisoners inevitably convey dread, threat, and intimidation. We learned at the prestudy stage that tattooed and rough-edged men and women have real fears when they return after many years to the changed world and society. Ordinary technology also creates great anxiety, because it has been transformed dramatically over the years. For example, a person incarcerated in the 1980s knows simply the coin-operated or dial phone and may never have used Droid-based smartphones or 4G broadband.

Informed consent. The participants were given a brief explanation of the interview process and problem statements and then asked whether they would be opposed to the interview being audio-recorded. No monetary incentive was offered to any participant. All of the participants signed the consent forms prior to data collection. To ensure the highest protection against personal incrimination of paroled persons who were willing to participate, parolees were informed verbally, as well as on the consent form, that participation in no way positively or negatively affected their probation and parole. Parole officers offered verbal and written assurance that parolees' participation would not have any effect on their probation or parole terms.

Interviews. The interview settings were important to protect the privacy and any perceived threat or intimidation to the parolee persons in disclosure for the purpose of this research project. Parolees participated in a focus group at the Department of Corrections meeting room without the presence of administrators or parole officers. The social work students completed their interview during one regularly scheduled class in the spring of 2008 at the University of Wyoming. Parole officers and corrections administrators were interviewed by telephone during their office hours.

Results

The challenges of reentry for incarcerated persons are complex and extensive, including aspects such as housing, employment, financial assistance, family reunification, educational needs, mental health care, and lingering social stigma. We present narratives obtained from individual interviews and focus groups to illustrate the serious challenges anticipated by various parties in the reentry process.

Personal Fears

Most Americans have an impression of a prisoner as tough, insensitive, ruthless, and fearless, without realizing the real anxieties of those released from prison. Many former prisoners have compelling fears and anxieties related to reentry success or failure. When these fears are not addressed or acknowledged, it can lead to a higher rate of recidivism through social alienation and inappropriate behaviors. Although parolees face many fears on reentry, this study examined the fears related to prison release, social stigma, social resources, police and criminal justice systems, and ordinary societal facilities such as unfamiliarity with information technology or megastores, such as WalMart.

Freedom. Embracing freedom after many years of incarceration is the natural expectation from and perception of the public. Parole officers and corrections administrators understand, however, that freedom is a real fear, not always a privilege, for many paroled persons. One parole officer commented:

> if they have been down for more than 5 years, just dealing with everyday life is very difficult; getting up on your own, having a job, making it, paying your bills—all of those things that were taken care of for so long—it's a big adjustment to doing it on their own.

Similarly, an administrator agreed:

> I think that they have a lot of anxieties about being released. I am sure, when they know their release dates coming up, they start getting pretty crazy about what it is going to be like. I think the other thing is fears setting in: fear of getting a job, fear of being back in the community and having to figure it out on their own, fear of seeing their family in the community (outside of prison) and having to do their own budget or having to get into a relationship.

The administrator continued:

> I would say they are probably worried about how their families are going to react when they get home; how society has changed, since they were incarcerated; how

their kids have grown, since they were away; how their family has managed to go on without them, since they have been gone; whether they still have job skills.

Prisoner stigma. A social perception commonly agreed on by parolees, parole officers, and administrators is the outcast stigma of a felony conviction lingering and impeding personal ability to reintegrate. This fear is already initiated prior to leaving prison or immediately following release. A parolee worries about how the world is going to react to his or her felony conviction. In this instance, a parolee stated that "with myself being gone from society for that long, sometimes I don't have a choice to talk about where I have been, because it is obvious to others that I have not been around."

A parole officer with intimate knowledge and extensive firsthand experience about the functioning of paroled persons' lives after reentering society discusses the unrelenting stigma felt in job search or during employment:

> Well, it's just that some places don't hire felons flat out, and so, if they are a felon, they have a really hard time obtaining a good paying job. They can work at Burger King, but sometimes McDonalds won't even hire felons.

Other privileges of the rural culture, such as hunting licenses, are also unavailable to felons. An administrator affirms, "the less criminal things like voting, hunting, but here in Wyoming and the culture, people get really excited about hunting season, and [felons] are not able to fit into that situation either."

Penal system. Anticipating compound disadvantages and challenges on reentry, paroled persons have an immediate fear of failing, thus becoming another public statistic in the revolving door of incarceration. Many former prisoners have seen this prison recycling routine, in which many individuals were released at or near the same time as they were but did not succeed in reentering society. A parolee divulged his fear of becoming another statistic, "I think the anxieties that I felt right before I got out were [about] not being that statistic that you kept watching go in and out [of prison]." Parolees and corrections personnel also acknowledge the reluctance of parolees to call on the justice of peace or public-safety personnel (police) for assistance after reentry. A parole officer confirms:

> Another big fear is just dealing with law enforcement, cops, on a positive basis. They have huge anxieties of trying to ask for help or reporting something without

feeling like they are a criminal again and harassed. I have some guys that have been out for 2–3 years, and they are starting to do well, but every time they have to have a law enforcement contact they shake and get real nervous, and they haven't done anything wrong but just their stresses of the past are still with them.

Having choices and freedom to choose are privileges the public naturally assumes or expects in the daily routines. When parolees transition into the community, they face enormous choices in their actions or decisions that can cause severe anxiety and psychological stress. Each parolee who was interviewed reluctantly shared his embarrassing experience of the first time he entered a large store. One shared this experience:

> I had so many years of thoughts and visions of what could be out here, to be nonviolent, to be nonthreatening, and successful. So, I got overconfident and a false sense of security, and a false sense of how the world was. A friend took me to Walmart for the first time, and I had to use the restroom. When I came out, I couldn't see him, and I went into a panic attack. Almost like a form of dementia, I was lost when I couldn't see him and ended up going around the entire store the longest way possible.
>
> That was very embarrassing, painful, and shameful. There wasn't really anything positive about it; scared, probably embarrassed most of all. As time goes on I find that you "don't run before you walk." You have to crawl then walk. Then keep walking, and, to me, that is the way that you are going to have a successful transition into society.

Resources

Perceived need for a person on parole to succeed. Individuals with criminal convictions face considerable barriers, often needing transitional services and support to improve their ability to acquire gainful employment and transition after incarceration. Former prisoners may be ineligible for Temporary Assistance for Needy Families (TANF), Social Security Income, and food stamp benefits. A parolee who has been convicted in a drug-related felon is barred for life from receiving federally funded cash assistance through the TANF program and food stamps. Currently, 22 states have imposed the ban in part and 14 states completely enforce the ban.

If parolees are still eligible for these benefits, parole mandates often conflict with the work requirements for benefit programs. For example, work hours or location of employment may be beyond the authorized curfew or place of residence.

In this study parolees offered diverse opinions on their immediate and long-term needs for successful reentry. Several important areas of need were identified: having a social support system, being able to reconnect with people, obtaining work and a living wage, and gaining skills in technology and education. A parole officer affirmed:

I just think [we] need education and support and people to identify the right resources in order to help [us] succeed. I think [we] need some sort of balance in [our] lives and some sort of discipline in [our] lives as well.

Another parole officer commented:

Probably the biggest thing is motivation, their own self-motivation to stay away from drugs, alcohol, their old friends, and then having a positive support system of people who are not going to bring those things around. Then having a good job, family, and friends—those types of supports are always good.

Another big thing is being honest with themselves about what's going on, being willing to talk about the problems, issues, and asking for help when the problem does come up, instead of trying to hide from it.

An administrator laments the uphill challenge for all parolees: "It seems to me that if you don't have the ability to make money or get yourself into a decent housing situation, than its just always going to be an uphill battle, a struggle from the get-go."

When a parolee reenters society, many initial resources are very critical, as expressed by one administrator:

I just think that there is a hierarchy of stuff that they need, and I think that it's kind of a domino situation when they don't get it, so I would say that the housing is an issue, but jobs are a bigger issue, and then, of course, a support network is probably critical.

Education. Many former prisoners have minimal education or outdated skills from being away for many years. As mentioned, they cannot receive federal student financial aid. Without obtaining more education, the parolee is destined to work at a dead end job, or, worse, continue doing what they know best—criminality. An administrator offered a grim assessment:

> I think that, even if they get into college, and let's just say that they get a degree, which would be pretty amazing, and then you bring an inmate that has been in prison for 10 years, and then you put them in the college situation, and they are already 10 years older, even if they get the degree, they still have to apply and report that they are a felon.

A student shared in this view:

> I just feel like there is a huge setback being in prison and not being aware of what's going on outside of prison—technology, education. Many of the jobs require vocational training or some kind of post-secondary education, not just needing a minimum GED.

Housing. Parolees face challenges in obtaining the very basic need of housing, stemming from the inability to qualify for low-income state funded housing to background checks, mostly stemming from the stigma of being a felon. Other housing exclusions include moving into a federally subsidized housing facility or participating in a federally assisted housing program. "Housing authorities sometimes will not allow them (paroled persons) to receive benefits or live with someone receiving benefits because of their record," one paroled officer said. In addition, it is difficult for a former prisoner to get housing in the private market, because they often lack the financial resources for a security deposit and lack the employment and housing references for applications. A parole officer confirms that "many apartment complexes, mobile home parks, and things will run background checks, and, if you have any kind of felony record, they automatically disqualify you, so people are having a harder and harder time finding a place to live." The cycle of rejection is predictable, according to a student: "I think that a lot of them don't have a place to live when they get out, and you cannot get a job if you do not have an address or a phone number."

Health and social services. When reentering their communities, former prisoners or paroled persons often do not receive proper medical and substance abuse treatment. This is especially a concern because of the high incidence of medical problems (HIV and AIDS, tuberculosis, hepatitis C, etc.), substance abuse, and mental illness in the prison population. A parole officer explains service availability to parolees who enter the transitional housing services in Cheyenne, WY:

> We do have one program that is going in town here that seem to be helping a lot, and it's a church-based group that do a 12-step group and a Bible study type of thing, and it's through Second Change Ministries.

Although treatment services remain a priority at reentry, "very few take parenting classes when we have such limited resources available for those things," according to one parole officer.

Information technology lag. Keeping up with technology is difficult for anyone. Imagine being away from it for 5, 10, or more years. Technology, particularly computer and communication equipment, has changed exponentially from the 1980s to present. One man shared his view while serving parole:

> Oh yes, that is huge. When I was incarcerated, cell phones were not in much use and the Internet had only been around for like a year, so to come out now, with all the new advances in technology, is really frightening. I was a typical person who thought that I didn't need to learn how to use a computer, and it is essential.

A student empathetically affirms:

> I think that they need skills with technology. If you look at a person who has been in prison for 5 years, for them to know just how much our society has progressed would be very important for their reentry success.

Similarly, a parole officer elaborates:

> They didn't have cell phones, don't know how to get one, or operate one. You know, people   pay their bills online. Nowadays, computer skills and understanding what the new technology is with cell phones and computers are always a big help. Financial skills in dealing with their checkbooks, bank accounts, loans and not getting in over their heads, understanding the consequences of impulse purchases and things like that.

Work

Criminal records are easily available to potential employers, landlords, and other general community members, so former prisoners are frequently discriminated against and denied access to many resources critical to reintegration and successful reentry. Federal and state statutes prohibit employment in certain fields (e.g., law enforcement or the military), as related to particular criminal convictions, and prohibit former prisoners from obtaining licenses for several occupations. Former prisoners also are discriminated against in the hiring process because of their criminal history, regardless of whether the position is related to the convicted crime.

Finding an occupation in rural Wyoming that pays a living wage is very difficult for many individuals. Work opportunities are limited, industries are scattered across the state, and former prisoners' travel distance is limited by parole restrictions. Paroled persons have a very difficult time finding a living wage in Wyoming or elsewhere. Although there is always work in the oil fields or construction industry in Wyoming, these jobs require the parolees to move to rural Wyoming, where there are not many other resources (e.g., counseling, Alcohol/Narcotics Anonymous, or family support) to help their reintegration. An administrator confirms: "The real crucial things, like getting good employment, are always going to be one of the negative side effects or conditions of committing a felony and going to prison." A parole officer says of the employment barriers affecting the parolees:

> Most of them have job skills in the construction-type industry and labor industry, oil industry, and that's where they tend to be very focused on the work thing. But some of them really have not completed much education. They don't know how to go on a job interview, fill out a job application, and present themselves to get that employment. Some of them don't even know where to begin.

Job skills. An individual lacking job skills and past work experience is not a marketable individual in the contemporary workforce. Adding the information of being a convicted felon to that job application, the paroled persons' chances of obtaining a living wage are slim to none. Wyoming lacks the resources to provide job skill training for incarcerated persons, which results in many parolees leaving prison with very limited or no job skills. Although there are steps to address the limited job skill training in prison, the result of leaving prison and entering the labor market without these skills is highly predictable. Parole officers commented on the general status of the corrections systems in their vocational programs in and after prison:

> If they [prisoners] are up at the forestry camps, some of them get the opportunity to go through their fire programs. Also, at the farm, they have some fire-related work activities, which could potentially aid them with work on the outside.
>
> It's hard to address job skills when you are in prison, but so many of them lack job skills. Interpersonal relationship skills, such as how to talk to people and present themselves [at job interviews], are just basic skills you would assume they know. Many of them don't.

An administrator reflects on ways to overcome these barriers:

> It might be that prison could be the place where they could get the job skill...I just think that it is an area that we need to be educated a little bit more as to what they need. A lot of them may be releasing without the job skills that they will need in order to go into the workforce that they may have never been in before in the first place.

One student shared a thought on these barriers: "I think that, if people know that parolees are coming out of prisons and they have had all of these services, they might be more willing to hire."

Social Support

Families of prisoners struggle with a range of challenges that are often exacerbated by the imprisonment of a family member. Broadening our perspective to include incarceration's effect on prisoner families—from the arrest, to imprisonment, and on to release—raises a number of important questions (Travis & Waul, 2003). Some of these questions are: How can family bonds be strengthened during the prison term? Are there ways to help families cope with the period of incarceration? How should a parent and child be reunited? Is there a risk that the stress of incarceration will limit inmates' ability to be effective parents after release? Is there a heightened risk of domestic violence and child abuse as prisoners adjust to their new reality? Can the process of reentry be viewed as an opportunity for intervention with these families?

A parolee lamented the isolation from society and social support:

The most important part of my support system is finding the understanding of compassion toward my situation, because after being in the penitentiary for so long, you feel embarrassed, because you need to ask questions that people who haven't been in prison for 16 years do not need to ask... it's just that I need and want to learn, whether it is how to use a computer or cell phone. Support systems to me are the most awesome thing in the world. The healthy support system that you know you are living in, and people who are responsible—living with people who think healthily and make healthy decisions. Being without a support system is huge, because someone coming out of the penitentiary has all these anxieties, fears, hopes, questions, paranoia.

Having the support of family is important, one administrator believes: "the importance of the family: I think it would be important to develop while they are in prison and try to bring that group together a little closer and build that network while they are in prison." Another administrator agrees on the role of family support:

I think they lean on their families quite a bit...I think part of it is they need to build up their community relationships before they leave, if possible, so they can reestablish their community links and support system that may or may not be there anymore.

Having the ability to reconnect with others through socialization is very important in successful reentry. Parolees have been away from society, and they need help readjusting to the social changes that occurred while they were gone. A parole officer explains:

In my opinion, they just don't know how to socialize, and I think their fear sometimes is larger groups of people. Some of them are just really scared socially about how everything works in the world, because they have been away for a while.

Conclusion

In this chapter we discussed information drawn from qualitative interviews and a brief online questionnaire from the following stakeholders: (a) parolees through their perceptions, experience, and knowledge of policy and programs of incarceration and reentry; and (b) parole officers, corrections administrators, and social work students to assess their perceptions, knowledge, and interest in the reentry status of state incarceration. Most Americans pay little or no attention to people coming back from prison. Successful outcomes in reentry have enormous financial and personal costs to every community in America. The 2008 fiscal crisis has catapulted the taxing problem of incarceration across the country. According to the Justice Policy Institute (2009), 40 out of 50 states were at 90% capacity or more, with 23 of those states operating at more than 100% capacity in 2006. The public attitudes toward increases in drug imprisonment, decrease in releases from prison, and reincarceration for technical parole violations have created overcrowded conditions, spiraling costs, and state corrections budgets that have been exceeded.

Western (2008) proposes a prisoner reentry program that would be phased in over time and adjusted based on evidence of what works. The program would comprise four elements: (1) expanded in-prison correctional programs, such as education and work training; (2) transitional employment after release; (3) parole reform to support the effectiveness of transitional jobs; and (4) the elimination of bans on some federal benefits for people with criminal records.

Some changes have occurred in federal legislation to emphasize adequate resources and support at reentry to prevention of "recycling" into prison. The Second Chance Act was signed into law in April 2008. The 2008 omnibus included $10 million for an offender reentry program, which was used for the third and final year of funding for the Prisoner Reentry Initiative administered by the Department of Justice. The services to be funded under the Second Chance Act include mentoring programs for adults and juveniles leaving prison; drug treatment during and after incarceration, including family-based treatment for incarcerated parents; education and job training in prison; alternatives to incarceration for parents convicted of nonviolent drug offenses; supportive programming for children of incarcerated parents; and early release for certain elderly prisoners convicted of nonviolent offenses. Unfortunately, the level of funding is minimal and lacks long-term investment in the future of prisoners and protection of reimprisonment costs to society.

An individual's transition from prison back into a home and a community is difficult, and avoiding crime can be the least of his or her problems. Understanding these pathways and the reasons for and the dimensions of an individual's success or failure is the focus of recent scholarly attention to the problem of prisoner reentry, the process of leaving prison and returning to free society. However, most of the existing research on prisoners' lives after release focuses solely on recidivism and ignores the reality that recidivism is directly affected by postprison reintegration and adjustment, which, in turn, depends on factors such as personal and situational characteristics, including the individual's social environment of peers, family, community, and state-level policies (Visher & Travis, 2003).

The reintegration into society of incarcerated persons is complex and requires a variety of services, some help from others, and governmental policies that encourage reentry.

References

Beale, C. (1993). Prisons, population, and jobs in non-metro America. *Rural Development Perspectives*, 8(3), 16–19.

Beale, C. (1996). Rural prisons: An update. *Rural Development Perspectives, 11*(2), 25–27.

Bureau of Justice. (2009). *Statistics correctional surveys: Prisoners, probation and parole, and jail inmates at midyear 2009—statistical tables*. Washington, DC: U.S. Department of Justice.

Bureau of Justice Statistics. (2002). *Recidivism of prisoners*. Retrieved from http://bjs.ojp.usdoj.gov/index.cfm?ty=pbdetail&iid=1134

Chesney-Lind, M. (Eds.). (2002). *Invisible punishment: The collateral consequences of mass imprisonment*. New York, NY: The New Press.

Frontier Education Center. (2003). *Frontier: A new definition; the final report of the Consensus Development Project*. Retrieved from http://www.frontierus.org/documents/consensus_paper.htm

Huling, T. (2002). Building a prison economy in rural America. In M. Mauer & M. Chesney-Lind (Eds.), *Invisible punishment: The collateral consequences of mass imprisonment* (pp. 254–282). New York, NY: The New Press.

Justice Policy Institute. (2009). *Pruning prisons: How cutting corrections can save money and protect public safety*. Retrieved from http://www.justicepolicy.org/images/upload/09_05_REP_PruningPrisons_AC_PS.pdf

Kusmin, L., & Hertz, T. (2010). Rural American at a glance. *Economic Information Bulletin, 68*, 1–6.

Langan, P. A., & Levin, D. J. (2002). *Recidivism of prisoners.* Washington, DC: U.S. Bureau of Justice Statistics.

Petteruti, A., Walsh, N., & Velázquez, T. (2009). Pruning prisons: How cutting corrections can save money and protect public safety. Washington, DC: Justice Policy Institute.

Travis, J., & Waul, M. (2003). *Prisoners once removed: The impact of incarceration and reentry on children, families and communities*. Washington, D.C: Urban Institute Press.

Visher, C. A., & Travis, J. (2003). Transitions from prison to community: Understanding individual pathways. *Annual Review of Sociology, 29*, 89–113.

Walmsley, R. (2009). *World prison population list*, 8th ed. Retrieved from http://www.kcl.ac.uk/depsta/law/research/icps/publications.php?id=8

Western, B. (2008). *From prison to work: A proposal for a national prisoner reentry program*. Retrieved from http://www.brookings.edu/papers/2008/12_prison_to_work_western.aspx

Wodalh, E. (2006). The challenges of prisoner reentry from a rural perspective. *Western Criminology Review, 7*(2), 32–34.

Wyoming-Map.org. (2008). *Wyoming Map*. Retrieved from http://www.wyoming-map.org/

13 Resiliency and Behavioral Health Challenges Among American Indians and Alaska Natives in Rural Communities

PAT CONWAY, DOLORES SUBIA BIGFOOT,
AND ELANA PREMACK SANDLER

Rural American Indian and Alaska Native families live in geographically diverse areas throughout the United States, from remote communities in Northern Alaska, to rural Northern Plains reservations, to isolated communities in the Grand Canyon. Behavioral health challenges experienced by American Indians and Alaska Natives living in rural, frontier, and remote areas include high rates of depression, suicide, and substance use (Substance Abuse and Mental Health Services Administration [SAMHSA], 2008, 2010; Smith, N.D.; U.S. Department of Health and Human Services, 2010). Factors that may contribute to these challenges include a population that is younger than the national average, a higher percentage of single adult-headed households, a lower median income, and a lower high school graduation rate (Ogunwole, 2006) than the overall population. The rates are even more striking for American Indians and Alaska Natives living in rural tribal areas (Ogunwole, 2006). These challenges are, at least in part, the result of historical and current trauma, such as repressive federal policies that decimated families and communities, widespread poverty, and lack of access to resources in rural areas (Samuels, Probst, & Glover, N.D.). This chapter describes the current behavioral health status of American Indians and Alaska Natives in rural communities as a backdrop to identifying programs based on culture that builds on resiliency among American Indian and Alaska Native families and the use of evidence-based practices. The role of social work in this endeavor concludes the chapter.

American Indians and Alaska Natives in Rural Communities

The 565 federally recognized tribes and many other nonfederally recognized Indian communities, such as the Lumbee Tribe in rural North Carolina, are scattered across the "lower 48" and Alaska (see Figure 1; www.bia.gov). Thirty-nine percent of all American Indians and Alaska Natives live in rural areas, and 40% of those live in rural minority counties, usually reservations in the upper plains, the Southwest, and Alaska (Wagner, 2007/2008). Rural minority counties are counties where at least one third of the populations are minorities (Bowers & Cook, 1999). Some communities are in remote areas, such as the Turtle Mountain Band of Chippewa on the North Dakota/Manitoba border, with 30,995 enrolled members. The 2010 Census reports 8,656 people living within the Turtle Mountain reservation boundary; 96% are American Indian (North Dakota Indian Affairs Commission, 2011). Many enrolled members also live in farming communities surrounding the reservation; American Indians comprise 76% of Rolette County, where the reservation is located, compared with the state rate of 5.8% and 1.5% of the U.S. population (Murphy & Bishop, 2008; Ogunwole, 2006). This county is considered rural (a nonmetropolitan, completely rural, county that does not contain a town with at least 2,500 people); all the counties surrounding it are frontier, with fewer than six people per square mile.

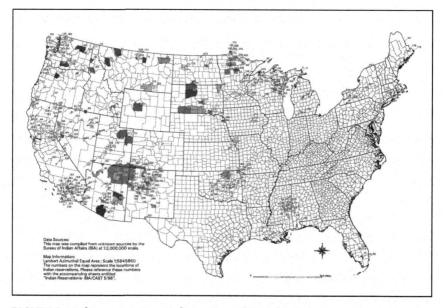

FIGURE 1   Indian reservations in the continental United States.

The types of rural areas in which American Indians and Alaska Natives live vary; the Census Bureau designated six Tribal Statistical Areas (U.S. Census, 2009). For instance, the Turtle Mountain Band of Chippewa has a designated reservation with tribal land. Many tribes in Oklahoma, such as the Chickasaw Tribe, are Oklahoma Tribal Statistical Areas (U.S. Census, 2009); these tribes previously had a reservation but no longer do. A high percentage of American Indians and Alaska Natives are young, with 33% below the age of 18. Correspondingly, a smaller percentage is age 65 and older, 5.6% compared to the national average of 12.4%. A higher percentage of families have female heads of households than the national average also (Ogunwole, 2006). Other areas of disparity include higher rates of poverty, lower educational attainment, and fewer economic opportunities (Samuels, 2002).

American Indians and Alaska Natives in rural areas experience the pleasures and dilemmas of all rural communities, such as trading lower crime rates for increased barriers for access to consistent health care, especially specialty care, such as treatment for behavioral health issues (SAMHSA, 2010). Even when economic times are tight, American Indians and Alaska Natives may prefer to remain in their home community. A study of residents in Southeast Alaska found that, in spite of the recent economic downturn, only 11% of Alaskan Natives planned to leave (Ulrich & Safford, 2011). Their top reasons for remaining, in order, were the quality of life, natural beauty, fishing and hunting, family, and cultural and religious roles. Rural areas are affected by behavioral health workforce shortages, provision of primary health care that does not incorporate behavioral health, fewer referral options for more specialized behavioral health care or treatment, and lack of training and specific skills among providers (STIPDA Rural Youth Suicide Prevention Workgroup, 2008). This is especially significant, considering the limitation of services available for children and adolescents, when immediate interventions would be most effective but are unavailable.

In addition to the typical issues regarding behavioral health, American Indians and Alaska Natives face unique challenges, especially when they live within reservation boundaries in one of the many small communities established as permanent settlements prior to 1880. A guiding factor in placement of settlements was the removal from conflict with encroaching settlers and mining interests. Therefore, many reservations are located in remote areas, creating educational and economic challenges.

The primary behavioral health care providers in rural areas are general practitioners and midlevel service providers, such as social workers and paraprofessionals (Gale, Shaw, Hartley, & Loux, 2010). In many tribal communities the

Indian Health Service (IHS) is the primary behavioral health care provider, in conjunction with other health care providers in their rural areas. The service delivery system includes IHS behavioral health; tribal health; community mental health; IHS, tribal, and/or community hospitals; private for and nonprofit service providers; and state residential facilities, leading to a complex and inconsistent service delivery system (Manson, 2004). Access to more specialized services, such as hospitalization, psychiatrists, and other specialists such as child psychologists, are many miles away. *Resolana: Voice of the People*, a documentary regarding stigma and access to health care in rural and tribal communities in Western North Dakota, vividly describes behavioral health issues among American Indians and Alaska Natives in rural communities (Mental Health America North Dakota [MHAND], 2009). Vivian Hall, a consumer of mental health services and an enrolled member of the Mandan, Hidatsa, Arikara Nation, states in the documentary, "Three to four months pass before you actually get the help that will benefit you. Emotionally it was hard—I felt like there was no way out." Donna Coffey, a behavior health technician in Ms. Hall's community, stated, "I really do feel that not enough people care. Unless it is on their doorstep, it's not a priority." Lack of services is interpreted as lack of caring, which, for those who have an immediate need, seems the same. The outcome, however, is the same, regardless of the cause.

Current Behavioral Health Status

Concerns about the behavioral health of American Indians and Alaska Natives took a very public and national focus in fall 2010, when the National Alliance for Suicide Prevention established suicide among American Indians and Alaskan natives as one of their three task forces' focus. Data regarding the current behavioral status of American Indians and Alaska Natives in rural communities is problematic, however (Beals et al., 2009; Letiecq & Bailey, 2004; O'Hare, 2010). Generally, people living in rural areas are underrepresented in research studies, due to lack of participation (infrastructure), lack of invitation (ignoring population), and lack of access (no transportation, no phone or Internet service). Commonly reported measures of behavioral health, such as the Behavioral Risk Factor Surveillance Survey (BRFSS), have underrepresented American Indians and Alaska Natives, perhaps because of lack of access through phone-based data collection (Poltavski, Holm, Vogeltanz-Holm, & McDonald, 2010). Even when data is collected, if numbers are small, they are frequently suppressed or combined with other groups, as is done within the articles "Youth Risk Behavior Surveillance—Unites States, 2009"

(Eaton et al., 2010) and "The Changing Faces of America's Children and Youth" (Johnson & Lighter, 2010). To obtain more reliable information, some studies have used community participatory action research methods to collect similar data in American Indian and Alaska Native communities. Using the 2003 BRFSS survey, Poltavski and colleagues (2010) surveyed 404 people living on four reservations on the Northern Plains. Using an adapted version of the 2010 BRFSS, Conway and Azure (2011) surveyed college students at Cankdeska Cikana Community College to collect accurate health and behavioral health data to support planning, prevention, and intervention programs.

Depression and Suicide

Rates of mental health issues in rural American Indian and Alaska Native communities such as depression, suicide, and substance use are high (U.S. Commission on Civil Rights, 2004). The rates among American Indians and Alaska Natives were highlighted in the *Surgeon General's Call to Action to Prevent Suicide*, which reported that American Indians and Alaska Natives' suicide rate was 1.5 times higher than the national average (U.S. Public Health Service, 1999). In 2007, the most recent year for which data are available, the Centers for Disease Control and Prevention reported the suicide rate among American Indian and Alaska Native adolescents and young adults ages 15–34 as 19.7 per 100,000, 1.8 times higher than the national average for that age group (11.1 per 100,000; Centers for Disease Control and Prevention [CDC], 2007). American Indian and Alaska Native males age 20–24 have the highest rates of suicide of all population and age groups (Smith, N.D.; CDC, 2007). Rates vary by IHS region; the highest rates are in the IHS regions of Alaska, followed by the Tucson and Aberdeen areas (Smith, N.D.). At 38.5 per 100,000 for Alaska, 23.1 per 100,000 for the Tucson region, and 22.4 per 100,000 for the Aberdeen area, the rates are much higher than the national average for all IHS regions (17 per 100,000) and the overall U.S. rates (10.6 per 100,000; age-adjusted suicide death rates for 1999–2001). The typical means for suicide varies by race. Nationally, firearms are the most common means of suicide for males (CDC, 2007). In the IHS Aberdeen Area, between 2005 and 2008, 75% of suicide completions were by hanging (Smith, N.D.). The correlation between suicide and substance use is higher among American Indians and Alaska Natives than other racial and ethnic populations (Alcohol and suicide, 2009). In the MMWR study, American Indians and Alaska Natives who died by suicide were more likely than other groups to have alcohol detected in their blood and blood alcohol concentrations above the legal limit.

Substance Use

Rates of substance use by American Indians and Alaska Natives vary by region of the country and type of substance use. The 2009 National Survey on Drug Use and Health reported lower rates of alcohol use and binge drinking for American Indians and Alaska Natives, compared with Whites (37.1 vs. 56.7% and 22 vs. 24.8%; SAMHSA, 2010). The rate of "heavy" alcohol and substance dependence or abuse was higher among American Indians and Alaska Natives than other groups, however. Rates vary by region, by all races, and for American Indians and Alaska Natives. For instance, in North Dakota in 2009, 32% of persons age 12 and older reported binge drinking, among the highest in the nation; 58% between age 18 and 25 reported binge drinking. Eighteen- to 25-year-olds also had the highest rate of alcohol use in the past month. Based on data from 1998–2007, American Indians in North Dakota were more likely to report binge drinking (North Dakota State Epidemiological Outcomes Workgroup, 2009).

Historically, American Indians and Alaskan Natives have always had high usage of ceremonial tobacco; unfortunately, they also reported the highest rate of addictive tobacco usage among all groups.

Factors that Impact the Behavioral Health

Walters, Simoni, and Evans-Campbell (2002) created an "indigenist" stress coping model, building on resiliency of American Indians, which "emphasizes cultural strengths, such as the family and community, spirituality and traditional healing practices, and group identity attitudes" (p. S104). Although recognizing the effect of historical and current trauma (see the next section in this chapter for information regarding historical and current trauma), Walters and colleagues (2002) suggest that cultural buffers, identify attitudes, enculturation, spiritual coping, and traditional health practices increase resiliency.

Historical and Current Trauma

The need for basic safety for children living in Indian Country is great. Historically, American Indian and Alaska Native children have had the advantage of knowing they were the center of the circle, which, for generations of child rearing, was sufficient to protect and prepare them for their place on this Great Turtle Island. The labeling of locations has always been important. Not knowing that others would call this land the Americas, many indigenous teachings call the land "this Great Turtle Island." They were reared knowing where they came from, why they were here, and where they were going. Being the center of the circle entitled them, in a blessed way, to have multiple caregivers and protectors, to have connections beyond just their immediate siblings and parents, to the extended family relations including cousins, aunts, uncles, grandparents, great aunts, and great uncles. Each of those relatives was once the center of the circle, during their own birth and growth through childhood. Children were reared with supervision, protection, guidance, watchfulness, and teachings. They responded by feeling connected, knowing they were sacred, and recognizing the honor of being a human being. Confronting tragic events has always been part of living on the Great Turtle Island. Although the human experience has always been difficult, full of dangerous and life-threatening elements, ceremonial and ritual activities have assisted in the adjustment to new demands or dealing with losses and disharmony (Bigfoot & Schmidt, 2010).

Today, the world is a very different place for American Indian and Alaska Native children, when they encounter traumatic challenges. They are in need of basic safety that will allow them to grow and flourish. Unfortunately, children are not all being supervised adequately; they receive little protection from exposure to many of the traumatic childhood experiences. Struggling parents find it hard to provide guidance and sufficient attentiveness to their children. Children do not feel connected to their families or their indigenous roots; they do not believe they are sacred or that they are honored. The kinds of trauma that American Indian and Alaska Native children experience comes in waves and reverberates among all the generations into cumulative and collective trauma (Bigfoot & Schmidt, 2010).

The current level of violence in Indian Country must be viewed from understanding that tribal and village infrastructure is compromised by and reflects historical, political, and economic disruptions. The military action, missionary efforts, the Federal Indian Boarding School Movement, the Dawes Act, the Indian Self-Determination and Education Assistance Act, and the Indian Child Welfare Act forever changed the economic, physical, and social lives of American Indian and Alaska Native people (BigFoot, 2000; Manson, 2004). Once self-reliant and self-sufficient, the policies of the federal government forced tribes/indigenous people toward removal; relocations; isolation; and, in some cases, termination and extinction, resulting in social, economic, and spiritual depravations. (Bigfoot & Schmidt, 2010)

Over the past 200 years, American Indian and Alaska Native people have suffered from a lack of education, unemployment, economic disadvantage, family disorganization, and personal despair (Manson, 2004; Walters et al., 2002). Most tribes, especially in Alaska Native villages, have limited financial and economic options to create jobs, build policing support, tax residents, or draw on the surrounding natural resources for sustainability. A significant portion of services within tribes and native villages depend on funding streams from federal, state, or nonprofit entities. Limited entrepreneurship and individual business ownership exist to generate the critical mass for sustainable revenue (Bigfoot & Schmidt, 2010).

Trauma in Indian Country includes different kinds of violence (i.e., assault, homicides, domestic violence, and bullying); substance abuse and addictions; child maltreatment and child fatalities; suicide and self-injuries; and loss and death due to car accidents, exposure, and a wide range of resulting health disparities. These current traumas are affected by poverty, oppression, and historical events that are unresolved and reexperienced with anniversaries or other recurrent events. The exposure to traumatic situations increases the vulnerability of children with each exposure. According to Felitti (Anda et al., 2005) in his Adverse Childhood Experience Study, exposure to specific conditions exponentially increases the vulnerability of children, resulting in poor adolescent and adult mental and physical health and early death. Unfortunately, the status of American Indian and Alaska Native children parallel those identified conditions (Bigfoot & Schmidt, 2010). Such conditions include:

(1) Physical abuse status. American Indian and Alaska Native children are over represented in the foster care system, due to child maltreatment.

(2) Emotional abuse. American Indian and Alaska Native youth have higher rates of disruptive behavior and substance abuse disorders than other, same age youth from other ethnic groups.

(3) Sexual abuse. An estimated 75% of caseloads in the U.S. Attorney's Offices, which cover Indian Country, are child sexual abuse allegations.

(4) Alcohol and/or drug abuser in the household. National statistics reveal that 12–16% of American Indian and Alaska Native adults are drug dependent, compared to 4–6% of non-American Indian and Alaska Native adults.

(5) Incarcerated household members. American Indians and Alaska Natives adults have a 38% higher incarceration rate than other groups http://www.lenapeprograms.info/Articles/Prison.htm). This does not address the number of incarcerated juveniles in state and federal custody and the number of adults on probation, parole, or under the custody of law enforcement in other legal status.

(6) Someone who is chronically depressed, mentally ill, institutionalized, or suicidal. American Indians and Alaska Natives have the highest rate of suicide for all groups. In addition, they lead the nation in deaths due to injuries and homicides. It is understandable that this is correlated with high levels of depression, anxiety, and posttraumatic stress disorder.

(7) Mother is treated violently. American Indian and Alaska Native women experience the highest rate of assaults and violence directed toward them, 50% higher than the typically noted rate of Black on Black violence (Bureau of Justice Statistics, 2004).

(8) One or no parents. Once considered an unusual condition, being an orphan or with few relatives, now 40% of our children live with only one parent. Increasingly, families are becoming less attached to their extended family members, and children are not being reared within the concept of being the center of the circle of relatives.

(9) Emotional or physical neglect. Historically, American Indian and Alaska Native children were not neglected. Many relatives tended to them. This is not the case for children today. According to the National Child and Neglect Data System (2002), American Indian and Alaska Native children have the highest rate of neglect (Bigfoot & Schmidt, 2010).

Access to Care

Barriers to access to care include individual, geographic, community, and organizational challenges. In the documentary *Resolana: Voice of the People*, MHAND (2010) identified barriers to access to care for persons living in rural, tribal areas: being under- or uninsured; transportation and distance; stigma; lack of collaboration, communication, and coordination between existing behavioral health care providers; layers of bureaucracy; demand for behavioral health services, including residential care that exceeds the capacity of existing services and the myth that IHS serves all the behavioral health needs on reservations; and disparity in the provision of timely services for mental illness/substance use when compared to traditional medical issues, such as heart disease and diabetes.

Distance and transportation. Several tribes have been successful in offering limited bus services and improving road conditions for better traffic safety. This is a recent effort for select tribes that established working relationships with state transportation offices or sought federal highway dollars (Brusin & Dwyer, 2002). Public transportation is not a common feature of rural or reservation roads. More common is the lack of transportation, that is, picture the "rez cars" in *Smoke Signals*, a movie based on a Sherman Alexie short story, with two young women traveling everywhere backwards, because their car's transmission was impaired, or the broken down van at the crossroads that served as the radio station (Estes & Eyre, 1998).

The behavioral health care system. Tribal health and IHS are consistently the most common partners in provision of health care, including behavioral health care, to American Indians and Alaska Natives (www.ihs.gov). Federal legislation (The Snyder Act, 1921, and the Indian Health Care Improvement Act of 1976–2001) established the Bureau of Indian Affairs' responsibility for health care. That care is compromised by discrimination, limited funding, and difficulties recruiting health care professionals, documented in the U.S. Commission on Civil Rights (2004) report, "Broken Promises: Evaluating the Native American Health Care System." Some unique programs, such as telemedicine, enhance access to specialty care, in spite of challenges related to rural access (Shore et al., 2008).

Evidence-Based Behavioral Health Practice Based on Old Wisdom

National attention is now focused on prevention and treatment of behavioral health issues, based on programs that build on family and community resiliency (U.S Department of Health and Human Services, 2010). Many American Indian and Alaska Native families demonstrate resiliency, including a commitment to strong families and vibrant communities. As Novalene Goklish said in testimony before the Senate Committee on Indian Affairs (March 25, 2010), "Native American communities have tremendous resiliency." Her community, the White Mountain Apache Tribe in the southwestern United States, has taken a proactive stance to improve behavioral health outcomes, becoming a model for other communities. It created a suicide surveillance system to monitor self-injury and substance use and instituted an aggressive system of case management for follow-up with persons demonstrating suicidal ideation or behaviors (Mullany et al., 2009). Through collaboration with Johns Hopkins University, the White Mountain Apache Tribe is creating an evidence-based system of care to prevent self-injury.

Efforts have been made to bring together American Indian and Alaska Native values and culture with the Western concept of evidence-based practice. Science has to support indigenous knowledge. The First Nations Behavioral Health Association (FNBHA) published a list of "mental health and culturally focused practices," indicating whether the program had been manualized (the creation of a treatment manual) and replicated and its level of evidence (2008, p. 1). Organized by six categories (community prevention and education, cultural and subsistence skill developments, workforce training and funding for positions, early intervention and skill building, individual and family treatment, recovery services and supports), evidence-based practices include strategies at the community, organization, family, and individual levels. As part of the Practice-Based Evidence: Building Effectiveness from the Ground Up project, Friesen and colleagues (2010) sought to better articulate mental health outcomes that incorporate both (a) outcomes considered nationally to be appropriate for evidence-based programs and (b) values from American Indian and Alaska Native youth and families. Outcomes found to be common in both "communities" included community-mindedness (helping others in one's community), positive cultural identity, school belongingness (engagement), reduced perceived discrimination, hope, spirituality, positive relationships with adults, and conflict resolution. Although based on American Indian and Alaska Native families in an urban setting, the program and its findings provide guidance for development of evidence-based strategies with American Indian and Alaska Native families in rural areas.

Prevention: American Indian Life Skills

To encourage the use of evidence-based practice to prevent suicide among American Indian and Alaska Native youth and young adults, SAMHSA (2010) published *To Live To See the Great Day That Dawns: Preventing Suicide by American Indian and Alaska Native Youth and Young Adults*. Although the evidence-based strategies focus only on individual youth, the manual also offers guidance for community development. One such program, American Indian Life Skills (AILS), was developed by Teresa LaFromboise, associate professor, Stanford University, to reduce adolescent suicide in tribal communities (FNBHA 2009). Initially developed as the Zuni Life Skills Development Curriculum (LaFromboise & Howard-Pitney, 1995;

LaFromboise & Lewis, 2008), the program emerged from one community's self-identified need. It has since been adapted in many other communities, including the Cherokee Nation and the Kiowa Tribe in Oklahoma and other tribal locations, including Alaska, Nevada, California, Nebraska, and Montana. A shorter version of the curriculum has been created and is being prepared for use. AILS is based on social cognitive theory to explain the "cause" of suicidal behaviors and to guide the intervention (skills training; LaFromboise & Lewis, 2008). The curriculum covers seven areas: self-esteem, emotions and stress, communication and problem solving skills, self-destructive behaviors (pessimism, anger reactivity), suicide information, suicide intervention training, and setting goals. Research has demonstrated the success of this curriculum in reducing hopelessness and suicidal thinking and improving skills in the Zuni community (LaFromboise & Howard-Pitney, 1995). Dr. LaFromboise designed the curriculum to allow each tribal community to adapt or customize the stories and activities to fit their region and culture.

Another SAMHSA initiative, the Garrett Lee Smith Youth Suicide Prevention Program (GLS), encourages evidence-based, culturally appropriate prevention strategies, such as community coalitions and skills building, with youth adapted for each community. The national Suicide Prevention Resource Center (SPRC), a technical assistance and resource center supporting the GLS grantees, disseminates information regarding evidence-based practices. In addition to the SPRC/American Foundation for Suicide Prevention Best Practices Registry, which features AILS, the component of the SPRC website focused on American Indian and Alaska Native suicide prevention links to other registries of best practices and local efforts that include culturally appropriate practices.

The FNBHA Catalogue of Effective Behavioral Health Practices for Tribal Communities, mentioned above, includes 26 programs, processes, or approaches selected based on criteria determined by FNBHA membership. The catalogue specifies each program's levels of evidence and outcomes (i.e., evidence-based practice with science validation, evidence-based practice with American Indian/Alaska Native cultural adaptation, practice-based evidence/nonculturally based, practice-based evidence with cultural validation, and local cultural, spiritual practices with community validation).

The IHS Health Promotion/Disease Prevention Online Search, Consultation, and Reporting (OSCAR) system includes evidence-based, promising practice, and local effort resources and policies (http://www.ihs.gov/oscar/index.cfm?module =slc). OSCAR is searchable based on criteria, including IHS service areas, health indicators (e.g., mental health, substance abuse, and traditional healing), and key-words (e.g., capacity building and empowerment, community directed intervention, and school health).

Intervention: Honoring children—mending the circle. The Indian Country Child Trauma Center developed Honoring Children—Mending the Circle, an American Indian and Alaska Native enhancement of the evidence-based child trauma treatment, Trauma-Focused Cognitive-Behavioral Therapy. Honoring Children—Mending the Circle guides the therapeutic process through a blending of American Indian and Alaska Native traditional teachings with cognitive-behavioral methods (BigFoot & Schmidt, 2010). The empirical research on child trauma treatment has improved considerably in recent years, due in large part to national initiatives such as the SAMHSA-funded National Child Traumatic Stress Network (http://www.nctsn.org/) and Systems of Care. According to BigFoot and Schmidt (2010), American Indian and Alaska Native partners assisted in the adaptation process to assure treatment fidelity while incorporating beliefs, practices, and understandings consistent with their individual tribal culture. The framework for Honoring Children—Mending the Circle is the circle, a sacred symbol that has long been used by many indigenous peoples to understand the world (Willmon-Haque & Bigfoot, 2008).

Spirituality has played and continues to play an important role in the life of American Indians (Bryde, 1971) and is the center of the circle. As such, there is no separation of the physical from the spiritual; they are interwoven and intertwined.

Honoring Children—Mending the Circle has adopted core constructs based on American Indian and Alaska Native worldviews: (a) all things are interconnected, (b) all things have a spiritual nature, and (c) existence is dynamic. Central to wellness and healing is the core American Indian and Alaska Native belief that all things, human and earth, have a spiritual nature. Well-being is balance and harmony both within and among one's spiritual, relational, emotional, mental, and physical dimensions (see Figure 2). The concept of "relationship" is broadened to include the natural helpers and healers critical to the child's recovery, including extended family, traditional helpers and healers, and the child's relationship with elements within the natural and spiritual world. The adaptation of Trauma-Focused Cognitive-Behavioral Therapy within an American Indian and Alaska Native well-being framework enhances healing through the blending of science and indigenous cultures (BigFoot & Schmidt, 2009, 2010).

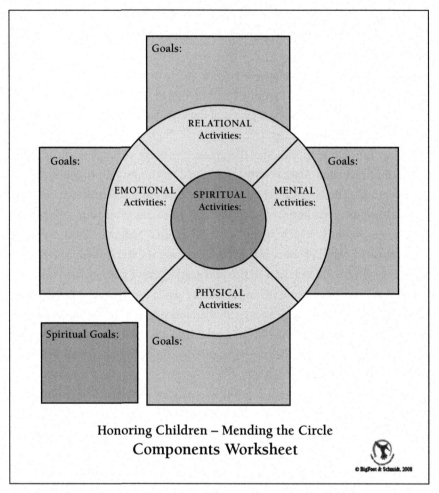

Honoring Children – Mending the Circle
Components Worksheet

FIGURE 2   **Honoring Children—Mending the Circle components worksheet.**

Conclusion

Social work's mission, "to enhance human well-being and help meet the basic human needs of all people, with particular attention to the needs and empowerment of people who are vulnerable, oppressed, and living in poverty" (National Association of Social Workers, 2008), sets the stage for identifying social work's purpose in addressing behavioral health issues and American Indians in rural areas. Social work values, such as respecting the dignity and worth of others and the central importance of human relationships (NASW Code of Ethics), undergird the role of social work in promotion, prevention, treatment, and maintenance of behavioral health issues with American Indian and Alaska Native families and their rural communities (National Research Council and Institute of Medicine, 2009). Social workers can, and in many cases already do, play a key role in many sectors, such as school-based screening and awareness programs; early childhood home visitation programs; wrap around services; injury prevention campaigns; mental health treatment through tribal health, the Indian Health Service, and mental health organizations in the broader community who are part of referral systems; community development; program planning; and research and evaluation (U.S. Department of Health and Human Services, 2010). That role includes supporting indigenous practices, participating in the development of their evidence base, and assisting with the adaptation of practices with evidence supporting their efficacy in other communities.

Social work may play a role with individuals, families, communities, and broader society when addressing behavioral health and American Indians. At the individual level, social workers may incorporate learning about American Indian constructs, such as the "indigenist" stress-coping model, to guide their practice. For instance, Duran and Walters (2004) suggest that the cultural buffers, enculturation and identify attitudes, are particularly important when conducting mental health assessments and planning interventions.

Social work may partner with other professions to support the development of evidence for successful practices. In an effort to bring together the diverse and divergent views on "culturally sensitive" practice, Gone (in press) reviewed related literature and proposed a method for achieving an "innovative integration approach" (p. 57). His model proposes a different approach to creating evidence-based practice for American Indian and Alaska Native families through "recover[ing] and reclaim[ing] indigenous therapeutic practices and understandings of wellness" and documenting their outcomes (Gone, [in press], p. 61). Rather than adapting Western therapeutic methods to a specific community, Gone argues that the focus should be indigenous traditions, determining their effectiveness. The Wiconi Ohitika Youth Suicide Prevention Project at Spirit Lake provides and exemplifies a culturally enriched approach to youth suicide prevention. It is based on the culture, language, values, and history of the Spirit Lake Dakota (Mni Wakan Oyate) and promotes positive self-identity, increased self-esteem, and increased knowledge of the Dakota way of life. Wiconi Ohitika's primary purpose is to educate, save lives, and aid in recovery for survivors of suicide, persons who have experienced the death of a loved one by suicide. The Wiconi Ohitika project is one of two Garrett Lee Smith projects nationally that operate in a tribal college setting.

Cankdeska Cikana Community College (CCCC) supports the strong cultural focus of the project in many ways, including CCCC's theme, "Think Dakota, Live Dakota," its courses in Dakota language and culture, and the Elder Language Advisory Committee. Wiconi Ohitika has sponsored cultural events designed to increase wellness, awareness of suicide prevention, and family and community engagement. For instance, after several deaths by suicide in the community, CCCC instituted a monthly day of prayer as a community-wide opportunity to gather to support each other, share a meal, and increase community engagement through cultural strengthening. Monthly day of prayer activities, such as the Wiping of Tears Ceremony and a presentation by Chief Arvol Looking Horse (the 19th Generation Keeper of the Sacred White Buffalo Calf Pipe) and the Red Road Approach (presented annually by Rick Thomas, Dakota, and Gene Thin Elk, Lakota, from South Dakota) engage indigenous practices in building resilience and healing. Initial evaluation of the Red Road Approach indicated a high level of success with community engagement, based on the level of community participation and qualitative feedback from people attending the events. Participants identified both professional and personal benefits.

The presentation was good at traditional thought integrated with today's works.

[I should] listen to not only what is being said, but watch body language. Know I am a safe place to turn in time of need.

I will take back what I learned and report it to the counselors at our program.

The feeling of spiritual healing. A feeling of lightness as I moved from more negative thoughts to one's of hopefulness. (Conway, 2011)

The challenge for evaluation is to develop reliable and valid methods for assessing outcomes, as recommended by Gone, to learn more about what one participant in the Red Road Approach said, "Many women and children suffer from abuse, but don't speak of it and these [trainings] help change that." Identifying the long-range effect of cultural strengthening is the challenge to be tackled.

Social work may support change in academic and research settings. Some social work programs have a focus on American Indians and Alaska Natives, such as the Department of Sociology, University of Wisconsin-Stevens Point, which offers a minor in Native American and Rural Social Work (http://www.uwsp.edu/sociology/).

In academic settings social work education can work to "dismantle the individual, community, and institutional barriers to academic advancement among aspiring AIAN [American Indians and Alaska Natives] investigators" (Walters & Simoni, 2009, p. S75). This change in a community academic organization might contribute to broader societal changes as American Indian and Alaska Native researchers more fully participate in creating and disseminating knowledge. Research can support the development of evidence to support American Indian and Alaska Native practices and also the effectiveness of interventions developed with non-American Indian and Alaska Native people (Duran & Walters, 2004, p. 192).

At the community level, social work educators can advocate change. Many resources are available for support of this endeavor, such as the Rural Community Assistance Corporation, which supports basic services such as water development in 13 western states (www.rcac.org); the American Indian Disability Technical Assistance Center at the University of Montana (http://aidtac.ruralinstitute.umt.edu/); the Indian Health Service American Indian and Alaska Native Suicide Prevention website (http://www.ihs.gov/NonMedicalPrograms/nspn/); the National Resource Center on Native American Aging (http://ruralhealth.und.edu/projects/nrcnaa/); and the Federal Collaboration on Health Disparities Research established in 2009 (http://minorityhealth.hhs.gov/fchdr/).

Finally, it is important to avoid assuming that all tribal and native people have similar traditions. In fact, most American Indian and Alaska Native people wish to maintain their uniqueness and their cultural integrity. Respect can be given to unique traditions, while recognizing the overall values that seem to be held by American Indian and Alaska Native groups collectively (BigFoot & Schmidt, 2010).

References

Alcohol and suicide among racial/ethnic populations—17 States, 2005–2006. (2009). *Morbidity and Mortality Weekly Report, 58,* 637–641.

Anda, R. F., Felitti, V. J., Bremner, J. D., Walker, J. D., Whitfield, C., Perry, B. D., …Giles, W. H. (2005). The enduring effects of abuse and related adverse experiences in childhood. A convergence of evidence from neurobiology and epidemiology. *European Archives of Psychiatry and Clinical Neuroscience, 256*(3), 174–185.

Beals, J., Belcourt-Dittloff, A., Freedenthal, S., Kaufman, C., Mitchell, C., Whitesell, C., & Walters, K. (2009). Reflections on a proposed theory of reservation-dwelling American Indian alcohol use: Comment on Spillane and Smith (2007). *Psychological Bulletin, 135,* 339–343.

BigFoot, D. S. (2000). History of victimization. In D. BigFoot (Ed.) *Native American topic-specific monograph series.* Washington, DC: Office for Victims of Crime.

BigFoot, D. S., & Schmidt, S. R. (2009). Science-to-practice: Adapting an evidence-based child trauma treatment for American Indian and Alaska Native populations. *International Journal of Child Health and Human Development, 2*(1), 33–44.

BigFoot, D. S., & Schmidt, S. (2010). Honoring Children–Mending the Circle: Cultural adaptation of trauma-focused cognitive-behavioral therapy for American Indian and Alaska Native Children. *Journal of Clinical Psychology, Special Issue: Culture-Sensitive Evidence-Based Practices, 66,* 847–856.

Bowers, D. E., & Cook, P. (Eds). (1999). *Rural conditions and trends: Socioeconomic conditions issue, 9*(2). Retrieved from http://www.ers.usda.gov/Publications/RCAT/RCAT92/

Brusin, J., & Dwyer, K. (2002). *Tribal transportation: Barriers and solutions, brief #5.* Missoula, MT: he University of Montana Rural Institute.

Bryde, J. F. (1971). *Modern Indian psychology.* Vermillion, SD: Dakota Press.

Bureau of Justice Statistics. (2004). *A BJS statistical profile, 1992–2002: American Indians and crime.* Retrieved from http://www.ojp.usdoj.gov/bjs/pub/pdf/aic02.pdf

Centers for Disease Control and Prevention (CDC). (2007). *Web-based Injury Statistics Query and Reporting System (WISQARS); National Center for Injury Prevention and Control, CDC.* Retrieved from www.cdc.gov/injury/wisqars/index.html

Conway, P. (2011). *Evaluation of the Wiconi Ohitika Project.* Fort Totten, ND: Cankdeska Cikana Community College.

Conway, P., & Azure, L. (2011). *Health status of tribal college students and staff.* Fort Totten, ND: Cankdeska Cikana Community College.

Duran, B., & Walters, K. L. (2004). HIV/AIDS prevention in "Indian Country": Current practice, indigenist etiology models, and postcolonial approaches to change. *AIDS Education and Prevention, 16*(3), 187–201.

Eaton, D. K., Kann, L., Kinchen, S., Shanklin, S., Ross, J., Hawkins, J., ... Wechsler, H. (2010). Youth risk behavior surveillance—United States, 2009. *Morbidity and Mortality Weekly Report, 59*(SS-5), 1–148.

Estes, L. (Producer), & Eyre, C. (Director). (1998). *Smoke signals* [Motion picture]. United States: ShadowCatcher Entertainment.

First Nations Behavioral Health Association (FNBHA). (2009). *FNBHA catalogue of effective behavioral health practices for tribal communities.* Portland, OR: Portland State University.

Friesen, B. J., Gowen, L. K., Lo, P., Bandurraga, A., Cross, T. L., & Matthew, C. (2010). *Literature support for outcomes in evaluating culturally- and community-based programs. Indicators of success for urban American Indian/Alaska Native youth: An agency example.* Portland, OR: Portland State University.

Gale, J. A., Shaw, B., Hartley, D., & Loux, S. (2010). The provision of mental health services by rural health clinics. Portland, ME: University of Southern Maine.

Gone, J. P. (in press). Psychotherapy and traditional healing for American Indians: Exploring the prospects for therapeutic integration. *The Counseling Psychologist.*

Johnson, K. M., & Lighter, D. T. (2010). The changing faces of America's children and youth. *Carsey Institute Issue Brief, 15.*

LaFromboise, T. D., & Howard-Pitney, B. (1995). The Zuni Life Skills Development Curriculum: Description and evaluation of a suicide prevention program. *Journal of Counseling Psychology, 42,* 479-486.

LaFromboise, T. D., & Lewis, H. A. (2008). The Zuni Life Skills Development Program: A school/community-based suicide prevention intervention. *Suicide and Life-Threatening Behavior, 38,* 343–353.

Letiecq, B. L., & Bailey, S. J. (2004). Evaluating from the outside: Conducting cross-cultural evaluation research on an American Indian reservation. *Evaluation Review, 28,* 342–357.

Manson, S. M. (2004). *Cultural diversity series: Meeting the mental health needs of America Indians and Alaska Natives.* Washington, DC: National Technical Assistance Center for State Mental Health Planning.

Mental Health America North Dakota (MHAND). (2009). *Resolana: Voice of the people.* Retrieved from www.mhand.org

Mullany, B., Barlow, A., Goklish, N., Larzelere-Hinton, F., Cwik, M., Craig, M., & Walkup, J. (2009). Toward understanding suicide among youths: Results from the White Mountain Apache Tribally Mandated Suicide Surveillance System, 2001–2006. *American Journal of Public Health, 99,* 1840–1848.

Murphy, T., & Bishop, B. (2008). *Counties with minorities in the majority grow in rural America.* Retrieved from http://www.dailyyonder.com/

National Association of Social Workers (NASW). (2008). *Code of ethics of the National Association of Social Workers.* Retrieved from http://www.socialworkers.org/pubs/code/code.asp

National Child and Neglect Data System. (2002). *Child maltreatment 2002.* Washington, DC: Department of Health and Human Services.

National Research Council and Institute of Medicine. (2009). *Preventing mental, emotional, and behavioral disorders among young people: Progress and possibilities.* Retrieved from http://www.iom.edu/Reports/2009/Preventing-Mental-Emotional-and-Behavioral -Disorders-Among-Young-People-Progress-and-Possibilities.aspx

North Dakota Indian Affairs Commission. (2011). *Statewide data.* Retrieved from http://www.nd.gov/indianaffairs/?id=37

The North Dakota State Epidemiological Outcomes Workgroup. (2009). *Alcohol, tobacco, and illicit drug consumption and consequences in North Dakota: The North Dakota epidemiological profile*. Bismarck, ND: North Dakota Department of Human Services.

Ogunwole, S. U. (2006). *We the people: American Indians and Alaska Natives in the United States*. Washington, DC: U.S. Census Bureau.

O'Hare, W. P. (2010). Rural areas risk being overlooked in 2010 Census. *Carsey Institute Issue Brief, 12.*

Poltavski, D., Holm, J., Vogeltanz-Holm, N., & McDonald, L. (2010). Assessing health-related quality of life in Northern Plains American Indians: Prominence of physical activity as a health behavior. *American Indian Alaska Native Mental Health Research, 17*(1), 25–48.

Leavitt, M. O., McSwain, R. G., Church, R. M., & Paisano, E. L. (N.D.). *Regional differences in Indian health 2002–2003 edition*. Rockville, MD: Indian Health Service.

Samuels, M. E. (2002). *Minorities in rural America*. Columbia, SC: University of South Carolina.

Samuels, M. E., Probst, J., & Glover, S. (N.D.). *Rural research focus: Minorities in rural America*. Columbia, SC: University of South Carolina.

Shore, J. H., Brooks, E., Savin, D., Orton, H., Grigsby, J., & Manson, S. M. (2008). Acceptability of telepsychiatry in American Indians. *Telemedicine and Health, 14*, 461–466.

Smith, C. B. (N.D.). *American Indian suicide*. Presentation at Johns Hopkins School of Public Health. Aberdeen, SD: Northern Plains Tribal Epidemiology Center, Area Tribal Chairmen's Health Board.

State and Territorial Injury Prevention Directors Association. (2008). *Preventing youth suicide in rural America: Recommendations to states*. Atlanta, GA: Suicide Prevention Resource Center. Retrieved from www.safestates.org and www.sprc.org

Substance Abuse and Mental Health Services Administration (SAMHSA). (2008). *The NSDUH Report—major depressive episode among youths aged 12 to 17 in the United States: 2004 to 2006*. Rockville, MD: Author.

Substance Abuse and Mental Health Services Administration (SAMHSA). (2010). *Results from the 2009 National Survey on Drug Use and Health: volume I. Summary of national findings* (NSDUH Series H-34A, HHS Publication NO. SMA 10-4586Findings). Rockville, MD: Author.

Ulrich, J. D., & Safford, T. G. (2011). Enduring ties to community and nature: Charting an alternative future for Southeast Alaska. *Carsey Institute Issue Brief, 22*, 1–8.

U.S. Census. (2009). *2010 Census Tribal Statistical Areas Program guidelines for delineating state designated tribal statistical areas*. Washington, DC: U.S. Government Printing Office.

U.S. Commission on Civil Rights. (2004). *Broken promises: Evaluating the Native American health care system*. Washington, DC: Author.

U.S. Department of Health and Human Services. (2010). *To live to see the great day that dawns: Preventing suicide by American Indian and Alaska Native youth and young adults*. [DHHS Publication SMA (10)-4480]. Rockville, MD: Substance Abuse and Mental Health Services Administration.

U.S. Public Health Service. (1999). *The surgeon general's call to action to prevent suicide*. Washington, DC: Author.

Wagner, J. M. (2007/2008). Improving Native American access to federal funding for economic development through partnerships with rural communities. *American Indian Law Review, 32*, 526–576.

Walters, K., & Simoni, J. M. (2009). Decolonizing strategies for mentoring American Indians and Alaska Natives in HIV and mental health research, *American Journal of Public Health, 99* (S71-S76).

Walters, K. L., Simoni, J. M., & Evans-Campbell, T. (2002). Substance use among American Indians and Alaska Natives: Incorporating culture in an "indigenist" stress-coping paradigm, *Public Health Reports, 117*(Suppl 1), S104–S117.

Willmon-Haque, S., & BigFoot, D. S. (2008). Violence and the effects of trauma on American Indian and Alaska Native populations. *Journal of Emotional Abuse, Special Issue: Children Exposed to Violence: Current Issues, Interventions and Research, 8*(1), 51–66.

14 Amish Society: *Clinical Approaches and Community Services*

GRETCHEN H. WALTMAN

The Amish are an important special population in rural areas, yet there is very little in the social work literature about their culture or how social workers can work effectively with Amish people. For example, a September 2010 review of the *Social Work Abstracts* database yields three references on the Amish (Kreps, Donnermeyer, Hurst, Blair, & Kreps, 1997; Piercy & Cheek, 2004; Reiling, 2002b). Most of the professional literature about the Amish is found in the health care field, especially medical and nursing journals (Beachy, Hershberger, Davidhizar, & Giger, 1997; Buccalo & Echelbarger, 1997; Wenger, 1991).

There have been a few presentations on the Amish at the National Institutes for Social Work and Human Services in Rural Areas, for example Lee (1984), Waltman (1989, 1996b, 1999), and Zook and Heikes (1990). Bean (1993) and Zook (1993) have written articles on the Amish in the journal *Human Services in the Rural Environment*, which is no longer published. Earlier editions of the current volume, *Social Work in Rural Communities*, have not included content on the Amish or how rural social workers should interact with them.

Amish communities are very self-reliant, and their Amish members usually wish to avoid contact with traditional social services. However, social workers in rural areas may have contact with Amish persons in child welfare, medical, and mental health settings and therefore need a basic understanding of Amish culture and culturally sensitive practice with Amish clients. The focus of this chapter is two-pronged:

first, to give a description and understanding of Amish culture and, second, to demonstrate and discuss how social workers can work effectively with Amish clients in clinical and community practice. Except where noted, the term *Amish*, as used in this chapter, refers to the Old Order Amish, the predominant group in the United States and Canada.

Understanding Amish Culture

The Amish are a socioreligious group, who wish to be visibly separate from the outside world. They are simultaneously a culture, a religion, and a way of life. The concept of *Gelassenheit*, meaning submission or yielding to a higher authority, embodies the Amish philosophy of life. *Gelassenheit* emphasizes obedience, humility, self-denial, submission, thrift, simplicity, and community well-being over individual rights (Kraybill, 2001).

Overview of the Amish Lifestyle

Amish people are not homogeneous. There are different Amish groups, such as the conservative Swartzentruber and Andy Weaver, traditional Old Order, and the more liberal New Order. All of these groups use horse-and-buggy transportation. In addition, there are car-driving groups, called Beachy Amish and Amish Mennonites. Kraybill and Hostetter (2001) offered this guideline to help identify Amish group affiliation:

> In general, the more conservative the group, the longer the beard, the wider the hat brim, the darker the color of clothing, the larger the head covering for women, the slower the singing in church, the longer the sermons, the greater use of Pennsylvania German, and the more traditional the technology. (p. 67)

Members of the more conservative Amish groups are less willing to accept technology or referral to traditional community health, mental health, or social services. Therefore, it is important for the social worker to determine, by asking, the Amish client's or family's group affiliation. Additionally, the social worker must still remember to individualize the client and not make assumptions about the client's values or choices based on his or her affiliation.

The Amish symbolic lifestyle serves as a boundary from the outside modern world. Hostetler (1993) explains that "the Amish perceive as their highest goal eternal life, which they seek to achieve by conforming to the ways of the early

Christians as described in the New Testament, including separation from the un-believing world" (p. 390). However, interaction with the outside world cannot be avoided altogether, so the Amish are continually defining and negotiating their place in modern society. Amish distinguish between themselves and outsiders by calling non-Amish people "English," referring to the outsiders' primary language.

Amish lifestyle is based on European peasant culture and includes a language, called Pennsylvania German or Pennsylvania Dutch, and a distinctive, plain cloth-ing style. They shun the use of electricity from public utility lines, but some may use batteries and generators for power. Horses are used for farming and trans-portation. Formal education ends at the eighth grade, whether in public or Amish parochial school, affirmed by the United States Supreme Court decision on *Wisconsin v. Yoder* (Lindholm, 2003). Worship services every other Sunday are not held in a church building, but in homes in the winter and barns in the summer. In addition to traditional Christian holidays, two special religious holidays are Old Christmas, observed on January 6, and Ascension Day, which falls 40 days after Easter. An unwritten set of rules called the *Ordnung* establishes the religious prac-tices and lifestyle for individual Amish church districts.

To the outsider, there seem to be some inconsistencies in applying the *Ordnung* to the Amish lifestyle. For example, Amish persons are not permitted to own cars but can ride in someone else's car to go to work, shopping, or to appointments. They can use a neighbor's telephone but cannot have one in their own homes. Zippers are not permitted on clothing, but Velcro-fastened shoes are acceptable. No computers are found in Amish homes, but an Amish person employed in an English-owned business may use a computer at work. Tradition, rather than logic, guides these rules. If an Amish person is asked to explain the observed inconsis-tencies, the response is often a shrug and a comment, "That's just our way." According to Kraybill (2001), "The Amish adopt technology selectively, hoping that the tools they use will build community rather than harm it. In short, they pre-fer technology that preserves social capital, rather than depletes it" (p. 188).

Historic Background

Today's Amish people trace their roots to the Anabaptist movement during the 16th century European Reformation. The Anabaptists (meaning "rebaptizers") practiced adult baptism and advocated separation of church and state, peace and nonresistance, literal translation of the Bible, and mutual aid (Nolt, 2003). The Anabaptists were rejected and persecuted by Catholics and Reformation Protestants for these beliefs and customs. *Martyrs Mirror* (Van Braght, 1972), a book found in most Amish homes, preserves illustrated stories of torture, murder, and imprisonment of these early Anabaptists and serves to remind today's Amish of their heritage of persecution for religious beliefs. The *Ausbund*, a German language hymnal used in Amish worship services, contains lyrics (but no musical notes) written by imprisoned martyrs. Contemporary Anabaptist groups include Amish and also the Brethren, Hutterite, and Mennonite denominations (Kraybill & Hostetter, 2001).

The Amish began in 1693, in Europe, when the followers of Jakob Ammann broke away from the Mennonite followers of Menno Simons to establish a more conservative Anabaptist group. They arrived in America in the early 1700s and first settled, in Pennsylvania (Hostetler, 1993). According to the website Amish Studies (www2.etown.edu/amishstudies), an estimated 250,000 Amish people live in the United States, including adults and children. They live in 427 geographic communities, called settlements, in 28 states and the Canadian province of Ontario. The states with the highest Amish population are Pennsylvania, Ohio, and Indiana. The four largest settlements are Lancaster County, PA; Holmes County, OH; Elkhart/LaGrange, IN; and Geauga County, OH. In the 20-year period from 1991 to 2010, the Amish population and number of settlements doubled and expanded into seven additional states. These figures are current as of July 2010 and include all Amish groups who use horse-and-buggy transportation. Thus, Amish communities are present in many rural areas where social workers live and work.

Each Amish settlement has church districts composed of 20–40 families. These individual congregations each have a bishop, two ministers, and one deacon, all serving for life. Bishops, ministers, and deacons are laypeople and are chosen by lot from among the married men in the church district. The bishop is the chief authority of the congregation and influences members' lifestyle; for example, one bishop may permit use of power mowers and another bishop may approve only push mowers. It is important for the social worker to respect this Amish church hierarchy and remember to approach an Amish community through its bishops. A listing of Amish church districts, bishops, ministers, and deacons in Amish communities throughout the United States and Canada is found in Raber's *New American Almanac* (2011).

Mutual Aid

As an outgrowth of their Anabaptist heritage, Amish society is a very strong mutual aid society. Mutual aid was a survival strategy for Anabaptists persecuted in

Europe and aided new arrivals in America. In today's Amish settlements a barn raising, after a fire or tornado, is the most visible example of mutual aid to tourists and English neighbors. More subtle examples are group harvesting of crops or a smaller building project called a "frolic." A sudden death, accident, or serious illness brings an immediate response of emotional support and assistance with daily activities from the local Amish community. Waltman (1992) observed that "there is a prescribed, ritualistic response to human tragedy and common disaster" (p. 104).

The Amish do not limit mutual aid activities to their own society. Many participate in local fire departments, benefit auctions, and relief projects sponsored by the Mennonite Church. For example, some Amish men joined the Mennonite Disaster Service home repair and building projects after Hurricane Katrina struck the Southern coast of the United States.

Because of the Amish tradition of community caring for each others' needs, social workers need to be mindful not to prematurely refer Amish clients to traditional social services. First, one should check with the Amish client or patient about services, and even financial assistance, available within the Amish community, because most Amish people would rather not use outside government or community services.

Communication Patterns

Amish people are bilingual (Pennsylvania Dutch and English), and some are trilingual (Pennsylvania Dutch, English, German). Pennsylvania Dutch is the language used within the home and Amish community, so preschool children may not understand English, and a parent may have to translate for them. Therefore, language is not a barrier between Amish and non-Amish, so social workers should be mindful not to "talk down" to an Amish patient or client.

Face-to-face verbal communication is important to the Amish and helps preserve cohesiveness within their community, and because of this value, most Amish homes do not have landline telephones. Some Amish-owned businesses, however, do have telephones. Visitors to Amish areas will see small shanty buildings along the road and think they might be outhouses, but these shanties house a community telephone used by several families in the area and may provide voicemail accounts for different persons. It is now rather common to see Amish people using cell phones; in fact, the cover of Hurst and McConnell's book, *An Amish Paradox* (2010), shows a photo of a young Amish girl talking on a cell phone. Thus, today's Amish families are not as isolated from the business and professional world as they once were, and this development facilitates communication with Amish clients.

On a national level, the Amish communicate with each other through weekly correspondent newspapers published in English for Amish readers. *The Budget* is published in Sugarcreek, OH, and *Die Botschaft* (The Message) is published in Millersburg, PA. Letters written by Amish writers, called scribes, report happenings in various Amish church districts and communities. According to Nolt (2008), the scribes' letters "create a sort of public, collective diary" (p. 184). This process might be compared with the modern world's phenomenon of social networking. The newspapers also contain ads for patent medicines; health care professionals, such as chiropractors; Amish clothes; battery-operated appliances; solar panels; auctions; and other items of interest to Amish people. Reading the correspondent newspapers promotes cultural unity for the Amish and is an effective way for non-Amish readers to gain insight into the Amish way of life.

Family Structure and Roles

Men and women are assigned definite traditional roles in Amish society. Letters in *The Budget* report the birth of a baby girl as a "dishwasher," whereas a new baby boy is described as a "woodchopper" or a "farmer." Amish men and women follow traditional rituals for courtship, marriage, childbearing and rearing, family life, and death and burial.

The Amish father is the spiritual head of the family and provides for his family through farming, a trade such as carpentry, or a job in the local community. Amish wives manage the household, take care of the yard and garden, and may help with some of the farm work. Some Amish families have home-based businesses, in which all family members work together to produce a product.

Amish women are expected to serve and please others and be helpers to their husbands. Although an Amish wife and mother is consulted about major decisions, such as health care for a child, the husband would communicate a final decision to a health care provider. Thus, it is important for social workers and other professionals to approach an Amish family through the father and patiently wait for him to communicate final decisions.

Child Rearing Practices

Because most Amish couples do not use birth control to limit family size, which is seen as interfering with God's will, it is not uncommon for an Amish family to have seven or more children. Hurst and McConnell (2010), using random sampling of data in the 2005 *Ohio Amish Directory, Holmes County and Vicinity*, found that Amish families average five children, well above the national average of two children per family. They also found that Amish farmers had more children than nonfarmers and surmised that this reflects a decreased need for labor as the Amish move away from farming as an occupation. It should be noted that the directory includes data on Old Order, Andy Weaver, and New Order groups, but not the more conservative Swartzentruber Amish, who tend to have larger families.

All children are welcomed and cherished in Amish families. Births and first appearances in church are reported regularly in *The Budget*. Intermarriage among the Amish, with some as closely related as second cousins, may result in children born with congenital hereditary conditions such as cystic fibrosis, dwarfism, hemophilia, and metabolic or neuromuscular disorders. A child born with a congenital health problem is called a "special child" in *The Budget*. Families with special children often have their own support groups that meet informally to socialize and exchange information on their children's conditions and care. These children are accepted as God's will, and an Amish couple will not limit their family due to the presence of a hereditary medical condition. Therefore, genetic counseling is probably inappropriate for most Amish couples, and sterilization would only be considered for the mother's health.

Children are expected to help with household and farm chores at an early age, as these activities teach appropriate gender roles in Amish society. Older children, especially girls, help care for younger brothers and sisters. However, involving young children in potentially dangerous tasks, such as driving large work horses, can result in untimely accidents and even deaths. These often preventable injuries and deaths present a dilemma for child welfare social workers, who must balance protecting children with respecting Amish cultural practices.

Rumspringa—*Staying and Leaving*

In many Amish communities, Amish teenagers experience a period of *rumspringa* ("running around") as a rite of passage to adulthood. They may drive cars, go to movies, dress in English clothes, and experiment with smoking, alcohol, or drugs, because they are not yet baptized and under the authority of the Amish church. Their parents largely ignore this behavior, because they may have experienced it themselves and know that for most youth it will end with a conscious decision to give up the worldly ways, be baptized, and join the Amish church. The alternative, however, is to choose to leave the Amish community. Stevick (2007) conducted extensive research on Amish adolescents and their families by visiting more than 60 Amish settlements in the United States and Canada over a period of 10 years. His book, based on the research, offers valuable insight into the "running around" experience for Amish adolescents, their families, and the communities. Despite being exposed to the many temptations of the outside modern world, a surprising number of Amish young adults choose to stay in their Amish communities. Kraybill (2001) estimated that more than 90% of Lancaster County Old Order children join the church. Hurst and McConnell (2010) calculated a retention rate of 86% among the Old Order Amish in the Holmes County settlement.

If an Amish young adult chooses not to join the Amish church, the parents and family are disappointed but usually retain some degree of relationship with that family member. However, if a baptized Amish church member decides to leave, the family may shun that person and break off all contact. Many people who leave the Amish faith become Mennonites and therefore are still under the Anabaptist faith umbrella, which may moderate estrangement from their family of origin. "Go high" and "jump over" are phrases used to describe leaving the Amish church.

The reasons for leaving and the resultant effects on family relationships are varied and should be considered on an individual basis. When working with a former Amish client, it is critical for the social worker to find out, perhaps in the context of a social history, if the person left the Amish church before or after baptism and what the current relationship with his or her family and the Amish community is. If the former Amish client is isolated from family and community, he or she loses the mutual aid safety net that protects an Amish person for life.

Intergenerational Family Life—Care of the Elderly

Because three or four generations live on an Amish farm, children grow up in intergenerational families and learn at an early age to respect their elders. The older grandparents live in a smaller house, called the *grossdaadi haus* ("grandpa house") or just *daadi haus*, which is attached or adjacent to the main farm house. Each family has its own separate living space, but the respective family members share some household or farming chores, such as canning food from their gardens.

Zook (2001) explained that "care of the elderly in Amish society is a part of their informal system of mutual aid, which permeates the entire culture and is a routine part of everyday life" (p. 143). When the elderly family members need assistance with activities of daily living, the younger generations are readily available to help with meals, nursing care, visiting, transportation, or whatever is needed. There is no stigma attached to being old, sick, or disabled. A recent letter to *The Budget* (Baltic, OH, scribe letter, 2010) reported that an older couple, ages 86 and 89 years, celebrated their 64th wedding anniversary. The letter reported that the wife's eyesight is failing, and she cannot read a newspaper; she is also mostly confined to a wheelchair. However, her son takes her to church in a buggy specially adapted to carry a wheelchair. The husband's mobility is restricted, but he is still able to hitch up his horse and go places by himself. Amish society mastered the art of aging in place long before mainstream society embraced the idea.

Family Breakdown

Although there is an emphasis on strong families and family life in Amish culture, there are instances of desertion, divorce, domestic violence, and child abuse. Much of the information on family breakdown is anecdotal within the Amish community and eventually finds its way to the larger surrounding English community. Occasionally, a very dysfunctional Amish family is sensationalized by the national news media, with the risk that the dysfunctional behavior will be generalized to all Amish families. Kraybill (2008) described the dilemma this poses for Amish community leaders who wish to provide accurate information to the news media, yet avoid unnecessary publicity.

Child abuse in Amish families is documented through reports to local authorities. Hurst and McConnell (2010) described a case in which a Holmes County Amish woman was convicted and jailed for abusing her baby by shaking him. They also interviewed the directors of Holmes County and Geauga County Jobs and Family Services agencies and found that the incidence of child abuse and neglect in Amish families is lower than in non-Amish families in those counties. Waltman (2000) advises, "Social service agencies serving Amish communities need to use culturally-sensitive approaches such as recognizing the patriarchal nature of Amish families and including their bishop in discussions of alleged abuse" (p. 55).

Current Trends in Amish Society

Perhaps the most dramatic change in Amish lifestyle is the shift from primarily farming to various nonfarm occupations. Kreps, Donnermeyer, and Kreps (1994) studied occupations of Amish males in the Holmes County, OH, settlement and reported that "farming as the primary occupation for males is declining and the occupational structure of the Amish is becoming more complex as more Amish males work away from the home" (p.716–717). They further concluded that these changes are due to the shortage of farms and farm-related jobs, the cost and scarcity of farmland, and the increase in the Amish population. Hurst and McConnell (2010) discovered that slightly less than 10% of nonretired Amish workers in a random sample from the 2005 *Ohio Amish Directory* were farmers, and this trend is also found in Pennsylvania and Indiana Amish communities. Amish men now work at local factories as laborers or on mobile construction crews as carpenters, painters, and masons. This nonfarm work exposes Amish men to what Kraybill and Nolt (2004) labeled the "lunch pail threat" (p. 149) because it threatens the Amish agrarian lifestyle. The Amish wife and mother is now in charge of the home and family, while the husband is away at work. She may have to make major decisions alone, such as whether to take a sick or injured child to a doctor or emergency room. If the child's condition is serious, the Amish mother may request hospital personnel to locate her husband and bring him in to participate in making decisions regarding a child's medical care. This request often goes to the hospital social worker to locate the father and make arrangements to transport him from his workplace to the hospital.

As an alternative to factory or mobile construction crew work, some Amish families establish home-based businesses, such as a greenhouses, bakeries, bulk food stores, or quilt shops. Producing wood products—furniture, gazebos, small storage barns—provides work for several family members and thus keeps the family unit together. Amish women are becoming entrepreneurs and establishing their own small businesses. Kraybill (2001) noted that 17% of Amish owned businesses in the Lancaster, PA, area are owned by women, giving them access to money, other resources, and the outside world. Waltman (2000) observed, "Similar to their non-Amish counterparts, Amish working women juggle the demands of their business with the demands of their husband, family, and social life" (p. 46).

The influx of tourism, especially in the Amish settlements in Ohio, Pennsylvania, and Indiana, has created further work and business opportunities for Amish men and women. Young unmarried Amish women now have a variety of vocations, ranging from waitresses in restaurants to clerks in stores and housekeepers in motels and bed and breakfast establishments. Some Amish cater to the tourists by opening retail businesses such as antique shops or furniture stores.

The development of these two trends—fewer Amish farmers and an increasing tourist industry in the larger Amish settlements—has caused some Amish families, especially those from the more conservative groups, to migrate to other geographic areas in search of affordable farmland to get away from the intrusions of curious tourists. When a group of Amish families arrives in an area not previously populated by Amish, local business and professional people can be quite perplexed and have some initial difficulty determining how to interact with this unfamiliar culture. Health and mental health professionals especially need to educate themselves about Amish culture and how best to serve Amish patients and clients.

Child Welfare Case Example: The Glick Family

At the 2007 Amish in America conference held at Elizabethtown College in Pennsylvania, Dr. D. Holmes Morton, founder and director of the Clinic for Special Children in Strasburg, PA, cautioned attendees that genetic metabolic diseases, especially those prevalent in the Amish population, can masquerade as common problems. The following case example, drawn from a scribe's letters to *The Budget* (Millersburg, PA, scribe letters, 1999–2000) illustrates Dr. Morton's point.

On December 22, 1999, an Old Order Amish couple, Samuel and Elizabeth Glick, took their very ill 4-month-old daughter to a local doctor, who referred them to a larger medical center in a neighboring county. The doctor at the medical center noted extensive bruises on the child's body and suspected child abuse, which he reported to the local child welfare agency. That same day, the child welfare workers visited the Glick family farm and removed their other children, seven boys ranging in age from 5 to 15 years old, and placed them in separate non-Amish foster homes. The baby died the next day and her death was declared a homicide. The Amish community responded by setting up a donor fund to help the family with court costs and other expenses. At the family's request, Dr. Morton entered the case and began looking for a possible genetic disorder that caused the child's illness and death.

The Glick's sons were, eventually, transferred to Amish foster homes, the school-age boys returned to school, and the parents were permitted to have supervised visits with their sons. Dr. Morton determined that the Glick baby died of a vitamin K deficiency and a genetic metabolic blood disorder, later verified by an independent expert from Philadelphia. In late February child welfare officials permitted the Glick children to return home, and a month later all child abuse and criminal allegations against the Glicks were dropped. In April, through their *Budget* scribe, the Glick family thanked the local and national Amish Community for their prayers and support during their ordeal.

What can be learned from this case example? Hurst and McConnell (2010) reported that child welfare personnel from Holmes and Geauga Counties in Ohio recommend placing Amish at-risk children with relatives or other Amish families who are part of the Amish community's natural helping network. It may also be advisable to involve the family's bishop in the case planning process and extended family members or other church members in the case management of ongoing cases. The goal for child welfare professionals is to practice cultural sensitivity and competency to build trust with the Amish community, while maintaining accountability to child protective laws.

Amish Community Services

The Clinic for Special Children (www.clinicforspecialchildren.org) in Strasburg, PA, is a nonprofit medical and diagnostic service for Amish and Mennonite children in the Lancaster County, PA, area with inherited metabolic disorders. Established in 1989 by Dr. D. Holmes Morton, the clinic provides clinical care, laboratory services, genetic disease research, and education in genetic medicine. In 2002 a similar clinic, Das Deutsch Center (DDC) Clinic for Special Needs Children (www.ddcclinic.org), opened in Middlefield, OH, to serve families in the Geauga County Amish settlement. The DDC Clinic provides outreach clinic services in the Holmes County Amish settlement. Both clinics also serve children from non-Amish families and are funded by local community support and foundations.

The Amish Youth Vision Project (http://ayvp.org) was established in 2005 in the Elkhart/LaGrange, IN, Amish settlement area to address alcohol and drug use and abuse among Amish youth. The project provides intervention, education, and prevention services for Amish youth and their parents. Local Amish persons are recruited and trained to serve as mentors for Amish teens and to co-lead, with professional counselors, the alcohol and drug education classes. Funding sources include community support, foundations, and fees. Government grants are used for administrative purposes only, as requested by local Amish leaders. It is important to involve Amish bishops as consultants in planning and carrying out community programs such as the Amish Youth Vision Project.

Amish Society's Response to Health and Mental Health Practices

Amish people experience some of the same social, health, and mental health problems as persons in the larger mainstream society: mental illness, mental retardation, illegitimacy, disability, and alcohol and drug abuse. Affected persons may look first to their immediate Amish community for help with such problems, but may also seek out and use mainstream community resources. Health and mental health professionals need to remember basic principles of acceptance, keeping a nonjudgmental attitude, and acknowledging client self-determination when responding to Amish clients and patients. Due to a lifestyle that values self-reliance, Amish communities may develop their own resources, which they often share with the outside world.

Health Care Beliefs and Practices

In the Amish culture, illness is defined not so much by symptoms as by the inability to work, sometimes delaying treatment. Amish health care habits are influenced by several factors, such as preferring a holistic approach and low-tech evaluation or treatment, evaluating costs that affect families and communities, knowledge about health and disease, and accessibility to health care services. Because of their Anabaptist heritage of suffering and martyrdom, some Amish persons choose to suffer in silence and await God's will regarding medical problems.

Health care systems used by the Amish. The Amish may use several health care systems, often simultaneously: professional care, alternative care, folk care, and self-care. Physicians working with Amish patients quickly learn to practice parallel medicine that tolerates the patient's use of other therapies along with the physician's treatment, as long as it is not detrimental to the patient.

Amish people get care from medical professionals such as physicians, dentists, nurses, and pharmacists, and they appreciate a professional who takes time to talk with patients and can accept an informal form of address, such as "Dr. Dan." There are no Amish medical professionals because of the required higher education and training. However, some practitioners may speak Pennsylvania Dutch, which adds to the patient's comfort level. Dr. Elton Lehman's (2004) account of his medical practice among the Amish in Wayne County, OH, includes a glossary of common Pennsylvania Dutch words and phrases, with English translations. Banks and Benchot (2001) recommended culturally specific nursing care for hospitalized Amish children, such as not turning on a television without parents' permission and offering plain gowns to replace those with cartoon characters. Medical social workers may be part of the professional health care team and need to be knowledgeable in regard to these nuances of care for Amish patients.

Chiropractors, herbalists, iridologists, and reflexologists are examples of alternative medical care providers used by the Amish. An iridologist examines the eye's iris to diagnose illness, whereas a reflexologist manipulates the feet to relieve symptoms in other parts of the body. Graham and Cates (2002) observed that Amish patients can be reluctant to discuss their use of alternative treatments and advised health care professionals to adopt a nonjudgmental manner when obtaining a health history, to get accurate information. Alternative care is not exclusively used by Amish patients, as non-Amish people also patronize these practitioners.

Folk care involves the use of indigenous Amish healers and lay midwives. An Amish folk practitioner called a "powwow" uses chants, charms, or physical manipulation to relieve symptoms such as backaches, headaches, or arthritis. The powwow may suggest helpful herbs and vitamins and accepts only donations for services, thus avoiding a charge of practicing medicine without a license. Amish lay midwives, in some states, preside over births in their homes or their patients' homes. Home remedies are an important adjunct to folk care, and recipes are passed down through generations. A family-owned drug store in Millersburg (Holmes County), OH, had a large Amish clientele who brought their recipes to the druggist to compound. Belladonna and similar drugs were popular ingredients in home remedies for human and veterinary use until they became controlled substances requiring a prescription. A column, "Information Please," in *The Budget* (2011) enables Amish readers to share health care information and home remedy recipes.

Self-care is based on self-diagnosis and the convenience of buying patent (non-prescription) medicines from local stores or by mail from various companies that advertise in *The Budget* or *Die Botschaft*. Popular patent medicines used by Amish customers are Lydia Pinkham Herbal Compound, cholera balsam, and Hyland's homeopathic combinations. Crawford, Manuel, and Wood (2009) described a pharmacist's experiences serving Amish patients in the Arthur, IL, Amish community, responding to their questions about self-care, which provided an opportunity for patient education. The Amish use of self-care is really no different from a non-Amish person who buys vitamins and supplements to promote health or patent medicines as a first response to signs of illness.

Mutual aid and health insurance. Because of a long history of mutual aid and caring for their own members, Amish people prefer not to buy commercial health insurance or participate in Medicaid or Medicare (Kraybill, 2001). Some Amish men working for English employers do participate in health care benefits, but most Amish communities have their own group health insurance, funded by contributions from member families. McCollum (1998) reported that hospitals and doctors may give substantial discounts to self-paying Amish patients, thus saving paperwork and payment negotiations with insurance companies. When an Amish family incurs an extraordinarily high medical expense, the local community will often give additional donations or organize a fund-raising event for the family.

To accommodate self-paying patients such as the Amish, Pomerene Hospital in Holmes County, OH, offers special pricing packages for a wide variety of services. An Amish advocate at the hospital assists patients with clinical and financial questions and also fields comments and complaints. The hospital also provides a limited transportation service for Amish patients and a nearby "Amish House" for family members who wish to stay close to hospitalized loved ones. These services are good public relations for the hospital and promote accessibility to health care for Amish patients and families.

Death and dying. According to Waltman (1996a), "within the Amish culture, death is accepted as a natural occurrence in the progression of life, a belief buoyed by a religious system that embraces the concept of eternal life" (p. 27). Therefore, an Amish family may decline extensive tests and heroic medical care for a family member, especially an elderly member, preferring to take the patient home and make him or her comfortable, while awaiting God's will. Other family members and friends then provide round-the-clock care, if necessary, bolstering a network of support for the patient and immediate family. Weyer and colleagues (2003) described home nursing care of a dying elderly Amish woman, while respecting the family's desire to provide only comfort care. Some Amish families use hospice care because it is compatible with their philosophy of death and dying. Funeral services, conducted by Amish clergy, are held in the deceased person's home.

Genetics. Amish people are an ideal population for conducting genetic studies, because they live in relatively closed communities, keep extensive genealogies, and have a large number of inherited recessive disorders in which both parents are carriers of a genetic condition (Francomano, 1996). Francomano, McKusick, and Biesecker (2003) documented a historical perspective on medical genetic studies with the Amish, initiated by researchers at Johns Hopkins University in Baltimore, MD, contributing greatly to general knowledge about genetics, which has benefited society as a whole.

Social workers and other human service professionals are especially interested in research to identify a gene or genes contributing to bipolar disorder in the Amish. Led by Egeland (1988) and others (Ginns et al., 1992; Kelsoe et al., 1989; LaBuda, Maldonado, Marshall, Otten, & Gerhard, 1996; Yang et al., 2009), the search continues and may involve very complex genetic origins. The National Institute of Mental Health recently placed ads in *The Budget*, obviously targeting the Amish population, for participants in a research study looking for genes that may affect a person's chances of developing bipolar disorder (Bipolar genetics research study, 2011).

Outsiders may wonder why Amish families participate in this human genetic research, when they will not necessarily use the information themselves. Francomano and colleagues (2003) explains that "the primary reason why the Amish share medical information with each other and with doctors and researchers is a commitment to help those in need and to provide the most help to those in greatest need" (p. 3). The Amish families may benefit from this research, because early diagnosis can lead to effective treatment for some children. The clinics for special children mentioned previously in this chapter are an important diagnostic and treatment resource for affected children.

Ethical issues in Amish health care. The predominant health care ethical issue is patient self-determination versus professional paternalism, complicated by children and adult protective services statutes. Whenever possible, it is best to avoid aggressive legal action to force an Amish family to accept heroic medical care for a family member. Lehman (2004) recommended using negotiation and compromise, within parameters of accepted medical practice, to resolve issues of patient self-determination regarding medical treatment decisions.

Other ethical scenarios involve beginning of life and end of life issues that affect not just the Amish, but everyone. Gibson (2008) described her experience caring for a critically ill, Amish, newborn baby boy and how her experience deepened her understanding of and respect for Amish culture. The hospital assisted with culturally sensitive care for this patient by allowing the family extended visitation and, eventually, moving the baby to a private room where the parents could stay with him. At the other end of this spectrum, Bryer (1979), a classic article on the Amish view of death, suggested "the real power in the Amish way of death is that they do not ignore it, thereby allaying the anxieties created by events they cannot fully understand or control" (p. 259). Breyer (1979) further explained that "the presence of the body in the home, the repeated viewing, the continuing community support, and the family participation in the actual disposition of the body all serve as constant reminders of the fact of death" (p. 259). Thus, Amish people's acceptance of death contrasts with an attitude of denial or delay that is often found in the larger society. These discussions remind health care professionals of an ethical obligation to not impose their own cultural values and preferences on their patients and families.

Case example: Baby Aaron (Clayton & Kodish, 1999). An Amish couple took their 3-month-old baby, Aaron, to a hospital emergency room, where he was diagnosed with congestive heart failure. A pediatric cardiologist recommended open heart surgery, predicting the baby would die within 3 months without surgery. The parents declined consent for surgery, stating religious grounds and preferring to take the baby home and accept God's will for the outcome. The cardiologist contacted a family physician in the Amish family's community, who suspected that economic concerns were influencing the family's decision. After talking with the family, the hospital social worker felt that the couple understood the consequences of their decision. This example poses some ethical dilemmas. Should the cardiologist discharge the baby without further medical procedures? Should medical personnel report the family to child protective services for possible child neglect? How would a report affect the family's trust in the health care system? Should the hospital ethics committee be consulted? As with other ethical dilemmas, there are no easy answers to these questions.

Amish community services. The Windows of Hope Project (www.wohproject.org) is an international undertaking organized in 2000 that focuses on identification, diagnosis, treatment, and prevention of genetic disorders among Anabaptist people, including Amish, Mennonites, and Hutterites. The website contains a searchable list of genetic disorders, research reports, genetics education, and a newsletter. In August 2009 the Windows of Hope Genetic Information Center (www.wohgeneticinfo.org) opened in Walnut Creek (Holmes County), OH, to help families and patients understand and cope with inherited disorders. A part-time nurse/educator is available on-site to provide information, referral, and coordination of care with family physicians.

The Rainbow of Hope Foundation (www.rohfoundation.org) is a nonprofit organization serving Amish and English families in Holmes, Coshocton, Wayne, and Tuscarawas Counties in Ohio who have incurred large medical expenses for their children. The foundation is an example of cooperation between the Amish and English to fill a community need. A professional social worker was involved in developing policies and procedures for the foundation and served on the governing board. The foundation's primary funding source is an annual auction of donated items such as quilts and furniture.

Support groups for Amish people with certain medical conditions, such as burn survivors, are available in various Amish settlements across the country. Organized by the Amish themselves, the support groups offer shared experiences, information, and social activities. Some support groups have a national following, and members communicate with each other through circle letters to update and share information regarding diagnosis, treatment, and recovery.

Mental Health Issues and Counseling Techniques

Compared to the professional literature available on Amish health care, there is very little to guide mental health professionals. This is due, in part, to some reluctance of Amish people to seek professional care for mental health issues, so psychiatrists, psychologists, counselors, and social workers do not have much experience to report in the professional literature. Reiling (2002a) identified two barriers for Amish persons seeking professional care for feelings of depression: first, a religious-based stigmatization of depression; and, second, a view of mental health providers as illegitimate help agents. An Amish person is more comfortable consulting a trusted family physician for the physical symptoms of depression, and the physician may then prescribe antidepressant medication. Eventually, the physician may be able to refer the patient to a mental health professional. Referral to a "Christian counselor" who uses scripture and prayer as part of treatment is more readily accepted by an Amish person who views mental illness as a spiritual problem. Speaking Pennsylvania Dutch is an added asset for a mental health provider.

Aberrations in behavior are easily tolerated in Amish society, and this can also be a barrier to seeking professional treatment for mental health problems. If the bishop is consulted, he may recommend only herbal remedies, rather than mental health treatment. Cates and Graham (2002) suggested meeting with Amish bishops to discuss psychological services available and to demonstrate sensitivity to the Amish way of life. In Cates' (2005) opinion, "the Amish clergy are also the frequent 'first line' of treatment for mental health problems, and will be the source of 'aftercare' when the client is terminated from a mental health center" (p. 378). A family therapy approach may involve the bishop in counseling sessions and planning case management. An Amish client or family will not likely be concerned about confidentiality issues, in doing so, and may actually request that the bishop be present.

Cultural aspects of diagnosis and treatment. Mental health professionals need to acknowledge the Amish culture's *Gelassenheit* principles influencing personal values and personality traits: humility, submission, obedience, modesty, and individual subordination to the good of the community. Humility may be mistakenly diagnosed as low self-esteem, submission as being withdrawn, obedience as a lack of self-expression, and modesty as difficulty accepting praise. Loyalty to the community over self limits opportunities for the personal growth and achievement affirmed by the dominant culture. Another expression of *Gelassenheit* is the use of silence to avoid conflict. Amish children are taught to suppress the expression of feelings and emotions other than pleasure. Cates and Graham (2002) observed that Amish clients sometimes display a flat affect to the outside world, and this should not be hastily interpreted as a mood disorder symptom. They also cautioned that traditional psychological test results can be skewed by the influence of Amish cultural and religious values of the client.

To establish an effective therapeutic relationship, Cates and Graham (2002) gave some practical suggestions, such as dressing in neutral or solid fabrics and providing a sense of equality by sitting with the client or family, rather than behind a desk. Amish clients may ask personal questions of the professional, such as whether the professional is married or has children, where he or she lives, or whether he or she is related to certain persons. This helps the Amish client individualize the professional and determine the professional's place within the overall community. These questions should be responded to briefly, but openly and honestly. Cates (2005) recommended accepting some emotional distance with Amish clients, because "often, the greatest rapport occurs as the client develops a respect, rather than the more commonly anticipated emotional closeness, for the therapist" (p. 373). Similar to health care professionals, mental health professionals may need to accept the client's use of herbal remedies concomitant with counseling.

Another cultural caveat involves the use of treatment and support groups with Amish clients. Amish clients are most likely comfortable with groups segregated by gender. SpringHaven, a nonprofit Christian counseling agency located within the Holmes County Amish settlement, announced an anxiety and depression psychoeducational group for women, led by a female licensed professional counselor. A similar group for men was formed with a male leader (Anxiety and depression group for women, 2010).

Former Amish. Social workers in rural communities are more likely to have former Amish persons as clients in mental health settings, because they will be more comfortable seeking professional help with mental health problems. These clients' Amish upbringing and cultural values remain with them, even though they live in the outside world. Clinical experience with former Amish clients indicates former Amish persons have a wide continuum of attitudes toward their Amish origins, somewhat dependent on whether the person left before or after baptism. Some former Amish persons are comfortable with leaving but still respect and cherish their Amish background. Others romanticize their earlier life and ignore the existence of serious problems within their past, such as child abuse. Still others are bitter and critical of their Amish experiences and have a demeaning attitude toward Amish people. It is important to evaluate a former Amish client's views of his or her Amish background and recognize that he or she may have very ambivalent attitudes toward his or her heritage.

Clinical issues. Several clinical issues surface for mental health professionals when working with Amish and former Amish clients. Understanding and dealing with these issues is crucial for establishing a helping relationship.

Amish clients' emphasis on humility and spiritual perfection may make it difficult for them to lower these self-expectations to a more realistic level. A learned cultural suppression of emotions and denial of feelings makes it difficult to verbalize psychosocial problems, so a counselor needs to listen patiently and observe nonverbal behavior. Remember the husband/father is the head of an Amish family; thus, he is the "window" to reach other members of the family. Respect for Amish cultural boundaries needs to be maintained, and a counselor may have to accept some limitations in developing treatment plans.

Former Amish clients may experience conflict with their earlier cultural influences, for example, submissive versus assertive behavior in interpersonal relationships. Because traditional Amish social relationships and activities are not present for former Amish clients, these clients may have difficulty with basic social skills and feel socially isolated. Estrangement from the Amish family of origin can cause feelings of guilt and even mourning for the loss of contact with extended family members. Lack of connection to the Amish mutual aid safety net may increase vulnerability and inability to deal with crisis situations.

Counseling techniques. Understanding and respecting Amish and former Amish clients' cultural context, and staying within those parameters, guides assessment, treatment planning, and counseling techniques. Obtaining a social history helps a counselor understand the client's psychosocial status as it relates to cultural context, and helps individualize the client. A social history is especially important with former Amish clients, to understand why they left and to determine their current relationships with their families of origin. Former Amish clients may need help learning new social skills to fit into the larger society. One may use journal writing to help the client express some feelings in writing, then venture toward verbal expression, if appropriate. Mental health professionals need to accept periods of silence with Amish and former Amish clients, as well as to respect the client's right to self-determination in decision making. Crisis intervention techniques may be needed intermittently, especially with former Amish clients who are isolated from strong social support networks.

Amish community services. The Counseling Center of Wayne and Holmes Counties (OH) has developed specialized programs and services for Amish clients and families. An Amish Family Support Group, for those dealing with a family member with mental illness, meets monthly in a school located within the Holmes County Amish settlement (Amish family support group, 2011). The Center also offers case management services and education programs targeted toward the local Amish community. De Rue, Schlegel, and Yoder (2002) reports on surveys the center conducted to determine mental health care needs of Amish consumers and family members.

Hoffnung Heim (Home of Hope) is an Amish facility housed in a farm house in Holmes County (OH), focusing on indigenous mental health assistance for the Amish. Counseling focuses on spiritual issues and relatively minor emotional problems. Persons with more serious psychiatric problems, however, are referred to licensed professionals for medication and therapy (Hurst & McConnell, 2010).

Former Amish Reunion (FAR) is a support group for individuals who have left the Amish church and is coordinated by a former Amish woman. The group meets twice a year at alternating sites in Ohio and Indiana for picnics and fellowship. Hurst and McConnell (2010) attended an Ohio picnic and reported that the activities included informal conversations among the attendees and music provided by a local evangelical church.

Conclusion

Social workers in rural areas may have a unique opportunity to interact with persons from Amish society who experience many of the same health, mental health, and social problems as do people in the dominant society. As presented in this chapter, culturally sensitive professional practice requires a basic understanding of Amish culture and knowledge of specific guidelines to use when working with Amish clients, families, and communities.

The pace of life in Amish society is slow—an Amish buggy travels about 10–20 miles per hour—so professionals need to adopt a calm and relaxed demeanor as they interface with this special population. Rural social workers will be comfortable in this cultural environment, because they know the art of chit-chat, taking time to talk about the weather, crops, local news, and events before introducing a more serious subject. Applying basic social work principles of individualization, acceptance, nonjudgmental attitude, and client self-determination further bolster the helping relationship with Amish clients.

Amish culture's *Gelassenheit* principles of humility, obedience, submission, and mutual caring guide their lives in their close-knit communities and in contacts with the outside world. When working with Amish clients, social workers need to be aware of the *Gelassenheit* philosophy and to practice patience, tolerate silent discourse, and accept some degree of negotiation and accommodation. This approach fosters an atmosphere of mutual respect between helping professionals and Amish clients.

Because they are continually growing in numbers and establishing new settlements in rural areas, the Amish are a special population of increasing importance to rural social workers. Armed with knowledge of Amish culture and professional guidelines, social workers in rural areas can provide appropriate clinical and community services to Amish client, families, and communities. There is also an opportunity to advocate for Amish people and assist them in accessing health and mental health services. In turn, the Amish can demonstrate how their stable and cohesive society builds social capital through networking and a high sense of community. Amish and English residents in rural areas can work together to improve the quality of life for everyone.

References

Amish family support group. (2011, January 12). *The Budget*, p. 5.

Amish Studies. (2010). *Amish population trends 2009–2010, one-year highlights.* Elizabethtown, PA: Elizabethtown College. Retrieved from www2.etown.edu/amishstudies/Population_Trends_2009_2010.asp.

Amish Studies. (2011). *Amish population trends 1991–2010, 20-year highlights.* Elizabethtown, PA: Elizabethtown College. Retrieved from www2.etown.edu/amishstudies/Population_Trends_1991_2010.asp

Anxiety and depression group for women. (2010, August 4). *The Budget*, p. 5

Ausbund (Selection). (1995). Lancaster, PA: Lancaster Press.

Baltic, OH, scribe letter. (2010, November 10). *The Budget,* p. 32.

Banks, M. J., & Benchot, R. J. (2001). Unique aspects of nursing care for Amish children. *MCN: The American Journal of Maternal and Child Nursing, 26,* 192–196.

Beachy, A., Hershberger, E., Davidhizar, R., & Giger, J. N. (1997). Cultural implications for nursing care of the Amish. *Journal of Cultural Diversity, 4*(4), 118–128.

Bean, N. (1993). Reaching out to isolated, rural families: A study of cooperative relationships developed with the Amish community by a center for developmentally disabled children. *Human Services in the Rural Environment, 16*(3), 18–23.

Bipolar genetics research study. (2011, July 6). *The Budget*, p. 20.

Bipolar genetics research study. (2011, July 13). *The Budget*, p. 42.

Bryer, K. B. (1979). The Amish way of death: A study of family support systems. *American Psychologist, 34,* 255–261.

Buccalo, S., & Echelbarger, M. E. (Eds.) (1997). Window on another world: Health practitioners look at the Amish culture and their health care beliefs. [Special issue]. *Journal of Multicultural Nursing & Health, 3*(2), 3–62.

Cates, J. A. (2005). Facing away: Mental health treatment with the Old Order Amish. *American Journal of Psychotherapy, 59,* 371–383.

Cates, J. A., & Graham, L. L. (2002). Psychological assessment of the Old Order Amish: Unraveling the enigma. *Professional Psychology: Research and Practice, 33,* 155–161.

Clayton, E. W., & Kodish, E. (1999). Baby Aaron and the elders. *Hastings Center Report, 29*(5), 20–21.

Crawford, S. Y., Manuel, A. M., & Wood B. D. (2009). Pharmacists' considerations when serving Amish patients. *Journal of the American Pharmacists Association, 49,* 86–94.

De Rue, D. S., Schlegel, R., & Yoder, J. (2002). *Amish needs and mental health care.* Retrieved from www.marshall.edu/jrcp/sp2002/amish.htm

Egeland, J. A. (1988). A genetic study of manic-depressive disorder among the old order Amish of Pennsylvania. *Pharmacopsychiatry, 21,* 74–75.

Francomano, C. A. (1996). Cultural and religious factors affecting the provision of genetic services to the Amish. In N. Fisher (Ed.), *Handbook on medical genetics and ethnocultural diversity* (pp. 176–197). Baltimore, MD: Johns Hopkins University Press.

Francomano, C. A., McKusick, V. A., & Biesecker, L. G. (2003). Medical genetic studies in the Amish: Historical perspective. *American Journal of Medical Genetics Part C (Seminar In Medical Genetics), 121C,* 1–4.

Gibson, E. A. (2008). Caring for a critically ill Amish newborn: An application of Leininger's theory of culture care diversity and universality. *Journal of Transcultural Nursing, 19,* 371–374.

Ginns, E. I., Egeland, J. A., Allen, C. R., Pauls, D. L., Falls, K., Keith, T. P., & Paul, S. M. (1992). Update on the search for DNA markers linked to manic-depressive illness in the Old Order Amish. *Journal of Psychiatric Research, 26,* 305–308.

Graham, L. L., & Cates, J. A. (2002). Health care and sequestered cultures: A perspective from the Old Order Amish. *Journal of Multicultural Nursing & Health, 8*(3), 53–59.

Hostetler, J. A. (1993). *Amish society* (4th ed.). Baltimore, MD: Johns Hopkins University Press.

Hurst, C. E., & McConnell, D. L. (2010). *An Amish paradox: Diversity and change in the world's largest Amish community.* Baltimore, MD: Johns Hopkins University Press.

Information please. (2011, September 14). *The Budget*, p. 33.

Kelsoe, J. R., Ginns, E. I., Egeland, J. A., Gerhard, D. S., Goldstein, A. M., Bale, S. J., ... Conte, G. (1989). Re-evaluation of the linkage relationship between chromosome 11p loci and the gene for bipolar affective disorder in the Old Order Amish. *Nature, 342*, 238–243.

Kraybill, D. B. (2001). *The riddle of Amish culture* (rev. ed.). Baltimore, MD: Johns Hopkins University Press.

Kraybill, D. B. (2008). Amish informants: Mediating humility and publicity. In D. Z. Umble & D. L. Weaver-Zercher (Eds.), *The Amish and the media* (pp. 161–178). Baltimore, MD: Johns Hopkins University Press.

Kraybill, D. B., & Hostetter, C. N. (2001). *Anabaptist world USA*. Scottdale, PA: Herald Press.

Kraybill, D. B., & Nolt, S. M. (2004). *Amish enterprise: From plows to profits* (2nd ed.). Baltimore, MD: Johns Hopkins University Press.

Kreps, G. M., Donnermeyer, J. F., & Kreps, M. W. (1994). The changing occupational structure of Amish males. *Rural Sociology, 59*, 708–719.

Kreps, G. M., Donnermeyer, J. F., Hurst, C., Blair, R., & Kreps, M. (1997). The impact of tourism on the Amish subculture: A case study. *Community Development Journal, 32*, 354–367.

LaBuda, M. C., Maldonado, M., Marshall, D., Otten, K., & Gerhard, D. S. (1996). A follow-up report of a genome search for affective disorder predisposition loci in the Old Order Amish. *American Journal of Human Genetics, 59*, 1343–1362.

Lee, K. K. (1984). *Amish society—in celebration of rural strength and diversity.* Paper presented at the Ninth National/Second International Institute on Social Work in Rural Areas, Orono, ME.

Lehman, E. (2004). *House calls and hitching posts.* Intercourse, PA: Good Books.

Lindholm, W. C. (2003). The national committee for Amish religious freedom. In D. B. Kraybill (Ed.), *The Amish and the state* (2nd ed.). (pp. 109–123). Baltimore, MD: Johns Hopkins University Press.

McCollum, M. J. (1998). Uncovered—and unfazed. *H&HN: Hospitals and Health Networks, 72*, 38.

Millersburg, PA, scribe letters. (1999, December 29–2000, April 5). *The Budget*.

Morton, D. H. (2007). *The Plain people and genetic medicine: What can the Plain communities teach us now?* Paper presented at the Amish in America conference, Elizabethtown, PA.

Nolt, S. M. (2003). *A history of the Amish.* Intercourse, PA: Good Books.

Nolt, S. M. (2008). Inscribing community: *The Budget* and *Die Botschaft* in Amish life. In D. Z. Umble & D. L. Weaver-Zercher (Eds.), *The Amish and the media* (pp. 180–198). Baltimore, MD: Johns Hopkins University Press.

Ohio Amish Directory. (2005). *Holmes County and vicinity*. Walnut Creek, OH: Carlisle Printing.

Piercy, K. W., & Cheek, C. (2004). Tending and befriending: The intertwined relationships of quilters. *Journal of Women and Aging, 16*, 17–33.

Raber, B. J. (2011). *The new American almanac*. Baltic, OH: Author.

Reiling, D. M. (2002a). Boundary maintenance as a barrier to mental health help-seeking depression among the Old Order Amish. *Journal of Rural Health, 18*, 428–436.

Reiling, D. M. (2002b). The "SIMMIE" side of life: Old Order Amish youths' affective response to culturally prescribed deviance. *Youth & Society, 34*, 146–171.

Stevick, R. A. (2007). *Growing up Amish: The teenage years*. Baltimore, MD: Johns Hopkins University Press.

Van Braght, T. J. (1972). *The bloody theater of martyrs mirror of the defenseless Christians*. (J. F. Sohm, Trans.). Scottdale, PA: Herald Press. (Original work published 1660).

Waltman, G. H. (1989). *Clinical issues with Amish and formerly-Amish clients*. Paper presented at the 14th National Institute on Social Work and Human Services in Rural Areas, Bemidji, MN.

Waltman, G. H. (1992). Clinical issues with Amish and formerly-Amish clients. In J. Borner, H. Doueck & M. Jacobsen (Eds.), *Emerging from the shadows: Selected papers from the Fifteenth National Institute on Social Work and Human Services in Rural Areas* (pp. 98–110). Mayville, NY: Chautauqua County Department of Social Services.

Waltman, G. H. (1996a). Amish health care beliefs and practices. In M. C. Julia (Ed.), *Multicultural awareness in the health care professions* (pp. 23–41). Boston, MA: Allyn & Bacon.

Waltman, G. H. (1996b, July). *Amish society's response to eldercare issues*. Paper presented at the 21st National Institute on Social Work and Human Services in Rural Areas, Kalamazoo, MI.

Waltman, G. H. (1999, July). *Understanding the Amish and their health care practices*. Paper presented at the 24th National Institute on Social Work and Human Services in Rural Areas, Salisbury, MD.

Waltman, G. H. (2000). Amish women: From martyrs to entrepreneurs. In M. C. Julia (Ed.), *Constructing gender: Multicultural perspectives in working with women* (pp. 35–67). Belmont, CA: Wadsworth/Thomson Learning.

Wenger, A. F. Z. (1991). Culture-specific care and the Old Order Amish. *NSNA/Imprint, 38*(2), 80–82, 84, 87.

Weyer, S. M., Hustey, V. R., Rathbun, L., Armstrong, V. L., Anna, S. R., Ronyak, J., & Savrin, C. (2003). A look into the Amish culture: What should we learn? *Journal of Transcultural Nursing, 14*, 139–145.

Yang, S., Wang, K., Gregory, B., Berrettini, W., Wang, L. S., Hakonarson, H., & Bucan, M. (2009). Genomic landscape of a three-generation pedigree segregating affective disorder. *PLoS One, 4*, e4474.

Zook, L. (1993). A case study of community prejudice: The Amish of Filmore County. *Human Services in the Rural Environment, 16*(3), 9–13.

Zook, L. (2001). Mutual aid and elders in Amish society. In L. K. Olson (Ed.), *Age through ethnic lenses: Caring for the elderly in a multicultural society* (pp. 134–145). Lanham, MD: Rowman & Littlefield.

Zook, L., & Heikes, J. (1990, August). *Advocating for the Amish in North America.* Paper presented at the 15th National Institute on Social Work and Human Services in Rural Areas, Fredonia, NY.

15 Living in a Rural Setting: *Implications of Increased Rural Diversity on Social Work Practice*

SHAWN D. KING

A review of the literature was conducted to determine the needs of the lesbian, gay, bisexual, transgender, and questioning (LGBTQ) population living in rural settings. Most rural studies have ignored inclusion of the LGBTQ population, making it more difficult to gain understanding of the health and social service needs of this population within the rural setting (Philo, 1992). Scholars have noted the lack of empirical research found within the literature specifically focusing on the LGBTQ population (Bell & Valentine, 1995; Boulden, 2001; Cody & Welch, 1997; Friedman, 1997; McCarthy, 2000; Yarbrough, 2003). What has been is that many LGBTQ individuals choose to leave rural life and move to more urban areas to feel safe and to develop a sense of community, including connecting with others who are similar. In these urban areas LGBTQ individuals find an appreciation for diversity often not found in their rural beginnings (Lindhorst, 1997; Smith, 1997). This chapter reviews the literature to aid better understanding of the social service and health needs of rural LGBTQ individuals.

The number of LGBTQ individuals living in rural areas has not been specifically accounted for in prior data collections or empirical research studies. Gates and Ost (2004) have conducted more recent analysis of census data, which reveals that gay and lesbian couples are found in 99.3% of all counties in the United States. The census information does not provide the total number of individuals, age, or options to identify sexual orientation, including bisexual or transgender, nor does it include those who wish to conceal their sexual orientation. Conversely, Otis (2008) finds that the census numbers suggest there is a substantial increase in the number of LGBTQ individuals living in rural communities. Smith and Mancoske (1997) acknowledge the migration of LGBTQ individuals to rural areas. However, they believe the movement to be much smaller. Overall, there is a need to better address the health and social service needs of LGBTQ individuals who choose to live in rural areas. Many of these individuals are faced with specific obstacles and challenges that are documented in the limited research available.

Many advances in equality that have resulted from the gay rights movement have not been realized in rural communities (Yarbrough, 2003). Rural communities often have traditional values, and many community members hold strong religious beliefs that require them to embrace these values as a way of life. Finding a sense of belonging and being integrated into these small rural communities requires subscribing to the rural traditions (Foster, 1997; Lindhorst, 1997; Smith, 1997). Frequently, diversity is not expressed or appreciated in rural settings, and the pressure to conform is emphasized by members (Ginsberg, 1998). Community members identifying as LGBTQ are considered threatening and are sanctioned for their lack of "conformity," or they are often subjected to "expulsion" from the communities (Oswald & Culton, 2003, p. 72). Conformity within rural environments has been defined as embracing family, community, and religious conservatism, along with a lack of real privacy within smaller communities (Oswald & Culton, 2003). These unique aspects of rural living add to the pressure to hide one's sexual orientation, which affects obtaining needed social and health care services. LGBTQ individuals face many difficulties within rural communities that are likely to have an effect on several systems with which they interact in their environment. Many of these difficulties stem from a lack of diversity which is, instead, replaced with a more homogenous and heterosexist existence for members of the rural community.

Lack of Diversity Found in Rural Settings

It has been reported that LGBTQ individuals are stigmatized within rural communities, which has been attributed to a heteronormative culture that does not allow for differences in sexual expression. Heteronormativity values heterosexual relationships and culture. Rural health and social services often focus on these heteronormative aspects surrounding heterosexual relationships. Gender specific behaviors are socially constructed with many variations from these socially acceptable behaviors, and those who do not conform are ostracized from the community

(Wilkinson & Pearson, 2009). Heterosexism is the belief that heterosexuality is the only acceptable form of sexual orientation, and that any variation should result in violators being sanctioned (Blumenfeld, 1992; Sears, 1997). The result is increased prejudicial and discriminatory attitudes from community members regarding anything that does not adhere to rural traditional community norms and standards. For the LGBTQ individual living in a rural area, the result can be homophobia, which fuels further marginalization and sometimes even violence (National Association of Social Workers [NASW], 1997).

Homophobia is the fear of an LGBTQ individual and further leads to marginalization and oppression (Yarbrough, 2003). Many LGBTQ individuals internalize homophobic attitudes. Internalized homophobia increases the LGBTQ individual's lowered self-esteem, self-hate, and the rejection of all aspects of homosexuality (Yarbrough, 2003). For adolescents who are questioning or identifying as LGBTQ, this self-hate can result in many maladaptive behaviors, which are perpetuated by the level of stigmatization found within schools. Stigmatization within the schools is thought to be an extension of the intolerance and hostility found in the broader rural community (Kosciw, Greytak, & Diaz, 2009). Snively (2004) attributes homophobia in rural settings to the lack of appreciation for diversity, holding conservative values, and having limited contact with those who are members of this sexual minority group. D'Augelli and Hart (1987) reports that many who move to urban settings do so to escape being stigmatized and oppressed in rural areas. These scholars also report that it is the homogenous nature of rural settings that puts demands on LGBTQ individuals to accept social conformity to fully integrate into their rural communities. As pointed out by Preston and colleagues (2004), "strong religious beliefs can play a major role in shaping social norms, and there is little tolerance for variations from the traditional family" (p. 292).

Remaining Invisible and Isolation

Many in rural areas will try to hide their sexual orientation to fit into the community. Boulden (2001) described this as a "don't ask, don't tell" understanding within these communities (p. 68). It often requires LGBTQ individuals to hide many aspects of their identities. If the individual chooses to reveal his or her sexual orientation and live in the community, researchers have noted that they are more likely to be ignored in the community at large. There are many psychological stress factors associated with hiding one's sexual identity. It requires keeping track of who knows this information and under what circumstances and making sure that the wrong person will not discover and reveal it to others who might retaliate. This leads to a fear for safety in the community (D'Augelli, 1988; King & Dabelko-Schoeny, 2009; Snively, 2004). Therefore, it stifles social options; the individual either refrains from involvement with others out of fear of discovery or spends large amounts of energy trying to pass as heterosexual (Leedy & Connolly, 2007). Additionally, as noted by Preston and colleagues (2004), when the identity of an LGBTQ individual is discovered in the community, he or she often experiences reprisal and rejection from friends and family because of the shame and stigma brought by the association with other LGBTQ individuals. Overall, the continued need to conceal one's identity in these rural settings results in a loss of social connections, community resources, and connections to services. These individuals often lack support or rely on informal support mechanisms out of fear (McCarthy, 2000).

Rural LGBT individuals often experience a sense of isolation, which is seen as a barrier to being able to stay in rural areas because it leads to the lack of access to social services and LGBTQ-specific information (Gottschalk, 2007; Leedy & Connolly, 2007; Lindhorst, 1997; Phillips & McLeory, 2004), Isolation stifles building a local gay culture for these individuals (King & Dabelko-Schoeny, 2009) and results in limited degrees of informal network connections (McCarthy, 2000). Snively (2004) proposes that isolation also increases homophobic attitudes within the rural setting, therefore contributing to the "lack of visibility" (p. 102).

Use of Internet

Haag and Chang (1997) report on the effects of isolation and loneliness resulting in the increased use of the Internet to connect with other LGBTQ individuals. Gay men in rural areas often use the Internet to identify other individuals for social and sexual encounters, sometimes in public places (Schnarrs et al., 2010). This form of socialization has been found to not always be a safe alternative to community-based organizations and connections. Researchers have connected rural community homophobia to the increase in internalized homophobia for LGBTQ individuals, which lowers self-esteem, increases stigma, and encourages more use of the Internet for sexual encounters that could result in unsafe sexual practices. There could be an increase in the chances for contracting human immunodeficiency virus (HIV) or other sexually transmitted diseases (STDs; Berry, 2000; Cohn, 1997; D'Augelli, Kassab, & Starks, 2007; Preston, D'augelli, Kassab, & Starks, 2007; Schnarrs et al., 2010). In their study of 99 men who identified as having sex with men, Preston et al. (2004) found that the lower the self-esteem experienced by gay men the higher the correlation with an increase in the amount of unprotected receptive anal intercourse. The same was found true for stigma associated with HIV and the homosexuality stigma that gay men experienced from family members. The outcome for higher stigma is a greater likelihood that gay men will engage in high-risk sexual behaviors. Furthermore, Sowell and Christensen (1996) note that resources that inform and educate rural gay and bisexual men of health risk and health care associated with HIV/AIDS are frequently missing.

Lack of Social and Community Supports

The lack of both informal and formal social support and services affects successful use of social and health care services by LGBTQ community members (Aday & Awe, 1997). Formal and informal social supports are found to be lacking for many rural LGBTQ individuals (King & Dabelko-Schoeny, 2009). Although researchers have found that family members rely on each other for informal supports in rural environments, this sometimes is not possible for rural LGBTQ individuals, who often do not have children (Angel, Dejong, Cornwell, & Wilmoth, 1995). Furthermore, the conservative nature of rural communities hinders development of a sense of community for LGBTQ individuals (Gottschalk, 2007; Lindhorst, 1997).

Very little empirical research can be found about the degree to which formal community support and services are available to LGBTQ individuals in rural settings. Available research denotes a lack of support services to assist this population from an affirmative perspective. Additionally, LGBTQ individuals living in rural areas are more likely to resist using formal community support systems (Snively, 2004). Researchers have found that rural LGBTQ individuals believe existing services lack the knowledge and understanding of the specific needs of their population (Eliason & Hughes, 2004). Additionally, researchers point out that some rural LGBTQ community members' feel that confidentiality is compromised by living in smaller communities (Preston et al., 2004; Rounds, 1988). Therefore, even if LGBTQ-specific formal support services are available, many will not seek out those services for fear of being exposed.

Researchers discuss the consistent absence of any formal or structural services and programs that address the needs of the rural LGBTQ population. This is coupled with homophobic attitudes found within the existing services (Hunter, Shannon, Knox, & Martin, 1998). When social and health care services are available, researchers find that many service providers, including doctors, dentist, nurses, and social workers, may have homophobic attitudes. Many of these health and social service providers are believed to take on the community values and traditions (Berkman & Zinberg, 1997; Lindhorst, 1997; Preston et al., 2004). Furthermore, empirical studies show that the fear, isolation, and oppression often encountered by rural LGBTQ community members adversely affect their use of services. This absence of LGBTQ individuals asking for services has allowed for the continuation of being marginalized and invisible within service delivery, further ignoring the specific needs of this population (Snively, 2004).

LGBTQ Youth in Rural Areas

LGBTQ youth in rural communities often struggle with their emerging sexual identities. These young people are at risk for mental and physical health concerns (Cohn & Hastings, 2010; Snively, 2004). Many LGBTQ youth are found to be at higher risk for self-harm and suicide (Snively, 2004). Cass (1979) and Troiden (1989) propose gay and lesbian identity models that emphasize the importance of developing a personal sense of gay community and synthesis into the broader community. These models put forth the importance of self-acceptance and balance of a person's sexual identity with other developmental tasks. However, many researchers have reported that a homophobic atmosphere supported by the broader community can be found within rural school systems. Therefore, many rural LGBTQ youth often struggle with homophobia as they attempt to resolve their emerging sexual identities with a positive self-identity (Epstein & Johnson, 1998; Wilkinson & Pearson, 2009).

Kosciw et al. (2009) found in their study that many LGBTQ youths experience bullying, harassment, and negative effects within the school setting. These scholars found that, although urban schools are thought to be more dangerous for LGBTQ youth, they may, in fact, be safer based on the varied social opportunities available. These scholars note that adherence to more rural, traditional values often carries into the school system. These strict beliefs make it impossible for gay youth to openly socialize without becoming victims. These authors suggest that school counselors and social workers have the obligation and the means to assist these young people who struggle with the negative effects of school-based homophobia and harassment. Another positive venue for LGBTQ youths struggling with their emerging sexual identity in rural school settings are gay–straight alliances. Although gay–straight alliances are met with resistance in many schools, they are now becoming more integrated within some schools. These nonclinical groups have given gay youth the ability to socialize with others who are either like themselves or supporting allies that build coping and resiliency skills needed to secure healthy development and well-being (Snively, 2004).

LGBT Older Adults in Rural Areas

Older LGBT adults are found to have the same barriers to services as their heterosexual counterparts in the rural community, including transportation issues and financial resources (King & Dabelko-Schoeny, 2009). The specific obstacles that face many older LGBT individuals who choose to age-in-place in rural communities include social isolation, homophobia, lack of a sense of community, and the lack of confidentiality and anonymity (Gottschalk, 2007; King & Dabelko-Schoeny, 2009). Many older LGBT individuals have experienced a lifetime of oppression and of hiding their sexual orientation. They often resort to reliance on informal support mechanisms, if available, as they age. Midlife and older LGBT adults living in rural areas are less likely to use available social support services because of their marginalized status (Sharma, 2006). They experience isolation and often have few close biological family ties (King & Dabelko-Schoeny, 2009). Therefore, as LGBT adults get older, there is a need to rely more on formal support services without knowing who will be accepting or intolerant of their sexual orientations (Snively, 2004). Consequently, many LGBT older adults continue to hide their sexual orientations from social and health care service workers. Some live out their lives with fewer resources and less formal support use, because they fear discrimination.

Additionally, there is a shortage in many rural areas of social services and health care workers. The barriers faced by the LGBT population include limited local access to health care and social services and access to social workers and health care practitioners who are knowledgeable, trained, and qualified to work with LGBT older adults in the rural setting (Lindhorst, 1997). The ability to access needed services in an efficient and timely manner for chronic conditions, especially for cancer, diabetes, and hypertension, is compromised by living in a rural area (Angel et al., 1995). Poor health outcomes are the result and may increase due to the barriers that affect many older adults living in rural areas, including those from the older LGBT adult population (Alley, Liebig, Pynoos, Banerjee, & Choi, 2007; Galambos, 2005). Those living in rural communities, including LGBT older adults, travel long distances to obtain medical services (Angel et al., 1995; King & Dabelko-Schoeny, 2009; Lindhorst, 1997). These obstacles combine to create concern for safety and security for all older adults in rural areas and especially this marginalized population (Gottschalk, 2007; Otis, 2008).

Older LGBT adults living in rural settings often continue to fear discrimination as they grow older, when services are needed the most. Social workers in rural communities should be knowledgeable about the obstacles faced by these older adults for receiving needed social and health care services. There is a need for LGBT community-based services that the target specific needs of this population, instead of approaching elderly services from a heterosexual perspective. For instance, isolation, financial needs, the lack of informal and formal supports, and civil rights that affect qualifying for needed services by gay and lesbian couples are found to be important (Moore, 2002; Oswald & Culton, 2003). Drumheller and McQuay (2010) propose needed education at the community level about the needs of the older LGBT population.

Implications for Social Work Practice

Identifiable obstacles need to be addressed for rural LGBTQ populations. Several important implications for rural social work practice with this population can be ascertained from the limited research available. One important point for practice is that social workers and health care practitioners should realize that, because of the small geographical area and conservative nature of most rural communities, many LGBTQ individuals may not feel comfortable accessing readily available mainstream services. Additionally, services may not be available that specifically address issues of isolation and the importance of identifying with other LGBTQ individuals (McCarthy, 2000); certain health issues, such as HIV/STDs; and preventive health care needs unique to LGBTQ individuals (Leedy & Connolly, 2007). There are many barriers to services, such as lack of specific knowledge of LGBTQ social service and health needs. Schnarrs and colleagues (2010) discusses the need for social workers to be aware of the "context of where their interventions are occurring" (p. 567). Similarly, social workers should examine any aspects of homophobia or heterosexism in their own attitudes that could interfere with service delivery (Rounds, 1988). Practitioners should strive to set aside personal values and morals to provide the unique services needed by LGBTQ individuals in the most appropriate ways (Moore, 2002; Oswald & Culton, 2003). This requires attention to all stages of the practice process (Eliason & Hughes, 2004).

Social workers in agencies are responsible for addressing stigma, making sure that the atmosphere of the agency is inclusive, and that it respects diversity with practice of cultural competency (Oswald & Culton, 2003; Rounds, 1988). Furthermore, any aspects of agency practice that silence this population through homophobia or heterosexism should be addressed (Moore, 2002). Several scholars recommend evaluating such tools as intake forms, agency policies, advertising, language, and waiting room materials for inclusion (Boulden, 2001; Eliason & Hughes, 2004; Oswald & Culton, 2003).

Social workers in rural schools also have an enormous task to address stigma and marginalization of LGBTQ adolescents who are questioning their sexual orientation in an environment that often sees heterosexuality as the only viable identity (Kosciw, Greytak, & Diaz, 2009; Snively, 2004). There are several recommendations specific to the rural setting where practice takes place. First, social workers should seek out community connections that address the needs of the adolescent in a safe and affirming environment (Snively, 2004). National organizations such as Parents, Families, and Friends of Lesbians and Gays (PFLAG) and the National Gay and Lesbian Task Force should also be considered as sources of support. The social worker may need to work with parents to help educate them about the child's emerging development (Kosciw et al., 2009). Second, social workers may need to focus on education and outreach, working with rural community practitioners and other resources that can help advocate and support the student (Kosciw et al., et al., 2009). Third, Yarbrough (2003) recommends ways that social workers, counselors, and teachers can frame conversations with LGBTQ adolescents to exhibit more understanding and provide empowerment and support. Fourth, social workers should be actively involved in the policy and administrative arena, carefully crafting ways to protect LGBTQ students and those within the school system who provide supportive services (Yarbrough, 2003). Finally, Kosciw and colleagues (2009) discuss supporting school-based organizations, such as gay–straight alliances, that reduce incidents of bullying and harassment and, instead foster an environment of acceptance and support.

Older LGBT adults living in rural settings often continue to fear discrimination, when services are needed the most. Social workers in rural communities should be knowledgeable about the obstacles faced by these older adults for receiving needed social and health care services. There is a need for LGBT community-based services that target specific requirements of this population, instead of approaching elderly services from a heterosexual perspective. For instance, the lack of informal and formal supports, isolation, financial needs, and civil rights that affect qualifying for needed services by gay and lesbian couples are found to be important (Moore, 2002; Oswald & Culton, 2003). Drumheller and McQuay (2010) propose education at the community level about the needs of the older LGBT population.

Boulden (2001) and Drumheller and McQuay (2010) stress the importance of informal collaboration with external resources and services, including health care providers, counselors, church organizations, and leaders from the LGBTQ population. These scholars believe that, because of homophobia and fear of discrimination, many rural LGBT older adults are fearful of using existing services in formal agency settings. Studies that examine successful HIV prevention and AIDS services support this finding (Rosser & Horvath, (2008).

D'Augelli and Hart (1987) point out that formal social service programs developed for gay men may be useless if the men will not seek access to the services (as cited in Boulden, 2001, p. 73). These scholars note that formal HIV/AIDS services provided in rural settings often are ignored by gay men who fear a lack of anonymity. Therefore, Boulden (2001) points out the importance of collaboration with gay organizations already found in rural areas and the adjacent larger communities within the area. Additionally, local services provided should be implemented using an informal approach that does not attach any stigma or clinical perception to the services offered (Boulden, 2001). Oswald and Culton (2003) propose working with LGBT community members to develop specific programs needed by the population.

Conclusion

In conclusion, rural social workers working with LGBTQ individuals in their rural communities should provide services and interventions that focus on the importance of the overall well-being of the gay, lesbian, or bisexual client. This approach incorporates affirming aspects of the client's sexual identity to increase self-esteem and produce more positive mental health and well-being outcomes (Gluth & Kiselica, 1994). The attitudes held by social workers and counselors are found to be an important aspect of providing effective social work services. Dillon and Worthington (2003) believe that social workers should be aware of heterosexual norms that further marginalize this population.

Kilgore, Sideman, Amin, Baca, and Bohanske (2005) add that, for social work practitioners to be more affirming in their practice with LGBTQ individuals, they must understand how homophobia and heterosexism affect individuals internally as well externally, which is especially relevant for those living in rural communities known for being more conservative and traditional. Many LGBTQ individuals internalize society's heterosexist and homophobic attitudes, causing lowered self-esteem, less self-confidence, and increased self-destructive behaviors. Social workers working with LGBTQ individuals in rural areas may find many of the obstacles to providing competent services and care outlined in this chapter. Social workers have a Code of Ethics obligation to seek ways to improve the outcomes for practice with vulnerable and marginalized populations, including the LGBTQ population.

Furthermore, research is scarce for the rural LGBTQ population. Research needs to explore the needs of this population, including studies related to different racial and ethnic members and those who are transgender and living in a rural community. These studies are needed to further advance understanding to provide services that will increase the health and well-being of rural LGBTQ populations.

References

Aday, L. A., & Awe, W. C. (1997). Health services utilization models. In D. S. Gochman (Ed.), *Handbook of health behavior research I: Personal and social determinants* (pp. 153–172). New York: Plenum Press.

Alley, D., Liebig, P., Pynoos, J., Banerjee, T., & Choi, I. H. (2007). Creating elder-friendly communities: Preparations for an aging society. *Journal of Gerontological Social Work, 49*(1/2), 1–18.

Angel, J. L., DeJong, G. F., Cornwell, G. T., & Wilmoth, J. M. (1995). Diminished health and living arrangements of rural elderly Americans. *National Journal of Sociology, 9*(1), 31–57.

Bell, D., & Valentine, G. (1995). Queer country: Rural lesbian and gay lives. *Journal of Rural Studies, 11*, 113–122.

Berkman, C. S., & Zinberg, G. (1997). Homophobia and heterosexism in social workers. *Social Work, 42*, 319–331.

Berry, D. E. (2000). Rural acquired immunodeficiency syndrome in low and high prevalence areas. *Southern Medical Journal, 93*, 36–43.

Blumenfeld, W. J. (1992). Squeezed into gender envelopes. In W. J. Blumenfeld (Ed.), *Homophobia: How we all pay the price* (pp. 1–23). Boston, MA: Beacon Press.

Boulden, W. T. (2001). Gay men living in a rural environment. *Journal of Gay and Lesbian Social Services, 12*(3/4), 63–75.

Cass, V. C. (1979). Homosexual identity formation: A theoretical model. *Journal of Homosexuality, 4*(7), 219–235.

Cody, P. J., & Welch, P. L. (1997). Rural gay men in Northern New England: Life experiences and coping styles. *Journal of Homosexuality, 33*(1), 51–67.

Cohn, S. E. (1997). IDS in rural America. *Journal of Rural Health, 13*, 237–239.

Cohn, T. J., & Hastings, S. L. (2010). Resilience among rural lesbian youth. *Journal of Lesbian Studies*, 14(1), 71–70.

D'Augelli, A. R. (1988). Lesbian women in a rural helping network: Exploring informal helping resources. *Women & Therapy*, 8(1/2), 119–130.

D'Augelli, A. R., & Hart, M. (1987). Gay women, men, and families in rural settings: Toward the development of helping communities. *American Journal of Community Psychology*, 15(1), 79–93.

D'Augelli, A. R., Kassab, C.D., & Starks, M. T. (2007). The relationship of stigma to the sexual risk behavior of rural men who have sex with men. *Starks in AIDS education and prevention*, 19(3), 218–230.

Dillon, F. R., & Worthington, R. L. (2003). The lesbian, gay, and bisexual affirmative counseling self-efficacy inventory (LGB-CSI): Development, validation, and training implications. *Journal of Counseling Psychology*, 50, 235.

Drumheller, K., & McQuay, B. (2010). Living in the buckle: Promoting LGBT outreach services in conservative urban/rural centers. *Communication Studies*, 61(1), 70–86.

Eliason, M. J., & Hughes, T. (2004). Treatment counselor's attitudes about lesbian, gay, bisexual, and transgendered clients: Urban vs. rural settings. *Substance Use and Misuse*, 39, 625–644.

Epstein, D., & Johnson, R. (1998). *Schooling sexualities*. Buckingham, UK; Open University Press.

Foster, S. J. (1997). Rural lesbians & gays: Public perceptions, worker perceptions and service delivery. *Journal of Gay & Lesbian Social Services*, 7(3), 23–35.

Friedman, L. J. (1997). Rural lesbian mothers and their families. *Journal of Gay & Lesbian Social Services*, 7(3), 73–81.

Galambos, C. M. (2005). Health care disparities among rural populations: A neglected frontier. *Health and Social Work*, 30(3), 179–181.

Gates, G., & Ost, J. (2004). *The gay and lesbian atlas*. Washington, D.C.: Urban Institute Press.

Ginsberg, L. H. (1998). An overview of rural social work. In L. H. Ginsbreg (Ed.), *Social work in rural communities*, 3rd ed. (pp. 3–22). Alexandria VA: Council on Social Work Education.

Gluth, D. R., & Kiselica, M. S. (1994). Coming out quickly: A brief counseling approach to dealing with gay and lesbian adjustment issues. *Journal of Mental Health Counseling*, 16(2), 163–174.

Gottschalk, L. H. (2007). Coping with stigma: Coming out and living as lesbians and gay men in regional and rural areas in the context of problems of rural confidentiality and social exclusion. *Rural Social Work and Community Practice*, 12(2), 31–46.

Haag, A. M., & Chang, F. K. (1997). The impact of electronic networking on the lesbian and gay community. *Journal of Gay and Lesbian Social Services, 7*(3), 83–94.

Hunter, S., Shannon, C., Knox, J., & Martin, J. I. (1998). *Lesbian, gay, and bisexual youths and adults: Knowledge for human service practice.* Thousand Oaks, CA: Sage.

Kilgore, H., Sideman, L., Amin, K., Baca, L., & Bohanske, B. (2005). Psychologists' attitudes and therapeutic approaches toward gay, lesbian, and bisexual issues continue to improve: An update. *Psychotherapy: Theory, Research, Practice, Training, 42,* 395–400.

King, S., & Dabelko-Schoeny, H. (2009). "Quite frankly, I have doubts about remaining": Aging-in-place and health care access for rural midlife and older lesbian, gay, and bisexual individuals. *Journal of LGBT Health Research, 5*(1), 10–21.

Kosciw, J. G., Greytak, E. A., & Diaz, E. M. (2009). Who, what, where, when, and why: Demograhic and ecological factors contributing to hostile school climate for lesbian, gay, bisexual, and transgender youth. *Journal of Youth and Adolescence, 38,* 976–988.

Leedy, G., & Connolly, C. (2007). Out in the cowboy state: A look at lesbian and gay lives in Wyoming. *Journal of Gay and Lesbian Social Sciences, 91*(1), 17–34.

Lindhorst, T. (1997). Lesbian and gay men in the country: Practice implications for rural social workers. *Journal of Gay & Lesbian Social Services, 7*(3), 1–11.

McCarthy, L. (2000). Poppies in a wheat field: Exploring the lives of rural lesbians. *Journal of Homosexuality, 39*(1), 75–94.

Moore, W. R. (2002). Lesbian and gay elders: Connecting care providers through a telephone support group. *Journal of Gay and Lesbian Social Services, 14*(3), 23–41.

National Association of Social Workers (NASW). (1997). *Social work speaks: NASW policy statements.* Washington, DC: Author.

Oswald, R. F., & Culton, L. S. (2003). Under the rainbow: Rural gay life and its relevance for family providers. *Family Relations, 52,* 72–81.

Otis, M. D. (2008). Issues in conducting empirical research with lesbian and gay people in rural settings. In W. Meezan & J. I. Martin (Eds.), *Handbook of research with gay, lesbian, bisexual and transgender populations* (pp. 280–299). New York, NY: Routledge.

Phillips, C. D., & McLeroy, K. R. (2004). Health in rural America: Remembering the importance of place. *American Journal of Public Health, 94,* 1661–1663.

Philo, C. (1992). Neglected rural geographies: A review. *Journal of Rural Studies, 8,* 193–207.

Preston, D. B., D'Augelli, A. R., Kassab, C. D., Cain, R. E., Schulze, F. W., & Starks, M. T. (2004). The influence of stigma on the sexual risk behavior of rural men who have sex with men. *AIDS Education and Prevention, 16*(4), 291–303.

Preston, D. B., D'Augelli, A. R., Kassab, C. D., & Starks, M. T. (2007). The relationship of stigma to the sexual risk behavior of rural men who have sex with men. *AIDS Education and Prevention, 19*(3), 218–230.

Rosser, B. R., & Horvath, K. J. (2008). Predictors of success in implementing HIV prevention in rural America: A state-level structural factor analysis of HIV prevention targeting men who have sex with men. *AIDS Behavior, 12*, 159–168.

Rounds, K. A. (1988). AIDS in rural areas: Challenges to providing care. *Social Work, 33*, 257–261.

Schnarrs, P. W., Rosenberger, J. G., Satinsky, S., Brinegar, E., Stowers, J. Dodge, B., & Reece, M. (2010). Sexual compulsivity, the Internet, and sexual behaviors among men in a rural area of the United States. *AIDS Patient Care and STDs, 24*, 563–569.

Sears, J. T. (1997). *Overcoming heterosexism and homophobia.* New York, NY: Columbia.

Sharma, S. (2006). Building a new culture in health and social care. *Nursing Standard, 20*(21), 26–27.

Smith, J. D. (1997). Working with larger systems: Rural lesbians and gays. *Journal of Gay and Lesbian Social Services, 7*(3), 13–21.

Smith, J. D., & Mancoske, R. J. (1997). Preface. *Journal of Gay & Lesbian Social Services, 7*(3), xvii–xx.

Snively, C. A. (2004). Building community-based alliances between GLBTQQA youth and adults in rural settings. *Journal of Gay and Lesbian Social Services, 16*(3/4), 99–112.

Sowell, R., & Christensen, P. (1996). HIV infection in rural communities. *Nursing Clinics of North America, 31*, 107–123.

Troiden, R. (1989). The formation of homosexual identities. [Special issue] *Journal of Homosexuality, 17*(1–2), 43–73.

Wilkinson, L., & Pearson, J. (2009). School culture and the well-being of same-sex–attracted youth. *Gender & Society, 23*(4), 542–568.

Yarbrough, D. G. (2003). Gay adolescents in rural areas: Experiences and coping strategies. *Journal of Human Behavior in the Social Environment, 8*(2/3), 129–144.

PART III

Specialized Agencies and Practice in Rural Areas

Laura S. Boisen, Nancy A. Rotenborg, and Lois A. Bosch have contributed this section's first chapter, which discusses the implications for social workers in rural areas of the immigrant and refugee migration to the United States. Assisting with the integration of such groups into rural community life is a challenge for many social workers.

Domestic abuse is also a problem, although sometimes ignored, in rural areas. In Chapter 17 Christina M. Chiarelli-Helmeniak and Jill Bradshaw describe the extent of the problem and some of the solutions provided in rural areas.

Health care social workers have a variety of resources and a myriad of challenges in rural areas—but these challenges can lead to opportunities. In Chapter 18 Suzie Cashwell and Saundra Starks cast social workers as agents of change for rural health care, using integrated practice skills to transform the system of services and improve the overall well-being of rural America.

Rural residents have high levels of depression, substance abuse, domestic violence, incest, and child abuse, like their urban counterparts. The prevalence and scope of mental health challenges in rural areas are discussed by Glenn Stone and Bill Frederick in Chapter 19. The chapter offers assessment tools to help social workers evaluate and improve practice in rural communities.

Cancer has adverse effects at all levels, including emotional as well as physical well-being. In rural areas, lack of access to psychosocial care can compromise cancer support for quality of life, ongoing emotional care, and uncertainty re-duction. In the final chapter in this volume, Sky Niesen Smith, Michael Glasser, and Wynne S. Korr offer case examples to demonstrate the reality of oncology so-cial work practice in a rural setting.

16 Implications for Rural Social Workers of Increasing Rural Diversity: *Immigration to Rural Areas*

Laura S. Boisen, Nancy A. Rodenborg, and Lois A. Bosch

In both rural and urban areas of the United States, immigration has increased the racial and ethnic diversity of many communities. Indeed, immigrants in rural areas represent a large proportion of nonmetropolitan growth since 1990 (Johnson, 2006). What are the implications of this increased racial and ethnic diversity for rural social work practitioners? In the context of rapid demographic change, what are some of the challenges faced and strategies adopted by social workers in rural communities?

This chapter describes some of the demographic shifts in rural communities, especially those associated with immigration, discusses some of the theories about means to decrease prejudice and discrimination associated with immigration, and discusses some of the ways social workers in rural communities can enhance cultural sensitivity and competence.

Demographic Shift

The increasing diversity of the United States is well-documented. Approximately 13% of the U.S. population was foreign-born in 2008 (Owen, Meyerson, & Otteson, 2010). The most common countries of origin were in Latin America (53%), Asia (27%), Europe (13%), and Africa (4%; Owen et al., 2010). In some states, such as California, as many as a third of the residents are foreign-born persons. However, other states have seen a surge in this population as well. For example, North

Carolina, Florida, Arkansas, Texas, and states throughout the Midwest and upper Great Plains have seen a heavy influx of immigrants in recent years (Jensen, 2006). Many of these immigrants and refugees dispersed from larger cities to rural areas for better schools, affordable housing, a more bucolic setting, and employment opportunities (Parra & Pfeffer, 2006; Shandy & Fennelly, 2006). In fact, due to localized employment opportunities in meat packing, food processing, agriculture, manufacturing, or tourism, some traditionally homogeneous small rural towns have experienced rapid increases in foreign born populations (Jensen, 2006).

Social work, in general, has faced challenges in practicing cultural competence, regardless of geographic location. For many social workers who reside and practice in rural areas, the influx of immigrants and refugees has also created a more complex practice environment. Traditionally, many rural social workers had clients who were of the majority culture (i.e., clients who identified as White, Christian, or groups that spanned age, ability, and socioeconomic categories, but were not dissimilar in terms of race or country of origin). Practicing with different color or nonnative born individuals and families can add additional factors for social workers in changing rural communities. Social workers must have awareness of their own identities and acquire both knowledge and skills sensitive to racial, cultural, and religious mores and traditions. Because many rural social workers have predominantly worked with clients from the majority culture, they may not have considered cultural difference as relevant to their practice. Language, food preferences, and family patterns may be different from those social workers may have previously encountered.

Social workers' social identity categories complicate the knowledge and skill sets required for rural practice. Like long-term residents of rural U.S. communities, many social workers who live and serve in those communities predominantly identify with majority cultures. The National Association of Social Workers (NASW) reported that 87% of their membership identified as White/Caucasian, and 11% of its membership identified as social workers of color (2003). Although not every social worker is a member of NASW, evidence from a study by the NASW and the Center for Health Workforce Studies also suggests that many rural social workers are likely to be White. In their 2004 survey of licensed social workers in the United States, Whitaker, Weismiller, and Clark (2006) found that social workers "are not as diverse as the populations they serve in terms of race, ethnicity and gender" (p. 9). A total of 86% of licensed social workers identified as non-Hispanic, White, compared to 68% of the U.S. population who identified as non-Hispanic, White (Whitaker et al., 2006).

Majority culture social workers are believed to have more challenges multiculturally than non-White social workers. Proctor and Davis (1994) asserted that work with people of color by White social workers could negatively affect the social work encounter. They found that some White practitioners did not adequately understand nonmajority culture verbal and nonverbal communication. This lack of understanding led, at times, to White workers assessing a problem more severely with clients of color than with White clients. Others have found that White practitioners are often less knowledgeable or comfortable with different color clients, tend to minimize the importance of color, and avoid discussions regarding color (Davis & Gelsomino, 1994; Green, Kiernan-Strong & Baskind, 2005; Proctor & Davis, 1994), even though color is important to discuss in cross-cultural practice (Chang, Hays, & Shoffner, 2003; Hepworth, Rooney, Rooney, Strom-Gottfried, & Larsen, 2010). Indeed, some White social workers insist that they do not see color, not understanding that this position denies the experiences and reality of their clients of color and suggests a lack of understanding and sophistication about privilege and oppression literature. Sue et al. (2007) assert that this colorblind attitude may reflect an exchange, often unconscious, that transmits a dismissive or denigrating message to people of color. Thus, a rural social worker who acts on his or her belief that people are "really all the same—just human" may demonstrate a negative attitude toward the client of color.

Theoretical Perspectives to Help Reduce Prejudice and Discrimination

Three theories from social psychology present three lenses through which to view the cultural competence challenges faced by rural social workers and are subsequently described: implicit bias theory, aversive racism, and intergroup contact theory.

Implicit Bias Theory

Even with the inclusion of multicultural curricula in all accredited social work programs, social workers are not immune from majority-culture stereotypes and bias—even if they identify as a member of the minority group. Indeed, a myriad of implicit association research has been conducted since the 1990s, with the development of the Implicit Association Test by the University of Washington and Yale. This research supports the premise that much of stereotyping is unconscious and unintended (Nosek, Bajaji, & Greenwald, 2002) and guides everyday life.

However, this unconscious and unintended process does not mean the results are inconsequential. For instance, McConnell and Leibold (2001) found that more negative implicit attitudes toward African Americans predicted more negative non-verbal behaviors in an interaction with an African American researcher than with a White researcher. Other researchers found that physicians with higher anti-Black implicit attitudes were more likely to misdiagnose serious medical conditions with Black patients than with White patients (Green, Carney, Pallin, Iezzoni, & Banaji, 2006, in Lane, Banaji, Nosek, & Greenwald, 2007). A comparable study of anti-African American implicit bias attitudes has not been replicated with social workers. However, there is no reason to believe professional social work education and training protects or immunizes social workers against the implicit forces present in the dominant culture.

Indeed, quantifying the degree of social workers' cultural competence is a discussion of some debate within the social work literature. The NASW Code of Ethics mandates that social workers practice in a culturally competent manner (Standard 1.05, NASW, 2008). Some, including NASW, have recommended retraining social work practitioners in multicultural practice (Bernard & Goodyear, 2004; Cary & Marques, 2007; Constantine, 1997). Some assert that people of color underutilize social services and end services prematurely because of insensitive cross-cultural practice (Sue & Sue, 1999). For those involuntary clients who cannot prematurely terminate services, the results can be sobering. Pedersen (1994) delineated some of the implications for inadequate cross-cultural training: an inability by the practitioner to anticipate other's worldviews, a lack of awareness of cultural differences, and the increased frequency of misunderstandings and miscommunication.

These issues are increasingly important in rural areas because of the changing demographics, especially those associated with immigration. Many immigrants to rural areas are non-Whites in areas that have had few non-White citizens. So, social workers in rural areas increasingly find themselves dealing with Asian and Pacific Islanders, Latinos, as well as African and Caribbean immigrants, and rural relocating African Americans.

How is implicit bias transmitted? Some believe that exposure to dominant-culture media is associated with increased bias and adherence to stereotypes (Dixon, 2008; Parenti, 2006). Parenti (2006) documents the concentration of major news media and press with six major companies controlling the U.S. market. These companies are owned and controlled by majority culture conglomerates that exercise control over news content and "offer little variety in perspective and editorial policy, ranging mostly from moderately conservative to ultraconservative" viewpoints (Parenti, 2006, p. 63). Parenti (2006) asserts the television and radio airwaves are filled with shows and commentary that are antiimmigrant and majority-culture positive and focused.

Dixon (2008) more closely associates exposure to network news to increased endorsement of stereotypes related to African Americans and more "racialized perceptions" (p. 330). His study suggests that, via framing—a technique whereby newscasts couple African American pictures with negative stories—racial perceptions and prejudice are shaped. No matter the transmission vehicle for implicit bias, it is essential that social workers, including those in rural areas, be aware of implicit bias and the implications for their practice.

Of course, media are available to persons in rural areas, including social workers, in the same form that they are influential in urban and metropolitan areas.

Aversive Racism

A second theory sheds further light on the cultural competence challenges faced by rural social workers. Similar to implicit bias, aversive racism theory is built on evidence suggesting that people experience prejudice, to which they are unconscious, and apply it to a specific group of individuals. As outlined by Dovidio and Gaertner (2000, 2002), aversive racism is a form of modern racism that applies to people who identify as politically liberal and believe themselves unbiased, but who actually hold unconscious negative beliefs about people of color and other outgroups (i.e., those groups of people against which the majority may have prejudice, including groups identified by race and ethnicity, religion, sexual orientation, gender, national origin, age, disability, social class, or other categorical differences). These individuals uphold egalitarian values and beliefs and are likely to see themselves as "good people" who are tolerant and open-minded. In fact, people characterized by aversive racism are likely to be vested in appearing unbiased, fair-minded, and essentially decent and are strongly motivated to maintain this self-image. This can result in anxiety around people perceived as different and concern about saying and doing something to negate their egalitarian self-image—of saying or doing "the wrong thing." Although understandable, this overriding worry about self-image makes aversive racism difficult to identify and address.

Aversive racism results in an insidious form of racism that occurs only subtly, in ambiguous situations, and in a manner that can be rationalized as something else (Dovidio & Gaertner, 2002). For example, aversive racism is suggested if a White social worker makes a more favorable decision on behalf of a White client than he or she would make on behalf of a Black client in similar circumstances. Evidence from research in a number of professional settings suggests that this very scenario repeatedly occurs. Evidence of subtle discrimination in ambiguous circumstances, as characterizes aversive racism, has been collected in medical (Penner et al., 2010) and legal (Hodson, Hooper, Davidio, & Gaertner, 2002) contexts. Additionally, social workers must be wary of the pull from bureaucratic cultures that may reinforce disparate service delivery (Glisson & Green, 2005). Glisson and Green (2005) suggest that practitioners employ ineffective or uneven practice strategies, in spite of their lack of effectiveness, to survive in an organization. Whaley (1998) found evidence of aversive racism in his review of research within mental health as well.

In addition to negative discrimination, when norms are not clear, aversive racism can lead to positive bias against African Americans. For example, Aberson and Ettlin (2004) found, if it was not clear which action would appear to be biased, African Americans received positively, instead of negatively, biased treatment. Thus, some social workers are likely to avoid confrontation or negative action against minority clients, even when such action is warranted.

Aversive racism is not thought to be pathological. Rather, it is believed to occur through the normal process of categorizing oneself and others into recognizable identity groups; people are seen to "belong" to certain groups and not others (Gaertner & Dovidio, 2005). A simple example occurs in the context of sports. Sports fans tend to associate with other like-minded people, preferring their own fans' company during games, rather than sitting with people from the "other side." The process of categorizing people according to team affiliation feels "natural" and is mostly harmless. However, unconsciously categorizing others by social identity in professional settings can be very serious, particularly when such unconscious categorization occurs about clients who are members of minority race, gender, religious, sexual orientation, or other stigmatized groups. Social workers' unconscious bias, in this context, is likely to conform to the negative stereotypes prevalent in the United States.

Evidence of aversive racism has been found in global as well as national contexts and extends over many years (Dovidio & Gaertner, 2008), and current research suggests that aversive racism affects a significant number of educated, liberal Whites in the United States (Dovidio & Gaertner, 2000). As educated people whose professional ethics require adherence to egalitarian values (NASW, 2008) and who are more likely politically liberal than conservative (Rosenwald & Hyde, 2006), rural social workers are just as susceptible to aversive racism as their urban colleagues. Intergroup contact theory presents one way in which social workers can learn to identify, confront, and reduce the discrimination associated with aversive racism. It should be noted, however, that rural social workers are more or less demonstratively prone to aversive racism than their metropolitan colleagues. Specific studies about rural social workers' possible aversive racism have, thus far, not been reported.

Intergroup Contact Theory

Part of the hope of desegregation was that increased contact between different color individuals would result in more positive racial attitudes (Myrdal, 1944). The belief was that prejudice was based on ignorance and misinformation and, through increased interracial contact, more informed opinions would emerge. In essence, increased cross-racial exposure would reduce prejudice and correct stereotypes. But, beginning with Allport's work in 1954, researchers have found that interracial contact alone does not reduce prejudice. Rather, the contact must occur under specific conditions to dispel stereotypes. Although numerous "contact conditions" have been proposed, Allport's (1954) four contact conditions remain central: (1) equal status, (2) cooperative pursuit of a common goal, (3) perceived common humanity, and (4) mutual support of an accepted institution.

Pettigrew (1998) systematically reviewed social contact research and found mixed results. Cross-racial social contact did not always result in more positive racial attitudes, but when more positive attitudes occurred, Allport's criteria were present. Pettigrew and others (Pettigrew, 1998; Pettigrew & Tropp, 2000) went on to find that personal friendships were especially vital in reducing prejudice cross-racially, and "friendship potential" is frequently cited as a central contact condition. In a meta-analysis of 515 studies undertaken between 1940 and 2000, Pettigrew and Tropp (2006) found that contact did, indeed, typically reduce prejudice, even if conditions were not perfect.

Others have contributed valuable nuance to social contact theory as well. Some have found that, if individuals are less anxious in the cross-racial exchange, there is a better chance of reducing prejudice (Eller & Abrams, 2003; Levin, van Laar, & Sidanius, 2003; Shelton & Richeson, 2005). Turner, Hewstone, Voci, and Vonofakou (2008) found that individuals who could empathize and see others as having a common identity were more apt to decrease their prejudice. Thus, the quality of contact has been a defining variable in much of the research.

The kinds of contacts suggested by Allport (1954) are increasingly available and possible in rural communities as means of increasing cultural competence and positive intergroup relations in rural areas.

Some of the more intriguing research has been related to "imagined" and "indirect" social contact. Turner, Crisp and Lambert (2007) found that prejudicial attitudes were reduced toward gay men through imagining interaction. Pettigrew, Christ, Wagner, and Stellmacher (2007) found that having a friend who had outgroup friendships could reduce prejudice for the individual having indirect contact. In fact, indirect contact (through the friend) was as effective at reducing prejudice as was direct contact.

Implications for Rural Social Work Practice

Social science theory, then, offers ample guidance related to cultural competence. Implicit association research suggests that bias and stereotypes are present in majority culture and difficult to rebuff in media-rich and media-biased U.S. society. Aversive racism identifies and delineates the dynamics of racism with today's educated, liberal-leaning individuals who support egalitarian principles and believe themselves to be unprejudiced. Finally, intergroup contact theory suggests the circumstances necessary to reduce prejudice and bias.

How can social workers, especially those in rural areas where diverse populations are still a small, albeit growing, proportion of the population, operationalize these theories to enhance their cultural competence? Four strategies are implied from these theories: (1) actively identify one's own bias and become proactive in remediation of biased thought; (2) diversify social contact; (3) make use of technology; and (4) become implicit-message savvy.

The issues and principles presented here are no more important in rural areas than in urban and metropolitan areas. However, it is likely that large city social workers have dealt with such issues for a long time, whereas they may be new phenomena for smaller community workers.

Identify and Correct

A person needs to learn how to identify and correct his or her own biases. This requires a two-pronged approach. First, a person must name his or her own bias. This may mean noting language, physical responses, or behaviors that tip off the biases. For example, using the phrase "those people" implies a biased feeling given that "those" infers difference. Another example may be if a person hesitates to speak or decides not to participate in a discussion related to difference or race. Another example might be if it becomes difficult for a person to articulate his or her feelings or thoughts. Some may decide not to participate because they are afraid of making a "mistake" or of what others might think of his or her attitude or comments. A physical response could also be a sign of bias, such as perspiring, reddening in the face, or exhibiting other physical tensions.

Second, a person must initiate a corrective response to bias. Cognitive behavioral strategies can be effective. Thus, once a possible bias is identified via a cue, the person analyzes the thought and hypothesizes about whether the meaning of the response was biased. Once aware that the view or response could be biased, the person would actively evaluate whether the view was correct for all people who were part of that social identity category. For example, if a White woman finds herself always clutching her handbag as she passes a Black male, this pattern must first be noted for change to occur. Once the pattern is recognized, the automatic thoughts and resulting behaviors must be identified and analyzed by exploring the veracity of the thought and actively replacing it with a more judicious outlook, if the original thought is found to lack validity and be biased.

Diversify Social Contact

The most obvious solution to decrease bias and stereotypical responses is to develop relationships with people who have different social identity categories, keeping the contact conditions in mind (equal status, shared goals, etc.). Of course, such efforts must be based on a genuine desire to develop new friendships or widen a person's social network, not an attempt to "collect" token friends. One way to do this would be to seek out social organizations or religious institutions within which increased diversity can be found. Others may take the social identity categories of others into account when deciding on a continuing education institution, a professional consultant, or a club choice when pursuing a hobby. Also important to remember is the research suggesting that being friends with others who have diverse networks can decrease a person's bias. Thus, a person may want to consider initiating conversation about friendship networks and connections with people who are already friends and begin to learn about others from them.

In rural communities, these attempts may be difficult because of the lack of diversity in a community. However, as rural areas grow in diversity, the possibilities also grow. When direct contact is difficult, more indirect contact may be considered. For instance, what books could enhance understanding of individuals or groups with differing social identity categories? What movies could help in this process? Even in rural areas, movies can be delivered easily and regularly. Becoming aware of playwrights, directors, and producers of films from groups other than one's own can offer opportunities to view and analyze the veracity of film portrayals of groups and cultures. Also, rural social workers should be mindful that diversity is not limited to color or ethnicity alone. Contact can help reduce prejudice against individuals of any social identity who someone perceives as "different," such as sexual orientation, gender, national origin, religion, or social class.

Use Technology

Technology and the Internet can assist in enhancing a person's cultural competence. Websites are available on which individuals review or chat about films, books, and other media. Depending on the site, multicultural perspectives may be available.

The Internet also provides connections to people the world over. Although people need to be savvy, connecting with people personally and investigating other cultures, beliefs, and rituals is as close as a click of the mouse. Routinely logging on to a non-U.S. news outlet is a very easy way to increase global understanding that could help reduce bias against others.

Combat Implicit Messages

Finally, becoming media-wise and critically analyzing the messages that are sent and reinforced by the media is essential in combating stereotype and prejudice. An enhanced awareness includes identifying what pictures and messages are coupled, as well as what language is used to describe individuals, groups, events, and processes. It is also important to identify which groups and messages are omitted from media.

Conclusion

In our globally connected world, rural social workers no longer live in homogenous isolation. Like social workers everywhere, their lives are affected by international connections. People who may be perceived as "different" by race, ethnicity, religion, gender, and sexual orientation live and work in their communities as clients and neighbors. Along with their other challenges, rural social workers must find ways to identify and reduce the bias and prejudice to which they, like everyone else, are susceptible. Suggestions for doing so within the rural context include identifying and correcting biases as they occur, diversifying social contact, taking advantage of new technologies to connect with others, and combating media-driven implicit messages.

References

Aberson, C. L., & Ettlin, T. E. (2004). The aversive racism paradigm and responses favoring African Americans: Meta-analytic evidence of two types of favoritism. *Social Justice Research, 17*(1), 25–46.

Allport, G. (1954). *The nature of prejudice.* Cambridge, MA: Addison-Wesley Publishing.

Armstrong, B., & Neuendorf, C. (1992). TV entertainment, news, and racial perceptions of college students. *Journal of Communication, 42*(3), 153–176.

Bernard, J. M., & Goodyear, R. K. (2004). *Fundamentals of clinical supervision,* 3rd ed. Boston: Allyn & Bacon.

Buselle, R., & Crandall, H. (2002). Television viewing and perceptions about race differences in socioeconomic success. *Journal of Broadcasting and Electronic Media, 46,* 265–282.

Cary, D., & Marques, P. (2007). From expert to collaborator: Developing cultural competency in clinical supervision. *Clinical Supervisor, 26*(1/2), 141–157.

Chang, C. Y., Hays, D. G., & Shoffner, M. F. (2003). Cross-racial supervision: A developmental approach for White supervisors working with supervisees of color. *Clinical Supervisor, 22*(2), 121–138.

Constantine, M. G. (1997). Facilitating multicultural competency in counseling supervison: Operationalizing a practical framework. In D. B. Pope-Davis & H. L. K. Coleman (Eds.), *Multicultural counseling competencies: Assessment, education and training and supervision* (pp. 310–324). Thousand Oakes, CA: Sage Publications.

Davis, L. E., & Gelsomino, J. (1994). An assessment of practitioner cross-racial treatment experiences. *Social Work, 39,* 116–123.

Dixon, T. L. (2008). Network news and racial beliefs: Exploring the connection between national television news exposure and stereotypical perceptions of African Americans. *Journal of Communication, 58,* 321–337.

Dovidio, J. F., & Gaertner, S. L. (2000). Aversive racism and selection decisions: 1989 and 1999. *Psychological Science, 11,* 315–319.

Dovidio, J. F., & Gaertner, S. L. (2002). Color blind or just plain blind? The pernicious nature of contemporary racism. *NonProfit Quarterly, 92,* 1–5.

Dovidio, J. F., & Gaertner, S. L. (2008). New directions in aversive racism research: Persistence and pervasiveness. In C. Willis-Esqueda (Ed.), *Motivational aspects of prejudice and racism* (pp. 43–67). New York: Springer Science & Business Media.

Ellers, A., & Abrams, D. (2003). Gringos in Mexico: Cross-sectional and longitudinal effects of language school-promoted contact on intergroup bias. *Group Processes and Intergroup Relations, 6*(1), 55–75.

Gaertner, S. L., & Dovidio, J. F. (2005). Understanding and addressing contemporary racism: From aversive racism to the common ingroup identity model. *Journal of Social Issues, 61,* 615–639.

Glisson, C., & Green, P. (2005). The effects of organizational culture and climate on the access to mental health care in child welfare and juvenile justice systems. *Administration and Policy in Mental Health and Mental Health Services Research, 33,* 433–448.

Green, A., Carney, D. R., Pallin, D., Iezzoni, L., & Banaji, M. (2006). [Physicians' implicit biases predict differential treatment of Black versus White patients.] Unpublished manuscript.

Green, R. G., Kiernan-Stern, M., & Baskind, F. R. (2005). White social workers' attitudes about people of color. *Journal of Ethnic and Cultural Diversity in Social Work, 14*(1/2), 47–68.

Hepworth, D. H., Rooney, R. H., Rooney, G. D., Strom-Gottfried, K., & Larsen, J. (2010). *Direct social work practice: Theory and skills,* 8th ed. Pacific Grove, CA: Brooks/Cole Cengage Learning.

Hodson, G., Hooper, H., Dovidio, J. F., & Gaertner, S. L. (2005). Aversive racism in Britain: The use of inadmissible evidence in legal decisions. *European Journal of Social Psychology, 35,* 437–448.

Jensen, L. (2006). *New immigrant settlements in rural America: Problems, prospects, and policies: A Carsey Institute report on rural America.* Retrieved from http://www.carseyinstitute.unh.edu/publications/Report_Immigration.pdf

Johnson, K. (2006). *Demographic trends in rural and small town America.* Durham, NH: University of New Hampshire.

Lane, K. A., Banaji, M. R., Nosek, B. A., & Greenwald, A. G. (2007). Understanding and using the Implicit Association Test: IV. What we know (so far) about the method. In B. Wittenbrink & N. Schwarz (Eds.), *Implicit measures of attitude: Procedures and controversies* (pp. 59–102). New York, NY: Guilford.

Levin, S., VanLaar, C., & Sidanius, J. (2003). The effects of ingroup and outgroup friendships on ethnic attitudes in college: A longitudinal study. *Group Processes and Intergroup Relations, 6*(1), 76–92.

McConnell, A. R., & Leibold, J. M. (2001). Relations among the Implicit Association Test, discriminatory behavior, and explicit measures of racial attitudes. *Journal of Experimental Social Psychology, 37,* 435–442.

Myrdal, G. (1944). *The American dilemma: The negro problem and modern democracy.* New York, NY: Harper and Brothers.

National Association of Social Workers (NASW). (2003). *Demographics of social workers.* Retrieved from http://www.socialworkers.org/pressroom/2003/100603.asp

National Association of Social Workers (NASW). (2008). *NASW code of ethics.* Washington, DC: Author.

Nosek, B. A., Banaji, M. R., & Greenwald, A. G. (2002). Harvesting implicit group attitudes and beliefs from a demonstration website. *Group Dynamics, 6*, 101–115.

Owen, G., Meyerson, J., & Otteson, C. (2010). *A new age of immigrants: Making immigration work for Minnesota.* Minneapolis, MN: Minneapolis Foundation.

Parenti, M. (2006). Mass media: For the many, by the few. In P. S. Rothenberg (Ed.), *Beyond borders: Thinking critically about global issues* (pp.60–74). New York: Worth Publishers.

Parra, P. A., & Pfeffer, M. J. (2006). New immigrants in rural communities: The challenges of integration. *Social Text, 24*(3), 81–98.

Pedersen, P. B. (1994). *A handbook for developing multicultural awareness,* 2nd ed. Alexandria, VA: American Counseling Association.

Penner, L. A., Dovidio, J. F., West, T. V., Gaertner, S. L., Albrecht, T. L., Dailey, R. K., & Markova, T. (2010). Aversive racism and medical interactions with Black patients: A field study. *Journal of Experimental Social Psychology, 46*, 436–440.

Pettigrew, T. (1998). Intergroup contact theory. *Annual Review of Psychology, 49*(1), 65–85.

Pettigrew. T., & Tropp, L. (2000). Does intergroup contact reduce prejudice? In S. Oskamp (Ed.), *Reducing prejudice and discrimination (Claremont Symposium on Applied Social Psychology)* (pp. 93–114). Mahwah, NJ: Lawrence Erlbaum Associates.

Pettigrew, T. F., & Tropp, L. R. (2006). A meta-analytic test of intergroup contact theory. *Journal of Personality and Social Psychology, 90*, 751–783.

Pettigrew, T. F., Christ, O., Wagner, U., & Stellmacher, J. (2007). Direct and indirect intergroup contact effects on prejudice: A normative interpretation. *International Journal of Intercultural Relations, 31*, 411–425.

Proctor, E. K., & Davis, L. E. (1994). The challenge of racial difference: Skills for clinical practice. *Social Work, 39*, 314–323.

Rosenwald, M., & Hyde, C. A. (2006). Political ideologies of social workers: An under explored dimension of practice. *Advances in Social Work, 7*(2), 12–22.

Shandy, D. J., & Fennelly, K. (2006). A comparison of the integration experiences of two African immigrant populations in a rural community. *Journal of Religion & Spirituality, 25*(1), 23–45.

Shelton, J. N., & Richeson, J. A. (2005). Intergroup contact and pluralistic ignorance. *Journal of Personality and Social Psychology, 88*(1), 91–107.

Sue, D. W., & Sue, D. (1999). *Counseling the culturally different: Theory and practice,* 3rd ed. New York, NY: John Wiley & Sons.

Sue, D. W., Capodilupo, C. M., Torino, G. C., Bucceri, J. M., Holder, A. M. B., Nada, K. L., & Esquilin, M. (2007). Racial microaggressions in everyday life: Implications for clinical practice. *American Psychologist, 62*(4), 271–286.

Turner, R. N., Crisp, R. J., & Lambert, E. (2007). Imagining intergroup contact can improve intergroup contact attitudes. *Group Processes and Intergroup Contact Relations*, *10*, 427–441.

Turner, R. N., Hewstone, M., Voci, A., & Vonofakou, C. (2008). A test of the extended intergroup contact hypothesis: The mediating role of intergroup anxiety, perceived ingroup and outgroup norms, and inclusion of the outgroup in the self. *Journal of Personality and Social Psychology*, *95*, 843–860.

Whaley, A. L. (1998). Racism in the provision of mental health services: A social-cognitive analysis. *American Journal of Orthopsychiatry*, *68*(1), 47–57.

Whitaker, T., Weismiller, T., & Clark, E. (2006). *Assuring the sufficiency of a frontline workforce: A national study of licensed social workers*. Executive summary. Washington, DC: National Association of Social Workers.

17 Victims of Interpersonal Abuse in Rural Communities

CHRISTINA M. CHIARELLI-HELMINIAK
AND JILL M. BRADSHAW

A common romantic notion is that rural communities are more tranquil or idyllic than urban or suburban communities. This myth about the peaceful nature of rural society might suggest that rural communities do not experience incidents of interpersonal violence, such as domestic violence, sexual assault, and child abuse. The reality is that violence within the home and community is present regardless of geographic location. This chapter begins with a case study before moving on to an overview of the various types of interpersonal violence. This chapter also presents the unique challenges to survivors of abuse in rural communities, ways to overcome barriers to service, and the role social workers can play in providing advocacy, services, and support.

Case Study

This case example is based on the work experience of one of the authors during her tenure as a child advocate at a domestic violence and sexual assault program in the rural South. This is the story of just one family, but, unfortunately, one that is far too common in families where violence is present. The reader will find many of the issues discussed throughout this chapter within this one example.

Ms. Beth Donahue was raised in a small community in the southern Appalachian Mountains. She became pregnant with her first child at the age of 16 and married the baby's father before the baby was born. Soon after being married, the abuse began, when her husband came home from work one night intoxicated. Ms. Donahue's husband struck her on the side of the face, when he realized that dinner was not prepared yet. Ms. Donahue quickly apologized and began preparing the meal and setting the table. On occasion, Ms. Donahue had witnessed her father hitting her mother and assumed this was part of a marriage. Ms. Donahue's mother had taught her that it was the wife's responsibility to keep up the house and make her husband happy, and that is what Ms. Donahue intended to do.

Following the birth of her first child, Mark, Ms. Donahue found the demands of being a new parent overwhelming and always felt tired. She also became less interested in sex with her husband. Six months after Mark's birth, however, Ms. Donahue's husband began to force himself on her sexually. Ms. Donahue began to dread going to bed each night, not knowing if she would need to fulfill her "wifely duties" that night. Ms. Donahue would silently cry each time her husband forced her to have sex, fearing what he might do to her if she said no. Her husband's drinking had increased, as did the frequency of him hitting her.

After about a year, Ms. Donahue decided to talk with the pastor of the church she had attended since she was a child, where she had been married, and where her son had been baptized. Ms. Donahue described how her husband would hit her on occasion, and she asked the pastor if this was okay in the eyes of the Lord. The pastor quoted a verse from the Bible and explained to Ms. Donahue that a wife must be subservient to her husband and that God will not provide her with more burdens than she is able to carry. The pastor, a revered community figure, reinforced the idea of violence as not only permissible, but normal.

When Mark was 4 years old, Ms. Donahue gave birth to a baby girl, Caroline. Then 2 years later, Heather was born. Ms. Donahue's husband was hoping for more boys, however, and took this out on Ms. Donahue, saying that she was weak and that was why she was giving him girls. Sons were prized in the community. Fathers hoped their sons would go on to play for the varsity football team or would plow the fields as their ancestors had done for generations. The abuse intensified one night, when Ms. Donahue's husband threatened to kill her with a shotgun, while Mark was in the next room watching television. Hearing the argument, Mark went into the room and saw his father pointing the shotgun toward his mother. Mark would later recount his father telling him, "this is the only way you can get a woman to listen to you." Ms. Donahue called the local sheriff's office, fearing her husband's threats. When the deputy arrived, he spoke with Ms. Donahue's husband first and then said to Ms. Donahue, "I know your husband is a good man. You just need to be a good wife."

Soon after the shotgun incident, Ms. Donahue was diagnosed with uterine cancer and, as a result, had to undergo a hysterectomy, eliminating the possibility of any future children. During her frequent visits to doctors' offices, medical professionals began to notice the bruises on her body and provided her information about the local domestic violence shelter. Ms. Donahue denied that she was being abused, claiming that, if she was a better wife, then her husband would not need to hit her. She assured the nurses and doctors that her children were safe and not being harmed in any way.

Many years passed before child protective services came to visit Ms. Donahue. When Caroline was 12 years old, she disclosed to her school guidance counselor that her father was coming into her bedroom at night and touching her. During an interview with child protective services, Heather also reported being touched by her father. The girls were taken into protective custody and placed in a foster home. Ms. Donahue was beside herself with grief and guilt that she had allowed this to happen to her daughters. The school guidance counselor provided Ms. Donahue the same information on the local domestic violence shelter that she had seen years before, but this time Ms. Donahue decided to call. The shelter's legal advocate assisted Ms. Donahue in obtaining a temporary protection order against her husband. As a result of the sexual abuse allegations, her husband was arrested and, ultimately, convicted. It was Ms. Donahue, however, who had to endure the long process of trying to get her daughters out of state custody. By this time, Mark had dropped out of high school, moved out of the family's home, and was staying with friends. Ms. Donahue filed for divorce from her husband, which enraged Mark, swearing he would never forgive his mother or sisters for what they had done to his father.

Without her husband's income, Ms. Donahue had little money to support herself, so she moved into the domestic violence shelter. The advocates assisted Ms. Donahue in working through the child protective services case plan, and her daughters were returned to her care. Through the domestic violence program, Ms. Donahue and her daughters were able to receive counseling. With the assistance of the advocates, Ms. Donahue learned she was eligible to receive Temporary Aid to Needy Families, as well as other assistance, and she was, eventually, able to save up enough money to rent a place to live with her daughters.

Types of Interpersonal Abuse

Defining Domestic Violence and Sexual Assault

Domestic violence is a term used to broadly define a pattern of abuse that occurs between two people in a close relationship. Domestic violence most often occurs between a current or former spouse or partner, a person with whom the abuser shares a child, or a current or former partner with whom the abuser shares or has shared a common residence. However, domestic violence can occur in any intimate relationship, such as dating relationships, between immediate or extended family members, or between friends (National Coalition Against Domestic Violence, 2011). Other terms commonly used to describe domestic violence include domestic abuse, intimate partner violence, abusive partner relationships, woman battering, family violence, and spousal abuse.

Domestic violence involves the use or threatened use of force or violence, and it is often part of a systematic pattern of dominance and control (Tjaden & Thoennes, 2000). Domestic violence is defined as including four main types of violence: physical violence, sexual violence, threats of physical or sexual violence, and psychological or emotional violence (Saltzman, Fanslow, McMahon, & Shelley, 2002). Domestic violence occurs on a continuum of frequency and severity, and existing issues such as economic stress, drug and/or alcohol abuse, and exposure to violence in childhood can increase the risk of violence between intimate partners (Bassuk, Dawson, & Huntington, 2006; Graham, Bernards, Wilsnack, & Gmel, 2011; Weissman, 2007).

Sexual assault is defined as rape, attempted rape, or any other unwanted sexual contact or threat of such contact. Sexual assault is defined as including four main types of violence: sexual contact, sexual coercion (i.e., sex out of obligation, verbal pressure, or misuse of authority), attempted rape, and rape (DeKeseredy & Joseph, 2006). The perpetrators of sexual assault could be intimate partners, friends, coworkers, acquaintances, or strangers. Sexual assault between intimate partners can be part of a pattern of domestic violence. Other terms used to describe sexual assault between intimate partners include marital rape, wife rape, spousal rape, or sexual assault in marriage. Sexual assault between acquaintances early in a dating relationship or between people who have met socially is often called date rape. Sexual assault between strangers is often described by the type of assault (i.e., rape or attempted rape).

Although there is evidence that domestic violence and sexual assault have existed for as long as written history, they were not topics of public discussion in the United States until the temperance movement and first wave of the feminist movement in the 1800s. It was the feminist movement of the 1970s, however, that brought forth a rush of public discussion about battered women, and it was during this time that the first shelters and support services for survivors were created.

Throughout the 1980s advocates continued to push for changes in legislation that would better protect women and increase funding for local programs. It was not until 1994 that the first federal legislation was passed to address this issue—the Violence Against Women Act (VAWA). VAWA is a comprehensive legislative package that includes funding for shelters, interventions, and education; increased penalties for offenders; requirements fot states to better enforce protection orders; and legal relief for immigrant survivors (U.S. Department of Health and Human Services [DHHS], 2011). VAWA was reauthorized in 2005, at which time it expanded protections for immigrants (Conyers, 2007). Research has shown that VAWA is associated with decreases in the overall incidence of domestic violence, increased police notification and perpetrator arrests, and reductions in rape and assaults (Boba & Lilley, 2008; Cho & Wilke, 2005).

The Centers for Disease Control and Prevention ([CDC], 2009) considers domestic violence a very serious public health problem, affecting millions of Americans. Although the actual rates of domestic violence are unknown because so many victims do not to report the crimes, research shows that women report 4.8 million domestic violence-related physical assaults and rapes each year, and men report 2.9 million domestic violence-related physical assaults (Tjaden & Thoennes, 2000). In 2005, domestic violence resulted in more than 1,500 deaths (Department of Justice, 2009). The National Violence Against Women Survey found that nearly 25% of women and 7.6% of men surveyed reported being raped and/or physically assaulted by a current or former spouse, cohabitating partner, or date at some point in their lives (Tjaden & Thoennes, 2000).

As with domestic violence, the true incidence rates for sexual assault are unknown, because many sexual assault survivors do not report the crimes (Kilpatrick & McCauley, 2009). A national study of sexual violence found that 1 in 6 women and 1 in 33 men reported experiencing an attempted or completed rape at some time in their lives (Tjaden & Thoennes, 2000). Among college women in the United States, 20–25% reported an attempted or completed rape during their college years (Fisher, Cullen, & Turner, 2000). A nationwide survey of high school students found that 7.4% reported having been forced to have sexual intercourse when they did not want to (CDC, 2010).

Defining Child Abuse and Neglect

In 1974 the Child Abuse Prevention and Treatment Act (CAPTA) was the first major federal legislation to address child abuse and neglect (Barusch, 2009). Today, federal regulations are imposed at the state level to ensure the safety and well-being of children across the nation, creating a system of unique child welfare agencies in each state. State legislation outlines the definitions of child abuse and neglect and the responsibilities of each state's Child Protective Services. Child abuse and neglect are defined by CAPTA (42 U.S.C.A. §5106g) as: "any recent act or failure to act on the part of a parent or caretaker which results in death, serious physical or emotional harm, sexual abuse or exploitation; or an act or failure to act, which presents an imminent risk of serious harm" (DHHS, 2010, p. xi).

According to DHHS (2010), in 2008 approximately 772,000 children in the United States were victims of some form of maltreatment. This total calculates into an average of 10.3 per 1,000 children who experienced abuse and neglect within a 1 year timeframe. Of the children found to be victims of maltreatment, 2.2% experienced medical neglect, 7.3% suffered psychological maltreatment, 9.1% were sexually abused, and 16.1% were physically abused. Most children (71.1%) suffered from neglect. An additional 9% were classified under "other" type of maltreatment.

Co-occurrence: Domestic Violence, Sexual Assault, and Child Abuse

Although domestic violence, sexual assault, and child abuse are distinct forms of interpersonal violence that can happen in isolation, multiple types of violence often occur in the same family. There are numerous studies that look at the co-occurrence of domestic violence and child abuse in the same home, showing an overlap of 30–60% (Bassuk et al., 2006; Cox, Kotch, & Everson, 2003; Ross, 1996; Tolan, Gorman-Smith, & Henry, 2006). In most cases it is the abusive partner in the domestic violence relationship who is also abusing the child (or children), but there is also research to suggest that battered women are more likely to abuse a child physically than women who are not abused (Straus & Gelles, 1990).

Children living in violent homes not only experience a higher risk for abuse and neglect, but they also risk observing traumatic events. Some experts believe that children who observe domestic violence may experience more harmful long-term effects than those who experience physical abuse (Margolin, 1998). Exposure to childhood violence is a risk factor for violence in adult interpersonal relationships (O'Keefe, 1995). Intergenerational abuse can occur when children are raised in a violent home, learn interpersonal violence as a normative behavior, and then model those same behaviors toward their own children (Marshall, Huang, & Ryan, 2011). Without a positive role model(s) to break this cycle of abuse, families can go on living within a cycle of violence for untold generations.

Incidence Rates in Rural Communities

More research is needed to truly understand incidence rates of interpersonal violence in rural communities. Some national statistics suggest that incidence rates are similar across the country, regardless of geographic location. A comparison of national domestic violence rates across urban, suburban, and rural populations found that women were equally at risk for intimate partner violence (Bachman, 1992). In contrast, some smaller studies suggest that incidence rates of interpersonal violence might actually be higher in rural areas. Johnson and Elliot (1997) found that women living in rural communities were more likely to be in a battering relationship with a violent partner than women living in larger communities. Another study of adult sexual victimization found that, although the number of sexual victimization cases reported was higher in urban areas, the rate of sexual assaults was higher in rural areas (Ruback & Menard, 2001).

A longitudinal study that included a sample of children living in a rural area of North Carolina found that 25% of the children reported exposure to a traumatic event, such as sexual abuse, physical assault, robbery, severe automobile accident, and so forth (Costello, Erkanli, Fairbanks, & Angold, 2002). The authors also concluded the likelihood of some traumatic events, such as sexual abuse, were increased by risk factors such as poverty. Slovak and Singer (2002) investigated children's exposure to violence through a survey of students in grades 3–8 attending school in a rural area of Ohio. Nearly one-half (45.1%) of the respondents reported being slapped, hit, or punched, and 13.3% reported being "beaten up" at home within the past year. Females reported being sexually abused two times more often than male students; and younger students (grades 3–5) reported being inappropriately touched almost three times more than older students (grades 6–8).

Although there is not yet enough clear evidence to indicate that rural communities experience higher rates of interpersonal violence, there are several well-established challenges to accessing services that are unique to survivors living in rural areas. A social worker seeking to advocate for survivors in a rural community would need to be aware of these barriers to services to appropriately organize and deliver the services and support that a survivor needs.

Unique Challenges to Survivors in Rural Areas

The availability of services and support for survivors of interpersonal violence in rural areas is limited in many ways, and there are a number of barriers to service delivery. Isolation, lack of transportation, high rates of poverty, and lack of community-based services all contribute to survivors facing increased difficulty in accessing appropriate services and ensuring their health and safety. The lack of appropriate legal response to reporting is another unique feature of rural living. Victim–offender relationships, patriarchal attitudes, and lack of access to criminal justice personnel are all barriers to service.

One of the major features of living in a rural area is isolation. The most obvious type of isolation is geographic; depending on the area, the nearest neighbor might be 1, 5, or even 25 miles away. Geographic isolation may be the most fundamental difficulty facing a survivor (Cook-Craig, Lane, & Siebold, 2010; Grama, 2000; Krishnan, Hilbert, & VanLeeuwen, 2001; Templeman & Mitchell, 2002). Geographic isolation often leads to social isolation; long distances between homes limits opportunities for social networking and opportunities to create and maintain friendships outside the home. Social isolation is often further limited by controlling patterns of the abusive partner, who limits the survivor's interactions with others. People living in rural areas might also feel culturally isolated; there are often customs and habits in rural communities that are quite different from those of mainstream society. And for survivors of interpersonal violence, there might be feelings of emotional isolation, "as part of the helpless, hopeless, and shameful feelings that characterize ... alienation, and loss of sense of self" (Davis, Taylor & Furniss, 2001, p.339).

One of the greatest barriers to accessing services noted by survivors in rural areas related to geographic isolation is lack of transportation (Lewis, 2003). Most rural areas do not have public transportation systems or even paid transportation services such as taxis, so survivors must rely on personal resources. For households that do have a vehicle, access to that vehicle may be limited or completely controlled by the abuser. The cost of gasoline may prevent a survivor from having the economic means to drive the vehicle. The rising cost of gasoline has greatly affected rural drivers, because commutes for daily activities are typically longer and vehicles are frequently larger, older models, which get less mileage per gallon (Krauss, 2008). Higher costs to operate a vehicle are problematic for the survivor, especially if the abuser also controls the finances. Additionally, the vehicle may be part of a family business (typical for a farm family), so taking the vehicle for personal use would not be an option. The geographic isolation of rural areas, paired with limited transportation options, keeps many survivors from ever discovering there are services available to help them (Grama, 2000). And even if survivors are aware of available services, lack of transportation makes them unable to access such services.

People living in rural areas are disproportionately affected by high rates of poverty (Albrecht, Albrecht, & Albrecht, 2000). The 2009 American Community Survey reported that the five states with the highest poverty rates (at or above 17%) were Alabama, Arkansas, Kentucky, Mississippi, and West Virginia—all states with significantly large rural communities (U.S. Census Bureau, 2010). For those living within 125% of income-to-poverty level, Mississippi reported the highest with 28.2%. Poverty affects a survivor's ability to gain access to any number of support services, because they are often unable to afford many basic necessities to connect with services, such as a telephone/cell phone, Internet access, and/or a car or some other mode of transportation.

Poverty also severely limits survivors' life choices, making the option of leaving an abusive partner often seem impossible due to financial constraints. Economic dependency is often cited as a major factor keeping many survivors in abusive relationships (Davis, 1999). Poverty is also associated with higher unemployment, substandard housing, increased mental health issues, addictive behaviors, and increased family stressors, which are all factors associated with increased risk for violence within the home (Krishnan et al., 2001). Children also are affected by poverty, due to increased health risks related to poor housing and inconsistent health care. Educational standards of public schools in low-income neighborhoods are not up to par with wealthier schools. And children from lower socioeconomic families have a greater risk of witnessing and/or experiencing abuse (Barusch, 2009; Templeman & Mitchell, 2002).

Poverty in rural areas is experienced not only at the personal level, but also at the community level. Many rural communities lack the resources for basic public services such as local police stations, hospitals, and road maintenance. Rural communities often rely on county funding to meet public service needs, and public services often are not available locally but require long distance travel to access. Many services critical to survivors, such health care, shelters, domestic violence/sexual assault advocacy services, children's advocacy centers, law enforcement, and courts, are not readily available in their own communities (Cook-Craig et al., 2010; Templeman & Mitchell, 2002). One study found that a sample of rural women lived an average of 11 miles or more from the nearest shelter and that 52% of those women had no access to transportation (Feyen, 1989).

The availability and quality of community-based healthcare has a significant effect on survivors of interpersonal violence. The type of hospital setting in which a child receives care makes a difference in whether their abuse is diagnosed and/or treated. One study found that child abuse victims brought to a children's hospital are 50% more likely to have their abuse identified, diagnosed, and treated, compared to children seen at general hospitals, where doctors typically do not receive specialized training in identifying the signs and symptoms of child abuse (Trokel, Waddimba, Griffith, & Sege, 2006). In some rural communities a child who has been abused has to be transported more than 2 hours to receive the specialized investigative services of a pediatric sexual assault nurse examiner and a forensic interviewer, both specially trained in child development and investigative interviewing, among other areas. A woman who has been abused may not have access to a mental health professional who has experience with posttraumatic stress disorder within her community, and, without reliable transportation, she may not even be able to travel to such a provider. Commonly, in this type of situation a local provider may treat a client without any training in the area of abuse (Paul, Gray, Elhai, Massad, & Stamm, 2006).

For survivors living in rural communities, issues related to reporting can present many challenges. Lack of anonymity in reporting is a significant problem in rural communities, which are often close-knit, and, even with the restraints of geographic isolation, rural community members often know each person living within their community. "Too often, the police officer that woman calls for help may also be a neighbor, the judge—a family friend or an advocate—an in-law of the batterer" (Grama, 2000, p. 177). The ability to report abuse and maintain anonymity in a rural community is often not possible, resulting in lower than average reporting rates.

The majority of sexual assaults in this country are nonstranger sexual assaults, and in rural communities this is especially true. Rural areas experience what is known as a "high acquaintance density," so the likelihood of a sexual assault victim knowing his or her abuser is higher in rural communities (Lewis, 2003). Research indicates that victim–offender relationships predict reporting, and the closer the relationship between the victim and the offender, the less likely it is that the crime will be reported (Ruback & Menard, 2001).

The "good ol' boys" system of patriarchy is still alive and well in many rural communities, and these patriarchal attitudes influence the legal response to reporting and addressing domestic violence and sexual assault crimes (Towns & Adams, 2009). Rural law enforcement officers tend to be more conservative than their urban counterparts, and they are often reluctant to become involved in domestic disputes (Grama, 2000). Legal services, such as access to lawyers, judges, and courts, are limited in rural areas. Courts in rural areas often meet at inconsistent times and locations, and the immediate needs of survivors cannot be met through these schedules.

There are numerous studies in which survivors from rural areas have expressed concerns with the criminal justice system. In a qualitative study of the experiences of rural survivors, many survivors reported they are afraid to call the police, because their abuser socially networks with criminal justice personnel and they feel that no action would be taken to help them (Websdale & Johnson, 1998). A study of African American women in the rural Deep South found mistrust of law enforcement as a primary barrier to receiving needed services (Lichtenstein & Johnson, 2009). A study of survivors in rural Texas found that survivors expressed concerns about criminal justice services, reporting inadequate protection, discourteous treatment, and insufficient information about their legal options. Additionally, the study found that criminal justice providers were reluctant to make arrests, often imposed lenient sanctions on batterers, questioned the survivor's credibility, and expressed victim-blaming attitudes (Van Hightower & Gorton, 2002).

In addition to these unique stressors facing survivors living in rural areas, a review of the literature highlights some other common challenges to rural survivors that warrant additional consideration. Travel limitations during periods of poor weather (Shepherd, 2001), increased likelihood of having weapons in the home, and strong religious teachings or beliefs that promote patriarchal attitudes are all issues that survivors in rural areas have raised as areas of concern (Krishnan, Hilbert, & McNeil, 2002; Towns & Adams, 2009; Websdale, 1998). Immigrant populations and persons of color living in rural communities are more likely to face racist attitudes (Grama, 2000). Immigrant survivors may face an additional barrier if they are not proficient in speaking English (Vidales, 2010). Rural communities offer limited opportunities for higher education, and survivors in rural areas report greater need with education/training than urban survivors (Grossman, Hinkley, Kawalski, & Margrave, 2005). One study of rural women found that they have significantly less social support, less education, less income, and more physical abuse than their urban counterparts (Logan, Walker, Cole, Ratliff, & Leukefeld, 2003).

Overcoming Barriers to Service Delivery

Rural programs supporting survivors of interpersonal violence must truly take a community-based approach to successfully overcome the barriers to service delivery that survivors in rural areas experience. Advocates for survivors need to reach out to social agencies, religious communities, businesses, legal officials, law enforcement, and local government to ensure that all bodies are working together and that everyone is educated about the realities of domestic violence, sexual assault, and child abuse in their community. Rural programs must address the unique needs of survivors in rural communities, with a primary focus on creating transportation networks and more locally available shelters or Safe Homes and children's advocacy centers. Although most rural communities do not have hospitals, many have health care clinics; a health care setting can be an ideal location to conduct screenings for abuse. A study of healthcare clinics in rural Pennsylvania found that they could rather easily implement domestic violence screening policies and help to refer their patients to domestic violence advocacy programs as needed. Patients were most likely to accept referrals when the advocate was on-site and able to meet with patients before they left (Ulbrich & Stockdale, 2002).

Informal networks and relationships and use of volunteers within rural communities are just as important as formal services. One study found it essential for rural women to have "supportive persons" in their lives who can help them access formal and informal networks and decrease isolation (Bosch & Bergen, 2006). The study found that "non-supportive persons" (e.g., persons who are judgmental, tend to foster traditional gender role values and expectations, and blame the victim) hinder a survivor's ability to access services, and their presence helps keep the survivor bound in abusive partner relationships. The social worker can take the role of being the "supportive person" in a survivor's life, or that role can be filled through informal networks of family, friends, or volunteer advocates. A study of survivors in Appalachia found that formal and informal community supports (e.g, family, friends, clergy, domestic violence organizations, legal systems) were important to successfully ending an abusive relationship (Gavin, 2009).

Advocacy, Services, and Supports

Treatment for survivors of domestic violence and sexual assault is typically conceptualized as a continuum of advocacy, services, and support provided by advocates and human service professionals with specialized training in understanding the needs of survivors. Peer counselors, who are themselves survivors, often work or volunteer within domestic violence/sexual assault programs, typically taking on advocate responsibilities. Emergency shelters, Safe Homes, and transitional housing are some of the most common residential services needed by survivors. Crisis hotlines, counseling, support groups, legal advocacy, medical care, and case management (e.g., help connecting with benefits) are commonly needed support services. Survivors also often need support with issues related to child custody, keeping pets safe, caring for farm animals, immigration issues, safe long-term housing, food, clothing, jobs and job training, education, and funds to pay for immediate needs. A study of domestic violence and sexual assault survivors found that the core services needed include crisis services, legal and medical advocacy, support groups, individual counseling, and shelter (Macy, Giattina, Sangster, Crosby, & Montijo, 2009).

Many survivors of domestic violence and sexual assault experience ongoing mental health effects such as depression, anxiety, and posttraumatic stress disorder (Dutton, 2009). Group therapy, one-on-one counseling, medication, and trauma-focused cognitive behavioral therapy are all interventions commonly used to help address the mental health issues faced by survivors. In rural communities access to mental health services often is limited. A solution to this barrier used in some rural communities is Internet-supported therapy, in which the therapist and survivor use Skype (or a similar program) to allow audio and visual interaction during their "web-based therapy" session (Barak, Klein, & Proudfoot, 2009, p.4). Similar interventions have been used by nurses to interact with survivors in shelters. A study of this approach found that survivors felt comfortable using the Internet as a medium to meet their health care needs (Mattson, Shearer, & Long, 2002).

Treatment for survivors of child abuse focuses on ensuring the child is currently living in a safe environment, and that a child welfare worker regularly monitors that environment. A common public misconception of the child welfare system is that all child protective services referrals result in a child being removed from a home. To the contrary, in 2008 only 20.9% of abuse victims were placed into foster care (DHHS, 2010). Foster care homes are in short supply in rural communities, and the ones in existence are often overburdened. Some children removed from the home are sent to foster homes outside of their rural community, possibly resulting in a need to change schools and loss of extended support systems. Alternatives to removing a child from the home include providing in-home services and individual and/or family counseling.

Based on a model developed in the 1980s, children's advocacy centers enhance the response to suspected child abuse cases by combining the wisdom and professional knowledge of various investigative agencies and other professionals. Team members come from a multitude of disciplines, such as prosecution, law enforcement, child protective services, and victim and medical advocacy, to conduct forensic interviews and make key decisions on the investigation together. These coordinated efforts can provide the knowledge, skills, and resources to assist alleged child abuse victims and their families (Jacobson, 2002). A children's advocacy center maintains focus on the child and helps ensure that the systems designed to protect children are able to do so effectively. As result of the Victims of Child Abuse Act of 1990, the National Children's Alliance is charged with increasing the number of rural communities using a multidisciplinary approach to child abuse (National Children's Alliance, 2009).

Many survivors of child abuse experience ongoing mental health effects such as depression, anxiety, behavioral outbursts, regression in daily living skills, and posttraumatic stress disorder. Mental health counseling with child abuse survivors uses a cognitive-behavioral therapy approach, and this approach is the most widely researched (Wolfe & Wekerle, 1993). A variant of cognitive-behavioral therapy that is increasingly used with this population is trauma-focused. Unfortunately, adopting research supported practices requires resources not often available in rural communities. Mental health providers and the community need to make a concerted effort to invest time for staff training, supervision, and ongoing monitoring.

Role of the Social Worker

The National Association of Social Workers (2011) has identified interpersonal violence as an area in which there is an overwhelming need for social workers involved in screening, early identification, and intervention. The National Association of Social Workers recommends that assistance take the form of a continuum of services to improve survivors' economic and psychological independence. The field of domestic violence/sexual assault promotes an empowerment approach to working with survivors. Given the geographic and social isolation experienced in rural areas, as well as limited resources, an integrated multilevel feminist approach within a multiservice agency is recommended to best meet the needs of survivors in rural areas (Davis et al., 2001; Websdale, 1998). It is important to remember that providing support to a survivor is a temporary and professional role, and, as dual relationships are often present within rural communities, boundaries must be protected and respected (Boisen & Bosch, 2005).

Social workers in rural communities need training specific to working within a rural community. A survey comparing rural and urban domestic violence service providers found that there are some specific and significant differences between working in these different geographic locations (Eastman & Bunch, 2007). Rural service providers are more likely to experience threats to personal safety and deal with limited resources within their agency and the community, and they will more frequently assume multiple roles when working with clients (Landsman, 2002). States with large rural areas, such as Montana, typically have social workers who perform functions such intake and assessment. Ideally, when a child is referred to child protective services regarding allegations of abuse, specialized units are used for intake, screening, investigation, and assessment of child abuse and neglect cases, but this is not always the case. Rural child protective service agencies may have generic caseworkers who perform investigations along with other functions (DHHS, 2010). A worker may feel additional stress related to working in multiple roles, so the rural social worker needs to pay special attention to balancing responsibilities and seeking help as needed. A study of rural child welfare workers found that efficacy and job satisfaction were important factors in reducing staff turnover rates (Strolin-Goltzman, Auerbach, McGowan, & McCarthy, 2008).

Additionally, social workers need to understand the societal norms of the communities in which they work. In a study of rural social workers, almost all of the respondents reported that they included "cultural information (the knowledge, information and beliefs that members of a community share)" in their daily practice (Saltman, Gumpert, Allen-Kelly, & Zubryzcki, 2004, p.525). Some of the rural cultural norms that were reported by more than two thirds of the social workers in the study included "slower pace of life; the importance of informal communication, suspicion of outsiders; suspicion of government; and pride in local history" (Saltman et al., 2004, p.526). Within many rural communities, maintaining the family is a strong value, and survivors may be more likely to remain living in an abusive relationship. Advocates need to understand the cultural norms related to survivors' decision-making processes and respect their choices.

Conclusion

Survivors of interpersonal abuse living in rural communities face many challenges to accessing needed support and services. The social worker in a rural community who seeks to advocate for survivors also faces multiple challenges and will likely be required to serve in multiple roles. In part, the role of the rural social work advocate is outreach and education regarding the realities of interpersonal violence and the needs of survivors. To ensure that needed supports are available for survivors, the social work advocate needs to develop strong working relationships with a broad range of community-based agencies, organizations, and the legal systems and engage those groups in creative planning to overcome barriers to service delivery. Additionally, the social work advocate in a rural setting needs to understand the cultural norms about interpersonal violence in that particular community and be supportive of survivors in their decision making and future planning.

References

Albrecht, D. E., Albrecht, C. M., & Albrecht, S. L. (2000). Poverty in nonmetropolitan America: Impacts of industrial, employment, and family structure variables. *Rural Sociology, 65,* 87–103.

Bachman, R. (1992). *Crime victimization in city, suburban, and rural areas: A national crime victimizations survey report.* Washington, DC: U.S. Department of Justice.

Barak, A., Klein, B., & Proudfood, J. G. (2009). Defining Internet-supported therapeutic interventions. *Annuals of Behavioral Medicine, 38,* 4–17.

Barusch, A. S. (2009). *Foundations of social policy: Social justice in human perspective,* 3rd ed. Belmont, CA: Brooks/Cole.

Bassuk, E., Dawson, R., & Huntington, N. (2006). Intimate partner violence in extremely poor women: Longitudinal patterns and risk markers. *Journal of Family Violence, 21,* 387–399.

Boba, R., & Lilley, D. (2008). Violence Against Women Act (VAWA) funding: A nationwide assessment of effects on rape and assault. *Violence Against Women, 15*(2), 168–185.

Boisen, L. S., & Bosch, L. A. (2005). Dual relationships and rural social work: Is there a rural code? In. L. H. Ginsberg (Ed.). *Social work in rural communities,* 4th ed. (pp. 189–203). Alexandria, VA: CSWE Press.

Bosch, K., & Bergen, M. B. (2006). The influence of supportive and nonsupportive persons in helping rural women in abusive partner relationships become free from abuse. *Journal of Family Violence, 21,* 311–320.

Centers for Disease Control and Prevention (CDC). (2009). *Intimate partner violence: Definitions.* Retrieved from http://cdc.gov/ViolencePrevention/intimatepartnerviolence/defintions.html

Centers for Disease Control and Prevention (CDC). (2010). *Youth risk behavior surveillance–United States, 2009. Morbidity & Mortality Report 59,* SS-5. Retrieved from http://www.cdc.gov/mmwr/pdf/ss/ss5905.pdf

Cho, H., & Wilke, D. J. (2005). How has the violence against women act affected the response of the criminal justice system to domestic violence? *Journal of Sociology and Social Welfare, 32*(4), 125–139.

Conyers, J. (2007). The 2005 reauthorization of the violence against women act: Why Congress acted to expand protections to immigrant victims. *Violence Against Women, 13,* 457–468.

Cook-Craig, P. G., Lane, K. G., & Siebold, W. L. (2010). Building the capacity of states to ensure inclusion of rural communities in state and local primary violence prevention planning. *Journal of Family Social Work, 13,* 326–342. doi:10.1080/10522158.2010.492498.

Costello, E., Erkanli, A., Fairbank, J. A., & Angold, A. (2002). The prevalence of potentially traumatic events in childhood and adolescence. *Journal of Traumatic Stress, 15*(2), 99–112. doi:10.1023/A:1014851823163.

Cox, C., Kotch, J. B., & Everson, M. D. (2003). A longitudinal study of modifying influences in the relationship between domestic violence and child maltreatment. *Journal of Family Violence, 18*(1), 5–17.

Davis, K., Taylor, B., & Furniss, D. (2001). Narrative accounts of tracking the rural domestic violence survivors' journey: A feminist approach. *Health Care for Women International, 22,* 333–347.

Davis, M. F. (1999). The economics of abuse: How violence perpetuates women's poverty. In R. A. Brandwein (Ed.), *Battered women, children, and welfare reform: The ties that bind* (pp.17–30). Thousand Oaks, CA: Sage.

DeKeseredy, W. S., & Joseph, C. (2006). Separation and/or divorce sexual assault in rural Ohio: Preliminary results of an exploratory study. *Violence Against Women, 12,* 301–311.

Department of Justice, Bureau of Justice Statistics. (2009). *Homicide trends in the United States.* Retrieved from http://www.ojp.usdoj.gov/homicide/tables/initimateestabl.htm

Dutton, M. A. (2009). Pathways linking intimate partner violence and posttraumatic disorder. *Trauma, Violence, & Abuse, 10*(3), 211–224.

Eastman, B. J., & Bunch, S. G. (2007). Providing services to survivors of domestic violence: A comparison of rural and urban service provider perceptions. *Journal of Interpersonal Violence, 22,* 465–473.

Feyen, C. (1989). Battered rural woman: An exploratory study of domestic violence in a Wisconsin county. *Wisconsin Sociologist, 26,* 17–32.

Fisher, B. S., Cullen, F. T., & Turner, M. G. (2000). *The sexual victimization of college women.* Washington, DC: U.S. Department of Justice.

Gavin, M. N. (2009). Intimate partner violence in Appalachia: Examining women's experiences with community support. *Dissertation Abstracts International, A: The Humanities and Social Sciences, 69,* 3340.

Graham, K., Bernards, S., Wilsnack, S. C., & Gmel, G. (2011). Alcohol may not cause partner violence but it seems to make it worse: A cross national comparison of the relationship between alcohol and severity of partner violence. *Journal of Interpersonal Violence, 26,* 1503–1523. doi:10.1177/0886260510370596.

Grama, J. L. (2000). Women forgotten: Difficulties faced by rural victims of domestic violence. *American Journal of Family Law, 14,* 173–189.

Grossman, S. F., Hinkley, S., Kawalski, A., & Margrave, C. (2005). Rural versus urban victims of violence: The interplay of race and region. *Journal of Family Violence, 20*(2), 71–81.

Jacobson, M. (2002). Local realities: A frontier perspective on child protection team practice. *Child Welfare, 81,* 737–755.

Johnson, M., & Elliot B. A. (1997). Domestic violence among family practice patients in midsized and rural communities. *Journal of Family Practice, 44,* 391–401.

Kilpatrick, D., & McCauley, J. (2009). *Understanding national rape statistics.* Retrieved from http://new.vawnet.org/Assoc_Files_VAWnet/AR_RapeStatistics.pdf

Krauss, C. (2008). *Rural U.S. takes worst hit as gas tops $4 average.* Retrieved from http://www.nytimes.com

Krishnan, S. P., Hilbert, J. C., & McNeil, K. (2002). *Understanding domestic violence in multiethnic rural communities: A focus on collaborations among the courts, the law enforcement agencies, and the shelters.* Retrieved from http://www.ncjrs.gov/pdffiles1/nij/grants/191863.pdf

Krishnan, S. P., Hilbert, J. C., & VanLeeuwen, D. (2001). Domestic violence and help-seeking behaviors among rural women: Results from shelter-based study. *Family Community Health, 24*(1), 28–38.

Landsman, M. J. (2002). Rural child welfare practice from an organization-in-environment perspective. *Child Welfare, 81,* 791–819.

Lewis, S. (2003). *Sexual assault in rural communities.* Retrieved from http://www.vawnet.org

Lichtenstein, B., & Johnson, I. M. (2009). Older African American women and barriers to reporting domestic violence to law enforcement in the rural deep south. *Women & Criminal Justice, 19*(4), 286–305.

Logan, T. K., Walker, R., Cole, J., Ratliff, S., & Leukefeld, C. (2003). Qualitative differences among rural and urban intimate violence victimization experiences and consequences: A pilot study. *Journal of Family Violence, 18*(2), 83–92.

Macy, R. J., Giattina, M., Sangster, T. H., Crosby, C., & Montijo, N. J. (2009). Domestic violence and sexual assault services: Inside the black box. *Aggression and Violent Behavior, 14,* 359–373.

Margolin, G. (1998). Effects of domestic violence on children. In P. K. Trickett & C. J. Schellenback (Eds.), *Violence against children in the family and the community* (pp.57–102). Washington, DC: American Psychological Association.

Marshall, J., Huang, H., & Ryan, J. P. (2011). Intergenerational families in child welfare: Assessing needs and estimating permanency. *Children & Youth Services Review, 33,* 1024–1030. doi:10.1016/j.childyouth.2011.01.004.

Mattson, S., Shearer, N., & Long, C. (2002). Exploring telehealth opportunities in domestic violence shelters. *Journal of the American Academy of Nurse Practitioners, 14*(10), 465–469. doi: 10.1111/j.1745-7599.2002.tb00077.x.

National Association of Social Workers. (2011). *The social work response to domestic violence.* Retrieved from http://socialworkers.org/pressroom/events/domestic_violence/response.asp

National Children's Alliance. (2009). *Child advocacy: Putting the needs of child abuse victims first.* Retrieved from http://www.nationalchildrensalliance.org

National Coalition Against Domestic Violence. (2011). *The problem.* Retrieved from http://www.ncadv.org/learn/TheProblem.php

O'Keefe, M. (1995). Predictors of child abuse in martially violence families. *Journal of Interpersonal Violence, 10,* 3–25.

Paul, L. A., Gray, M. J., Elhai, J. D., Massad, P. M., & Stamm, B. H. (2006). Promotion of evidence-based practices for child traumatic stress in rural populations: Identification of barriers and promising solutions. *Trauma, Violence, & Abuse, 7*(4), 260–273. doi: 10.1177/152483800629252.

Ross, S. M. (1996). Risk of physical abuse to children of spouse-abusing parents. *Child Abuse & Neglect, 20,* 589–598.

Ruback, B. R., & Menard, K. S. (2001). Rural-urban differences in sexual victimization and reporting: Analyses using UCR and crisis center data. *Criminal Justice and Behavior, 28*(2), 131–155.

Saltman, J., Gumpert, J., Allen-Kelly, K., & Zubrzycki, J. (2004). Rural social work practice in the United States and Australia: A comparison. *International Social Work, 47,* 515–531.

Saltzman, L. E., Fanslow, J. L., McMahon, P. M., & Shelley, G. A. (2002). *Intimate partner violence surveillance: Uniform definitions and recommended data elements, version 1.0.* Retrieved from http://www.cdc.gov/ncipc/pub-res/ipv_surveillance/initimate.htm

Shepherd, J. (2001). Where do you go when it's 40 below? Domestic violence among rural Alaska native women. *Affilia: Journal of Women & Social Work, 16,* 488–510.

Slovak, K., & Singer, M. I. (2002). Children and violence: Findings and implications from a rural community. *Child & Adolescent Social Work Journal, 19*(1), 35–56.

Straus, M. A., & Gelles, R. J. (1990). *Physical violence in American families: Risk factors and adaptations to violence in 8,145 families.* New Brunswick, NJ: Transaction Publishers.

Strolin-Goltzman, J., Auerbach, C., McGowan, B. G., & McCarthy, M. L. (2008). The relationship between organizational characteristics and workforce turnover among rural, urban, and suburban public child welfare system. *Administration in Social Work, 32*(1), 77–91. doi: 10.1300/J147v32n01_06.

Templeman, S. B., & Mitchell, L. (2002). Challenging the one-size-fits-all myth: Findings and solutions from a statewide focus group of rural social workers. *Child Welfare, 81,* 757–772.

Tjaden, P., & Thoennes, N. (2000). *Extent, nature, and consequences of intimate partner violence: Findings from the national violence against women survey.* Retrieved from http://www.ojp.usdoj.gov/nij/pubs-sum/181867.htm

Tolan, P., Gorman-Smith, D., & Henry, D. (2006). Family violence. *Annual Review of Psychology, 57,* 557–583.

Towns, A. J., & Adams, P. J. (2009). Staying quiet or getting out: Some ideological dilemmas faced by women who experience violence from male partners. *British Journal of Social Psychology, 48,* 735–754. doi:10.1348/014466608X398762.

Trokel, M., Waddimba, A., Griffith, J., & Sege, R. (2006). Variation in the diagnosis of child abuse in severely injured infants. *Pediatrics, 117,* 722–728.

Ulbrich, P.M., & Stockdale, J. (2002). Making family planning clinics an empowerment zone for rural battered women. *Women & Health, 35*(2), 83–100.

U.S. Census Bureau (2010). *Poverty: 2008 and 2009 American Community.* Retrieved from http://www.census.gov/prod/2010pubs/acsbr09-1.pdf

U.S. Department of Health and Human Services (DHHS), Administration on Children, Youth and Families. (2010). *Child maltreatment 2008.* Washington, DC: Government Printing Office.

U.S. Department of Health and Human Services (DHHS), Office on Women's Health. (2011). *Violence against women.* Retrieved from http://www.womenshealth.gov/violence-against-women/laws-on-violence-against-women/.

Van Hightower, N. R., & Gorton, J. (2002). A case study of community-based responses to rural woman battering. *Violence Against Women, 8,* 845–872.

Vidales, G. (2010). Arrested justice: The multifaceted plight of immigrant Latinas who faced domestic violence. *Journal of Family Violence, 25,* 533–544. doi:10.1007/s10896-010-9309-5.

Websdale, N. (1998). *Rural woman battering and the justice system: An ethnography.* Thousand Oaks, CA: Sage Publications.

Websdale, N. S., & Johnson, B. (1998). An enthnostatistical comparison of the forms and levels of woman battering in urban and rural areas of Kentucky. *Criminal Justice Review, 23*(2), 161–196.

Weissman, D. M. (2007). The personal is political—and economic: Rethinking domestic violence. *Brigham Young University Law Review, 2007*(2), 387–450.

Wolfe, D., & Wekerle, C. (1993). Treatment strategies for child physical abuse and neglect: A critical progress report. *Clinical Psychology Review, 13*(6), 473–500. doi:10.1016/0272-7358(93)90043-L.

18   Rural Health Care: *Access, Disparities, and Opportunities*

SUZIE CASHWELL AND SAUNDRA STARKS

The focus on national health care seems to be rising to new heights in a bubbling caldron of chaos and confusion. As this happens, attention should be drawn to health care in rural areas. Is there a crisis? How do rural areas measure up? Health care social workers have a variety of resources and a myriad of challenges that lead to opportunities in rural areas. Social workers practice in a variety of health care settings, such as hospitals, home health care, hospice, mental health, public health, and chronic care settings. Social workers are prepared to practice in the health care setting due to "their broad perspective on the range of physical, emotional, and environmental factors that have an effect on the well-being of individuals and communities" (National Association of Social Workers, 2005, p. 6). This generalist approach, which is intrinsic to social work, is grounded in systems theory and is especially valuable for rural health care.

Many people envision rural areas as "clean country living," where people live longer, free of pollution and the hectic pace of city life. However, in reality the long-term health (physical and mental) of rural citizens does not lead to an idyllic existence. According to the Agency on Healthcare Research and Quality, a unit of the U.S. Department of Health and Human Services, almost one in three adults living in rural America is in poor to fair health, with nearly 50% having at least one major chronic illness (Machlin & Kirby, 2009). However, individuals living in rural areas have less contact with physicians and mental health providers per year, on average, than their urban counterparts. Given these realities, social workers in rural areas have a multitude of opportunities to affect individuals, families, and rural communities.

Before exploring the challenges, resources, and opportunities for rural social workers in the health care arena, two terms need to be clarified. First, *health care* is a broad construct, which ranges in definition. *Health* emphasizes physical, social, and mental well-being (Harvey, 2009). For the purpose of this chapter, health care includes physical, mental, and oral care provided by educated and licensed professionals. This holistic approach provides a comprehensive picture of the rural health landscape. Second, what constitutes *rural*? How is it determined? Rurality is measured a variety of ways in the literature (Belanger & Stone, 2008; Cashwell & Just 2008; Cashwell & McNeece, 2000; Ginsberg, 2005; Scales & Streeter, 2003). For the purpose of this chapter, *rural* is defined as a continuum ranging from the smallest of communities to the least urban Metropolitan Statistical Area status communities (for more details refer to Chapter 1). Each community presents characteristics that are general and specific to issues of rural health care.

As challenges and resources are detailed, a framework can be applied that will analyze the interconnectedness of these challenges and resources in rural communities. Using the model of force field analysis (Lewin, 1951), social workers can identify opportunities to move toward a more adequate health care system in rural areas (see Figure 1). With force field analysis, helping forces (resources) can be identified, which will move the agenda toward the ideal status (adequate rural health care), as well as the restraining forces (challenges), which are maintaining the current status (current health care crisis).

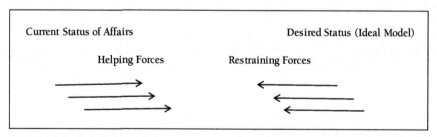

FIGURE 1   Force field analysis.

Elements of the framework represent energies that block progress or support the identification, development, and strengthening of resources to progress toward an ideal status. As we consider this framework (see Figure 1), a template for social work, integrated practice which includes collaboration, mobilization, and prevention (Parsons, Jorgensen, & Hernandez, 1994), becomes a critical part of intervening in the rural health care crisis.

An analysis of rural health care dynamics (see Figure 2) reveals challenges and strengths in moving toward an ideal health care status. These dynamics lead to opportunities for social workers to shift the balance between the helping forces and the restraining forces.

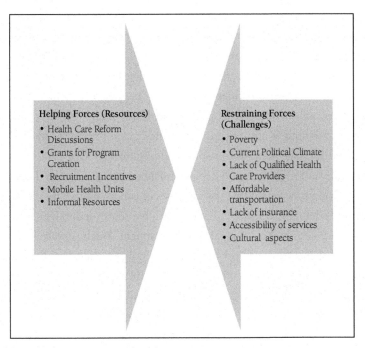

Helping Forces (Resources)
- Health Care Reform Discussions
- Grants for Program Creation
- Recruitment Incentives
- Mobile Health Units
- Informal Resources

Restraining Forces (Challenges)
- Poverty
- Current Political Climate
- Lack of Qualified Health Care Providers
- Affordable transportation
- Lack of insurance
- Accessibility of services
- Cultural aspects

FIGURE 2   Ideal rural health care.

Challenges

It is well-established that rural areas have higher rates of poverty than urban and suburban communities. Mueller (2009) stated "the causal connection between poverty and poor health status is well established" (p. 11). Beyond poverty, several barriers or restraining forces exist that make it difficult for rural Americans to access adequate health care. These barriers can be categorized into four areas: availability, accessibility, acceptability, and the arena (community setting). Although interrelated, these factors represent unique challenges to the recipient of care and the social work provider.

Availability

One challenge in rural areas is inadequately staffed resources. Rural Americans make up more than 20% of the population, whereas less than 9% of doctors, 10% of psychologists and psychiatrists, and 20% of social workers practice in rural America (Ziller, Coburn, & Yousefian, 2006). More than 65% of rural Americans receive mental health services from their primary physicians. Primary physicians may not have as much training and experience with differential diagnoses of complex mental health issues. With the rapidly developing psychotropic medications, primary care physicians may not be able to stay current with specialized knowledge regarding the management of these drugs. Physicians are only one aspect of comprehensive behavioral health intervention. The federal government has identified areas of health care provider inadequacies. Physicians, psychologists, and social workers are encouraged to practice in these areas. However, in a study examining recruitment and retention of primary care physicians in rural Health Professional Shortage Areas, Pathman, Konrad, Dann, and Koch (2004) found that recruitment was the challenge to keeping qualified practitioners in these areas.

The waiting time or waiting list for services can be quite long. Belanger and Stone (2008) found that the waiting list was a barrier for more than 40% of rural children and teens seeking mental health treatment. Due to the lack of primary caregivers, patients may wait 3–4 hours in rural walk-in clinics. In other rural areas they may be denied services entirely for lack of insurance or ability to pay.

According to Shah, Rajasekaran, Sheahan, Wimbush, and Karuza (2008), rural areas face a unique challenge because many first responders are volunteers and, although they may have good intentions, might be poorly trained and supervised. However, many small areas continue to train volunteers. Given the remote areas to which the professional responders have to travel, the availability of a volunteer could make the difference between life and death.

Roh (2007) suggests that rural health care patients may by-pass local hospitals, due to lack of available services or perceived lack of services. Patients who are dealing with cancer, for example, may bypass their local hospital for a regional or tertiary hospital to receive services that the local hospital may not have the equipment or knowledge to address (Hunter & West, 2010; McGrail & Humphreys, 2009; Roh, 2007, Tai, Porell, & Adams, 2005). This bypass of services becomes a complex issue. Patients who have bypassed local hospitals continue to stay away from local services (Roh, 2007). This creates issues of sustainability for many small hospitals.

The lack of qualified professionals in disciplines other than social work provides the social worker with a unique challenge to be transdisciplinary. Rural social workers find themselves with the need to understand health-care related terminology, techniques, and interventions that may be beyond the scope of their education and training.

Accessibility

Accessibility is a multifaceted barrier. The issues of transportation and proximity are familiar challenges to social workers in rural areas. Cultural concerns add to the barrier of adequate service provision (Quandt et al., 2009). The final issue of cost of care and insurance is not unique to rural areas, although individuals in rural areas are less likely to have health care insurance than those in urban areas. This cost issue, coupled with the fact that rural areas have a higher population of working poor, provides unique concerns for social workers.

Transportation. Transportation has long been identified as a barrier for most services in rural areas, including health care services. "Many rural residents with mental health problems must travel prohibitive distances to access care" (Bischoff, Hollist, Smith, & Flack, 2004, p. 79). Where there is no mass transit system, services are often located outside the patient's neighborhood. Other factors include rising costs of gasoline, reliability of transportation, and costs of operating a vehicle. When direct costs such as gas, insurance, depreciation, finance charges, routine maintenance, and repairs are considered, it becomes clear how personal transportation is the most expensive form of transit for an individual.

Proximity. Many researchers (Belanger & Stone, 2008; McGrail & Humphreys, 2009; Roh 2007; Shen & Hsia, 2010; Wood 2008) have focused on the issue of proximity of services in rural areas. Shen and Hsia (2010) found that individuals accessing emergency departments have to drive 26 minutes longer than a decade ago. Although 26 minutes may not seem long, it is a matter of life or death when the presenting condition is stroke, heart attack, or traumatic accident.

Belanger and Stone (2008) found that distance was a barrier for many young people in rural counties seeking substance abuse treatment. Most services are offered only in larger communities. After House Bill 100 (privatizing of mental health care) became law in Georgia, many of the small behavioral services offices closed. These offices moved to more urbanized areas. As a result, individuals could no longer walk to get services. Those in outlying areas have to drive additional miles to reach services. Given the findings of Shen and Hsia (2010) of 26 additional minutes to reach emergency rooms, one wonders if distance is similar for mental health services.

Cultural concerns. Cultural considerations, which may be overlooked, are restraining forces. For example, in communities with higher levels of Hispanic populations, Shen and Hsia (2010) found that the emergency services were at a greater risk of deterioration in regard to the facility and provision of health care. Thus, rural areas, which have higher levels of migrant workers, tend to require more travel time to an emergency room than areas with lower numbers of migrant workers. In addition, there are limitations in the traditional health care systems with diverse groups (Siegrist, 2011). For example, Villabla (2007) indicated that urban and rural Latino/a youth experience high rates of health disparities.

The U.S. Department of Health and Human Services and Health Resources and Services Administration indicate that these barriers are greater with minority individuals. More than 15% of the minority population live in rural areas and make up more than 30% of the individuals living in rural poverty. Nelson (2002) stated "Racial and ethnic disparities in health care exist even when insurance status, income, age and severity of conditions are comparable" (p. 666). This creates barriers beyond affordability and availability of qualified professionals. For example, one group, migrant workers, has issues with consistent care, as well as language barriers.

Cost/Insurance. Individuals in rural areas are less likely to have health insurance for a variety of reasons, including part-time or seasonal work, low paying jobs with no benefits, poverty, and cost of health care (Fordyce, Chen, Doescher, & Hart, 2007; Ziller, Coburn, & Yousefian, 2006). Even with insurance, the copay and type of insurance can create a barrier to obtaining quality services. In addition, mental health insurance access, parity, and stigmatization may create significant barriers.

Individuals employed in low-wage jobs may be at risk of severe impoverishment, due to medical crises and low social capital (Gringeri, 2008). Such individuals in rural areas tend to be in service positions, which pay minimum wage and provide no health care benefits. Workers who are able to handle the daily living cost are often one medical visit away from absolute poverty. Butler (2006) concludes that the elderly population in rural areas uses significant portions of its fixed incomes on health care, even if individuals have Medicare (which requires the individual to pay a percentage of the cost). For example, an elderly woman who pays approximately $80 per month for her Medicare was turned away from a doctor recently. The medical staff explained that the physician was not taking new Medicare patients. In rural areas, where the numbers of physicians are limited, doctors who are not accepting new Medicare patients complicate the matter further.

Acceptability

Although mental health services have long faced issues of stigmatization, physical health care services face stigmatization regarding the quality of health care as well. Health care services in rural areas are often perceived as inadequate and inferior. Attitudes often prevail that are cultural and generationally passed down, which prohibit using such health care facilities and products. Rural residents tend to view behavioral and mental health through the lens of stigmatization (Helfinger & Christens 2006; Sawyer, Gale, & Lambert 2006). Pullman and Heflinger (2009) found that rural judges were less likely to use substance abuse referral services, due to the courts' perception of the inadequacy of care. Distance from treatment may "increase the perceived stigma of therapy" (Bischoff et al., 2004, p. 188), whereas other rural patients may operate under the assumption that "better health care quality is available at bigger hospitals with more health care technology" (Roh, 2007, p. 77).

> In urban areas people encountering each other on the street generally do not know each other's mental or physical health history; however, in rural areas, it is not uncommon for everyone in town to have some knowledge about a person's condition. (Manning & Van Pelt, 2005, p. 261)

The fish bowl phenomenon (Cashwell & Just, 2008) exacerbates the issues with acceptability of health care and mental health services. The phenomenon of everyone seeming to know what everyone is doing in rural areas often interacts with the historical notion of health stigmas to prevent rural individuals from seeking services.

Arena

The arena for understanding the restraining forces in adequate health care delivery needs to be viewed from the perspective of the community. The unique barriers in rural communities are exacerbated by the impoverishment of many rural areas. This arena includes economic challenges, toxic dumps, landfills, pesticides, and drug manufacturing. Rural areas have commonly been sought out as convenient places to create toxic dumps and/or landfills. Often, community residents are not informed of the potential health hazards.

There are other economic challenges besides the availability of jobs or the availability of health insurance. When a young mother has to take off work to care for a sick family member, the loss of wages can be economically disabling (Ontai, Sano, Hatton, & Conger, 2008). When lack of access to birth control produces increased family sizes, even working families can become the working poor.

Where there were once fields of growing tobacco, corn, and peanuts with all the pesticides and chemicals, there are now homes, wells, and septic tanks. Rios and Meyer (2006) indicated that residents' health is endangered by exposure to pesticides. Beyond pesticides, they concluded that gastrointestinal illnesses were negatively affected by practices such as keeping garbage on the property for more than a week (not uncommon in rural areas), and by infrastructure issues such as outdoor toilets or inadequate plumbing.

According to Van Gundy (2006), youth in rural areas abuse alcohol at higher rates than urban youth, whereas adults in rural areas tend to have a greater problem with methamphetamine (meth) use. Rural areas, by their very nature, allow for the manufacturing of drugs. Over the last decade there has been an increase in meth labs, as well as marijuana fields. Remote roads and abandoned barns provide a natural location to manufacture drugs without detection. The space between "neighbors" also increases the likelihood that these activities will go undetected. National Public Radio (2004) indicated that meth labs in rural areas have increased by more than 800%. Rural areas, which once faced issues with illegal manufacturing of alcohol (moonshine), now face issues with manufacturing of meth and marijuana.

Resources

A critical part of a force field analysis is to determine the forces or resources that strengthen movement toward the ideal of adequate health care. Resources are considered elements that are supportive and enhance the potential of attaining adequate health care. Included in this group of elements for rural areas would be education; prevention; primary, secondary, and tertiary interventions; health care funding; and formal and informal support services. Although it is easy to quickly focus on the lack of formal resources in most rural areas, a brief exploration reveals informal resources as potential aids. In addition, the arena of rural areas also provides adaptability, which is often an invisible helping force.

Formal Resources

Government focus on rural health care issues has led to the establishment of rural centers, some of which function as clearing houses. They provide information on a variety of services such as education, networking, and brokering of services. Other rural networks are developed around services to a potential age group, such as senior citizens. Senior citizen centers and programs, such as Meals on Wheels, try to address social and health needs of older rural adults.

Many rural areas have rural health clinics. From Hoonah, AK, to Au Gres, MI, to Islesboro, ME, rural clinics are paid for through federal and state funding. An entire listing can be found at http://www.raconline.org. The Rural Assistance Center, described on this website, provides information on resources and grants for rural communities.

Research grants with universities provide resources for offering services to rural individuals. The National Institute on Aging funded Project to Enhance Aged Rural Living (Kaufman, Scorgin, Burgio, Morthland, & Ford, 2007) to research the effect of cognitive behavioral therapy on rural elderly caregivers. They were provided 10 sessions of cognitive behavioral therapy in their homes. Social workers traveled more than 1 hour each way, in some cases, to provide in-home services.

Evans and colleagues (2008) used school-linked mental health services to provide assistance in rural Florida. This partnership was between University of Florida's psychology department and local rural schools. Projects are often funded to address specific groups, such as grandparents raising grandchildren (Gidding & Cashwell, 1999; King, Kropf, Perkins, Sessley, & Lepore, 2009) or caregivers of the chronically ill (Cashwell & Cleveland, 1999).

Mobile health units are another example of formal resources for rural communities. In south central Kentucky, grants and donor gifts provided for a traveling unit that offers preventive, promotional, and treatment services to the medically underserved and uninsured of rural Kentucky. The target area is 10 counties of the local Area Development District. Services include dental cleaning and screenings; health screenings for diabetes, hearing, hypertension, speech, vision, and bone density; child safety seat inspections; and the provision of health education materials. In northeastern Alabama the Health Services Clinic—a private nonprofit organization—provides services to rural areas (Wood, 2008). The clinic uses a mobile unit to provide a wide variety of health and mental health services in the home, including free medications.

Another possible formal resource in rural communities is telecommunications (Bischoff et al., 2004). Although e-therapy and e-medicine might seem like science fiction to many, advances in technology are allowing rural practitioners to access services and specialists in other areas. Some regional hospitals partner with tertiary hospitals via telecommunications.

Informal Resources

Gringeri (2008) discusses the concept of social capital as a resource for battling the health care crisis. This concept is discussed as a safety net for poor and rural people. It is a personal exchange and sharing of resources. Given the culture of rural people, there is a tendency to create social capital. There is a tendency to be helpful, neighborly, and reciprocal.

Rural churches have provided many resources throughout time that assist in health care for rural residents. Spiritual aspects for various ethnic groups are considered sustaining forces (Starks & Whitlock, 2010). This is true for rural areas as well. Some rural churches are beginning to recognize the relationship between health, physical and emotional needs, and spirituality. Recently, in one small community more than 20 churches came together to provide a multitude of needs for the area. There were health care screening booths intertwined with the free clothes to give away. Rural churches often have members who will provide transportation to health care appointments. These competencies for organizing resources are often overlooked as a helping force in meeting the health care needs of rural America.

Valued informal resources, considered extremely important to this discussion, are indigenous health interventions, folk healers, and other alternative approaches to traditional health care. The traditional healer (shaman, midwife, herbalist, or religious leader) in rural ethnic communities is becoming somewhat extinct. "Folk healing practices may be beneficial to the patient and may be socially cohesive; healing ritual and sessions frequently involve the patient and patient's families and neighbors" (Cook, 2011, p. 28)

Arena

Rural areas, although diverse, have some common features that provide adaptability in the face of restraining forces. Rural areas tend to be closed communities, which are conservative by nature (Cashwell & Starks, 2003). These communities tend to respond by assisting others when a need is identified. According to Cashwell and Just (2008), there are four key values in rural areas: parochialism, patriotism, fundamentalism, and fatalism. These values combine to produce the adaptability of hard-working individuals with a strong sense of charity. "Friends and neighbors in rural areas typically provide services that private and not-for-profit associations provide in urban areas, such as child care" (Cashwell & Just, 2008, p. 346).

Opportunities

Social workers who are trained in the generalist perspective and skilled in multilevel interventions understand issues of context and psychosociophysical connections and can bring critical resources (helping forces) and skills together to meet the challenges (restraining forces) in rural health care. The following are critical elements needed to intervene with inadequate health care services: mobilization, collaboration, and prevention. These elements translate into roles that are all within the knowledge and skills of integrated social work practitioners (Parson et al., 1994).

Mobilization

One role of the social worker would be mobilizing and organizing informal support systems, while requiring formal support systems to be holistic, flexible, available, and acceptable. Martinez-Brawley (2000) suggested that bringing the community together to address the issues creates the best outcome. This is particularly relevant to maintain the standards of cultural competency. Restrictive health care is a form of oppression directed at the poor, both working and unemployed.

Social workers in rural communities have the opportunity to bring together informal resources, such as mutual aid, church transportation, food giveaways; and formal resources, such as mobile health units and established senior citizen centers. By creating opportunity for mobile health units to use rural isolated churches, social workers can increase the number of individuals receiving quality health care screenings. The use of churches and senior citizen centers reduces the stigma that may be associated with these services or resources.

Collaboration

Collaboration is the process by which two or more individuals, groups, or organizations gather to reach a common goal. This process may provide opportunity to create new helping forces. Mueller (2009) indicated that collaborations are needed to enhance health care. He recommends collaborations between local providers, as well as collaboration between local and regional providers. Social workers are often favorably placed to organize such collaborations because of the interdisciplinary nature of the profession. This collaboration may need to extend to tertiary levels of health care. Roh (2007) suggests rural hospitals become more competitive by building cooperative relationships with larger rural and urban institutions. This could mean an increase in beds, as well as in the scope of services provided.

Social workers can use leadership skills, as well as grant writing skills, to access a variety of funding sources, such as the U.S. Department of Agriculture or the National Institutes of Health. For example, a grant that brings health care screening and intervention to the home of the rural resident or the fields where migrants work would increase the early detection of chronic illness, requiring less expensive and lengthy treatment. These skills, as a part of building collaboration, can create pockets of resources. These are just a few of the myriad ways social workers can collaborate in the health care arena.

Prevention

Prevention is a critical component in making sure the next generation of society does not experience the devastation of inadequate health care. Prevention needs to be multifaceted and multidisciplinary. Prevention includes recruitment and retention of qualified health care providers in all disciplines of education, health care provision, health care literacy, political advocacy, use of technology, and economic and social development.

Recruitment and retention of qualified providers are critical in preventing inadequate health care. Pathman et al. (2004) concludes that "the principal dynamic by which rural shortage areas emerge is simply that too few physicians are recruited" (p. 1,726). This is equally true for social workers. Often, rural residents who attain formal social work education do so in urban settings and do not return home for a multitude of reasons, including job security or compensation. Programs of social work education must find ways to educate social workers in rural settings. Hopefully, this will encourage social workers to remain in underserved areas.

Another aspect of recruitment that needs to be addressed is culturally relevant service providers. According to Nelson (2002), ethnic and racial groups are underrepresented in the pool of service providers. This may be even more prevalent in rural areas. Recruiting social workers who are multilingual should be a priority.

Health care literacy is one opportunity for social workers. "Health care literacy is defined as (a) a patient's level of health knowledge and health-seeking skills and

(b) health providers' level of health knowledge and helping skills" (Carter, 2006, p. xix). Given the basic social work principles of "start where the client is" and "client right to self-determination," social work practitioners in rural areas need to conduct culturally responsive assessments and interventions to the context of the individual and the community. Social workers have the opportunity to build bridges across these two areas of health care literacy. While working with both the patient and the health care provider, a social worker's role as educator becomes paramount.

The enabler role, which includes organizationsl development, social planning, and community education (Parsons et al., 1994), is primary to health care literacy. "The use of community health care workers—such as non-medical personnel who help patients navigate the health care system—as well as multidisciplinary treatment and preventive care teams should be supported" (Nelson, 2002, p. 666). Social workers should be a part of those treatment and preventive teams. They can also address the literacy issue with the development of mandated health promotions and early health assessment. The development of person-centered program materials may increase the literacy of many rural communities.

Political advocacy, which at the very root of the profession, requires the social worker to intervene across practice levels to increase the helping forces needed to achieve adequate health care services. "Social policy makers interested in building a sense of community in the United States should be concerned about the severe shortage of health care in rural areas" (Bettencourt & Molix, 2003, p. 11). Political incentives to change rural health infrastructure need to be addressed as well. "Clearly, accessible health care is likely to influence not only the physical well-being but also the psychological well-being of rural citizens" (Bettencourt & Molix, 2003, p. 2). Any discussion of health care has to include the Patient Protection and Affordable Care Act. This act is considered, by some, the most innovative, far-reaching, and significant health care law since the creation of Medicare and Medicaid in 1965 (Reid, 2009). Although many believe this plan is the wrong direction for the United States, the debate will continue, and social workers must be at the forefront of this movement.

The use of technology is a resource that can be accessed and maximized by social workers for preventive care. Mobile health units, for example, could increase the early identification of health problems. Telemedicine is another example. Bischoff and colleagues (2004) discussed the use of telecommunications as a "promising solution to the inaccessibility of mental-health services in rural communities where more traditional treatment options do not exist" (pp. 180–181). Creating a cyber-infrastructure in rural areas will increase connection to a wider range of services while allowing quicker access to treat illness, decreasing the need for regional and tertiary treatment.

Although not a readily accepted practice, social workers using e-services to bring resources into the rural community may increase access to qualified case management and other health and mental health services. Linking individuals with unique needs to support can be a challenge in rural areas. The new "society," linked by technology, can be one way social workers network and broker services for the most remote locations.

Social change without economic change is ineffective. Along the same lines, economic change without social change is ineffective. This reciprocal relationship provides the foundation for policy intervention. Therefore, economic and social development must happen in tandem. As communities focus on economic development, social workers can advance social development, which should contribute to economic success. Additionally, universal health care across the life span must be addressed. "Health care coverage cannot be left to the voluntary, informal sector of social capital" (Gringeri, 2008, p. 28). This health care coverage must become a part of the social fabric. "A universal health care system covering all ages….might allow us to benefit from the superior health care outcomes of other countries" (Butler, 2006, p. 41).

For a universal health care system to be successful, economic improvement must be addressed. "Improving the economic well-being of a person, household or neighborhood requires policies addressing health care needs that contribute to sustained productivity" (Mueller, 2009, p. 11). Social workers have brokering skills, which are an asset to communities in identifying and developing economic resources. An influx of jobs and services could result from social workers assisting communities in identifying gaps (need assessment) and creating new resources.

Therefore, opportunities for improved and adequate health care services exist through linking the major systems of health care, education, and welfare. Using models of integrated practice, social workers can apply a multilevel approach to research, education, lobbying, brokering, and collaborating to create change in the system. "Rural communities should seize the opportunity to integrate services, thereby improving community mental [and physical] health, which in turn will be the local asset that attracts further economic development" (Mueller, 2009, 12). Social workers need to be active change agents, driving forces to move toward the ideal health care situation for individuals in rural communities.

Conclusion

This chapter explores the resources, challenges, opportunities, and implications for adequate health care reform in rural America. Clearly, the premise is that health care, in general, and rural health care, specifically, are in crisis. From a social work perspective, this creates an opportunity to address the challenges holistically, economically, and politically.

Using a force field analysis framework allows identification of forces needed to sustain, support, and strengthen, as well as forces that serve as barriers and challenges. These forces affect movement toward the ideal status of an adequate health care system for all citizens. This framework establishes a better clarification of the determining forces that hinder and those that promote the potential for adequate health care. Restraining forces, or challenges, were identified as impeding the progress. Helping forces, or resources, were identified as promoting and strengthening the potential for progress. Together, these forces need to be acknowledged and addressed as significant to understanding the dynamics and opportunities of the health care crisis that exists in rural America.

Bischoff and colleagues (2004) suggests that, if the crisis identified in this chapter is left untreated, the consequences could be disastrous health outcomes. Interdisciplinary collaboration, advocacy, health care literacy, treatment transparency, and culturally responsive assessments and service delivery are imperative. Accessibility, availability, and acceptability of services, as discussed in this chapter, need to be broadly defined while continuing the health care debate until coverage is attained for all citizens.

Responding to this health care crisis requires an integrated approach and a "think outside the box" paradigm. The opportunities available for social workers to affect the social, political, and economic systems related to health care are colossal. As agents of change, social workers with integrated practice skills are needed to transform the system of services and improve the overall well-being of rural America. Ultimately, social workers will have the opportunity to assist society in deciding whether health care for all is a "privilege" or a "right."

References

Aisbett, D. L. (2006). Interpretive phenomenological approaches to rural mental health research. *Rural Social Work and Community Practice, 11*, 52–58.

Arcury, T. A., Gesler, W. M., Preisser, J. S., Sherman, J., Spencer, J., & Perin, J. (2005). The effects of geography and spatial behavior on health care utilization among the residents of a rural region. *Health Services Research, 40*(1), 135–155.

Bailey, J. (2004). Health care in rural America: Part 1. *Center for Rural Affairs—A Newsletter Surveying National Events Affecting Rural America.* Retrieved from http://www.cfra.org/news_media/newsletter

Belanger, K., & Stone, W. (2008). The social service divide: Service availability and accessibility in rural versus urban counties and impact on child welfare outcomes. *Child Welfare, 87*(4), 101–124. doi:09–4021/2008/0408.

Bettencourt, B. A., & Molix, L. (2003). Satisfaction with health care and community esteem among rural women. *Analyses of Social Issues and Public Policy, 3*(1), 1–14. doi:10.1111/j.1530-2415.2003.00011.x.

Bischoff, R. J., Hollist, C. S., Smith, C. W., & Flack, P. (2004). Addressing the mental health needs of the rural underserved: Findings from a multiple case study of a behavioral telehealth project. *Contemporary Family Therapy, 26*(2), 179–198.

Butler, S. (2006). Low-income, rural elders' perceptions of financial security and health care costs. *Journal of Poverty, 10*(1), 25–43. doi:10.1300/J134v10n01_02.

Carter, C. S. (2006) Social work and women's health: Resources on health empowerment, advocacy and literacy. Alexandria, VA: CSWE Press.

Cashwell, S. T., & Cleveland, P. H. (1999). Getting the short end of the stick: Family caregivers, professional caregivers, and care receivers in rural America. *Conference Proceedings: The Changing Face of Rural America, The 24th Annual National Institute on Social Work and Human Services in Rural America,* 73–81.

Cashwell, S. T., & Just, M. M. (2008). Rural social work practice. In D. M. DiNitto & C. A. McNeece (Eds.), *Social work issues and opportunities in a challenging profession* (pp. 333–356). Chicago, IL: Lyceum Books.

Cashwell, S. T., & McNeece, C. A. (2000). Smoke and mirrors: The shifting dependency of former rural welfare mothers. *Rural Social Work, 6*(1), 17–25.

Cashwell, S. T., & Starks, S. H. (2003). The culture of rurality: It isn't the Beverly Hillbillies. *Presented at the 28th National Institute on Social Work and Human Services in Rural Areas. Innovative Social Work Practice in Rural Communities: Identifying Needs, Meeting Challenges.* University of New Hampshire, Durham, NH.

Cook, T. H. (2011). Historical factors: Community health nursing context. In M. A. Nies & M. McEwen (Eds), *Community/Public health nursing: Promoting the health of populations,* 5th ed. (pp. 18–34). St. Louise, MO: Elsevier.

Economic Research Service. (2002). *Rural income, poverty, and welfare: Rural poverty.* Retrieved June 28, 2003, from www.ers.usda.gov/Briefing/IncomePovertyWelfare/ruralpoverty/

Economic Research Service. (2003). *Briefing room: Rural population and migration.* Retrieved from www.ers.usda.gov/Briefing/Population/

Evans, G. D., Radunovich, H. L., Cornette, M. M., Wiens B. A., & Roy, A. (2008). Implementation and utilization characteristics of a rural, school-linked mental health program. *Journal of Child and Family Studies, 17*(1), 84–97. doi 10.1007/s10826-007-9148-z.

Evans, R. (2009). A comparison of rural and urban older adults in Iowa on specific markers of successful aging. *Journal of Gerontological Social Work, 52* 423–438. doi: 10.1080/01634370802609197.

Fiske, A., Gatz, M., & Hannell, E. (2005). Rural suicide rates and availability of health care providers. *Journal Community Psychology, 33,* 537–543. doi: 10.1002/jcop.20069.

Folta S. C., Lichtenstein, A. H., Seguin R. A., Goldberg, J. P., Kuder, F. J., & Nelson, M. N. (2009). The strong women-healthy hearts program: Reducing cardiovascular disease risk factors in rural sedentary, overweight and obese midlife and older women. *American Journal of Public Health, 99,* 1271–1277. doi:10.2015/AJPH.2008.145581.

Fordyce, M. A., Chen, F. M., Doescher, M. P., & Hart, L. G. (2007). *2005 physician supply and distribution in rural areas of the United States (Final Report #116).* Seattle, WA: University of Washington.

Giddings, M. M., & Cashwell, S. T. (1999). To grandma's house we go: Providing services to grandparents raising grandchildren in rural America. *Conference Proceedings: The Changing Face of Rural America, The 24th Annual National Institute on Social Work and Human Services in Rural America,* 29–35.

Ginsberg, L. H. (2005). *Social work in rural communities,* 4th ed. Alexandria, VA: Council on Social Work Education.

Gringeri, C. (2008). Cashing in on social capital: Subsidizing low-wage work in Utah's rural areas. *Rural Social Work and Community Practice, 13*(1), 20–30.

Harvey, D. (2009). Conceptualizing the mental health of rural women: A social work and health promotion perspective. *Rural Society, 19,* 353–362.

Helfinger, C. A., & Christens, B. (2006). Rural behavioral health services for children and adolescents: An ecological and community psychology analysis. *Journal of Community Psychology, 34,* 379–400. doi: 10.1002/jcop.20105.

Hunter, L. C., & West, C. (2010). Challenges in achieving positive outcomes for children with complex congenital conditions: Safety and continuity of care. *Health Sociology Review, 19*(1), 86–99. doi: 10.5172/hesr.2010.19.1.086.

Kaufman, A. V., Scorgin, F. R., Burgio, L. D., Morthland, M. P., & Ford, B. K. (2007). Providing mental health services to older people living in rural communities. *Journal of Gerontological Social Work, 48*, 349–365. doi:10.1300/J083v48n03_05.

King, S., Kropf, N. P., Perkins, M., Sessley, L., & Lepore, M. (2009). Kinship care in rural Georgia communities: Responding to needs and challenges of grandparent caregivers. *Journal of Intergenerational Relationships, 7*(4), 225–242. doi: 10.1080/15350770902852369.

Lewin, K. (1951). *Field theory in social science.* New York, NY: Harper and Row.

Machlin, S. R., & Kirby, J. (2009) *Health care in urban and rural areas, combined years 2004-2006. Requests for assistance on health initiatives: Update of content in MEPS Chartbook No. 13.* Retrieved from http://www.ahrq.gov/data/meps/chbook13up.htm

Manning, S. M., & Van Pelt, M. E. (2005). The challenges of dual relationships and care in rural mental health. In L. H. Ginsberg, L. H. (Ed.), *Social work in rural communities,* 4th ed. Alexandria, VA: Council on Social Work Education.

Martinez-Brawley, E. (2000). *Close to home: Human services and the small community.* Washington, DC: NASW Press.

McGrail, M. R., & Humphreys, J. S. (2009). A new index of access to primary care services in rural areas. *Australian and New Zealand Journal of Public Health, 33*(5), 418–423. doi: 10.1111/j.1753-6405.2009.00422.x.

Mueller, K. (2009). Advancing the health and well-being of rural communities. *Policy & Practice, 67*(5), 10–12.

National Association of Social Workers. (2005). *NASW standards for social work practice in health care settings.* Washington, D.C.: NASW Press.

National Public Radio. (2004). *Meth a growing menace in rural America.* Retrieved from http://www.npr.org/templates/story/story.php?storyId=3805074

Nelson, A. (2002). Unequal treatment: Confronting racial and ethnic disparities in health care. *Journal of the National Medical Association, 94*, 666–668. PMCID: PMC2594273.

Ontai, L., Sano, Y., Hatton, H., & Conger, K. J. (2008). Low-income rural mothers' perceptions of parent confidence: The role of family health problems and partner status. *Family Relations, 57*, 324–334. doi: 10.1111/j.1741-3729.2008.00503.x.

Parsons, R. J., Jorgensen, J. D., & Hernandez, S. H. (1994). *The integration of social work education.* Pacific Grove, CA: Brooks Cole.

Pathman, D. E., Konrad, T. R., Dann, R., & Koch, G. (2004). Retention of primary care physicians in rural health professional shortage areas. *American Journal of Public Health, 94*, 1723–1729.

Pullmann, M. D., & Heflinger, C. A. (2009). Community determinants of substance abuse treatment referrals from juvenile courts: Do rural youths have equal access? *Journal of Child & Adolescent Substance Abuse, 18,* 359–378. doi: 10.1080/10678280903185518.

Quandt, S. A, Chen, H., Bell, R. A., Anderson, A. M., Savoca, M. R., Kohrman, T., ... Arcury, T. A. (2009). Disparities in oral health status between older adults in a multiethnic rural community: The rural nutrition and oral health study. *Journal the American Geriatrics Society, 57,* 1369–1375. doi:10.1111/j.1532-5415.2009.02367.x.

Reid, T. R. (2009). *The healing of America: A global quest for better, cheaper and fairer healthcare.* New York, NY: Penquin Press.

Reif, S., Golin, C. E., & Smith, S. R. (2005). Barriers to accessing HIV/AIDS care in North Carolina: Rural and urban differences. *AIDS Care, 77,* 558–565.

Rios, J., & Meyer, P. S. (2006). Associations between health, utilities and practices in rural south Texas: The case of the Nueces county colonias. *101st American Sociological Association Annual Meeting,* Montreal, Quebec.

Roh, C. (2007). Health care utilization by rural patients: What influences hospital choice? *Social Work in Public Health, 23*(1), 75–94. doi:10.13(X)/J523v23n01_05.

Sawyer, D., Gale, J., & Lambert, D. (2006). *Rural and frontier mental and behavioral health care: Barriers, effective policy strategies, best practices.* Waite Park, MN: National Association for Rural Mental Health.

Scales, T. L., & Streeter, C.L (2003). *Rural social work: Building and sustaining community assets.* Pacific Grove, CA: Brooks Cole.

Shah, M. N, Rajasekaran, K., Sheahan, W. D., Wimbush, T., & Karuza, J. (2008). The effect of the Geriatrics Education for Emergency Medical Services Training Program in a rural community. *Journal of the American Geriatrics Society, 56,* 1134–1139. DOI: 10.1111/j.1532-5415.2008.01738.x.

Shen, Y., & Hsia, R. Y. (2010). Changes in emergency department access between 2001 and 2005 among general and vulnerable populations. *American Journal of Public Health, 100,* 1462–1469. doi: 10.2105/AJPH.2009.175828.

Siegrist, B. C. (2011). Family health. In M. A. Nies & M. McEwen (Eds.), *Community/Public health nursing: Promoting the health of populations,* 5th ed. (pp. 379–401). St. Louise, MO: Elsevier.

Starks, S. H., & Whitlock, S. (2010). African American women faculty in predominately White institutions: Health and well-being. In S. R. Moore, R. Alexander, & A. J. Lemelle (Eds.), *Dilemmas of black faculty at U.S. predominately white institutions* (pp. 29–48). Lewsiton, NY: Edwin Mellen Press.

Tai, W-T., Porell, F., & Adams, K. (2005). Hospital choice of rural Medicare beneficiaries: Patient, hospital attributes, and the patient-physician relationship *HSR: Health Service Research, 49:* 1903–1920.

Van Gundy, K. (2006). *Report on rural America: Substance abuse in rural and small town America.* Retrieved from http://www.carseyinstitute.unh.edu/publications/Report_SubstanceAbuse.pdf

Villabla, J. A. (2007). Health disparities among Lationa/o adolescents in urban and rural schools: Educators' perspectives. *Journal of Cultural Diversity, 14*(4), 169–174.

Wong, S. T., Kao, C., Crouch, J. A., & Korenbrot, C. C. (2006). Rural American Indian Medicaid health care services use and health care costs in California. *American Journal of Public Health, 96,* 363–370. doi:10.2105/AJPH.2004.050880.

Wood, S. (2008). Health care services for HIV-positive substance abusers in a rural setting: An innovative program. *Social Work in Health Care, 47*(2), 108–121.

Ziller, E. C., Coburn, A. F., & Yousefian, A. E. (2006). Out-of-pocket health spending and the rural underinsured. *Health Affairs, 25,* 1688–1699.

19 Assessing Clinical Social Work Practice in Rural Mental Health Settings

GLENN STONE AND BILL FREDERICK

Social work practitioners and researchers have long been aware of the special mental health issues that exist for rural Americans and the agencies that work to meet those needs. The prevalence and scope of mental health challenges in rural areas are significant. For example, research has found that rural residents have higher levels of depression, substance abuse, domestic violence, incest, and child abuse than residents of urban areas (Bushy, 1998; Cellucci & Vik, 2001). The problem of substance abuse has been demonstrated to be a critical issue for rural regions, because up to 40% of individuals in rural areas with a mental illness diagnosis also experience a substance abuse disorder (Gogek, 1992). Residents of rural areas have been found to have higher rates of suicide than urban residents. They have also been found to engage in higher levels of behavioral risk factors, such as obesity and smoking (Eberhardt, Ingram, & Makuc, 2001; Eberhardt & Pamuk, 2004). Mental health issues are not limited to adults; rural youths have been found to exhibit higher rates of depression and substance use than urban youths. Substance abuse issues include the use of alcohol, tobacco, methamphetamines, inhalants, marijuana, and cocaine (National Center on Addiction and Substance Abuse, 2000; Substance Abuse and Mental Health Services Administration, 2001). It has also been found that women in rural areas face particular pressures that affect their mental health, including increased risk for abuse, increased isolation, economic instability, and a lack of childcare support; these pressures also have been linked with mood disorders (Boyd & Mackey, 2000; Dimmitt & Davila, 1995).

Challenges for Rural Mental Health Agencies

It seems clear that mental health needs in rural areas are significant. At the same time, the mental health agencies serving these rural populations have their own special set of problems. Obviously, there is the challenge of trying to serve clients with a wide range of psychological issues. This is particularly challenging for rural mental health agencies, because they may lack specialists to serve the many issues presented by rural clients (Harman, Dong, Xu, Ewigman, & Fortney, 2010). Rural agencies also have difficulties recruiting and retaining workers. The insufficient supply of mental health providers results in several problems, as noted by Wagenfeld, Murray, Mohatt, and DeBruyn (1994):

> rural professionals often work in relative isolation and without many of the professional and personal amenities enjoyed in urban settings. Rural practitioners often lack professional peers to consult with on difficult cases and to share evening and weekend emergency coverage; frequently find appropriate continuing education programs inconvenient, inaccessible, or unaffordable; and often feel personally cut off from the cultural, educational, and recreational activities they grew accustomed to during their more urban and university-based training years. (p. 31)

This problem in recruitment and retention of workers affects the quality of services in other ways. Having limited professionals results in high caseloads and the assignment of additional responsibilities, such as administrative tasks. This reduces the time available for services and interagency coordination and contributes to the fragmentation that already exists among substance abuse, mental health, and primary health care providers (Wagenfeld et al., 1994).

Research also indicates that cancellation and no-show rates are particularly high among rural mental health clients (Gale, Shaw, & Hartley, 2010). This can seriously affect the quality of care clients receive, as well as interfere with the revenue stream that rural agencies rely on for fiscal solvency. The causes of these higher cancellation and no-show rates are numerous; however, a primary concern is the potential that clients are not keeping appointments because they may not feel the intervention efforts of their social workers are effective. These lapses in intervention may be connected to a variety of issues, including the challenge of supervision in rural agencies and the limited knowledge clinical social workers may have about evaluative options to improve the therapeutic relationship and subsequent practice outcomes.

Supervision Issues in Rural Agencies

Rural agencies may often lack the resources to provide adequate supervision and continuing education opportunities for clinical staff (Stamm, 2003). Therefore, it may be difficult for mental health practitioners to receive consistent feedback on the quality of their work with clients. Indeed, supervisors may only have time to evaluate the "quality of the paperwork" completed on a client, rather than the "quality of the service." This focus on paperwork and subsequent lack of feedback on treatment quality could seriously hinder the effectiveness of the social worker and his or her intervention efforts.

Roberts, Battaglia, and Epstein (1999) point out that the lack of adequate supervision and self-monitoring of practice can also lead to ethical dilemmas. They note that practitioners in rural settings must commonly serve in a "generalist" capacity. Essentially, clinicians in rural settings may be performing their work with expanded roles, with more autonomy, and with an increased need for specialist support. However, the paradox is that these clinicians may be working in these wide-ranging areas with less training and supervision and fewer resources than their urban counterparts. This issue of working in a wide range of specializations can have critical ethical ramifications, because working outside of one's area of competence in mental health care, except in emergencies, essentially violates ethical norms for the social work professional. Again, this raises the specter of competence. The issue of quality assessment seems especially crucial, as current trends, such as the shift of mental health services into the marketplace and the subsequent emergence of managed care, that have made practice effectiveness and accountability more pressing are considered (Baer, 2001). Given the dearth of time and resources available to the practicing mental health social worker in rural mental health agencies, it seems imperative that social workers establish reliable and valid ways to monitor their own practice to ensure they are engaging in effective intervention activities with their clients. This evaluation of practice also needs to occur in a manner that is neither overly time-consuming nor expensive. It is important that evaluation be feasible.

Role of Practice Assessment for Clinical Social Workers

According to Baer (2001), "the search for quality and effectiveness in social work is ubiquitous and longstanding" (p. 127). She notes that the ability to evaluate practice outcomes is vital to the profession. However, she also points out that, despite the importance of practice evaluation, "no true consensus about methods or measures for evaluating practice has been reached" (Baer, 2001, p. 127). The Council on Social Work Education (2008) believes evaluation is so important that they have included it in their Educational Policy and Accreditation Standards as a required competency of graduating social workers. In Educational Policy 2.1.10(d)—Evaluation standard, it is stated: "social workers critically analyze, monitor, and evaluate interventions" (Council on Social Work Education, 2008, p. 7). Thus, there is sufficient cause to believe that the social work profession believes in the importance of evaluating clinical practice; however, how to go about accomplishing the task may not always be agreed on.

Gardner (2000) notes some of the challenges that exist for social workers in attempting to assess the success of their work. First is how social workers assess their practice in a manner that is consistent with the way they do their work. They actively pursue models of practice that are collaborative, yet many forms of evaluation are not built on a client-centered, or even client-inclusive, model. Practice evaluation that does not focus on collaborative efforts with the client may be a process that is not empowering for the client. Knowledge may be created that does not result in clients gaining the information they need to make significant progress in their work with the clinical social worker. The evaluation efforts may not enhance the therapeutic relationship between social worker and client.

Another challenge is that any effort at practice evaluation needs to demonstrate a level of benefit to the social worker's agency (Gardner, 2000). This may be particularly relevant for efforts by "external" evaluators to set up evaluation plans for a social service agency. External evaluators may not fully understand the type of information that agency-based clinicians need to improve their practice. These evaluations completed externally, again, become a process of looking at paperwork. It might be more helpful if evaluations were conducted and analyzed by the individual practitioners themselves.

Research on Practice Evaluation

Since Eysenck (1952) showed that approximately two thirds of people diagnosed with neuroses recovered without any psychological intervention, there has been a degree of skepticism regarding the effectiveness of all forms of mental health therapy. Despite this skepticism, the field of social work at least has espoused the importance of taking the time and effort to assess clinical social work practice. In fact, in the 1990s there was an "explosion of interest" in practice evaluation strategies, as noted by Martin and Kettner (1997). However, they also point out that this interest seemed to diminish within a short amount of time. Despite a few notable exceptions, "the literature in human services has essentially ignored the concept of accountability over the last two decades" (Martin & Kettner, 1997, p. 17–18). Even though the Council on Social Work Education mandates that practice-based research be covered in the curriculum (Bloom, Fischer, & Orme, 1999), research indicates that social work practitioners have not taken what they learned in the classroom and implemented it in practice.

For example, a recent study by Baker, Stephens, and Hitchcock (2010) surveyed 134 social workers across different social work settings, positions, and level of preparation. The researchers examined the incidence and type of evaluation activity, training received, and barriers related to implementing practice evaluation in the practice setting. They reported that the majority of social workers are not involved in evaluation activities beyond collecting basic statistics.

Thus, it would seem that there may be a "significant 'disconnect' between what is taught in social work education and what is considered good practice in clinical settings" (Wade & Neuman, 2007, p. 52). It is possible that the fault lies in how social workers are taught practice evaluation in academic settings and that social workers intuitively understand this information is not truly connected to quality of care.

Practice Evaluation: What We Do Know

It is time for social workers in rural agencies to speak up for what they know is right—namely, quality of care for clients. So much is known about what works in clinical social work, yet social work practice continues to give full cooperation with what social workers sense is not helpful—namely, tending to the details of the insurance-directed paper work. Research indicates the following:

(1) Involvement of the client is the key ingredient. At this point, it is clear that the more the client is involved in the intervention, the more successful that intervention will be. This is the number one indicator of positive change (Connors & Carroll, 1997).

(2) The client's rating of alliance in the second session is the number one predictor of outcome. In contrast, the therapist's rating of relationship has zero correlation with outcome (Connors & Carroll, 1997).

(3) Early indication of change, as noted by the client, increases the likelihood of longer term change. Similarly, if there is no change by the third session, the possibility of change is greatly decreased. If there is no change by the sixth session, it is highly unlikely change will occur. Change in the way intervention is being pursued is then indicated. (Brown, Dreis, & Nace, 1999).

(4) It is arguable that all therapies are, in fact, "brief therapies," given that most therapy is done in 12 or fewer sessions. (Brown et al., 1999).

(5) People who receive therapy are better off than 80% of those that do not receive help (Wampold, 2001).

The question then is, "How do we reliably and validly know when these events transpire?" A social worker once asked one of the authors, "Are we just selling snake oil?" His question stated, in a dramatic way, what is often wondered about a specific client at a specific time: "Is this helping?" Much like the point of zero correlation with therapist opinion, the only way a social worker can know if what he or she is doing is helping is by obtaining reliable and ongoing feedback from each specific client at a specific times.

Similarly, there is a great difference in therapist performance. Clinical social workers, at the low end, are 20% effective and, at the high end, 70% effective (Wampold, 2001). There is no evidence that clinical social workers are any more or any less effective doing psychotherapy than psychologists or psychiatrists. Where do you want to be on this continuum? It is of interest that 80% of therapists rate themselves above average (Walfish, McAllister, & Lambert, Unpublished manuscript), which is self-evidently not the case. The answer to this question, then, is in contrast to wondering if what social workers are doing is helping. The key question, though, is how can rural social workers improve what they do? Clearly, each needs to first know how he or she is doing. What percentage of clients has significant improvement, and what percentage does not seem to improve?

Clients who are not improving challenge rural social workers in two ways. First, they stop coming. How they were doing is unknown, and the social worker is left to wonder. Second, they keep coming. In this case, they like the social worker, and, apparently, seeing a social worker is a pleasant experience for them, despite lack of improvement. If a social worker has many of these clients, they fill hours, and the social worker wonders if he or she is effective at all. However, there is evidence that supports the notion that these clients do want positive change (Miller & Duncan, 2000). Similarly, knowing that clients are improving can energize social workers.

There is also evidence to support the contention that most clients successfully complete therapy in 8–12 sessions (Miller & Duncan, 2000). One implication of this finding is that those who continue to come in and are no longer changing may be keeping others who are at that point of wanting to change from getting in the door of the rural agency, because the social workers are so busy. Conversely, the client that is taking up the time also wants to change but may be trapped in this habit of seeing the therapist. This is a crucial issue for rural practice settings, because the availability of trained clinical social workers may be limited. However, this is a seductive process; the therapist needs the hours to achieve agency-determined productivity rates, and the client, at least, feels good about trying something that is only 1 hour per week. It would seem that intervention efforts should have better goals than noted in this situation.

Client Directed Outcome Informed (CDOI) Tools

Fortunately, there is evidence that clinical social workers can examine their own practice to determine whether they have formed an effective working alliance with the client in the client's opinion and whether the work they are engaging in with clients is, in fact, leading to desirable changes from the client's perspective. There is also evidence that graduates from social work programs desire more information on practical and easy-to-use measures and strategies (Staudt, 2007). This section discusses the evidence-based measures easily used to explore these issues.

Outcome Rating Scale (ORS). The ORS was developed as a brief alternative to the Outcome Questionnaire (OQ) 45 (Lambert et al., 1996). It was discovered that clients and clinicians complained that the original instrument was too long. The specific items on the revised and abbreviated ORS were adapted from the three areas of client functioning assessed by the OQ 45; specifically, individual (or symptomatic) functioning, interpersonal relationships, social role performance (work adjustment, quality of life; Lambert & Hill, 1994), and an "overall" rating (general sense of well-being). With regard to the specific items on the ORS, the four areas of client functioning were simply translated into visual 10 cm lines, with instructions to place a hash mark on each line with low estimates to the left and high to the right. Changes in the first three areas are widely considered valid indicators of successful treatment outcome (Kazdin, 1994; Lambert et al., 1996; Lambert & Hill, 1994). A recent study (Miller, Duncan, Brown, Sparks, & Claud, 2003) found that the abbreviated ORS has adequate validity, solid reliability, and high feasibility.

Use of the ORS. Although the use of the instrument, at first glance, seems simple, the developers note that "You cannot over explain the ORS" (Miller et al., 2003, p. 91). It is simple, yet serious. If the social worker wants to pay clear attention to client progress and his or her own growth as a practitioner, the baseline, or first ORS, observation is particularly important. At the beginning of each session, the practitioner is instructed to hand the paper version of the ORS to the client with an explanation that asks the client to complete the form, and that this will be done at each subsequent session to make sure the client is getting what he or she wants from the meetings. Practitioners can have the client read the instructions themselves, or they can read it with the client. The practitioner is instructed to make sure the client understands that the rating is about the current session and the past week, and that they are to highlight concerns for which they are coming to see the worker. For example, if the client's rating of family is high (i.e., relatively problem-free) but there are marital difficulties, then the client should rate the marital difficulties. If work and friendships are going well but the client sees the social worker about school, then he client should rate the school issue. The social worker then scores the instrument by measuring each line (which is 10 cm long) with a centimeter ruler. The score is the length on each line of the measurement as measured in centimeters. The worker then adds up the scores. The summated scores range from zero to 40.

Next, the practitioner should begin to make a connection with the score and therapy. For instance, the social worker might say that, nationally, the average score of a first session is 19 and then talk of the level of distress the client rated in comparison to the national average. The practitioner can then ask the client whether this makes sense. In addition, a lower score on one line is likely an indication of the reason that the person came to see the worker. This can open the door for early talk involving the client's reasons for coming to therapy. It is widely accepted that therapy starts in the first session (Miller & Duncan, 2000), and this helps clients know practitioners are not all about getting paperwork done, but rather about clients' concerns. Following the completion of the ORS, the social worker conducts therapy as he or she would normally. One of the advantages of CDOI is that it is not a specific model, but rather a metamodel—one that can be used with any theoretical model of therapy.

At the same time, in the first interview the social worker should pay attention to the client in a way that allows the client to adjust that first score. It may go something like this: "As you tell me of the marriage concerns, I have to wonder if you did not fully consider that in your rating?" The worker can then invite the client to rescore that area (but not insist that the client do so). This is an honest question, not a means to get the baseline functioning level lower, but to ensure that this initial rating is reasonably accurate. This also makes further connection with ORS and treatment.

For clinical purposes, it is helpful to know that research shows a score of 25 on the ORS denotes a reasonable degree of psychological well-being. In addition, a score over 25 often suggests that remaining clinical issues are in a rather specific area, thus the social worker should avoid therapies designed to revisit old "issues" with which the client has reached an acceptable level of satisfaction. The dredging up of old issues has the possibility of doing harm, influencing the client to feel bad, whereas they previously felt good.

A further nuance is that mandated clients will often score high, as if to say "I do not have a problem," but rather, "my probation officer or my spouse thinks I do." It could be useful to then ask the client to rate what the referral source might rate them. These clients are at risk to not benefit from therapy. Conversely, mandated clients that rate themselves low are just as likely as others to have positive change (Connors & Carroll, 1997).

Session Rating Scale (SRS). Johnson (1995) recognized that different therapies can achieve similar results, and that it is the therapeutic alliance that proves most important. In response, he created SRS in the early 1990s to help track his own progress with clients. SRS was specifically designed as a clinical tool, not as a research instrument. The items on the initial SRS were a combination of elements from the Working Alliance Inventory (Horvath & Greenberg, 1989) and the Empathy Scale (Burns & Nolen-Hoeksema, 1992), which specifically address the clinical relationship. The SRS combined elements of each measure into a 10 item Likert-scaled instrument.

As with the ORS, clinicians and clients complained that the original version was too long. In response, a 4-item scale was created to address the complaints of clinicians and to encourage routine conversation between social workers and clients about the therapeutic alliance. The final version of the SRS is a 4-item visual analogue instrument that has its origins in several perspectives on what constitutes effective therapy. First, Bordin (1979) defined the alliance with three interacting elements: (1) a relational bond between the therapist and client, (2) agreement on the goals of therapy, and (3) agreement on the tasks of therapy. In addition, Gaston's (1990) slightly different perspective also influenced the SRS. She agreed with Bordin on the major alliance themes, but she also pointed out that the similarity between the client's and the therapist's beliefs about how people change in therapy are vital for a successful therapy alliance. Thus, the SRS can be viewed as a scale adapted from the definition of the alliance by Bordin, with a focus on the client's theory of change as suggested by Gaston. These perspectives make up the first three items assessed on the scale: (1) relationship with worker, (2) goals and topics of the session, and (3) approach or method used by the worker. There is a fourth item—the overall rating of the session by the client. Efforts have been made to assess the reliability of the SRS. In one study, a Cronbach's coefficient alpha of .88 was calculated for all administrations (N=420) of the instrument. Concurrent validity was also evaluated in the same study with acceptable levels reported.

Use of the SRS. At the end of each session, the worker asks the client to score the SRS. The statement should be similar to: "at the end of each session, I want to make sure that I am on track with you and what you are wanting out of therapy." As can be expected, this is relatively new territory for clients—to rate aspects of their service provider. How would you feel rating your MD as he or she sat waiting? The scoring is similar to ORS, in that each assessment area is measured and then the scores are summed. In the case of the SRS a summated score under 36, or any individual line under 9, merits an invitation for discussion. Again, involvement of the client is key. In addition, important information that helps in therapy may be attained. Although it may be tempting for clinicians to feel pleased with scores of 40, they should be reminded that there is evidence that criticism of therapists in early sessions is a good indication of the likelihood of positive change later in therapy. So, if the client rates the worker with three "10" ratings and one "9" rating, the worker can focus on the "9" rating by asking how the worker could serve the client better in that area. If the client offers a suggestion, the worker needs to acknowledge, clarify, make note, and refer to this issue in the next session. As with ORS, the score itself means nothing without client input. It cannot be assumed that one person's rating on the SRS of 32 is the same as someone else's rating of 32. Often, clients are quite pleased with the opportunity to evaluate their worker and simply offer the explanation that they are a "hard grader" and will not give out the best grades at the beginning of their therapy. What they offer as explanation suffices. One creative therapist asked for feedback as part of her own continuing education. The point is to do what is useful to productively engage the client. The correct response then is to thank the client for the feedback. As clinicians, the goal should be to reach the point at which critique is genuinely appreciated; after all, as noted earlier, the critique increases the possibility of success for that client.

For subsequent sessions, workers start each session with the ORS. The social worker should point out differences in scores, notice the differences line by line, and discuss concerns as related to therapy. For example, if the family score is high, the social worker might ask what is working or how they have accomplished the improvement. The question and listening can be focused with the model of therapy the social worker and the client are using at this time. If that score is down, the social worker might ask whether or how that is related to what needs to happen in the current session. By the third or fourth session, discussion of "is therapy helping" should be included. If there are no indications of change by the sixth to eighth sessions, it time to discuss how the social worker and the client might change efforts; research is clear (Miller & Duncan, 2000) that it is quite unlikely that change will happen by proceeding in the same way. Is it time to make referral to someone else, involve a group, or take a different tack within the therapy? The difference in approach needs to be a significant difference. Historically, this is often the point at which the therapist and client are comfortable working together, but change is not happening. As noted previously, the risk here is filling hours that may be pleasant and good for productivity levels, but, with increasing likelihood, unlikely to produce change. Making a change in treatment is not a negative reflection on either the therapist or the client, but rather on the fact that similar intervention methods do not always lead to the same outcomes, and the current model of therapy is not helping.

It is all important to note that these tools are not designed for job performance. Once someone says job performance is connected to ORS or SRS, it raises questions of possible adjustment of scores in a manner that puts more emphasis on the therapist, rather than the client's changing perspective on his or her therapy. However, it is important to understand that the score can be used constructively in supervision. The supervision sessions can focus on questions such as "What can be done to help the client raise the ORS" or "What can be done to improve relationship," because these are healthy discussions for supervision sessions. Finally, the use of these measures can assist a well-meaning therapist to provide his or her own "supervision," at least related to quality of care. This is an area that can be vital to the isolated clinical social worker practicing in a rural setting.

Socials workers should also continue to have clients complete the SRS throughout therapy. Social workers should use the client-based assessments to note and discuss any decrease in a specific score area. At some point, if the SRS score stabilizes and there is no longer feedback about the alliance, the worker can simply thank the client for completing the measure.

Case Examples

To gain a better understanding of the use of the ORS and SRS in a rural practice setting, three case examples are presented. These cases provide examples of the diverse nature of rural clients that clinical social workers might see in a rural agency.

Case Example 1: Importance of ORS Scores

Toni was a 40-year-old, single, White female who had been in the rural mental health system for some time without substantial progress. She was depressed, and she was also physically disabled and could not return to the work she had done for years. She worked with a Solution Focused therapist she liked. The SRS score was consistently 40, and she reported feeling better after sessions and looking forward to them. However, her ORS scores started at 8, and, through the eighth session, varied no more than two points. Normative data for the ORS reports that 50th percentile of change on the scale for someone starting at 8 is 18; essentially, Toni was not making any progress. Toni and her therapist began a discussion of what else could be done to improve things. They began to work in a way that was more cognitive behavioral and involved a group intervention; changing therapists was also discussed, but the client had no interest in that option. As no change continued through the 12th session, the discussion of transferring to another therapist was again broached, and this time the client agreed.

Toni's new therapist tried dialectical behavioral therapy, and the ORS rather rapidly began improving. By the 10th session Toni and the new therapist agreed she was, for now, done with therapy.

In Toni's case the use of the ORS was vital in helping both the social worker and the client acknowledge that, although their time together was perhaps enjoyable, it was not leading to significant therapeutic progress for Toni. The ORS opened the door to an honest discussion regarding the merit of the therapy for Toni and empowered her to realize that she deserved to be connected with a social worker who would be a better fit for finding ways to make progress.

Case Example 2: Importance of SRS Scores

A therapist, in his rural office, was a bit fascinated by the presence of Tom, a 24-year-old, single, White male who was a self-proclaimed Buddhist. The therapist was quite active in Tom's session, feeling an understanding of the religion and energized by this somewhat out of the ordinary presence in a rural setting. Afterward, the therapist felt brilliant. He did reframing and insights that were energized and per-haps accurate; then came the SRS scores. The ratings were 7, 8, 8, and 8, for a sum-mated total of 31. This was much lower than the guideline of 36. To give insight to the scores, the therapist addressed them with Tom in the following manner:

Therapist: "What could make this better for you?"

Tom: "I liked what you said, but it was hard for me to take it in. I felt you were giving ideas, without understanding who I am."

Therapist: "So you want to know, first, that I have some better understanding of who you are, and then, if I get there, you want ideas?"

Tom: "Yes, I like the ideas, but I need to feel you know where I am coming from first. I need to know I am understood."

Therapist: "Thank you. Next time, I will go slower and check with you about my understanding before offering ideas."

Tom: "Yes, you got it."

Tom did decide to come back, and therapy proceeded. The therapist made an effort to go slower and do more "checking out," but he did not feel as "brilliant." Tom later completed an additional SRS, and the score was 36, with verbal feedback provided that he perceived the therapist as understanding and that feedback within the session was useful. The client was then seen for six additional sessions, with regular headway in ORS (past the 50th percentile of change) and SRS scores at 36 or higher with no further suggestion of how to change therapy. The result was mu-tual termination.

In Tom's case the SRS scores were a pivotal force in therapy. The use of these scores enabled the client to provide valuable feedback to the therapist; namely, "this is not working." The worker was then able to adjust course early and make the necessary steps to collaborate with Tom, reaching a better understanding of what Tom wanted out of each session. These changes led to increased ratings on the client's perception of therapeutic outcomes via scoring on the ORS, as well as improved outcomes for Tom.

Case Example 3: Therapy Without ORS or SRS

This case example is in contrast to Tom's situation. Levi, a retired, 72-year-old, married, White male, began experiencing feelings of depression and decided to visit the community mental health center, although a bit tentatively. Levi presented as a client with little "sophistication." The therapist was pleasant and excited to give information related to the latest cognitive behavioral workshop she had attended. She enthusiastically suggested that Levi complete a homework assignment and instructed him to bring the completed papers back for the next session. She told him he could expect that completion of this homework would lead to new thinking. Levi blankly nodded affirmation. There was no SRS or ORS completed. Levi went home and told a relative, "What is wrong with these therapists? I have no idea how they can help anyone." He never returned.

This difference in feedback with Levi and Tom is dramatic. Tom was a save, a client that is helped who may not have to come back; Levi was a miss. These misses must be addressed, because many can be avoided. In one case, Tom felt understood and that the worker was interested in working toward a collaborative effort that would be client-directed and based on client feedback. For Levi, the social worker did not show that kind of interest. The focus was not really on Levi, but rather on therapeutic technique. The importance of the alliance was lost in the effort to try something new, regardless of Levi's true needs and concerns.

Research on the Effectiveness of the ORS and SRS

Although it is helpful to review case reports of the usefulness of the ORS and the SRS, it is also important to review any existing research that would provide additional evidence that using these instruments can make a difference in clinical practice. This section reviews research that supports the effectiveness of using the ORS and SRS in therapy.

The most compelling research on the effectiveness of the ORS and SRS can be found in a study by Miller, Duncan, Brown, Sorrell, and Chalk (2006). Their study involved 75 therapists and 6,424 clients over a 2-year period. The study found that "providing formal, ongoing feedback to therapists regarding clients' experience of the alliance and progress in treatment resulted in significant improvements in both client retention and outcome" (Miller et al., 2006, p. 10). They found that access to the client's experience of progress in treatment effectively doubled the overall effect size of services. They also found that improving a poor alliance at the beginning of intervention was associated with significantly better outcomes at the conclusion.

It is also useful to note that Miller and colleagues (2006) are not the only researchers to find that feedback from the client to the therapist is an effective way to improve the effectiveness of the interventions. For example, Whipple and colleagues (2003) found that clients whose therapists had access to progress and alliance information were less likely to worsen, more likely to stay in therapy longer, and twice as likely to experience significant improvements in their outcomes. Formal client feedback has also been shown to be particularly helpful in cases at risk for a negative or null outcome. A meta-analysis of three studies by Lambert and colleagues (2003) found that when therapists were aware of their clients' ratings of clinical progress the final outcomes of therapy were improved. Specifically, clients in these situations were better off than 65% of clients whose therapist did not received this information.

Conclusion

Serving the rural population is a difficult task under the best circumstances. Although knowledge of what works in mental health is growing, rural social workers must simultaneously deal with agency policies that are increasingly preoccupied with the manner and timeliness of completion of paperwork that, unfortunately, has been shown to have no correlation to quality of care. Furthermore, it seems quite likely that concurrent completion of paperwork has the potential to be detrimental to the number one predictor of progress in therapy—the client–therapist alliance.

It should be noted, however, that completing the ORS and SRS, in fact, does add to the paperwork load of the therapist. The difference is that proper use of these tools, in comparison to others, takes minimal time, and benefits to intervention efforts far outweigh the additional responsibility of the social worker. The completion of these measures can also be contrasted with the burdens of paperwork and procedures that offer no evidence of clinical usefulness. If social workers are to succeed in their challenging positions in rural-based mental health agencies, it is time for them to find ways to tend to the quality of care directly. The use of the ORS and SRS can provide a feasible way for rural clinicians to monitor their practice efficiently. This will help workers focus on doing "A+" clinical work with the clients in their office now, and be satisfied with perhaps a "C" on the paperwork needed to ensure the rural clinic gets paid in a timely way and does not have to repay funds. Standards of paperwork have perpetually been a moving target, but ethics require social workers to focus on quality of services. Social workers want to provide a high quality of care, and most, it is hoped, would like to improve as clinicians. Proper use of feedback tools and full involvement of clients can help this process.

This chapter serves as an effort to help rural social workers become more aware of an efficient way to engage in reflective practice in collaboration with clients. The tools put forth in this chapter originate in the field of psychology, and an increasing number of psychologists are advocating for the use of the ORS and SRS in practice. It would seem that these tools can also be used by social workers as a means to evaluate and improve practice. It seems imperative that, in this age of accountability and competency-based practice, social work should make efforts to use such tools to improve practice efforts. They are efficient, helpful, and could provide social workers with valuable feedback.

References

Baer, J. (2001). Evaluating practice: Assessment of the therapeutic process. *Journal of Social Work Education*, 37, 127–136.

Baker, L., Stephens, F., & Hitchcock, L. (2010). Social work practitioners and practice Evaluation: How are we doing? *Journal of Human Behavior in the Social Environment*, 20, 963–973.

Bloom, M., Fischer, J., & Orme, J. G. (1999). *Evaluating practice: Guidelines for the accountable professional*. Needham Heights, MA: Allyn and Bacon.

Bordin, E. S. (1979). The generalizability of the psychoanalytic concept of the working alliance. *Psychotherapy: Theory, Research & Practice*, 16(3), 252–260.

Boyd, M. R., & Mackey, M. C. (2000). Running away to nowhere: Rural women's experiences of becoming alcohol dependent. *Archives of Psychiatric Nursing*, 14(3), 142–149.

Brown, J., Dreis, S., & Nace, D. K. (1999). What really makes a difference in psychotherapy outcome? Why does managed care want to know? In M. A. Hubble, B. L. Duncan, & S. D. Miller (Eds.), *The heart and soul of change: What works in therapy* (pp. 389–406). Washington, DC: APA Press.

Burns, D. D., & Nolen-Hoeksema, S. (1992). Therapeutic empathy and recovery from depression in cognitive—behavioral therapy: A structural equation model. *Journal of Consulting and Clinical Psychology*, 60, 441–449.

Bushy, A. (1998). Health issues of women in rural environments: An overview. *Journal of the American Medical Women's Association*, 53(2), 53–56.

Cellucci, T., & Vik, P. (2001). Training for substance abuse treatment among psychologists in a rural state. *Professional Psychology: Research and Practice*, 32(3), 248–252.

Connors, G. J., & Carroll, K. M. (1997). The therapeutic alliance and its relationship to alcoholism treatment participation and outcome. *Journal of Consulting and Clinical Psychology, 65*, 588–598.

Council on Social Work Education. (2008). *Educational policy and accreditation standards.* Retrieved from http://www.cswe.org/File.aspx?id=13780

Dimmitt, J., & Davila, Y. (1995). Group psychotherapy for abused women: A survivor group prototype. *Applied Nursing Research, 8*, 3–8.

Duncan, B., Miller, S., & Hubble, M. (2007). How being bad can make you better. *Psychotherapy Networker, 57*, 36–45.

Eberhardt, M. S., Ingram, D. D., & Makuc, D. M. (2001). *Urban and rural health chartbook: Health United States 2001.* Hyattsville, MD: National Center for Health Statistics.

Eberhardt, M. S., & Pamuk, E. R. (2004). The importance of place of residence: Examining health in rural and nonrural areas. *American Journal of Public Health, 94*, 1682–1686.

Eysenck, H. J. (1952). The effects of psychotherapy: An evaluation. *Journal of Consulting Psychology, 16*, 319–324.

Gale, J., Shaw, B., & Hartley, D. (2010). *The provision of mental health services by rural health clinics.* Working paper #43, Portland, ME: University of Southern Maine.

Gardner, F. (2000). Design evaluation: Illuminating social work practice for better outcomes. *Social Work, 45*(2), 176–182.

Gaston, L. (1990). The concept of the alliance and its role in psychotherapy: Theoretical and empirical considerations. *Psychotherapy, 27*, 143-152.

Gogek, L. B. (1992). Letters to the editor. *American Journal of Psychiatry, 149*, 1286.

Harman, J. S., Dong, F., Xu, S., Ewigman, N., & Fortney, J. C. (2010). *Assessment of the mental health funding marketplace in rural vs. urban settings.* Retrieved from http://wiche.edu/info/publications/HarmanfundingmarketplaceYr4Proj3.pdf

Horvath, A. O., & Greenberg, L. S. (1989). Development and validation of the Working Alliance Inventory. *Journal of Counseling Psychology, 64*, 223–233.

Johnson, L. D. (1995). *Psychotherapy in the age of accountability.* New York, NY: Norton.

Kazdin, A.E. (19914). Methodology, design, and evaluation in psychotherapy research. In A. E. Bergin & S. L. Garfield (Eds.), *Handbook of psychotherapy and behavior change* (pp. 19–71). New York: John Wiley.

Lambert, M. J., Hansen, N. B., Umphress, V., Lunnen, K., Okiishi, J., Burlingame, G. M., … Reisinger, C. (1996). *Administration and scoring manual for the OQ 45.2.* Stevenson, MD: American Professional Credentialing Services.

Lambert, M. J., & Hill C. E. (1994). Assessing psychotherapy outcomes and processes. In A. E. Bergin & S. L. Garfield (Eds.), *Handbook of psychotherapy and behavior change.* (pp. 72–113). New York, NY: John Wiley & Sons.

Lambert, M. J., Whipple, J. L., Hawkins, E. J., Vermeersch, D. A., Nielsen, S. L., & Smart, D. W. (2003). Is it time for clinicians routinely to track patient outcome? A meta-analysis. *Clinical Psychology*, *10*, 288–301.

Martin, L. L., & Kettner, P. M. (1997). Performance measurement: The new accountability. *Administration in Social Work*, *21*(1), 17–29.

Miller, S. D., & Duncan, B. L. (2000). The heroic client: Doing client-directed, outcome-informed therapy. San Francisco, CA: Jossey-Bass.

Miller, S., Duncan, B., Brown, J., Sorrell, R., & Chalk, M. (2006). Using formal client feedback to improve retention and outcome: Making ongoing, real-time assessment feasible. *Journal of Brief Therapy*, *5*, 5–33.

Miller, S. D., Duncan, B. L., Brown, J., Sparks, J., & Claud, D. (2003). The outcome rating scale: A preliminary study of the reliability, validity, and feasibility of a brief visual analog measure. *Journal of Brief Therapy*, *2*(2), 91–100.

National Center on Addiction and Substance Abuse. (2000). *No place to hide: Substance abuse in mid-size cities and rural America.* New York, NY: Author.

Roberts, L., Battaglia, J., & Epstein, R. (1999). Frontier ethics: Mental health care needs and ethical dilemmas in rural communities. *Psychiatric Services*, *50*, 497–503.

Stamm, B. H. (2003). *Rural behavioral health care.* Washington, DC: American Psychological Association.

Staudt, M. (2007). Two years later: Former students' perceptions of a clinical evaluation course and current evaluation practices. *Journal of Teaching in Social Work*, *27*, 125–139.

Substance Abuse and Mental Health Services Administration. (2001). *Summary of findings from the 2001 National Household Survey on Drug Abuse.* Rockville, MD: Office of Applied Studies.

Wade, K., & Neuman, K. (2007) Practice-based research: Changing the professional culture and language of social work. *Social Work in Health Care*, *44*(4), 49–64.

Wagenfeld, M. O., Murray, J. D., Mohatt, D. F., & DeBruyn, J. C. (1994). *Mental health and rural America: 1980–1993. An overview and annotated bibliography.* [ORHP, U.S. DHHS NIH Pub. No. 94-3500]. Washington, DC: Government Printing Office.

Walfish, S., McAllister, B., & Lambert, M. J. (in press). *Are all therapists from Lake Wobegon? An investigation of self-assessment bias in mental heal providers.* Manuscript submitted for publication.

Wampold, B. E. (2001). *The great psychotherapy debate: Models, methods, and findings.* Hillsdale, NJ: Lawrence Erlbaum.

Whipple, J. L., Lambert, M. J., Vermeersch, D. A., Smart, D. W., Nielsen, S. L., & Hawkins, E. J. (2003). Improving the effects of psychotherapy: The use of early identification of treatment and problem-solving strategies in routine practice. *Journal of Counseling Psychology*, *50*, 59–68.

20 Rural Oncology Social Work: *Culture, Context, and Care in the Rural Setting*

SKY NIESEN SMITH, MICHAEL GLASSER, AND WYNNE S. KORR

This chapter addresses psychosocial oncology practice in a rural community. It examines the cultural and practical realities of practice in the rural context as it affects cancer patients and the family system and considers the ethical dilemmas embedded in such practice. Although much of the literature on rural social work practice emphasizes the generalist model (e.g., Davenport & Davenport, 2008), specialized practice should be considered, when resources allow it, to address specific conditions, especially those known to have poorer outcomes (i.e., increased health disparities) in rural communities.

Culture and Context

Our focus is on a rural, three-county area in northwest Illinois. This region is characterized as agricultural and industrial with pockets of minority populations and "rust belt" de-industrialization—many industries having relocated, resulting in high unemployment. The residents are hard-working, proud people, who rely heavily on family for support, both financially and emotionally. In this culture, a person's last name is very important: Judgments and assumptions may be made immediately based on the name and community gossip about a person and family. Physicians are often regarded as infallible. Outsiders, especially those from "the big city," are sometimes admired, sometimes avoided. Within this context, the client with cancer, the family, and social connections become part of practice, not always in a facilitating way.

Need for Specialized Cancer Care

Cancer has adverse effects at all levels, affecting physical health and emotional well-being. It brings uncertainties regarding not only the ability to be treated and survive, but also related to quality of life because of the cost of treatment and related care and the need for continuing medical and social support. The burden of cancer is felt by individuals, their families, their communities, and the health care system. Not surprisingly, one of the primary objectives related to cancer in Healthy People 2020—the blueprint for equitable and quality health care in the United States—is to "increase the mental and physical health-related quality of life of cancer survivors" (U.S. Department of Health and Human Services, 2011.

According to the Institute of Medicine ([IOM], 2007) report, *Cancer Care for the Whole Patient: Meeting Psychosocial Health Care Needs*, cancer care is often incomplete in terms of access and availability of psychosocial services.

> Many people living with cancer report that their psychosocial health care needs are not well-addressed in their care. At the most fundamental level, throughout diagnosis, treatment, and post treatment, patients report dissatisfaction with the amount and type of information they are given about their prognosis, available treatments, and ways to manage their illness and health. Health care providers often fail to communicate this information effectively, in ways that are understandable to and enable action by patients. (Epstein & Street, 2007)

Cancer care can be problematic in rural areas. Nearly one quarter of Americans live in rural areas, where there are consistent reports of higher cancer mortality rates, higher cancer rates overall, and people are more likely to be smokers, compared to their urban and suburban counterparts (Albert Einstein College of Medicine, 2010; Jones, Parker, Ahearn, Mishra, & Variyam, 2009). Additionally, although more than 20% of the population in the United States resides in rural communities, just 10% of the physician workforce practices in rural America (Rosenblatt, 2004). Overall, as Lancaster (2011) reported,

> rural people have higher levels of poverty, a larger percentage of older adults tend to be in poorer health and have fewer physicians and other health care professionals to provide care, and they are less likely to have insurance than people who live in urban areas. (p. 89)

Cancer Experiences of Residents of These Three Rural Counties

In 2009 two of the present authors were part of a research team that conducted a pilot study of the needs of cancer survivors in a three-county region of northwest Illinois. One of the authors is a social worker who was practicing in this rural community. The research team was interested in learning about the experiences and psychosocial needs of cancer survivors, in particular, to tailor programs to better meet local needs. This region was the catchment area for Home of Hope Cancer and Wellness Centers. Home of Hope is a cancer wellness and counseling center providing free psychosocial health services for individuals diagnosed with cancer and their support networks. This agency is not officially affiliated with any medical providers and is miles from medical oncology/hematology clinics, yet close in proximity to a radiation oncology clinic. These counties are classified as "rural" using the Rural Urban Commuting Area classification system, a census tract-based classification scheme that uses the standard Bureau of Census Urbanized Area and Urban Cluster definitions in combination with work commuting information to characterize all of the nation's census tracts in terms of rural and urban status and relationships (UW Rural Health Research Center, 2010).

Local needs assessments through the Illinois Department of Public Health Project for Local Assessment of Need process found that the top three health problems in each of the three targeted counties, respectively, were (1) heart disease, diabetes, and cancer; (2) heart disease, mental health, and access to care; and (3) obesity, tobacco use, and youth development. Cancer, mental health, and tobacco were health issues of particular interest, given the focus of the study. Very importantly, other chronic conditions such as heart disease, diabetes, and obesity, were also identified—comorbid conditions that can make addressing the needs of cancer patients and survivors all the more difficult.

In our study a pretested survey addressed demographics and general health; mental health, using instruments such as the National Comprehensive Cancer Network Distress Thermometer (Jacobsen, 2004); responses to a depression scale—the Durham GRECC (Koenig, Meador, Cohen, & Blazer, 1988) and a series of quality of life questions; and status regarding level of need using CaSUN (the Cancer Survivor's Unmet Needs measure), developed by Hodgkinson and colleagues (2007). A total of 13 cancer survivors in the rural areas confirmed the existence and general types of needs of rural cancer (61.5% women; mean age=65.7, SD=10.5; range=44–80). On average, the survivors reported more than two additional chronic medical conditions. On the standardized depression scale, nearly

54% of the cancer survivors were at risk for depression—scoring four or higher on the scale. According to the National Comprehensive Cancer Network Distress Thermometer criteria, 31.4% of the cancer survivors were also at risk for some type of psychosocial problem in their lives requiring assistance (National Comprehensive Cancer Network, 2007). Using the measure of CaSUN (Hodgkinson et al., 2007), we found that survivors who expressed some level of need, compared to those who did not, also consistently scored higher in distress and lower in quality of life.

The Practice Model

The oncology social worker provided psychosocial health services, drawing on a chronic care model. Psychosocial health services are defined as those psychological and social services that enable patients, their families, and health care providers to optimize biomedical health care (IOM, 2007). Management of the psychological, behavioral, and social aspects of illness and its consequence has been demonstrated to promote better health and quality of life. Psychosocial oncology includes (a) identifying patients with psychosocial health needs that are likely to affect their health or health care; (b) developing, with the patients, appropriate plans for linking patients to appropriate health services; (c) supporting patients in managing their illness; (d) coordinating psychosocial with biomedical care; and (e) following up on care delivery to monitor the effectiveness of services and determine whether changes are needed. The practice model is implemented, taking into consideration the rural culture and the rural service delivery context.

Addressing the needs of rural cancer patients and survivors requires a comprehensive care model, taking into account the interface of cancer with other chronic conditions and the role of social support in enhancing quality of life and well-being. The Chronic Care Model (CCM) is such a comprehensive care framework (Bodenheimer, Wagner, & Grumbach, 2002; Lennon-Dearing, Florence, Garrett, Click, & Abercrombie, 2008; Wagner, 1998). The CCM represents a paradigm shift from a focus on acute problems to prevention and chronic care management. The CCM's premise is that quality care is not delivered in isolation, but rather is enhanced by community resources, self-management support, decision-making support, and organizational support. The CCM recognizes the roles of the individual, the practice team, the community, and the healthcare system.

Ethical dilemmas that occur in applying these models in the rural context also need to be considered. Many authors (e.g., Boisen & Bosch, 2005; Galambos, Watt,

Anderson, & Danis, 2006; Gumpert & Black, 2005) have highlighted the problems of applying general ethical principles to rural social work practice. Most have focused on the problem posed by dual relationships, the need to avoid boundary violations that could lead to coercion and harm to patients, and the difficulties in maintaining confidentiality. The National Association of Social Workers Code of Ethics (National Association of Social Workers, 1996) describes dual relationships as happening "when social workers relate to clients in more than one relationship, whether professional, social, or business" (Standard 1.06[c]). Dual relationships occur with greater frequency in the rural context, because social workers and clients are more likely to encounter one another in multiple contexts (Boisen & Bosch, 2005). As Ginsberg (2005) aptly described, "One's friends, fellow church members, grocers, auto dealers, and organizational colleagues may also be clients or may be related to clients" (p. 7). Gumpert and Black (2005) outlined three approaches to dual relationships: rule-based safeguards, differential criteria for practitioner decision making, and appropriate boundary crossing for therapeutic impact (p. 160). They also highlighted the difficulties that may be encountered in maintaining confidentiality.

Three cases are subsequently presented that illustrate the challenges in applying best practices, according to the approaches previously outlined within the context of rural culture and constrained, splintered, and sometime nonexistent resources. Ethical dilemmas are also highlighted in these cases. Finally, implications are drawn from the cases for the design of new protocols to creatively enhance the standard of care for rural oncology practice.

The Cases

The following case examples include three fictional situations that a practitioner may encounter when working in oncology social work in a rural setting. The cases were chosen to illustrate the range of social work interactions with rural clients. The presentations include a summary of the psychosocial assessment, interventions employed, and ethical considerations. The cases also illustrate factors common to many environments, as well as those mostly associated with the rural culture and communities.

Sally Smith

Identifying information. Mrs. Sally Smith is a 40-year-old, married, Caucasian woman who was diagnosed with Stage II Breast Cancer 5 years ago. She has been considered "cancer-free" for the past 5 years, following chemotherapy and radiation treatment. She is employed as an attorney. Mrs. Smith has two children, 12 and 15 years of age. Both children reside in her home.

Referral. Primary care physician

Chief complaint/purpose of visit. Sally Smith was referred to the social worker for psychosocial assessment, due to her report that she is having difficulty coping with her past diagnosis of breast cancer. Her family physician reports that Sally contacts his office multiple times per day with concerns that her cancer has returned. Her physician feels that Sally could benefit from counseling and an antidepressant medication. The family physician reported that Sally felt afraid to attend an appointment at a cancer counseling center and that she requested that a social worker meet with her at her physician's office. There are few counselors in the rural area where Sally resides. She lives 30 minutes from this social worker's office. Throughout Sally's cancer treatment, she was not given any information about psychosocial care or mental health services.

Sally Smith: Systems Review

Current stressors. Fear of cancer recurrence

Symptoms. Panic episodes, anxiety, fear, distress, headaches, sleeplessness, nightmares, intrusive thoughts, and avoidance of stimuli with cancer association

Coping. Sally Smith identified talking to her husband as her coping skill.

Mental health history. Sally Smith reported that she does not have a history of mental health concerns. She has not previously attended counseling or psychotherapy. She reports no family history of mental health diagnoses.

Social history. Sally Smith was the youngest of a sibship of three born to an intact family. She was born and raised in rural Illinois. Sally reports that her childhood and development were stable and that all of her basic developmental needs were met. She and her husband have been married for 15 years. They have two children, 12 and 15 years of age. She describes her children as doing well and says they did not seem to be affected by her breast cancer diagnosis. Sally attended Rural High School, Country College, and Law School. She is currently employed as a partner by the area's largest law firm.

Support system. Sally Smith's husband seems to provide her primary support. In addition, Sally reports an extensive support network of family members, colleagues, and friends. Despite this solid support, Sally reports that she does not discuss her breast cancer diagnosis with any of her friends or colleagues. In fact, there are few people who know that Sally was diagnosed with breast cancer.

Sally Smith: Discussion

Sally Smith was quite reluctant to meet with a social worker to discuss her thoughts and feelings surrounding her breast cancer diagnosis. She appeared quite nervous that someone would see her in the physician's office with this social worker. In Sally's rural environment, there is often a negative stigma attached to attending counseling/social work appointments. Many residents in Sally's community know Sally well, both personally and professionally. Once Sally was engaged in conversation, she relaxed and was able to provide a history of precipitating events. Sally shared that she was diagnosed with breast cancer 5 years ago. She described that during surgery and treatment she experienced a high level of distress and remembers, in detail, nearly every moment of the experience. She stated that, from the time she was given her diagnosis and every visit after, she would enter the oncology office in tears. To maintain privacy, Sally took an extended leave of absence from work during chemotherapy treatments. She spent months indoors for fear that she would encounter someone in her community who knows her. She reported high distress when she would attend oncology appointments for fear that someone would recognize her. When she returned to work, her colleagues merely believed that she had received a short haircut. Sally reported that she only shared her cancer experience with her husband, children, and parents.

Through Sally's treatment, she shared with her medical staff that she had been having difficulty coping. When her treatment was completed, Sally experienced significant distress regarding fear of disease recurrence. She stated that her local medical staff suggested she speak with a breast cancer survivor to instill hope. Sally was extremely frightened to do so, based on her privacy concern.

Sally is currently experiencing nightmares about her cancer returning. She contacts her family physician frequently to schedule check-ups. She reports that her fear consumes her on a daily basis. It is the first thought she has in the morning. The thought of cancer recurring interferes in work meetings, when Sally will suddenly run out of the room and become tearful in the break room. She reports that these episodes are becoming more and more difficult to hide. She has not been offered any social work services until recently.

Sally would like to continue to see the social worker for counseling. However, she is clear that she will not meet at the social worker's office, which is located at a cancer center, due to issues of privacy, specifically someone in the rural community seeing her vehicle parked at the counseling center. Sally also has concerns about people seeing her with a social worker, if someone she knows is also at her family physician's office.

This social worker faces the challenges of meeting Sally's needs, in terms of privacy and confidentiality, while at the same time providing services that allow Sally to feel comfortable and open. The social worker must be prepared to use creative interventions to ensure Sally's safety and privacy is maintained. In the context of the rural environment, confidentiality can certainly become problematic when many social work clients, such as Sally, feel nervous about where their car is parked, because many in their local community recognize vehicles, as well as names and faces.

The interventions that the social worker employed were designed to meet Sally's needs under these circumstances. The social worker agreed to meet with Sally once weekly at an off-site, private counseling office. Also, since psychosocial health services were not provided to Sally during her cancer treatment, the social worker will then discuss the psychosocial side effects of a cancer experience with Sally as if she were just diagnosed with cancer. The psychoeducation added to Sally's therapy will then allow Sally to process her cancer experience in a normalized way. Sally will no longer feel that she is "going crazy," but rather will understand that clinically significant distress is a common experience among people diagnosed with cancer (Zabora, BrintzenhofeSzoc, Curbow, Hooker, & Piantadosi, 2001).

The social worker will then provide distress management interventions that will provide some relief to the traumatic distress that Sally, unfortunately, has been experiencing for years. Again, due to the lack of access to psychosocial services, Sally's cancer care could be considered as substandard, in that her cancer team treated her disease, but did not treat the "whole" person. The social worker may need to reach out to Sally's primary oncology medical team to create a multidisciplinary approach to Sally's medical care, including psychosocial care. This may involve educating the medical team about the relevance and importance of psychosocial care in cancer care.

Samantha Larson

Identifying information. Samantha Larson is a 9-year-old girl, diagnosed with childhood acute myeloid leukemia 4 years ago. She currently resides with her mother, father, and 11-year-old brother, in Rural, IL. Due to limited access to pediatric oncology care, she has received medical treatment from a facility that is 2 hours away and now is seen for quarterly follow-up care and is followed by her local pediatrician.

Referral. Walk-in appointment, with mother and brother/Samantha's school

Chief complaint/purpose of visit. Samantha's mother reported that Samantha has been physically and verbally acting out in school. She has been hitting children on the bus and calling children names. She has concerns that Samantha's cancer experience may have caused Samantha to react this way. She felt that discussing her experience with an oncology social worker would help Samantha's school behaviors. When questioned, Samantha's mother reported that Samantha's school had encouraged the family to contact this oncology social worker for counseling.

In discussing this referral, Samantha's mother reported some difficulty at home. She stated that these behaviors may be learned, because she and Samantha's father fight often. When questioned about abuse, Samantha's mother reported that her husband frequently calls his wife degrading names and, at times, becomes physically violent by hitting his wife. Samantha and her brother are present during these moments.

Samantha Larson: Systems Review

Current stressors. Violence in the home, previous leukemia diagnosis, financial difficulties, difficulty with school behavior

Current symptoms. Acting out in school—physical aggression and name calling

Coping. Samantha and her brother are very close.

Mental health history. Unknown

Social history. Samantha is the youngest of a sibship of two born to an intact family. Her parents have separated several times, due to domestic violence. Most of Samantha's childhood was spent in Florida. The family was displaced by a tropical storm and then moved to rural Illinois, when Samantha was 4 years old, to be near Samantha's father's family. Currently, Samantha's school is concerned about acting-out behaviors. Samantha's paternal grandfather is the Rural City chief of police. Samantha's paternal aunt is the supervisor of the local child protective services office.

When questioned about safety, Samantha's mother reported that she would like to escape from the violence in her home, but that her husband's father's position makes it impossible for her to run away. He is closely involved, professionally, with the local domestic violence shelter. She also stated that Department of Children and Family Services (DCFS) has become involved in the past, but that her husband's aunt's position seemed to influence the case, and that she had been indicated in the report, since she pushed one of the children away to avoid being hit by their father. Samantha's mother reports that she feels trapped and that there is no way out. She feels that she must endure the emotional and physical abuse or her children will be taken away from her. On another note, this DCFS supervisor is a dear personal friend of the social worker's supervisor. Samantha's mother fears another DCFS report.

Support system. Samantha's mother states that she has no friends or family members in the local community. Her mother resides in Florida and is terminally ill. She has some friends throughout the country, but she feels that they have given up supporting her in her abusive marriage. Samantha has the support of her school staff and has some friends at school.

Samantha Larson: Discussion

The interconnectedness of this rural community poses a challenging dilemma for Samantha and her mother. Ensuring both Samantha and her mother access to resources and safety for the mother and children will be extremely difficult. It appears that Samantha's mother must leave her local community to access unbiased services. For the social worker, the reaction or intervention does not easily follow a prescribed protocol. The literature on dual relationships focuses on the social worker's need to avoid dual relationships. In this case, the problematic dual relationships are between other key persons in the service network and the client. For example, a call to the child abuse hotline must be made per mandated reported laws, but the investigator may have a dual relationship with the husband, allowing the domestic abuse to easily go unaddressed.

The social worker may need to develop creative interventions to facilitate the family's access to services outside of the rural community, such as in a metropolitan area that may provide the safety of anonymity. The interconnectedness and lack of privacy present for this family makes application of the care model and of traditional ethical guidelines much more difficult. The social worker needs to probe about dual relationships with other providers who may need to interact with the client. The social worker needs to be aware of how to access services outside the immediate community, if dual relationships limit the ability to address client needs.

Gwen Johnson

Identifying information. Ms. Gwen Johnson is a 52-year-old, divorced, Caucasian woman who resides in Rural, IL. Gwen is employed as a legal assistant. She has three adult children and two grandsons. Gwen's 25-year-old daughter was recently diagnosed with Hodgkin's lymphoma.

Referral. Gwen saw a brochure for the cancer center oncology social work counseling and scheduled an intake consultation with an oncology social worker.

Chief complaint/purpose of visit. Gwen is struggling with her daughter's diagnosis and feels that she is having difficulty coping. She expressed that she would like to receive weekly counseling appointments to learn stress management techniques and to talk to someone who will listen. She stated that her daughter is doing well psychologically and does not want counseling at this time.

Gwen Johnson: Systems Review

Current stressors. Daughter's diagnosis of lymphoma

Current symptoms. Anxiety, distress, tearfulness, feeling "out of control"

Coping. Art, music, talking to others

Mental health history. Gwen reports no history of mental health concerns.

Social history. Gwen was the oldest of a sibship of three born to an intact family. She reports that during her early childhood development her needs were met and family members were supportive. In adulthood, Gwen was married for 20 years. She divorced 7 years ago and reports that she and her ex-husband have remained friends.

Support system. Gwen describes a solid support system of friends, coworkers, and family members.

Gwen Johnson: Discussion/Intervention

Gwen was openly engaged in participating in hour-long counseling sessions with the oncology social worker, which focused on cognitive-behavioral anxiety reduction techniques. After four sessions Gwen reported that talking to this social worker has improved her symptoms dramatically. She said that she would like to continue weekly sessions. At the fifth session Gwen bounded into the social worker's office and reported that she had amazing news: She and the social worker were actually cousins and neighbors who only lived one block away from each other. She reported that she felt even closer to the social worker and that she called the social worker's parents and informed them of how happy she was that a family member had helped her. She begged the social worker to continue seeing her, if not professionally, then possible once weekly for coffee.

At this point, the social worker's professional ethics are questioned, in terms of the dual relationship that has unknowingly arisen. This scenario, although seemingly farfetched, is not unreasonable in the rural context, where very large extended families exist to the point that many do not realize who they may be related to. As a social work practitioner, privacy and confidentiality are even more challenging to maintain because clients may also be a part of the practitioner's social and family networks.

The social worker needs to have plans for dealing with her own dual relationships and boundary issues, including those that emerge during treatment. Preferably, the social worker's approach to these issues should be explained earlier in the relationship with the client (e.g., how the social worker handles encounters with the client at a family event). Even more challenging may be the common issue of lack of access to care. If the social worker deems it ethically inappropriate to continue sessions with this client, the nearest social worker could be more than an hour away. Issues then arise with ethical termination and appropriate referrals for ongoing care.

Furthermore, if this client is, indeed, the social worker's cousin, family reunions or gatherings might provide unique challenges in maintaining professional and personal boundaries. As is common among many rural practitioners, even in private life, the social worker must maintain his or her professional identity. This certainly provides challenges in creating boundaries and maintaining client confidentiality, while at the same time allowing the social worker to have a private existence outside of the professional role.

Conclusion

The case examples highlighted in this chapter (Sally Smith, Samantha Larson, and Gwen Johnson) demonstrate the reality of oncology social work practice in a rural setting. Psychosocial interventions in cancer care must focus on assessment, interventions, distress screening, problem-solving, cognitive behavioral therapy, and patient advocacy. Although empirically supported as essential to cancer care, reports indicate that many patients do not have access to psychosocial health services (IOM, 2007). Yet, as demonstrated in our pilot research and case studies, rural cancer patients express needs in relation to changes in quality of life, ongoing emotional support, and help in uncertainty reduction. In rural areas lack of access to psychosocial care compromises cancer support in all of these areas and is further exacerbated by a greater prevalence of cancer, as well as a shortage of physicians and other providers in rural communities.

Finally, the evidence suggests the importance of a comprehensive model to cancer care in rural communities. Cancer sets a course for complex interactions and relationships, often not currently addressed in the rural community, for many reasons. The

Chronic Care Model is valuable in pointing to essential components to be considered in interventions. It prescribes components that include using community resources in managing health, offering case management services, organizational support, and decision-making support (Improving Chronic Illness, 2007). In the case examples presented in this chapter, the Chronic Care Model proves complex in practical application, as the community resources available to the clients often involve working with people who have ethically questionable roles. In providing decision-making and case management support, these resource roles must be analyzed by the social worker. Due to the greater difficulty in accessing both general and psychosocial care and the dilemmas posed by the tight-knit rural culture, the rural practitioner may find it quite challenging to provide professional and ethical support in the rural context.

References

Albert Einstein College of Medicine (2010). *Cancer care in rural America.* Retrieved from http://www.sciencedaily.com/releases/2010/12/101203113235.htm

Bodenheimer, T., Wagner, E. H., & Grumbach, K. (2002). Improving primary care for patients with chronic illness. *Journal of the American Medical Association, 288,* 1775–1779.

Boisen, L. S., & Bosch, L. A. (2005). Dual relationships and rural social work: Is there a rural code? In L. H. Ginsberg (Ed.), *Social work in rural communities,* 4th ed. (pp. 189–204). Alexandria, VA: Council on Social Work Education.

Davenport, U. A., & Davenport, J. (2008). Rural practice. In T. Mizrahi & L. E. Davis (Eds.), *Encyclopedia of social work,* 20th ed., vol. 3. (pp. 536–541). Washington, DC/New York, NY: NASW Press/Oxford University Press.

Epstein, R. M., & Street R. L. (2007). *Patient-centered communication in cancer care: Promoting healing and reducing suffering.* [NIH Publication No. 07-6225]. Bethesda, MD: National Cancer Institute.

Galambos, C., Watt, J. W., Anderson, K., & Danis, F. (2006). Ethics forum: Rural social work practice. *Journal of Social Work Values and Ethics.* Retrieved from http://www.socialworker.com/jswve/index2.php?option=com_content&do_ pdf =1&id=23

Ginsberg, L. H. (2005). The overall context of rural practice. In L. H. Ginsberg (Ed.), *Social work in rural communities,* 4th ed. (pp. 1–14). Alexandria, VA: Council on Social Work Education.

Gumpert, J., & Black, P. N. (2005). Walking the tightrope between cultural competence and ethical practice: The dilemma of the rural practitioner. In L. H. Ginsberg (Ed.), *Social work in rural communities,* 4th ed. (pp. 157–174). Alexandria, VA: Council on Social Work Education.

Hodgkinson, K., Butow, P., Hunt, G. E., Pendlebury, S., Hobbs, K. M., Lo, S. K., & Wain, G. (2007). The development and evaluation of a measure to assess cancer survivors' unmet supportive care needs: The CaSUN (Cancer Survivors' Unmet Needs Measure). *Psycho-Oncology, 16*, 796–804.

Improving Chronic Illness Care. (2007). *Improving chronic illness care.* Retrieved from http://www.improvingchroniccare.org/index.html

Institute of Medicine (IOM). (2007). *Cancer care for the whole patient: Meeting psychosocial health needs.* Washington, DC: National Academies Press.

Jacobsen, P. B. (2004). Screening for psychological distress in cancer patients: Challenges and opportunities. *Journal of Clinical Oncology, 25*, 4526–4527.

Jones, C. A., Parker, T. S., Ahearn, M., Mishra, A. K., & Variyam, J. N. (2009). *Health status and health care access of farm and rural populations.* [Economic information bulletin no. 57]. Washington, DC: U.S. Department of Agriculture.

Koenig, H. G., Meador, K. G., Cohen, H. J., & Blazer, D. G. (1988) Self-rated depression scales and screening for major depression in the older hospitalized patient with medical illness. *Journal of the American Geriatrics Society, 36,* 699–706.

Lancaster, J. (2011). From the editor. *Family and Community Health, 34,* 89.

Lennon-Dearing, R., Florence, J., Garrett, L., Click, I. A., & Abercrombie, S. (2008). A rural community-based interdisciplinary curriculum: A social work perspective. *Social Work in Health Care, 47,* 93–107.

National Association of Social Workers (1996, revised 1998). *Code of ethics of the National Association of Social Workers.* Washington, DC: Author.

National Comprehensive Cancer Network. (2007). *Distress management.* Retrieved from http://www.nccn.org/professionals/physician_gls/PDF/distress.pdf

Rosenblatt, R. A. (2004). A view from the periphery: Health care in rural America. *New England Journal of Medicine, 351,* 1049–1051.

U.S. Department of Health and Human Services. (2011). *Healthy people 2020 summary of objectives.* Retrieved from http://www.healthypeople.gov/2020/topicsobjectives2020/pdfs/Cancer.pdf

UW Rural Health Research Center. (2010). *Rural urban commuting area codes (RUCA). UW departments Web server.* Retrieved from http://depts.washington.edu/uwruca/

Wagner, E. H. (1998). Chronic disease management: What will it take to improve care for chronic illness? *Effective Clinical Practice, 1,* 2–4.

Zabora, J., BrintzenhofeSzoc, K., Curbow, B., Hooker, C., & Piantadosi, S. (2001). The prevalence of psychological distress by cancer site. *Journal of Psycho-Oncology, 10,* 19–28.

About the Authors

Dexter Alexander, PhD, MBA, is an adjunct lecturer in the School of Public Affairs, Morehead State University, where he teaches "Ideology and Policy Development in Appalachia." Dr. Alexander is emeritus faculty and retired dean of Institutional Effectiveness and Research at Somerset Community College (Kentucky). He formerly was a banker and a soldier.

Dolores Subia BigFoot, PhD, an enrolled member of the Caddo Nation of Oklahoma, is an assistant professor in the Department of Pediatrics, University of Oklahoma Health Sciences Center. She directs the Indian Country Child Trauma Center, part of the National Child Traumatic Stress Network. As a doctoral-level counseling psychologist, Dr. Bigfoot provides consultation, training, and technical assistance to tribal, state, and federal agencies on child maltreatment, child trauma, and cultural issues. Dr. BigFoot is recognized for her efforts to bring traditional and spiritual practices and beliefs into the formal teaching and instruction of American Indian people, as well as the professionals working with indigenous populations.

Laura S. Boisen, PhD, LICSW, is associate professor and MSW field coordinator, Department of Social Work at Augsburg College in Minneapolis, MN. She has previous practice experience in child welfare, hospital social work, and administration in rural areas. Her current research interests include dual relationships and ethics and multicultural competence.

Lois A. Bosch, PhD, LISW, is associate professor and MSW program director, Social Work Department at Augsburg College in Minneapolis, MN. She has extensive practice experience as a school social worker in rural areas. Her current research interests include dual relationships in rural social work practice, international social work, and multicultural competence in macro social work practice.

Jill Bradshaw is a recent graduate of the University of Connecticut School of Social Work PhD program. She is currently the research coordinator for the national Domestic Violence Non-Residential Services & Supports study. Ms. Bradshaw's doctoral dissertation was an evaluation of two parent education videos aimed at preventing Shaken Baby Syndrome. She received her MSW from the University of Washington, Seattle, and her BSW from Brigham Young University in Utah.

N. Yolanda Burwell is working on poverty reduction and asset development as a senior fellow with North Carolina Rural Economic Development Center. Prior to this position, she taught for 25 years in social work programs in Louisiana and North Carolina. Her research and writings focus on social welfare history in African American communities. She holds a PhD from Cornell University, an MSW from Washington University, and earned her BSW from North Carolina A&T State University.

Iris Carlton-LaNey is professor in the School of Social Work at the University of North Carolina at Chapel Hill. Her research focuses on African American social welfare history and rural aging. Her publications include *African American Leadership: An Empowerment Tradition in Social Welfare History* (2001) and *African Americans Aging in the Rural South* (2005). She has a PhD from the University of Maryland, an MA from the University of Chicago, and a BSW from North Carolina A&T State University.

Suzie Cashwell, PhD, is associate professor with Herzing University. She has taught social work for more than 10 years. Her practice experiences include child welfare, health care, community development, and social welfare policy. She has served as president of the National Rural Social Work Caucus. She has been on the editorial board of the *Journal of Rural Social Sciences* and the Georgia NASW Ethics committee. She has completed some 70 presentations and publications.

Christina M. Chiarelli-Helminiak is a doctoral student at the University of Connecticut School of Social Work, where she also teaches in the MSW program.

Ms. Chiarelli-Helminiak led the development of a children's advocacy center, providing community-based services to abused children in rural north Georgia. She received her BA in social work from Shippensburg University and an MSW from Marywood University, where she was the first social work student to receive the Sister M. Eva Connors Peace Medal.

Pat Conway, PhD, LCSW, senior research scientist with Essentia Institute of Rural Health, conducts research with health and behavioral health programs and is the editor of the *Journal of Family Social Work*. She has been a social worker in the fields of family violence, health and behavioral health, and gerontology and a social work educator. Dr. Conway has a BA and MSW from the University of Oklahoma and a PhD from the University of Texas at Austin.

Michael Daley is professor and director of the Social Work Program at the University of South Alabama in Mobile, AL. He is president of the Association of Baccalaureate Social Work Program Directors and a past president of the Rural Social Work Caucus. Rural social work is one of his primary areas of interest, and he has published a number of pieces in the field.

Heather Dodson, MSW, is a native of Wyoming and an alumna of the University of Wyoming Division of Social Work. She is the coproprietor of a licensed case management service company in Cheyenne, WY, that provides comprehensive services to individuals living with developmental disabilities. Ms. Dodson is an advocate for community integration for all of her clients with the least restrictive service in the rural and frontier communities.

Paul DuongTran, PhD, is director of the Social Work Program at Dominican College in Orangeburg, NY. He has extensive social work and research experience in urban and rural health and mental health services spanning the states of Oregon, Hawaii, Wyoming, and New York. His research seeks evidence to support social work-grounded health promotion using cross-cultural methodology. His research focuses on health services, including mental health, with an emphasis on health behavior and health communication aimed at eliminating health disparities across racial and ethnic groups.

Bill Frederick, LCSW, ACSW, currently maintains a private mental health practice in Muncie, IN, and also has extensive practice experience in community mental health. He is a leader in Indiana for training and using Solution Focus Therapy. He has presented at the National Association of Social Workers Indiana State Conference on "Client Directed Outcome Informed Therapy" and "Becoming an Effective Therapist." He received his MSSW from the University of Tennessee, Knoxville, and BS from DePauw University.

Vanda Galen is professor and chair of the Social Work Program at the University of Wisconsin-Eau Claire. She was a social services supervisor in her home state of Kentucky and has held academic positions at Morehead State University (KY) and at Minnesota State University Mankato, where she retired as an emeritus professor. She holds an MSW from Virginia Commonwealth and a PhD from the University of Minnesota.

Leon Ginsberg has written extensively on social work in rural areas and edited the first four editions of this volume. He was a 2011 recipient of the Council on Social Work Education Lifetime Achievement award.

Michael Glasser, PhD, is associate dean for rural health professions, University of Illinois Health Sciences campus in Rockford, IL, and codirector of the National Center for Rural Health Professions. Dr. Glasser is a medical sociologist whose research focuses on rural workforce development, chronic disease outcomes and management, and international health professions education. He is a member of the W. K. Kellogg Foundation Rural People, Rural Policy initiative and coeditor of the journal *Education for Health*.

Karen V. Harper-Dorton earned her PhD in social work from The Ohio State University, served on the faculty there, and is currently at West Virginia University. Her research, presentations, and publications include rural poverty, child welfare, and intervention from existential and cognitive behavioral perspectives. She is coauthor of *Cross-Cultural Social Work: An Existential Approach* and *Working with Children, Adolescents and Families*. She serves as principal investigator of Public Social Services Education and Training Project, Title IV-E at West Virginia.

Shawn D. King earned his MSW and PhD from The Ohio State University in social work. He is an assistant professor at Marshall University in West Virginia, where he teaches in the BSW program. His research interests include rural health care and social service access and mental health and preventive care for vulnerable and marginalized populations. He has several publications and research presentations at national and state conferences.

Wynne S. Korr, PhD, is dean and professor at the School of Social Work, University of Illinois at Urbana-Champaign. Previously, she was a faculty member at the School of Social Work, University of Pittsburgh, and at the Jane Addams College of Social Work, University of Illinois at Chicago. She has published on evaluation of mental health services and on mental health policy and services, including rural issues.

Larry W. Kreuger began teaching at the University of Missouri in Columbia in 1983, retired in 2009, and became chair of the Social Work Department, Southern Illinois University Edwardsville. He has published on homelessness, natural disasters, and hypertechnology and coauthored two textbooks. In addition, he is adjunct faculty at Addis Ababa University, Ethiopia.

Paul Force-Emery Mackie is associate professor and BSSW program director at Minnesota State University, Mankato. Dr. Mackie received a BS in psychology from Northern Michigan University, an MSW from the Brown School at Washington University in St. Louis, and a PhD from the Graduate School of Social Work at the University of Denver. His research areas address rural social service labor force concerns, rural community organizing, and rural socioeconomic development.

Aaron Metzger is assistant professor of Life-Span Developmental Psychology in the West Virginia University Department of Psychology.

Abigail Nelson, MSW, is a licensed therapist at Northern Wyoming Mental Health Center in Sheridan, WY. Her clinical and research experiences include the identification and design of services to assist persons who leave incarceration to resume their lives in rural Wyoming communities. Currently, her work in substance abuse focuses on spirituality and creating opportunities for client involvement in social justice activism.

Barbara Pierce is a PhD candidate at Case Western Reserve University and associate professor of social work at Northwestern State University of Louisiana. She has 12 years of experience as a social work educator and more than 30 years of experience in social work. Her main research interests during the past 12 years have been competency education in rural social work and child welfare and identifying student perceptions of learning gaps between the classroom and field.

Suzanne Pritzker, PhD, is assistant professor in the University of Houston Graduate College of Social Work.

Komalsingh Rambaree is a senior lecturer in social work at the Department of Social Work and Psychology, University of Gävle, Sweden. He holds a PhD in social work and social policy from University of Manchester in England. Before moving to Sweden in 2009, he served as a lecturer in England and Mauritius. He is currently involved in teaching international social work. His research areas include poverty and environment, community mobilization and empowerment, and teaching and learning of social work.

Elana Premack Sandler, LCSW, MPH, specializes in violence and injury prevention and adolescent health promotion, having worked in program development, implementation, evaluation, and consultation at the community and national levels. Sandler writes the blog *Promoting Hope, Preventing Suicide* on PsychologyToday.com. She is currently based at the Education Development Center, where she works on initiatives related to health and human development, including suicide and domestic violence prevention.

J. Sky Smith, LICSW, OSW-C, is a social worker at Mayo Clinic in Rochester, MN, for the blood and marrow transplant and hand/arm transplant programs. She has worked as an oncology social worker since 2007, with an interest in psychosocial oncology in the rural context. Sky recently presented research on psychosocial distress in rural communities at the American Society of Clinical Oncology annual meeting.

Saundra Starks, EdD, is associate professor at Western Kentucky University (WKU). She has more than 25 years of social work education and social work clinical practice. She has served on the national boards of NASW and the Association of Social Work Boards. She serves on the editorial board of *Journal of Indigenous Social Work Practice* and is coauthor of *Women of Color as Social Work Educators.* She is the director of the Family Resource Program of WKU's Clinical Education Complex.

Glenn Stone, PhD, is professor and chair of the social work program at Ball State University. He has more than 10 years of social work teaching experience and more than 15 years of direct clinical social work practice in rural and semirural settings. He researches in the area of practice evaluation and men's mental health. He received his MSW and PhD from The Ohio State University.

Gretchen H. Waltman is an independent social work consultant, trainer, and author of published articles on social work practice in rural areas and on Amish culture. She obtained her MSW from The Ohio State University and has been an adjunct instructor for the university. Having lived among the Amish in Holmes and Tuscarawas Counties (OH) most of her life, Ms. Waltman has had a unique opportunity to observe Amish culture and lifestyle.

Index